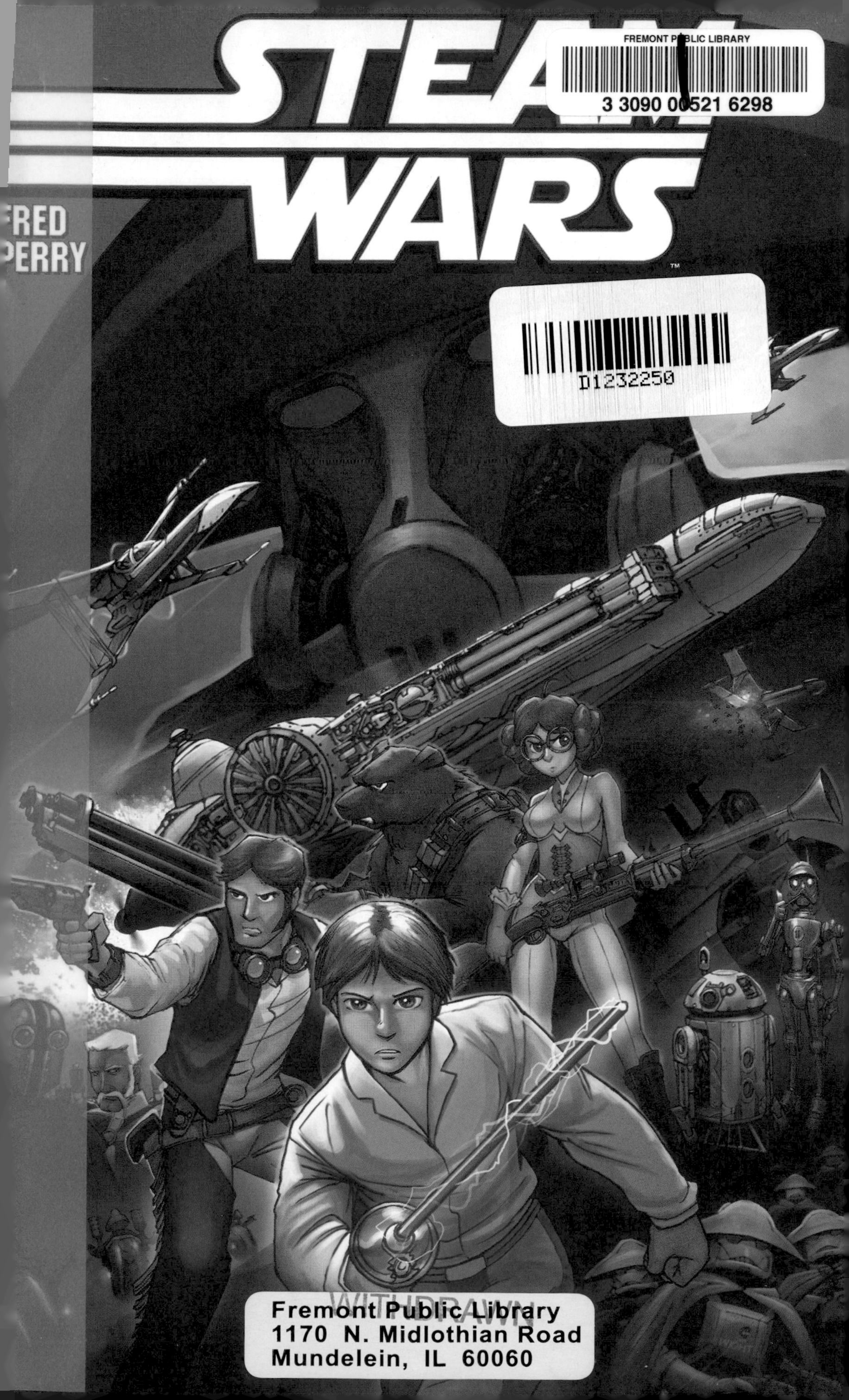
STEAM
WARS
™
FRED
PERRY

STEAM WARS

STORY & ART BY
Fred Perry
fredgdperry.deviantart.com
gd200fanmail@gmail.com

EDITED BY
Doug Dlin
Joe Wight

Episode I
AN EMBER OF HOPE

It is a period of civil war. Resistance troops, striking from within a hidden base, have won their first victory against the tyrannical Hegemonic Crux.

During the battle, Resistance spies managed to steal the secret formula for the Hegemony's ultimate asset, WARP COAL, a power source that allows them to build enormous, steam-powered dreadnoughts that move in absolute silence.

Pursued by the Hegemony's shock troops, Duchess Imoen and her Resistance cell race to escape aboard a waiting supply ship piloted by honorary Royal Navy officer Hansel Lowe. Imoen carries the stolen formula that can save her people and their allies and restore freedom to their world...

Steam Wars TPB #1 July
Collects Steam Wars #1-4, first published in 2013 by Ant
Press. Steam Wars is published by Antarctic Press.
Wurzbach, Suite #204, San Antonio, Texas, 78240. FAX#
593-0692. Story and art © Fred Perry. All other materia
and © Antarctic Press. No similarity to any actual chara
and/or place(s) is intended, and any such similarity is
coincidental. Nothing from this book may be repro
without the express written consent of the author, exce
purposes of review or promotion. "Crose SOOPAH
doahs!" Printed and bound in

PRESIDENT
Joe Dunn

ART DIRECTOR
Joseph Wight

IN-HOUSE ARTISTS
Fred Perry
Brian Denham
Rod Espinosa
David Hutchison
Robert Acosta

FOUNDER
Ben Dunn

VP OF PRODUCTION
Wes Hartman

EDITOR IN CHIEF
Jochen Weltjens

PUBLISHING MANAGER
Robby Bevard

PROD. ASSISTANTS
Tony Galvan
Zech Gray
Hughston Mund

SALES DIRECTOR
Lee Duhig

OFFICE MANAGER
Doug Dlin

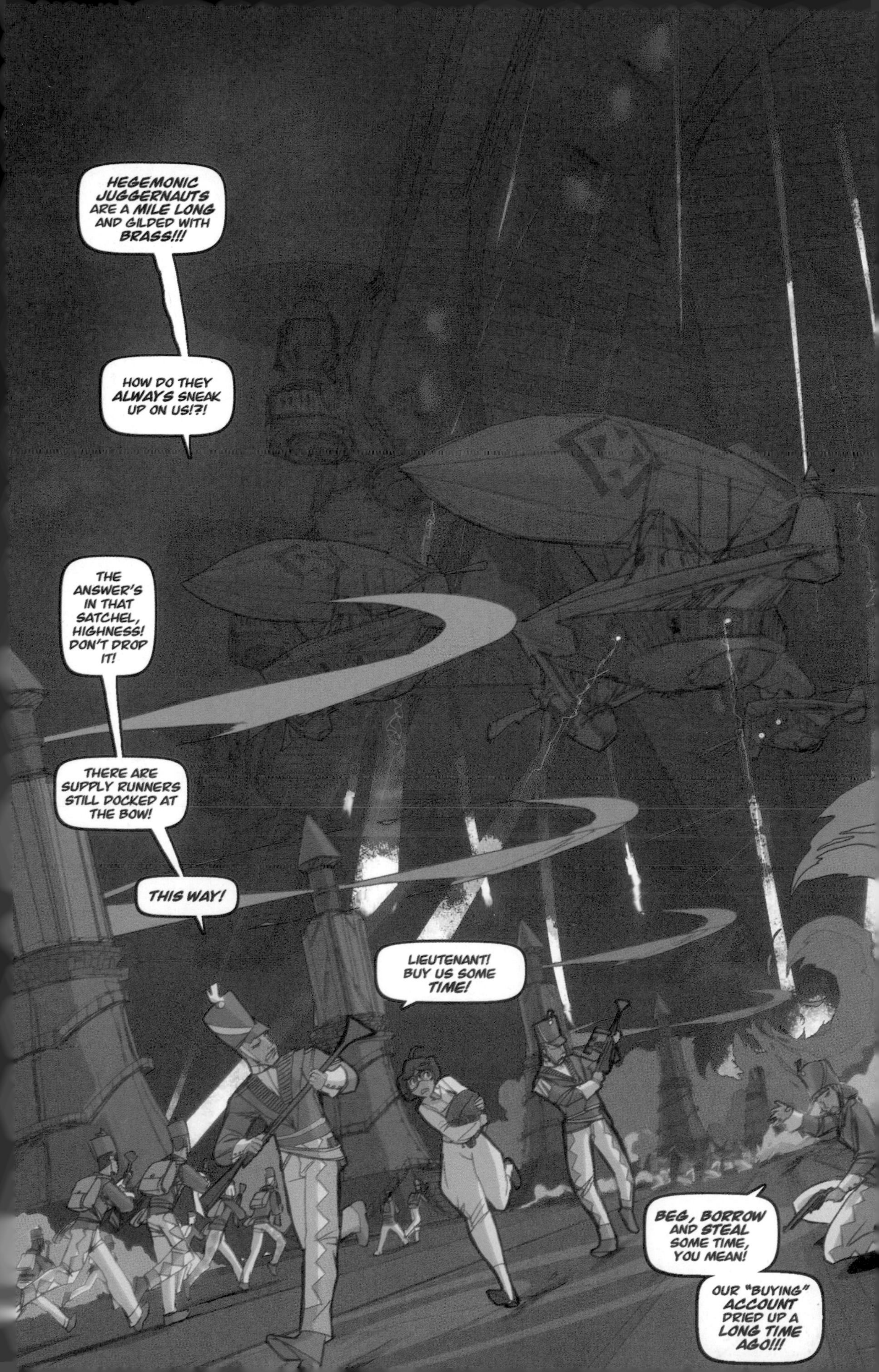
HEGEMONIC JUGGERNAUTS ARE A MILE LONG AND GILDED WITH BRASS!!!
HOW DO THEY ALWAYS SNEAK UP ON US!?!
THE ANSWER'S IN THAT SATCHEL, HIGHNESS! DON'T DROP IT!
THERE ARE SUPPLY RUNNERS STILL DOCKED AT THE BOW!
THIS WAY!
LIEUTENANT! BUY US SOME TIME!
BEG, BORROW AND STEAL SOME TIME, YOU MEAN!
OUR "BUYING" ACCOUNT DRIED UP A LONG TIME AGO!!!

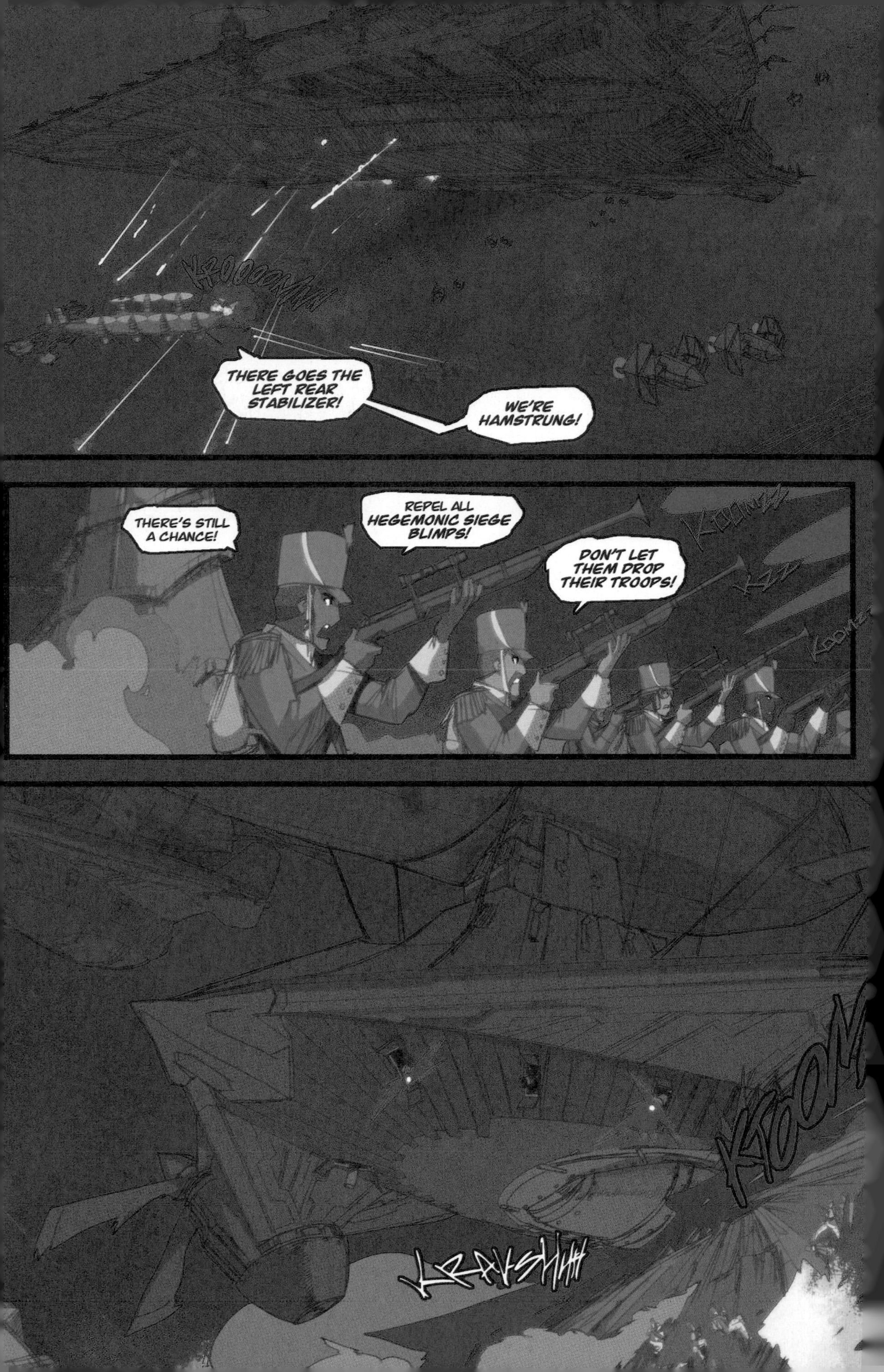
THERE GOES THE LEFT REAR STABILIZER!
WE'RE HAMSTRUNG!
THERE'S STILL A CHANCE!
REPEL ALL HEGEMONIC SIEGE BLIMPS!
DON'T LET THEM DROP THEIR TROOPS!
KROOM

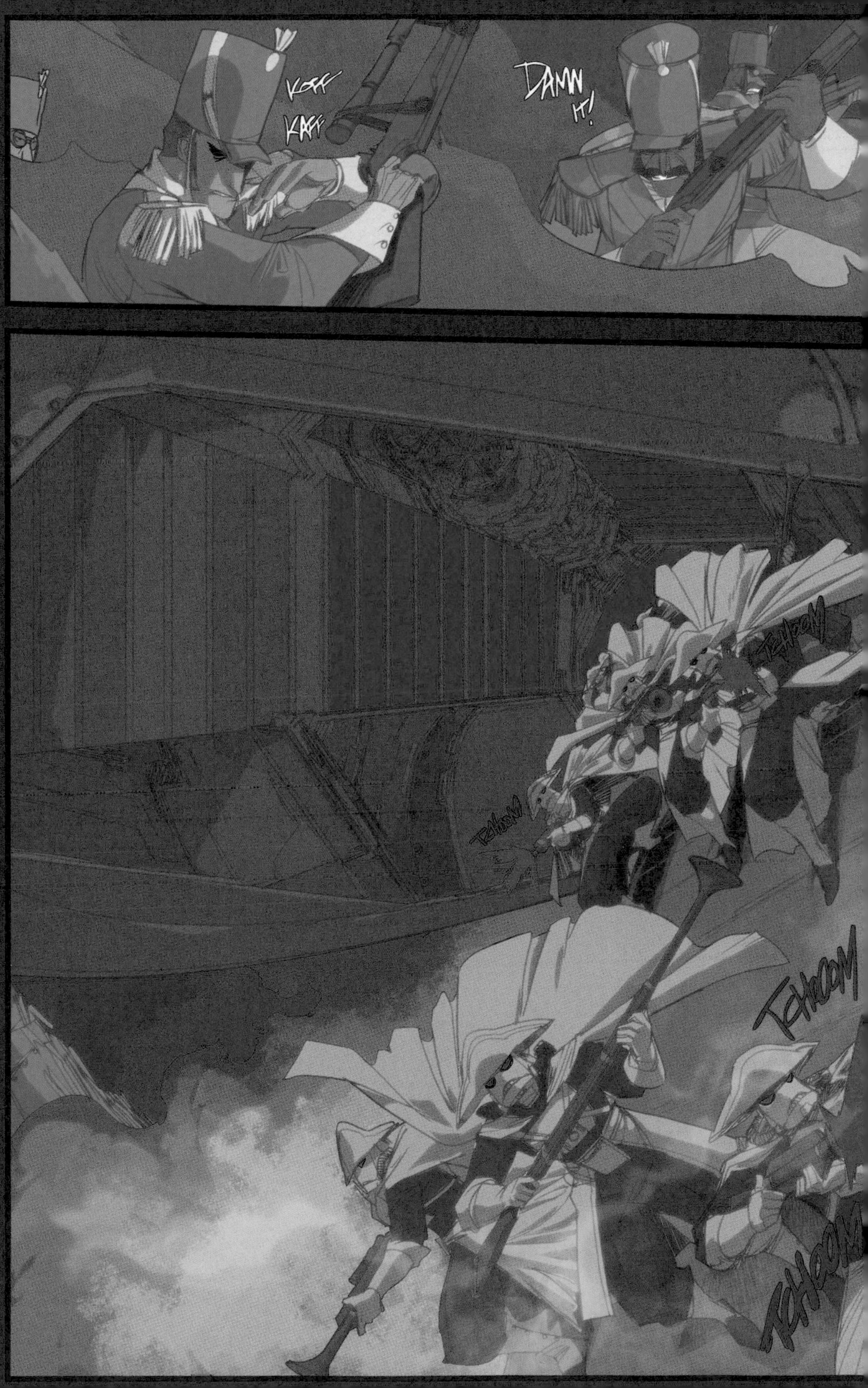
KOFF
KAFF
DAMN IT!
TCHOOM
TCHOOM
TCHOOM
TCHOOM

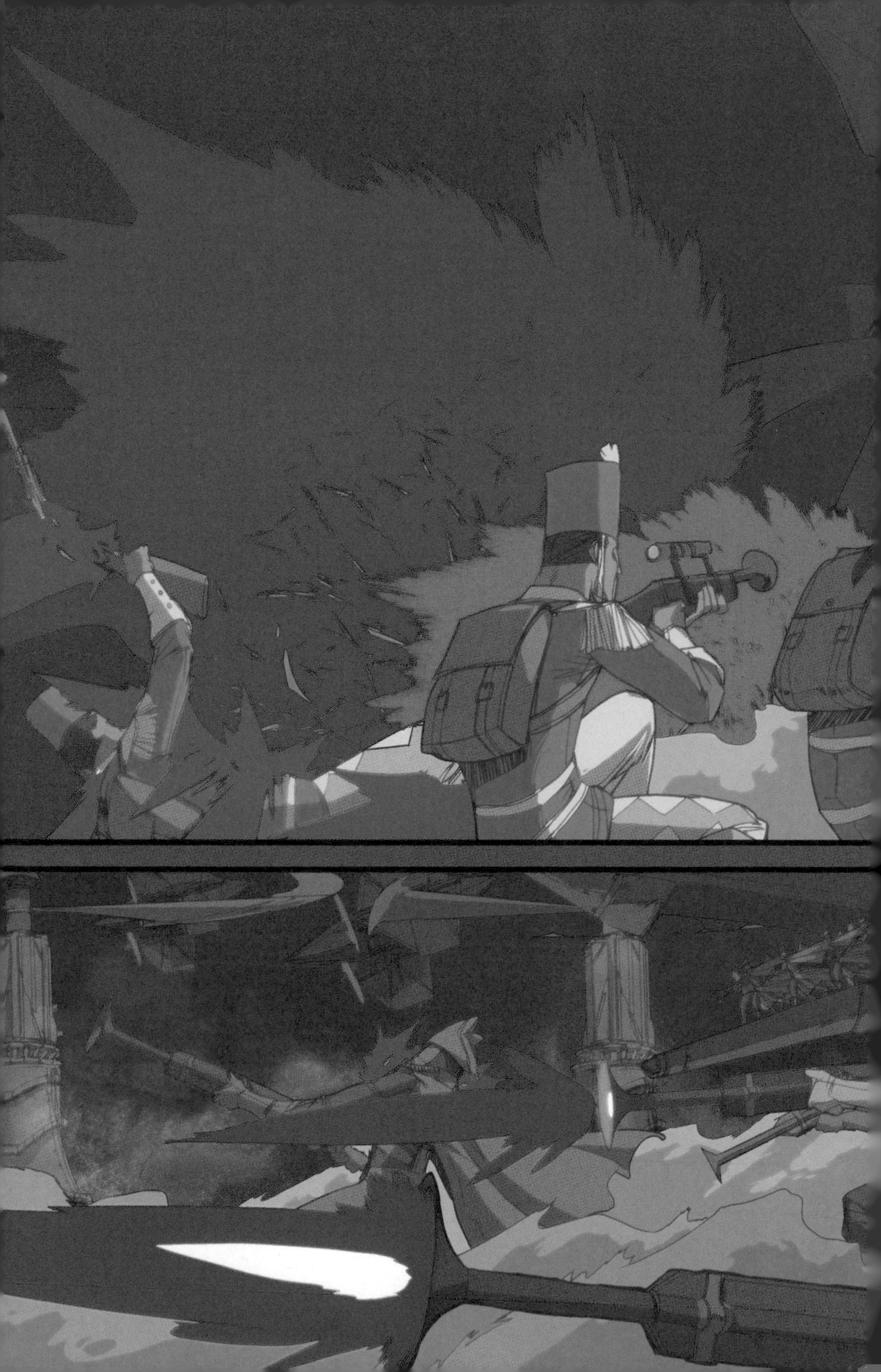

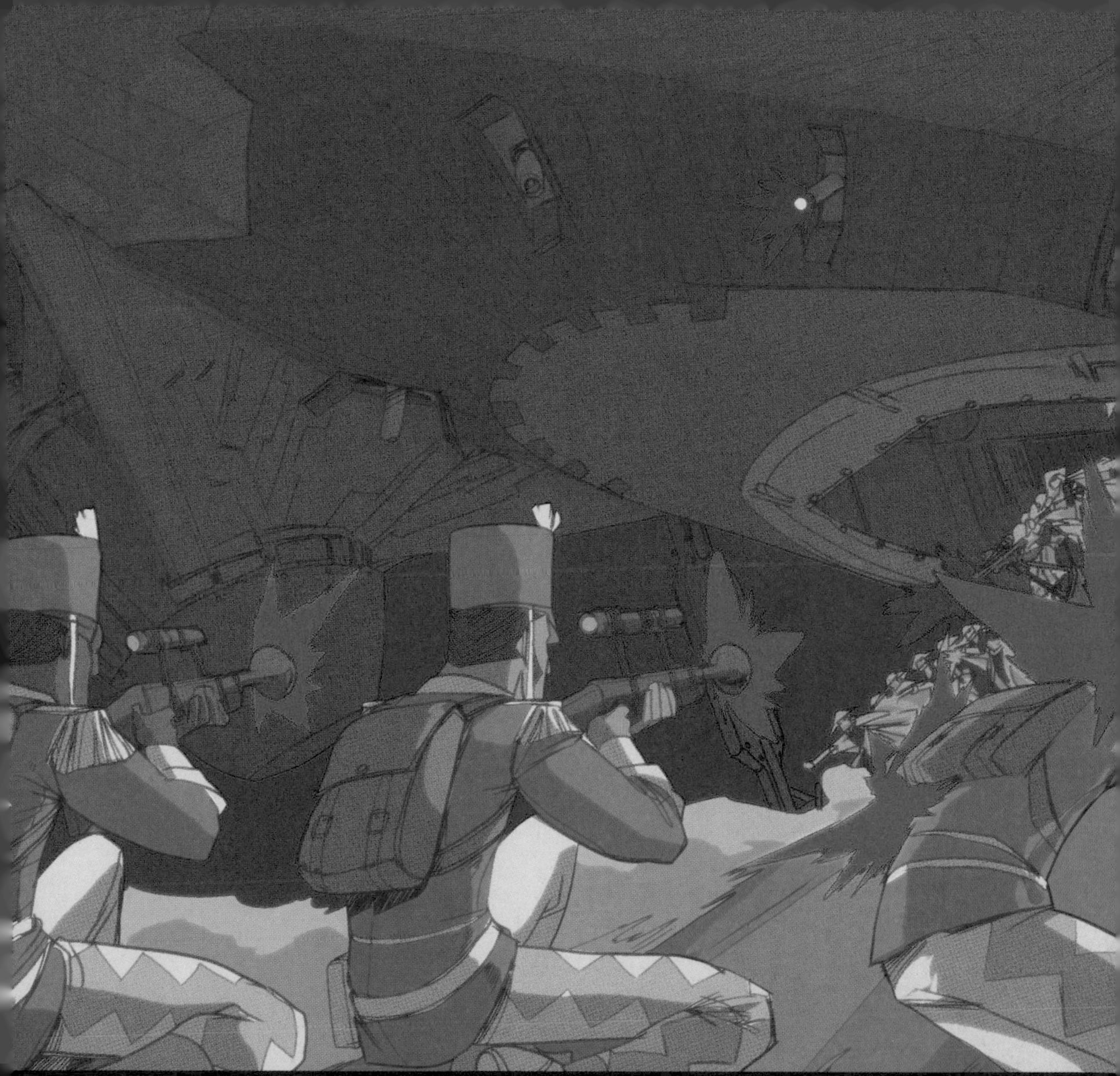
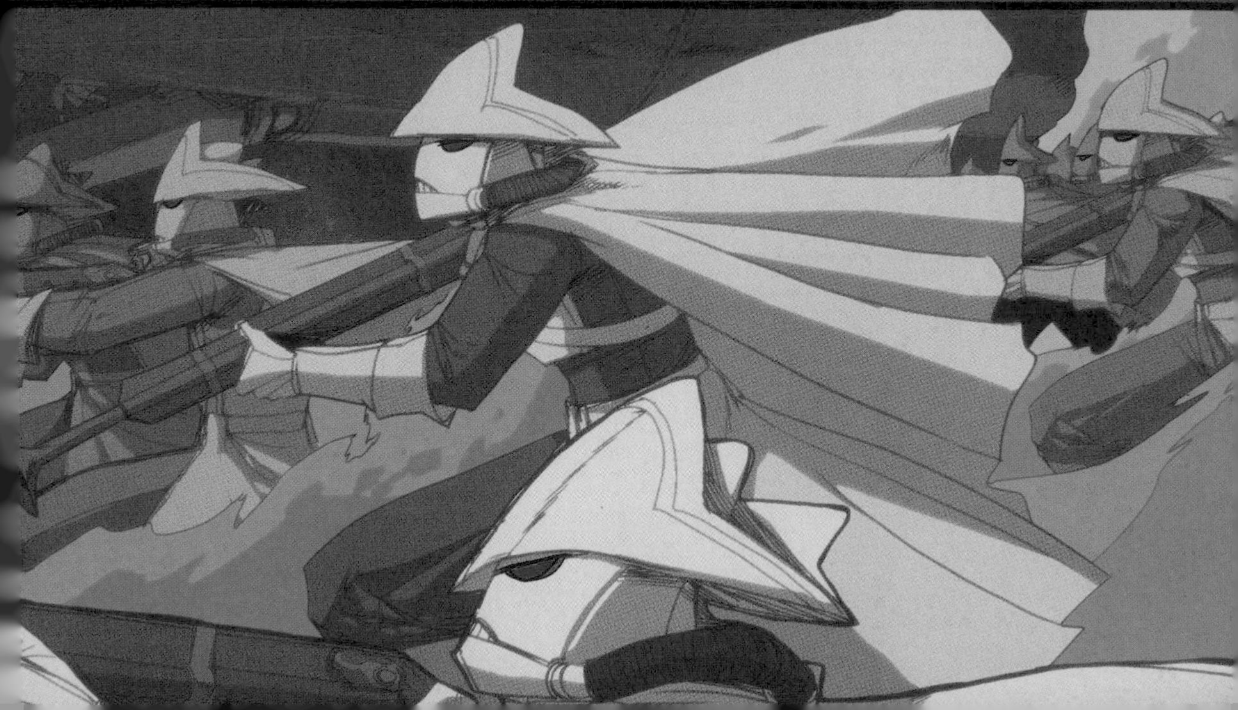

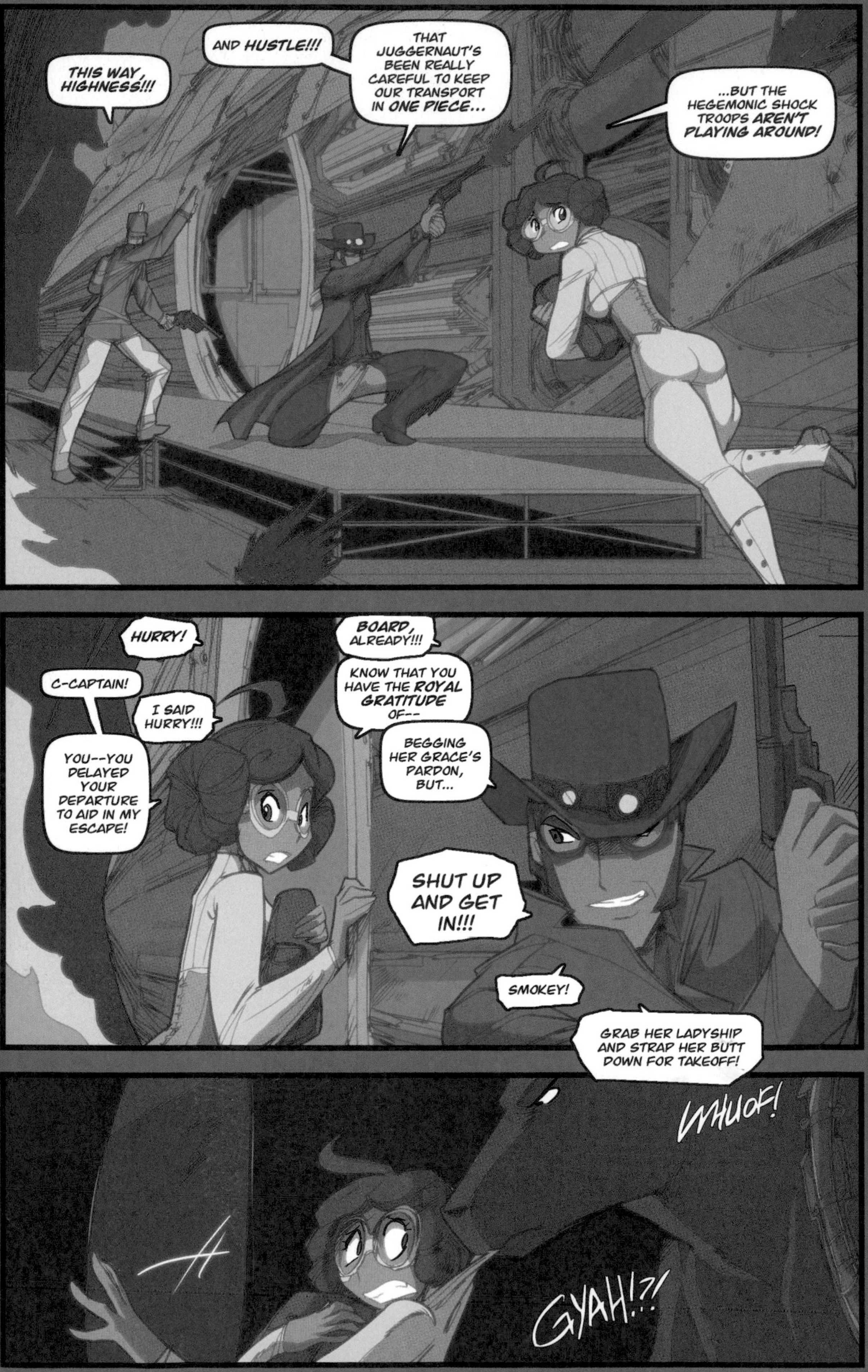
THIS WAY, HIGHNESS!!!
AND HUSTLE!!!
THAT JUGGERNAUT'S BEEN REALLY CAREFUL TO KEEP OUR TRANSPORT IN ONE PIECE...
...BUT THE HEGEMONIC SHOCK TROOPS AREN'T PLAYING AROUND!
HURRY!
BOARD, ALREADY!!!
KNOW THAT YOU HAVE THE ROYAL GRATITUDE OF--
C-CAPTAIN!
I SAID HURRY!!!
YOU--YOU DELAYED YOUR DEPARTURE TO AID IN MY ESCAPE!
BEGGING HER GRACE'S PARDON, BUT...
SHUT UP AND GET IN!!!
SMOKEY!
GRAB HER LADYSHIP AND STRAP HER BUTT DOWN FOR TAKEOFF!
WHUOF!
GYAH!?!

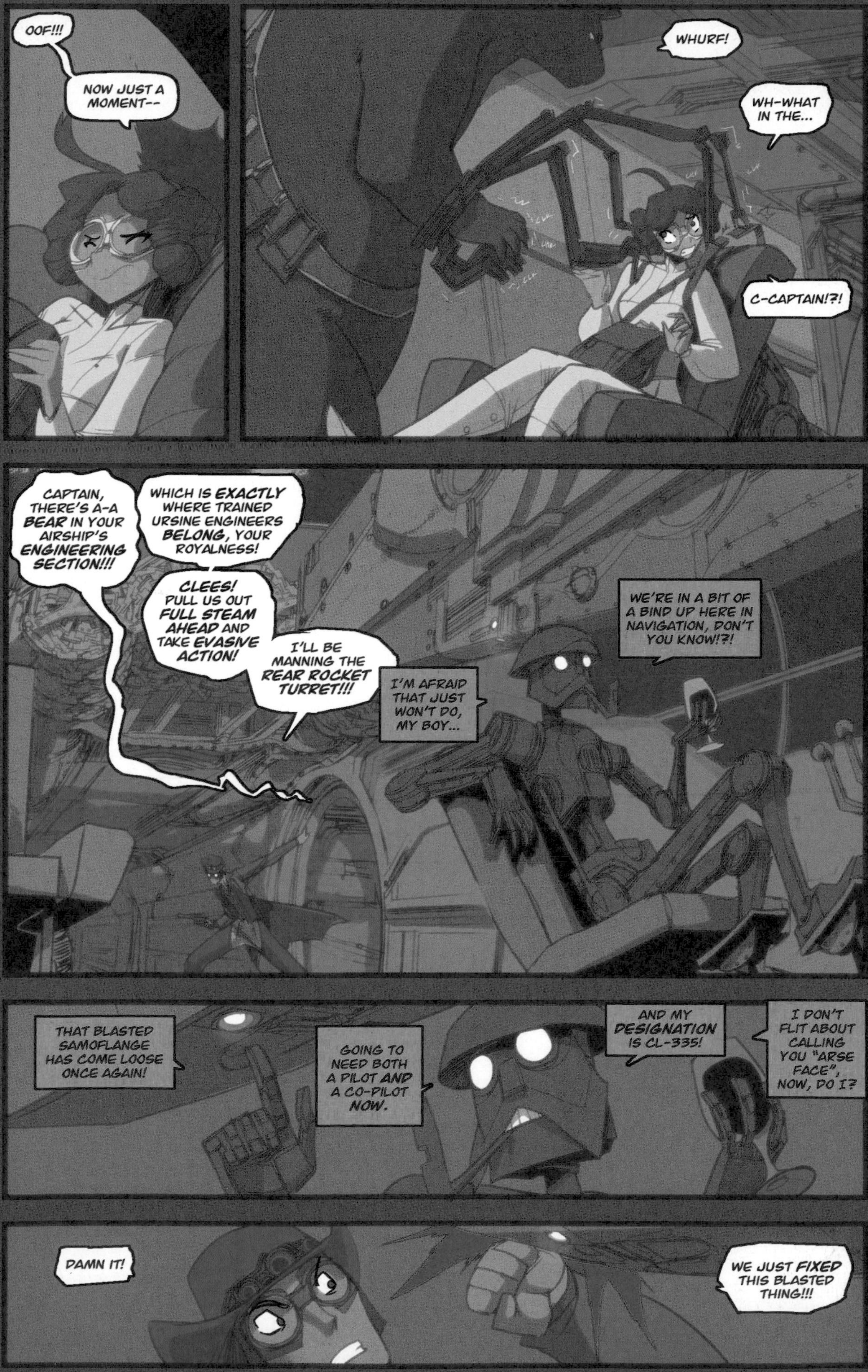
OOF!!!
NOW JUST A MOMENT--
WHURF!
WH-WHAT IN THE...
C-CAPTAIN!?!
CAPTAIN, THERE'S A-A BEAR IN YOUR AIRSHIP'S ENGINEERING SECTION!!!
WHICH IS EXACTLY WHERE TRAINED URSINE ENGINEERS BELONG, YOUR ROYALNESS!
CLEES! PULL US OUT FULL STEAM AHEAD AND TAKE EVASIVE ACTION!
I'LL BE MANNING THE REAR ROCKET TURRET!!!
I'M AFRAID THAT JUST WON'T DO, MY BOY...
WE'RE IN A BIT OF A BIND UP HERE IN NAVIGATION, DON'T YOU KNOW!?!
THAT BLASTED SAMOFLANGE HAS COME LOOSE ONCE AGAIN!
GOING TO NEED BOTH A PILOT AND A CO-PILOT NOW.
AND MY DESIGNATION IS CL-335!
I DON'T FLIT ABOUT CALLING YOU "ARSE FACE", NOW, DO I?
DAMN IT!
WE JUST FIXED THIS BLASTED THING!!!

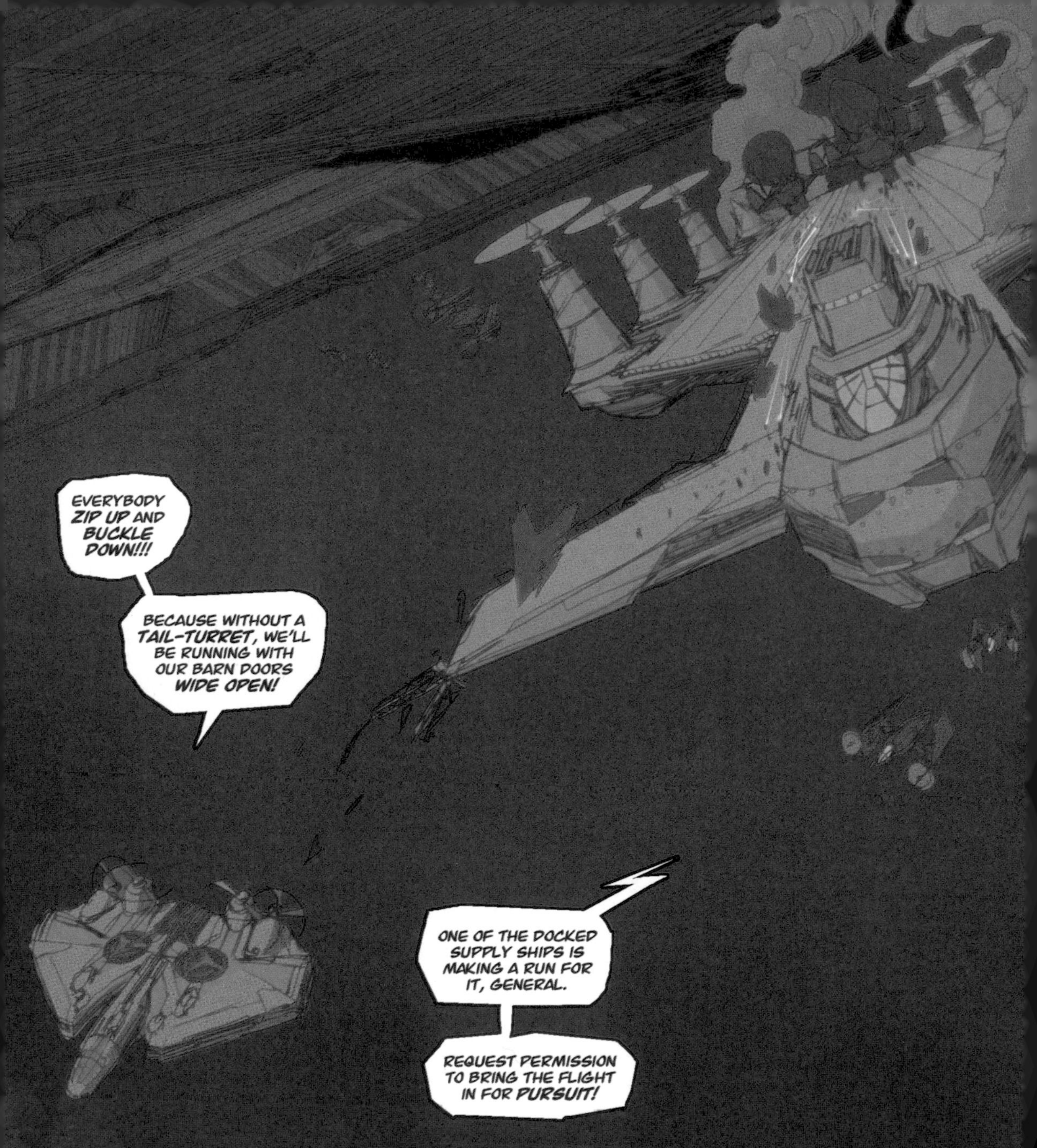
EVERYBODY ZIP UP AND BUCKLE DOWN!!!
BECAUSE WITHOUT A TAIL-TURRET, WE'LL BE RUNNING WITH OUR BARN DOORS WIDE OPEN!
ONE OF THE DOCKED SUPPLY SHIPS IS MAKING A RUN FOR IT, GENERAL.
REQUEST PERMISSION TO BRING THE FLIGHT IN FOR PURSUIT!

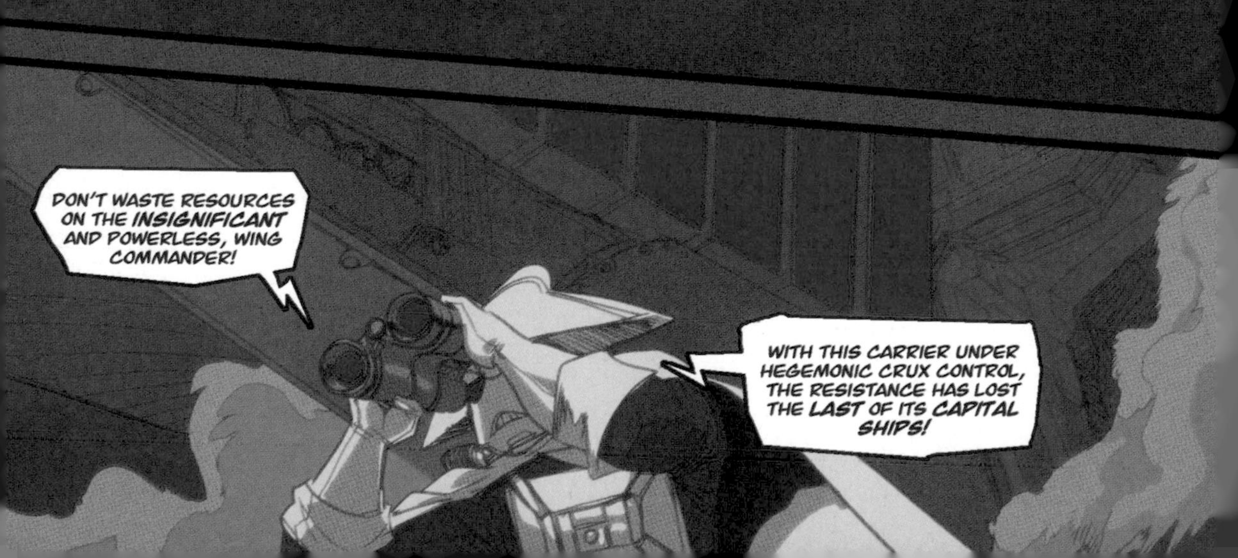
DON'T WASTE RESOURCES ON THE INSIGNIFICANT AND POWERLESS, WING COMMANDER!
WITH THIS CARRIER UNDER HEGEMONIC CRUX CONTROL, THE RESISTANCE HAS LOST THE LAST OF ITS CAPITAL SHIPS!

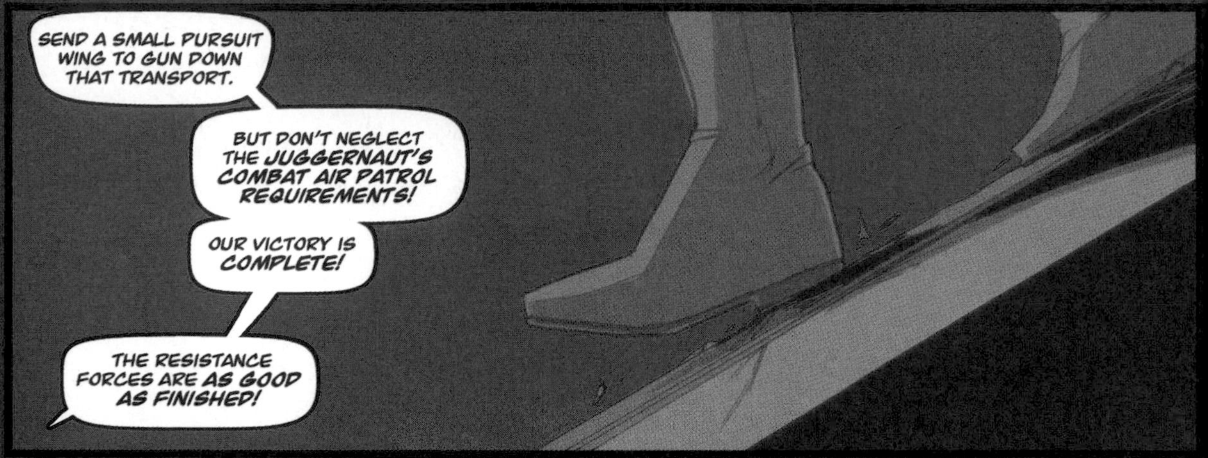
SEND A SMALL PURSUIT WING TO GUN DOWN THAT TRANSPORT.
BUT DON'T NEGLECT THE JUGGERNAUT'S COMBAT AIR PATROL REQUIREMENTS!
OUR VICTORY IS COMPLETE!
THE RESISTANCE FORCES ARE AS GOOD AS FINISHED!

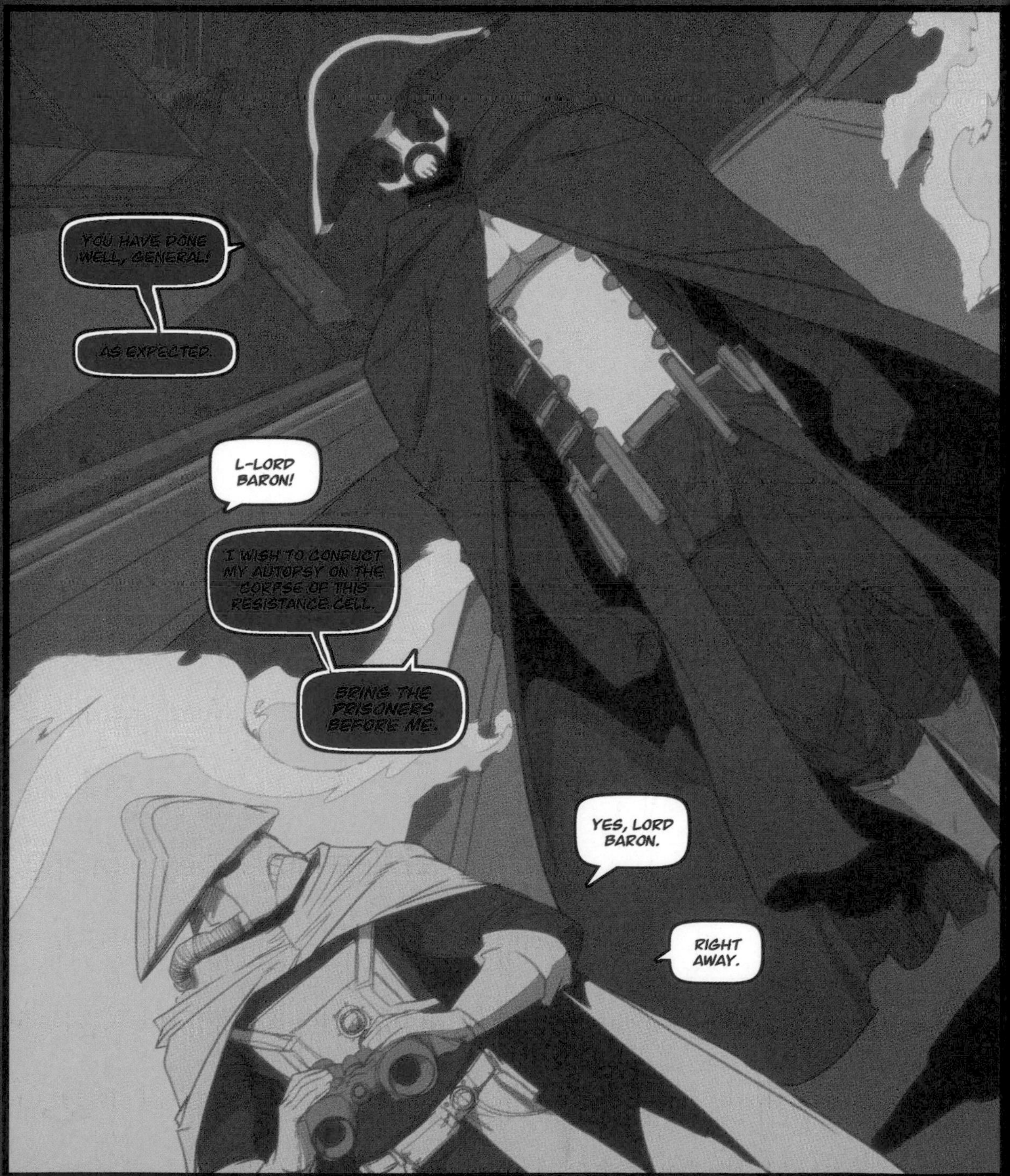
YOU HAVE DONE WELL, GENERAL!
AS EXPECTED.
L-LORD BARON!
I WISH TO CONDUCT MY AUTOPSY ON THE CORPSE OF THIS RESISTANCE CELL.
BRING THE PRISONERS BEFORE ME.
YES, LORD BARON.
RIGHT AWAY.

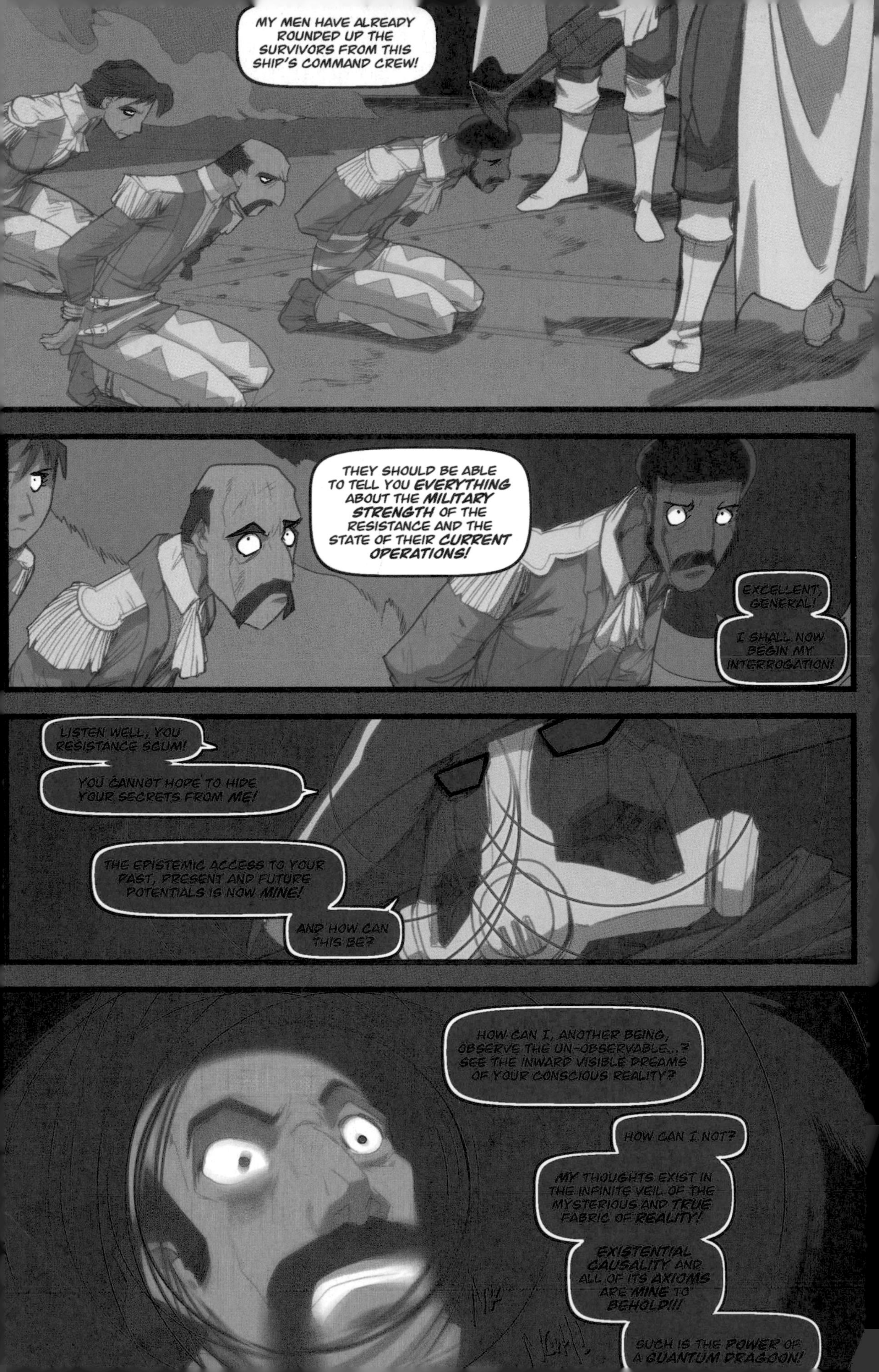
MY MEN HAVE ALREADY ROUNDED UP THE SURVIVORS FROM THIS SHIP'S COMMAND CREW!
THEY SHOULD BE ABLE TO TELL YOU EVERYTHING ABOUT THE MILITARY STRENGTH OF THE RESISTANCE AND THE STATE OF THEIR CURRENT OPERATIONS!
EXCELLENT, GENERAL!
I SHALL NOW BEGIN MY INTERROGATION!
LISTEN WELL, YOU RESISTANCE SCUM!
YOU CANNOT HOPE TO HIDE YOUR SECRETS FROM ME!
THE EPISTEMIC ACCESS TO YOUR PAST, PRESENT AND FUTURE POTENTIALS IS NOW MINE!
AND HOW CAN THIS BE?
HOW CAN I, ANOTHER BEING, OBSERVE THE UN-OBSERVABLE...? SEE THE INWARD VISIBLE DREAMS OF YOUR CONSCIOUS REALITY?
HOW CAN I NOT?
MY THOUGHTS EXIST IN THE INFINITE VEIL OF THE MYSTERIOUS AND TRUE FABRIC OF REALITY!
EXISTENTIAL CAUSALITY AND ALL OF ITS AXIOMS ARE MINE TO BEHOLD!!!
SUCH IS THE POWER OF A QUANTUM DRAGOON!

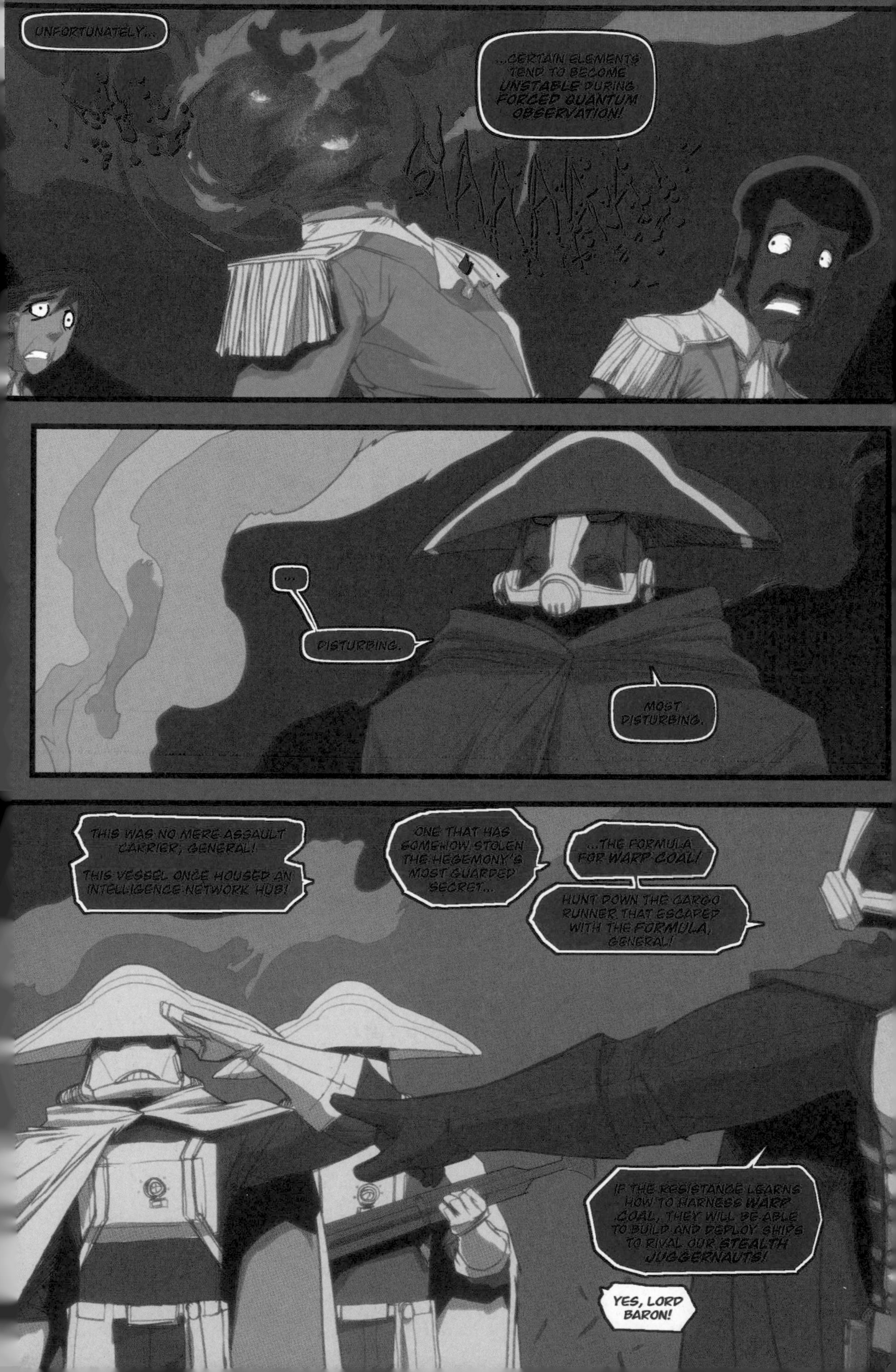
UNFORTUNATELY...
...CERTAIN ELEMENTS TEND TO BECOME UNSTABLE DURING FORCED QUANTUM OBSERVATION!
...
DISTURBING.
MOST DISTURBING.
THIS WAS NO MERE ASSAULT CARRIER, GENERAL!
THIS VESSEL ONCE HOUSED AN INTELLIGENCE NETWORK HUB!
ONE THAT HAS SOMEHOW STOLEN THE HEGEMONY'S MOST GUARDED SECRET...
...THE FORMULA FOR WARP COAL!
HUNT DOWN THE CARGO RUNNER THAT ESCAPED WITH THE FORMULA, GENERAL!
IF THE RESISTANCE LEARNS HOW TO HARNESS WARP COAL, THEY WILL BE ABLE TO BUILD AND DEPLOY SHIPS TO RIVAL OUR STEALTH JUGGERNAUTS!
YES, LORD BARON!

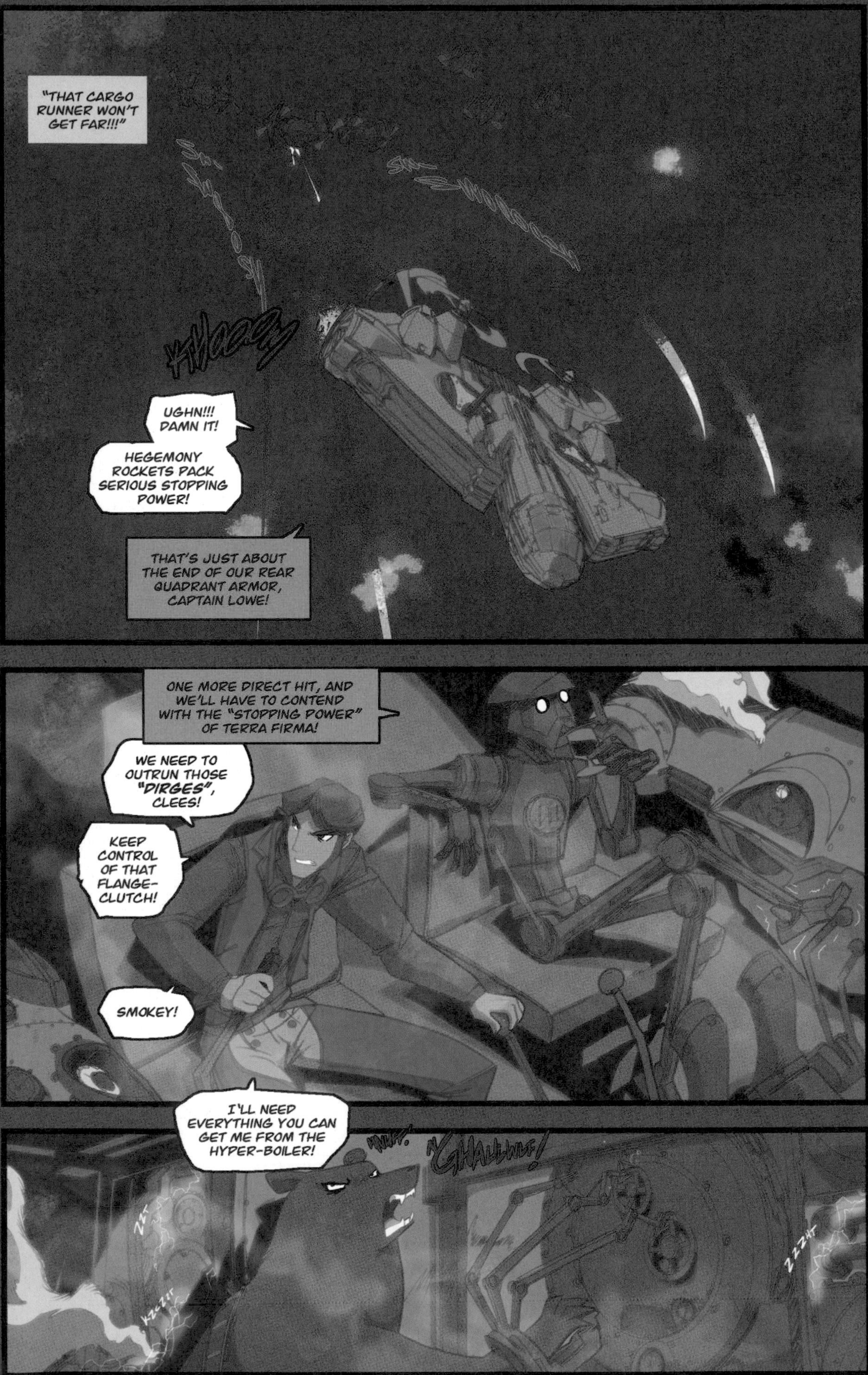
"THAT CARGO RUNNER WON'T GET FAR!!!"
UGHN!!! DAMN IT!
HEGEMONY ROCKETS PACK SERIOUS STOPPING POWER!
THAT'S JUST ABOUT THE END OF OUR REAR QUADRANT ARMOR, CAPTAIN LOWE!
ONE MORE DIRECT HIT, AND WE'LL HAVE TO CONTEND WITH THE "STOPPING POWER" OF TERRA FIRMA!
WE NEED TO OUTRUN THOSE "DIRGES", CLEES!
KEEP CONTROL OF THAT FLANGE-CLUTCH!
SMOKEY!
I'LL NEED EVERYTHING YOU CAN GET ME FROM THE HYPER-BOILER!

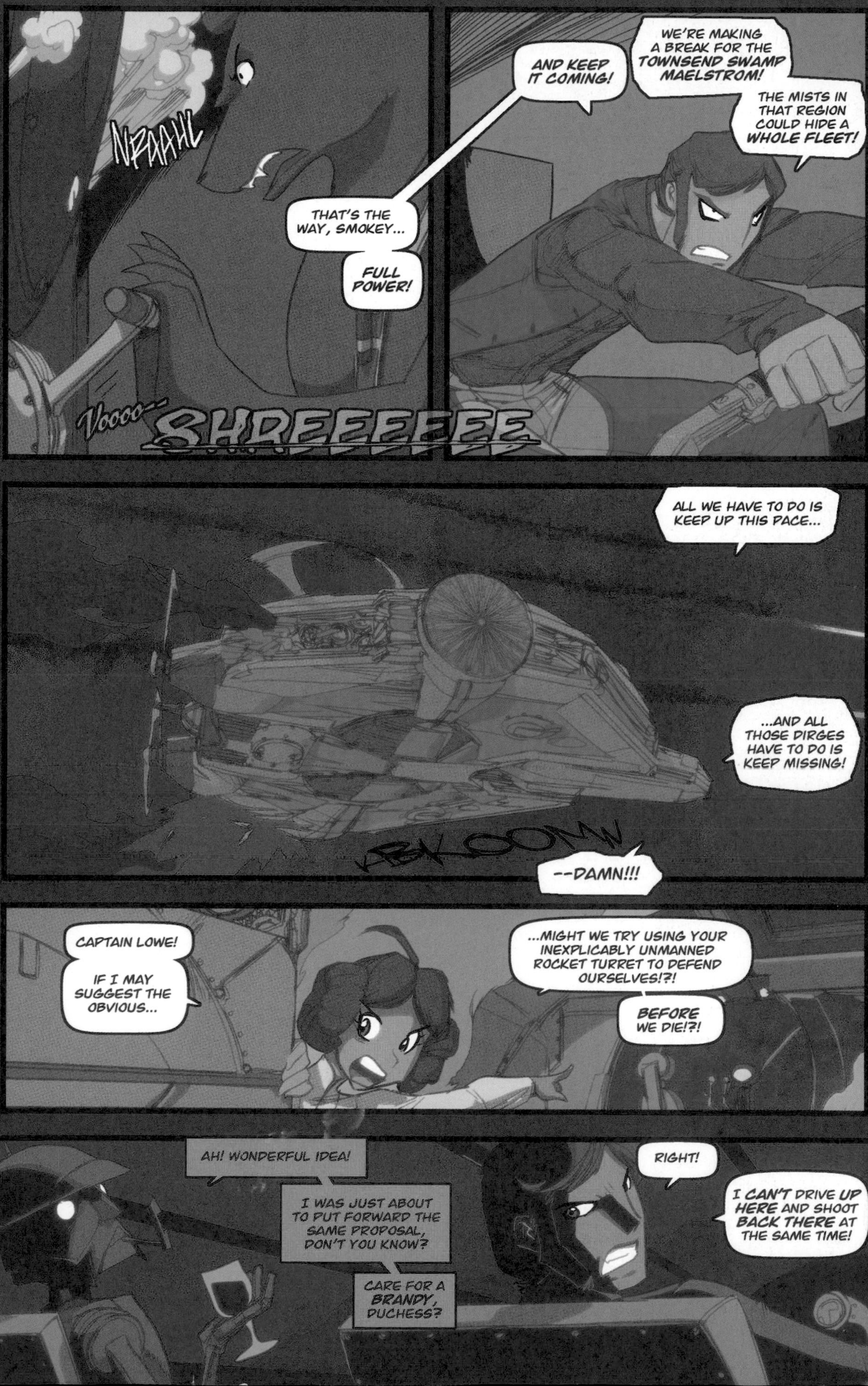

NRAAHL
THAT'S THE WAY, SMOKEY...
FULL POWER!
Voooo--SHREEEEEE
AND KEEP IT COMING!
WE'RE MAKING A BREAK FOR THE TOWNSEND SWAMP MAELSTROM!
THE MISTS IN THAT REGION COULD HIDE A WHOLE FLEET!
ALL WE HAVE TO DO IS KEEP UP THIS PACE...
...AND ALL THOSE DIRGES HAVE TO DO IS KEEP MISSING!
--DAMN!!!
CAPTAIN LOWE!
IF I MAY SUGGEST THE OBVIOUS...
...MIGHT WE TRY USING YOUR INEXPLICABLY UNMANNED ROCKET TURRET TO DEFEND OURSELVES!?!
BEFORE WE DIE!?!
AH! WONDERFUL IDEA!
I WAS JUST ABOUT TO PUT FORWARD THE SAME PROPOSAL, DON'T YOU KNOW?
CARE FOR A BRANDY, DUCHESS?
RIGHT!
I CAN'T DRIVE UP HERE AND SHOOT BACK THERE AT THE SAME TIME!

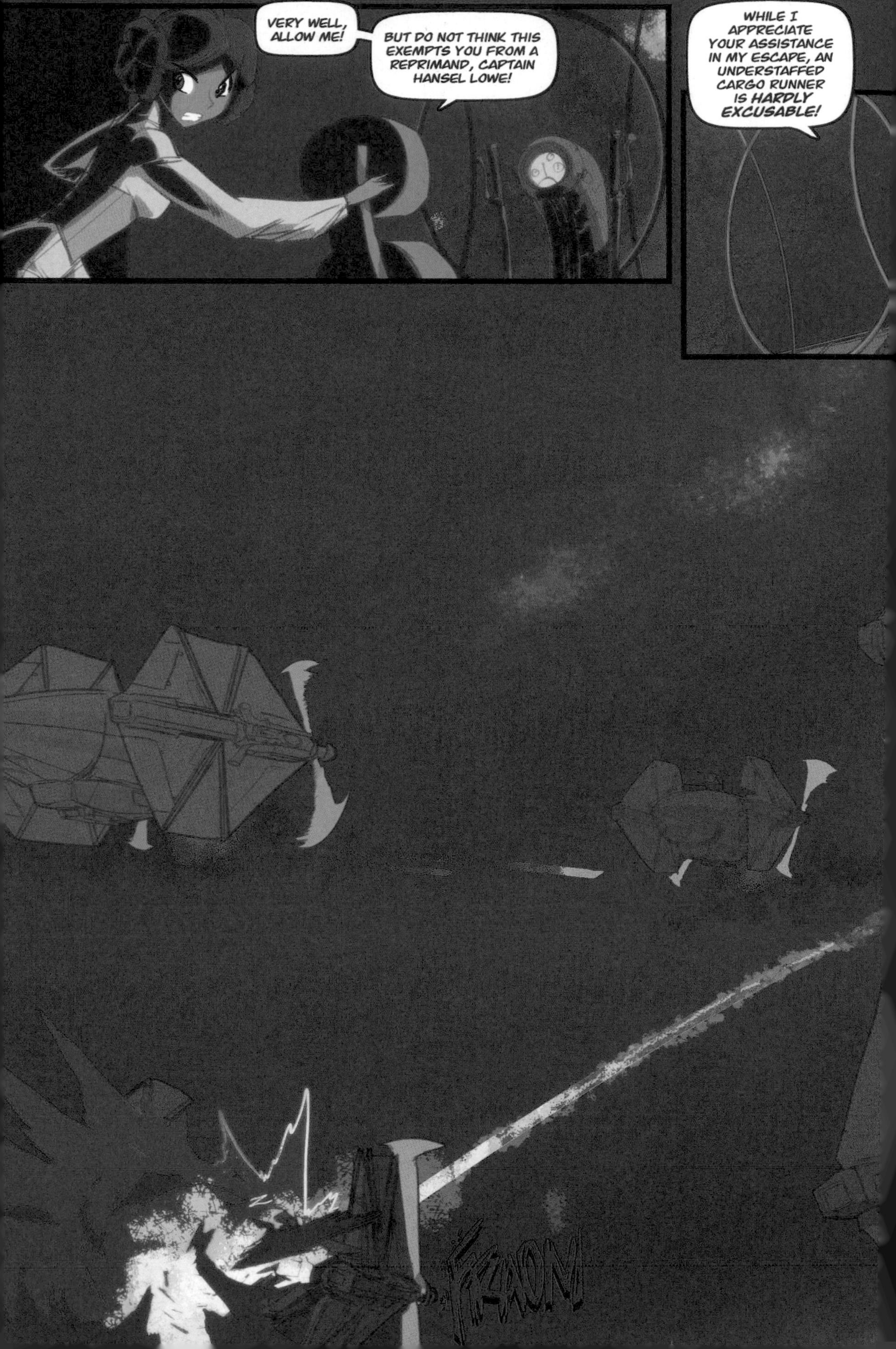
VERY WELL, ALLOW ME!
BUT DO NOT THINK THIS EXEMPTS YOU FROM A REPRIMAND, CAPTAIN HANSEL LOWE!
WHILE I APPRECIATE YOUR ASSISTANCE IN MY ESCAPE, AN UNDERSTAFFED CARGO RUNNER IS HARDLY EXCUSABLE!

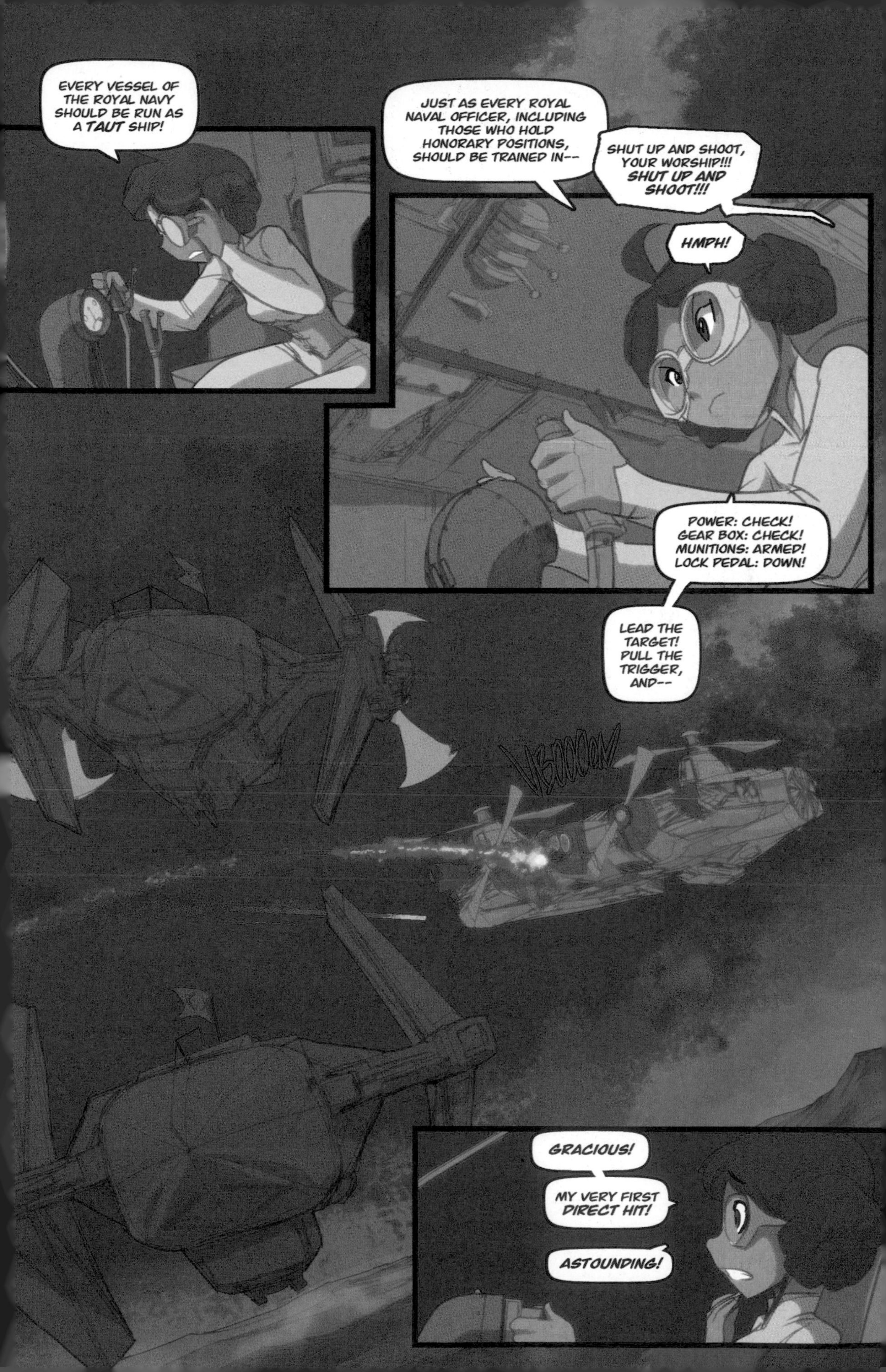
EVERY VESSEL OF THE ROYAL NAVY SHOULD BE RUN AS A TAUT SHIP!
JUST AS EVERY ROYAL NAVAL OFFICER, INCLUDING THOSE WHO HOLD HONORARY POSITIONS, SHOULD BE TRAINED IN--
SHUT UP AND SHOOT, YOUR WORSHIP!!! SHUT UP AND SHOOT!!!
HMPH!
POWER: CHECK! GEAR BOX: CHECK! MUNITIONS: ARMED! LOCK PEDAL: DOWN!
LEAD THE TARGET! PULL THE TRIGGER, AND--
VBOOOOM
GRACIOUS!
MY VERY FIRST DIRECT HIT!
ASTOUNDING!

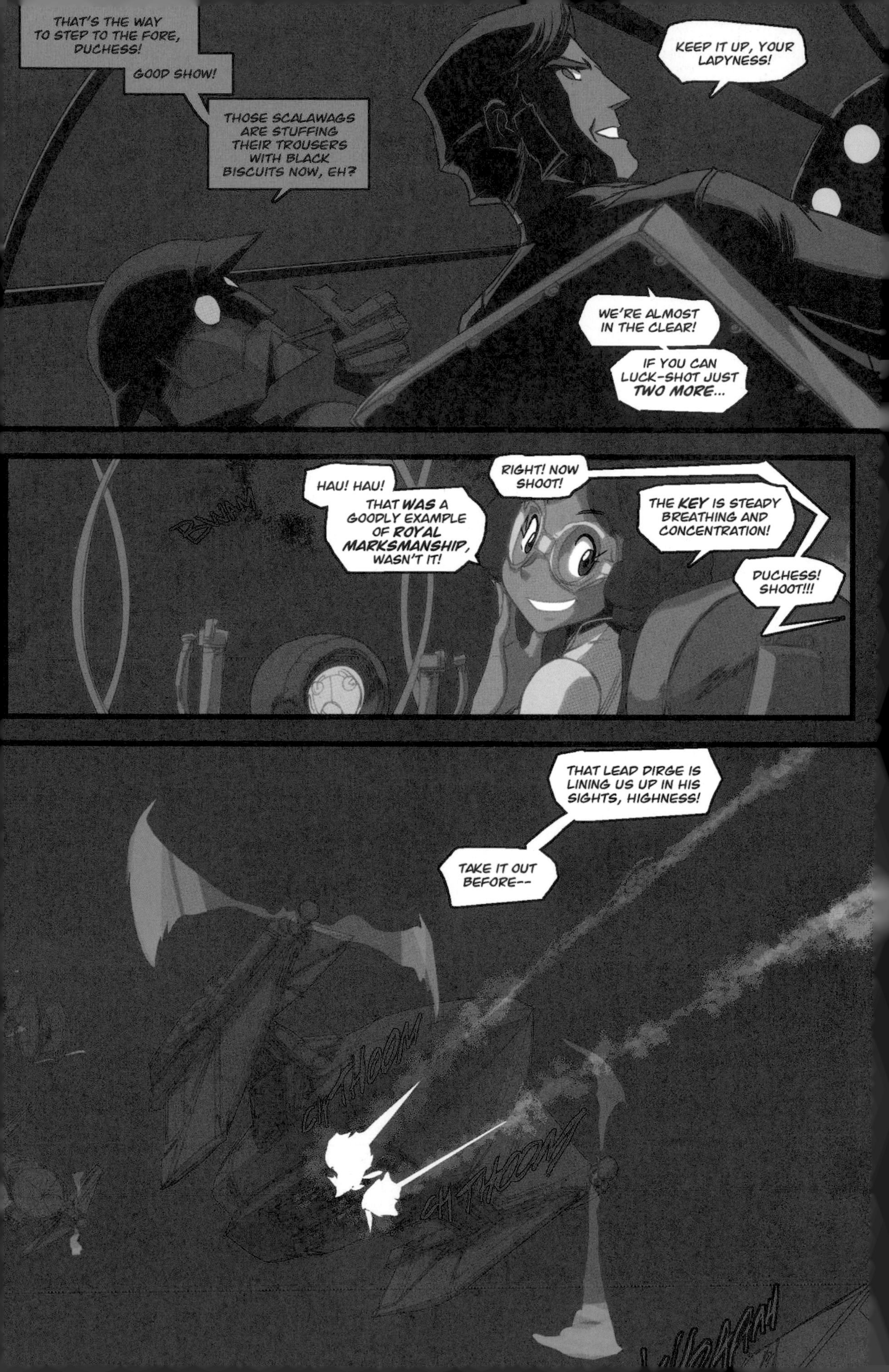
THAT'S THE WAY TO STEP TO THE FORE, DUCHESS!
GOOD SHOW!
THOSE SCALAWAGS ARE STUFFING THEIR TROUSERS WITH BLACK BISCUITS NOW, EH?
KEEP IT UP, YOUR LADYNESS!
WE'RE ALMOST IN THE CLEAR!
IF YOU CAN LUCK-SHOT JUST **TWO MORE**...
HAU! HAU!
THAT ***WAS*** A GOODLY EXAMPLE OF ***ROYAL MARKSMANSHIP***, WASN'T IT!
RIGHT! NOW SHOOT!
THE ***KEY*** IS STEADY BREATHING AND CONCENTRATION!
DUCHESS! SHOOT!!!
THAT LEAD DIRGE IS LINING US UP IN HIS SIGHTS, HIGHNESS!
TAKE IT OUT BEFORE--

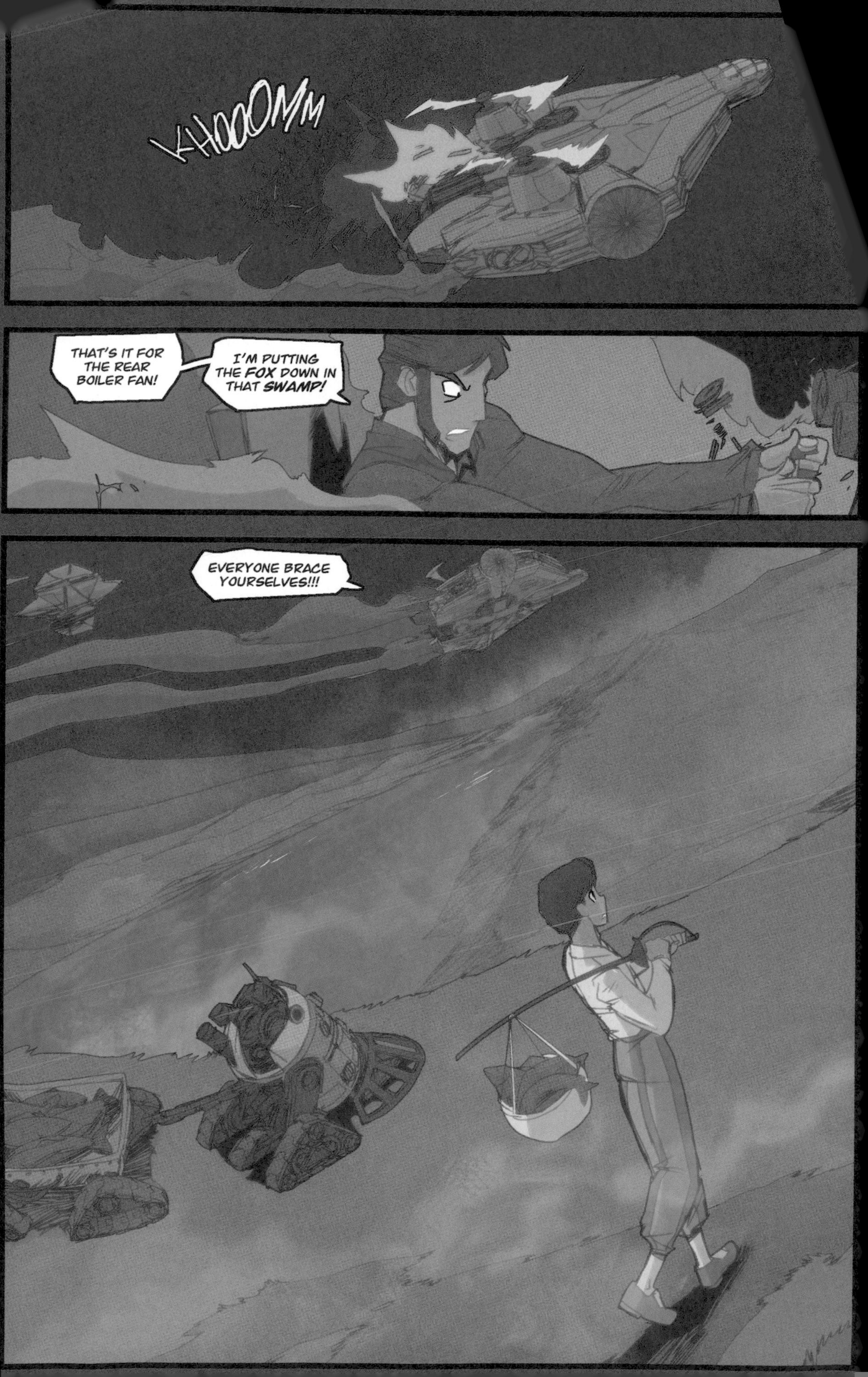
KHOOOMM
THAT'S IT FOR THE REAR BOILER FAN!
I'M PUTTING THE FOX DOWN IN THAT SWAMP!
EVERYONE BRACE YOURSELVES!!!

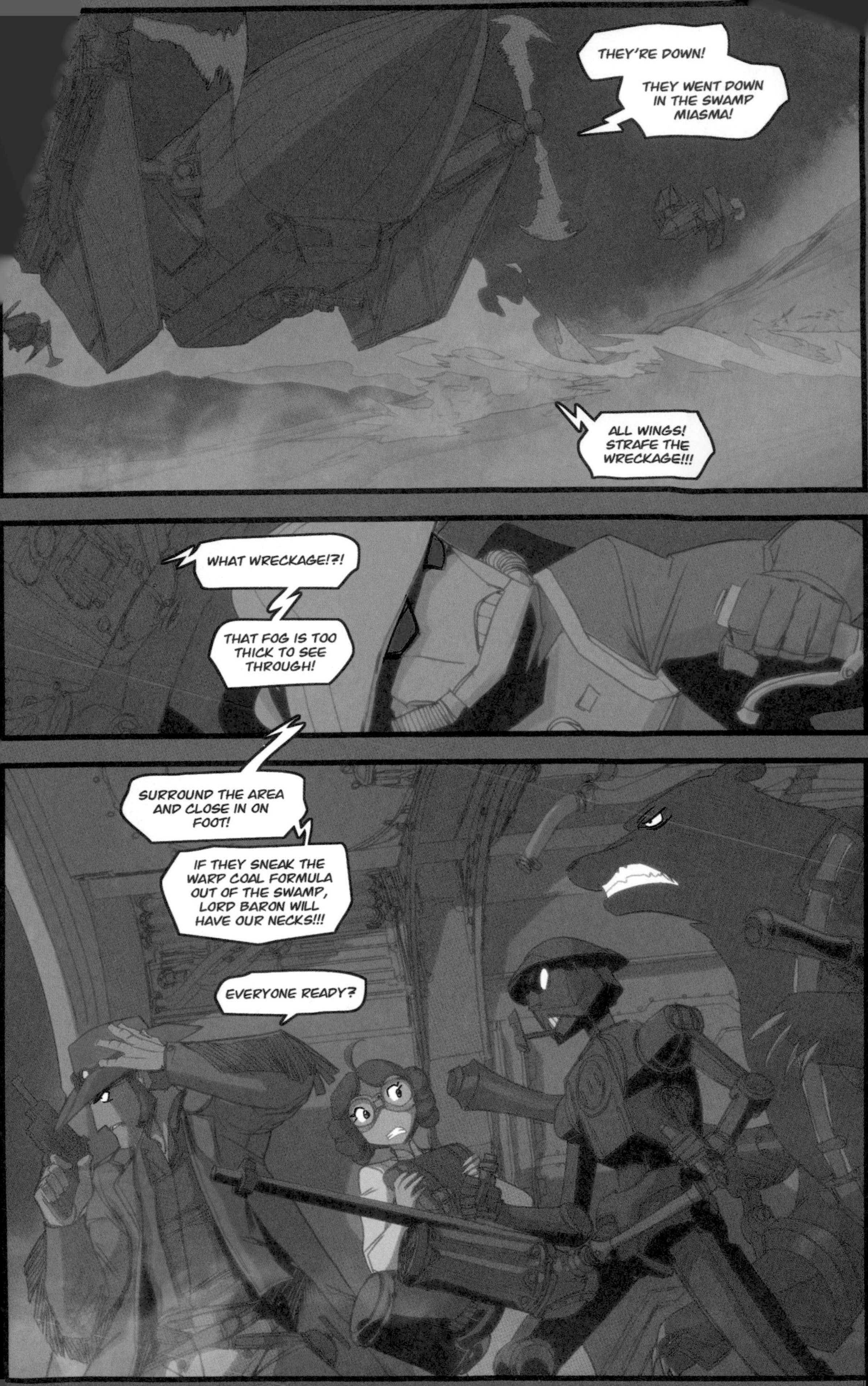
THEY'RE DOWN!
THEY WENT DOWN IN THE SWAMP MIASMA!
ALL WINGS! STRAFE THE WRECKAGE!!!
WHAT WRECKAGE!?!
THAT FOG IS TOO THICK TO SEE THROUGH!
SURROUND THE AREA AND CLOSE IN ON FOOT!
IF THEY SNEAK THE WARP COAL FORMULA OUT OF THE SWAMP, LORD BARON WILL HAVE OUR NECKS!!!
EVERYONE READY?

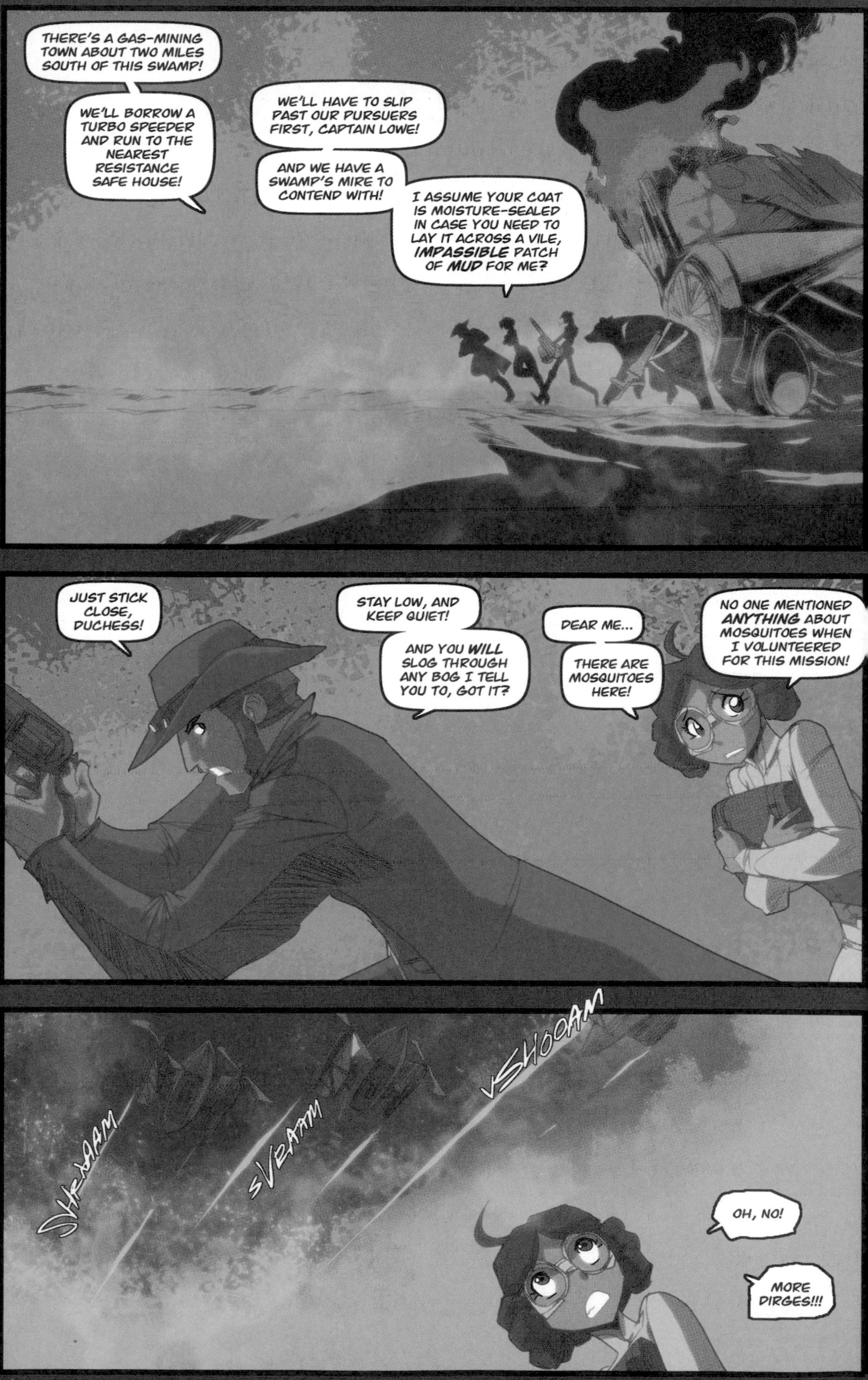
THERE'S A GAS-MINING TOWN ABOUT TWO MILES SOUTH OF THIS SWAMP!
WE'LL BORROW A TURBO SPEEDER AND RUN TO THE NEAREST RESISTANCE SAFE HOUSE!
WE'LL HAVE TO SLIP PAST OUR PURSUERS FIRST, CAPTAIN LOWE!
AND WE HAVE A SWAMP'S MIRE TO CONTEND WITH!
I ASSUME YOUR COAT IS MOISTURE-SEALED IN CASE YOU NEED TO LAY IT ACROSS A VILE, **IMPASSIBLE** PATCH OF **MUD** FOR ME?
JUST STICK CLOSE, DUCHESS!
STAY LOW, AND KEEP QUIET!
AND YOU **WILL** SLOG THROUGH ANY BOG I TELL YOU TO, GOT IT?
DEAR ME...
THERE ARE MOSQUITOES HERE!
NO ONE MENTIONED **ANYTHING** ABOUT MOSQUITOES WHEN I VOLUNTEERED FOR THIS MISSION!
SHRAAM
SVRAAM
VSHOOAM
OH, NO!
MORE DIRGES!!!

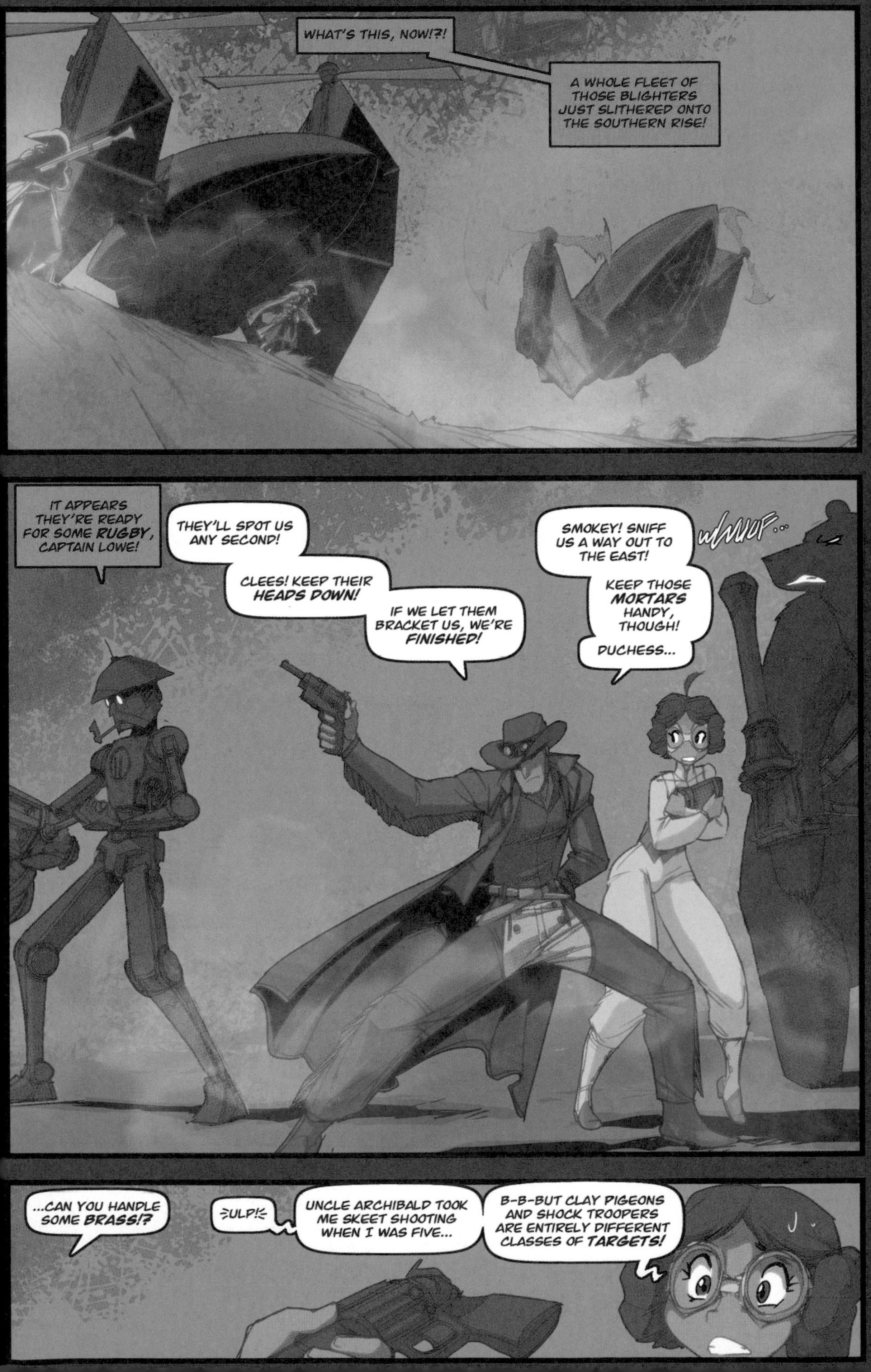
WHAT'S THIS, NOW!?!
A WHOLE FLEET OF THOSE BLIGHTERS JUST SLITHERED ONTO THE SOUTHERN RISE!
IT APPEARS THEY'RE READY FOR SOME RUGBY, CAPTAIN LOWE!
THEY'LL SPOT US ANY SECOND!
CLEES! KEEP THEIR HEADS DOWN!
IF WE LET THEM BRACKET US, WE'RE FINISHED!
SMOKEY! SNIFF US A WAY OUT TO THE EAST!
KEEP THOSE MORTARS HANDY, THOUGH!
DUCHESS...
WUUF...
...CAN YOU HANDLE SOME BRASS!?
ULP!
UNCLE ARCHIBALD TOOK ME SKEET SHOOTING WHEN I WAS FIVE...
B-B-BUT CLAY PIGEONS AND SHOCK TROOPERS ARE ENTIRELY DIFFERENT CLASSES OF TARGETS!

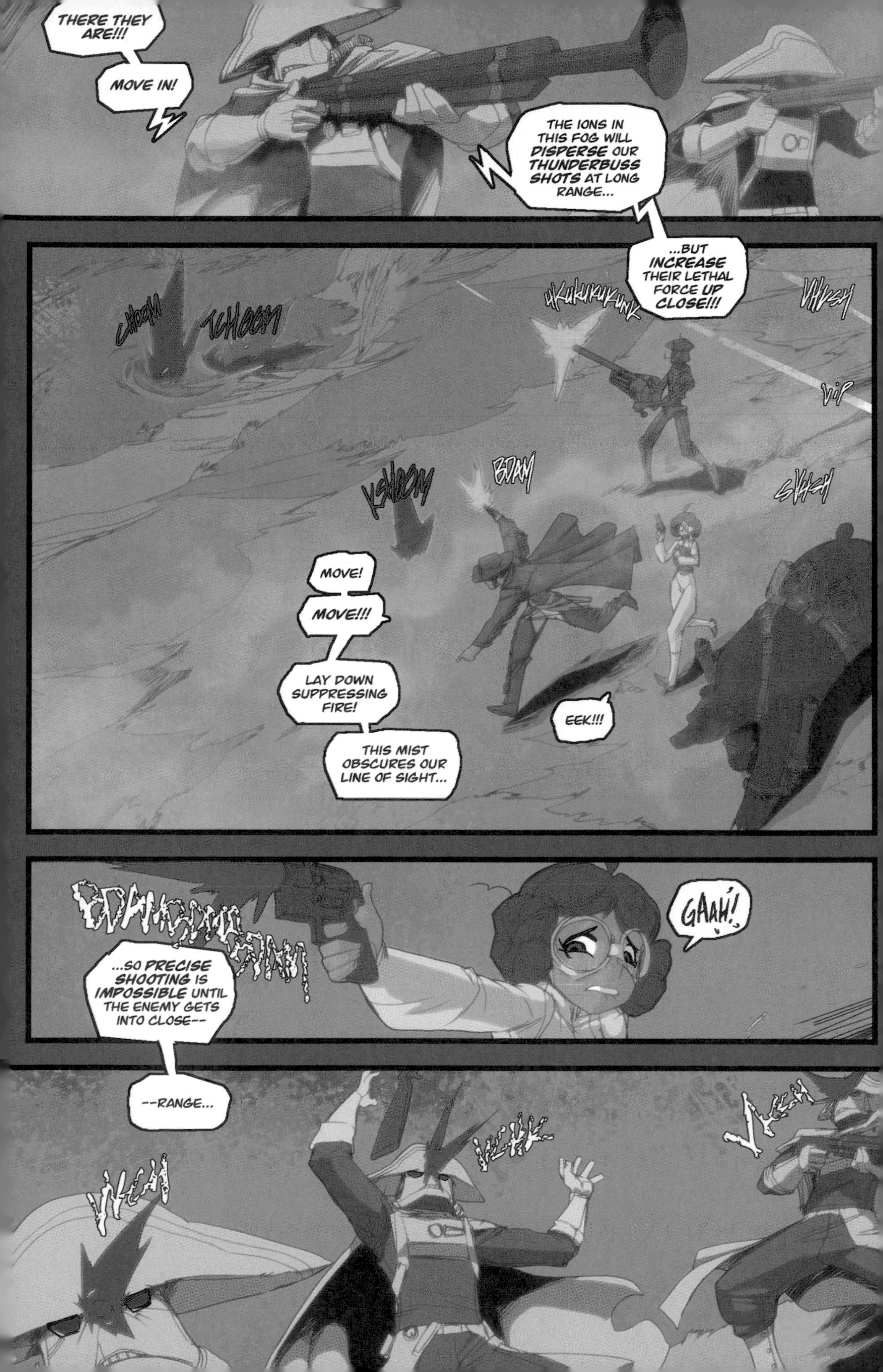

THERE THEY ARE!!!
MOVE IN!
THE IONS IN THIS FOG WILL DISPERSE OUR THUNDERBUSS SHOTS AT LONG RANGE...
...BUT INCREASE THEIR LETHAL FORCE UP CLOSE!!!
TCHOOM
BDAM
MOVE!
MOVE!!!
LAY DOWN SUPPRESSING FIRE!
THIS MIST OBSCURES OUR LINE OF SIGHT...
EEK!!!
GAAH!
...SO PRECISE SHOOTING IS IMPOSSIBLE UNTIL THE ENEMY GETS INTO CLOSE--
--RANGE...

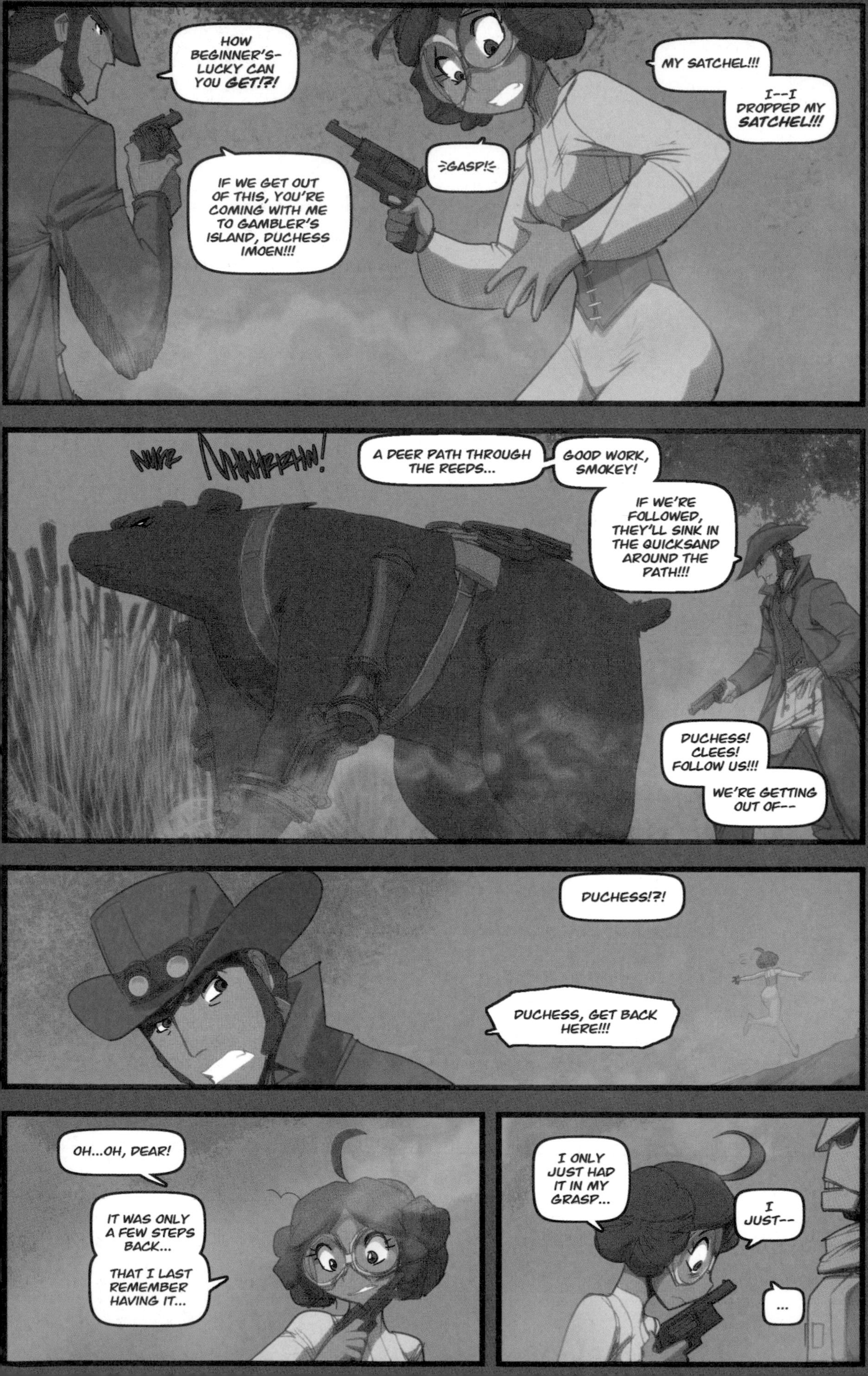
HOW BEGINNER'S-LUCKY CAN YOU GET!?!
IF WE GET OUT OF THIS, YOU'RE COMING WITH ME TO GAMBLER'S ISLAND, DUCHESS IMOEN!!!
GASP!
MY SATCHEL!!!
I--I DROPPED MY SATCHEL!!!
A DEER PATH THROUGH THE REEDS...
GOOD WORK, SMOKEY!
IF WE'RE FOLLOWED, THEY'LL SINK IN THE QUICKSAND AROUND THE PATH!!!
DUCHESS! CLEES! FOLLOW US!!!
WE'RE GETTING OUT OF--
DUCHESS!?!
DUCHESS, GET BACK HERE!!!
OH...OH, DEAR!
IT WAS ONLY A FEW STEPS BACK...
THAT I LAST REMEMBER HAVING IT...
I ONLY JUST HAD IT IN MY GRASP...
I JUST--
...

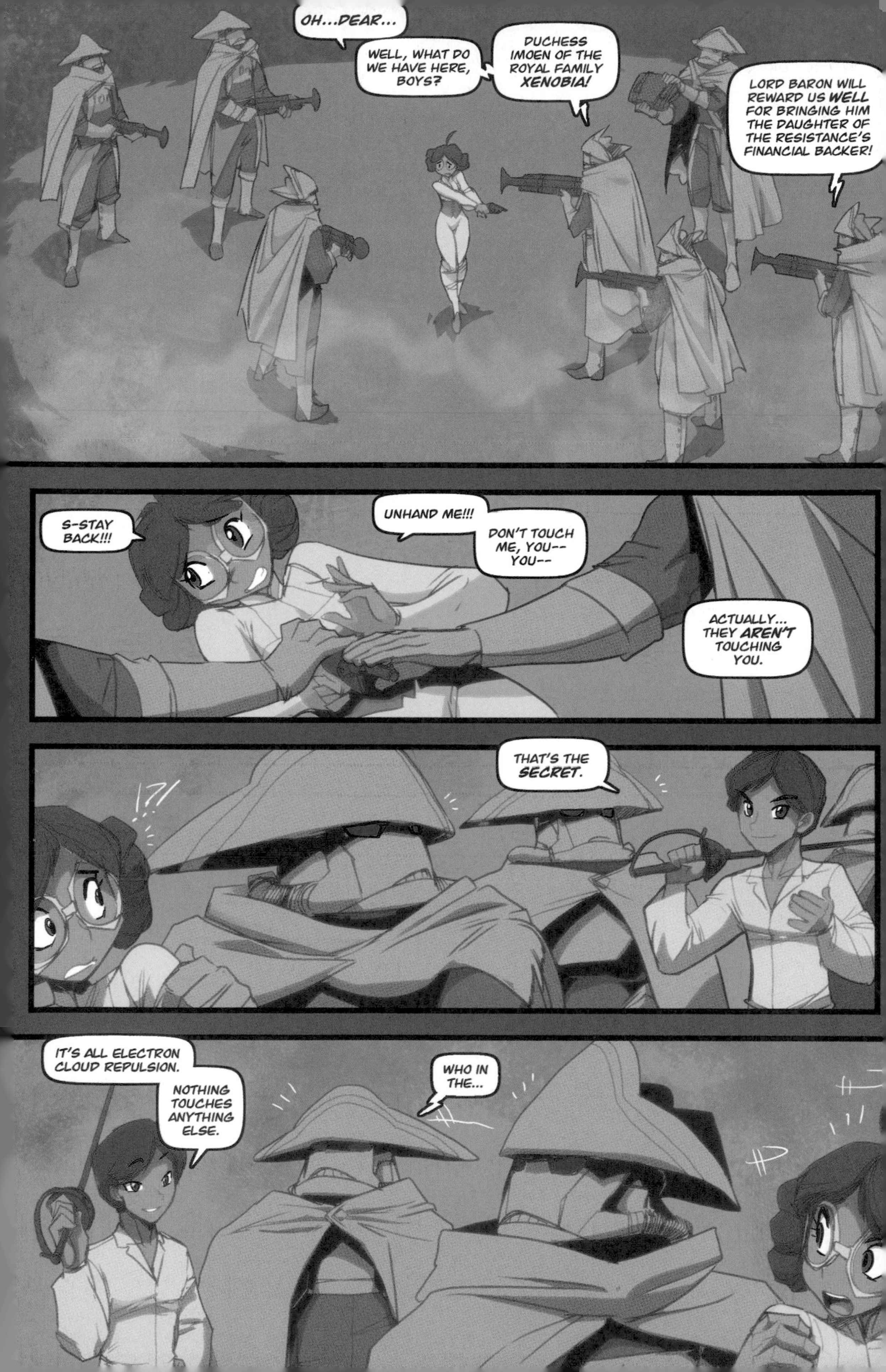

OH...DEAR...
WELL, WHAT DO WE HAVE HERE, BOYS?
DUCHESS IMOEN OF THE ROYAL FAMILY XENOBIA!
LORD BARON WILL REWARD US WELL FOR BRINGING HIM THE DAUGHTER OF THE RESISTANCE'S FINANCIAL BACKER!
S-STAY BACK!!!
UNHAND ME!!!
DON'T TOUCH ME, YOU-- YOU--
ACTUALLY... THEY AREN'T TOUCHING YOU.
!?!
THAT'S THE SECRET.
IT'S ALL ELECTRON CLOUD REPULSION.
NOTHING TOUCHES ANYTHING ELSE.
WHO IN THE...

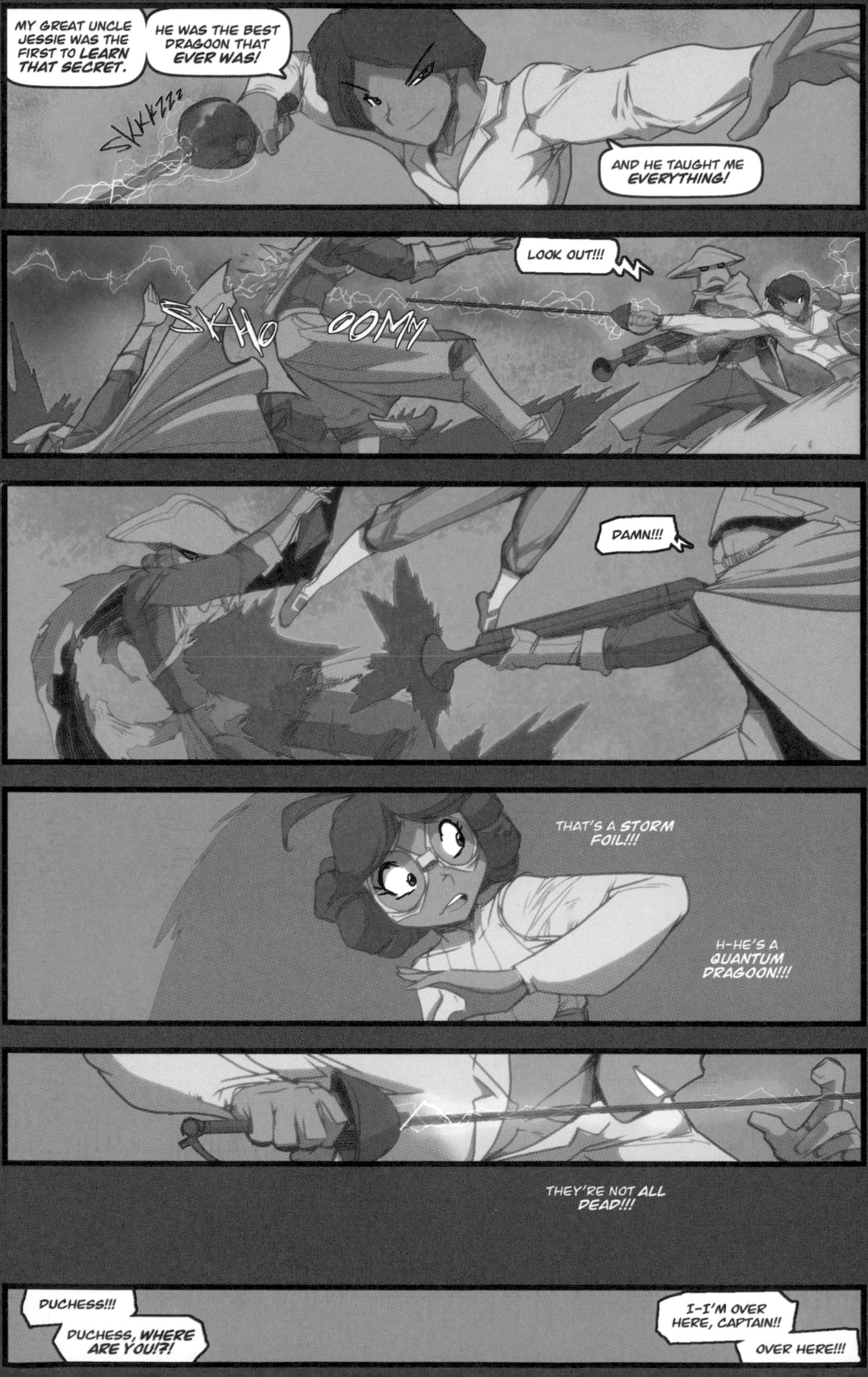
MY GREAT UNCLE JESSIE WAS THE FIRST TO LEARN THAT SECRET.
HE WAS THE BEST DRAGOON THAT EVER WAS!
SKKKZZZ
AND HE TAUGHT ME EVERYTHING!
LOOK OUT!!!
SKHOOOMM
DAMN!!!
THAT'S A STORM FOIL!!!
H-HE'S A QUANTUM DRAGOON!!!
THEY'RE NOT ALL DEAD!!!
DUCHESS!!!
DUCHESS, WHERE ARE YOU!?!
I-I'M OVER HERE, CAPTAIN!!
OVER HERE!!!

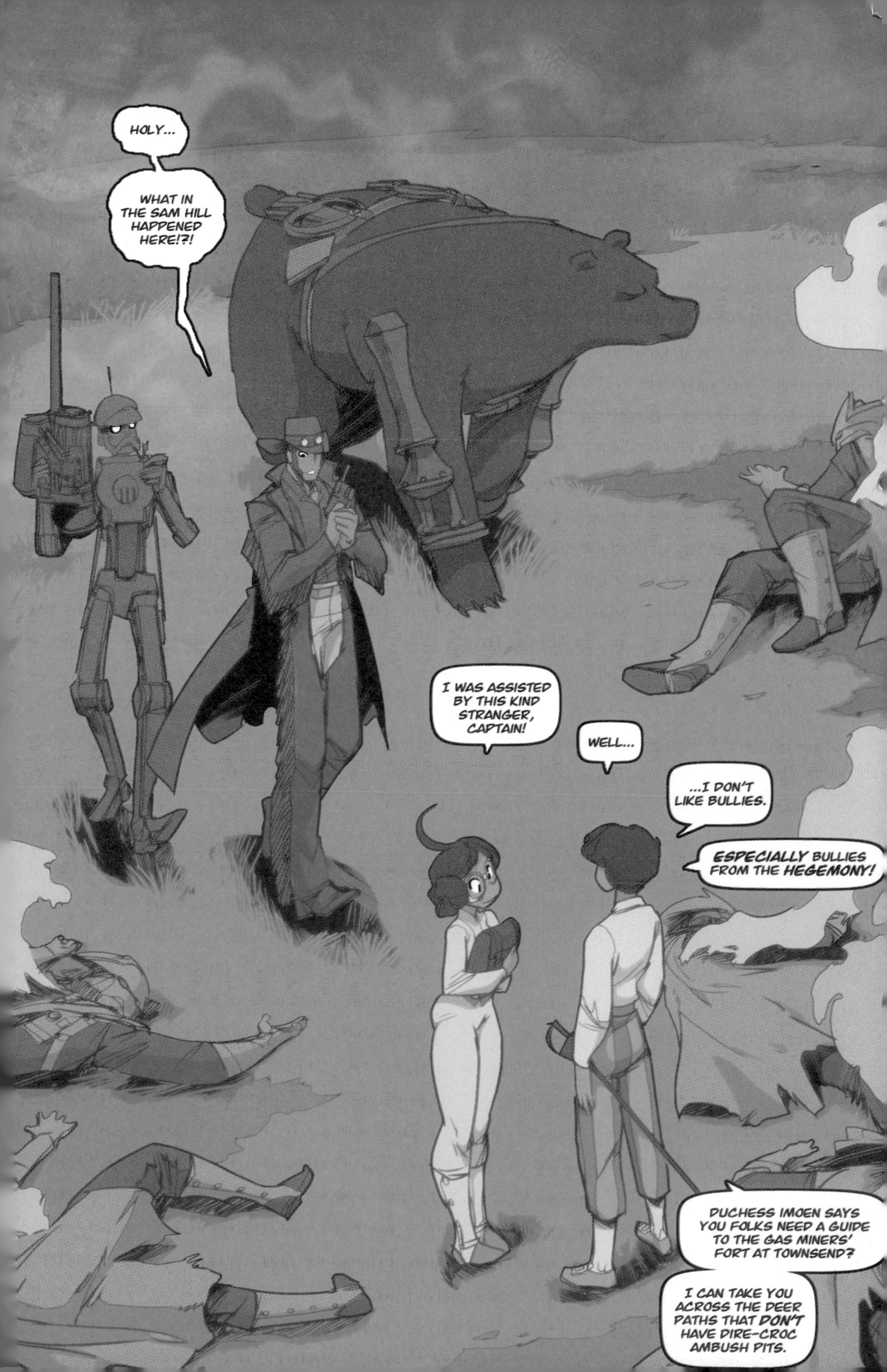
HOLY...
WHAT IN THE SAM HILL HAPPENED HERE!?!
I WAS ASSISTED BY THIS KIND STRANGER, CAPTAIN!
WELL...
...I DON'T LIKE BULLIES.
ESPECIALLY BULLIES FROM THE HEGEMONY!
DUCHESS IMOEN SAYS YOU FOLKS NEED A GUIDE TO THE GAS MINERS' FORT AT TOWNSEND?
I CAN TAKE YOU ACROSS THE DEER PATHS THAT DON'T HAVE DIRE-CROC AMBUSH PITS.

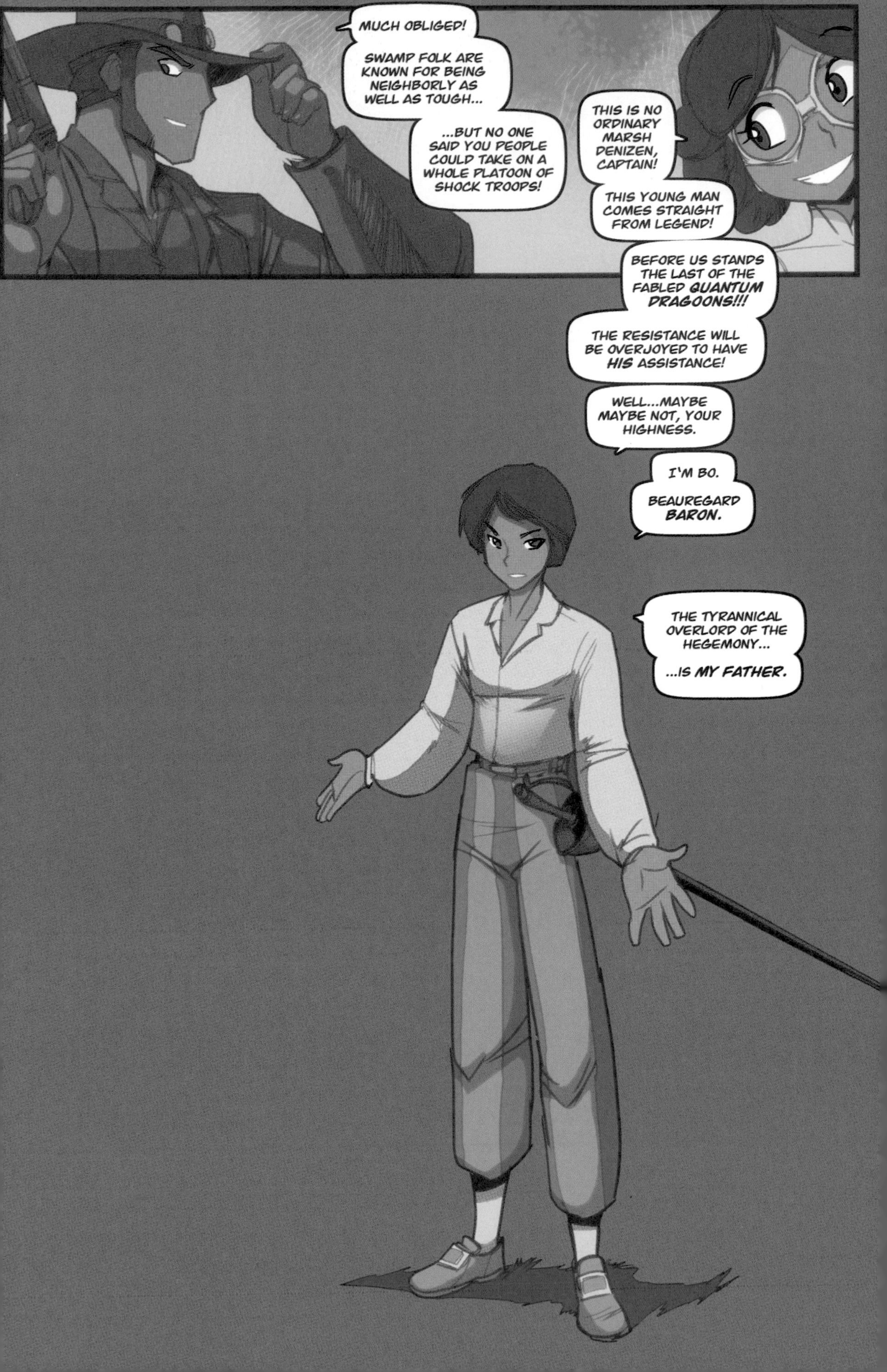
MUCH OBLIGED!
SWAMP FOLK ARE KNOWN FOR BEING NEIGHBORLY AS WELL AS TOUGH...
...BUT NO ONE SAID YOU PEOPLE COULD TAKE ON A WHOLE PLATOON OF SHOCK TROOPS!
THIS IS NO ORDINARY MARSH DENIZEN, CAPTAIN!
THIS YOUNG MAN COMES STRAIGHT FROM LEGEND!
BEFORE US STANDS THE LAST OF THE FABLED QUANTUM DRAGOONS!!!
THE RESISTANCE WILL BE OVERJOYED TO HAVE HIS ASSISTANCE!
WELL...MAYBE MAYBE NOT, YOUR HIGHNESS.
I'M BO.
BEAUREGARD BARON.
THE TYRANNICAL OVERLORD OF THE HEGEMONY...
...IS MY FATHER.

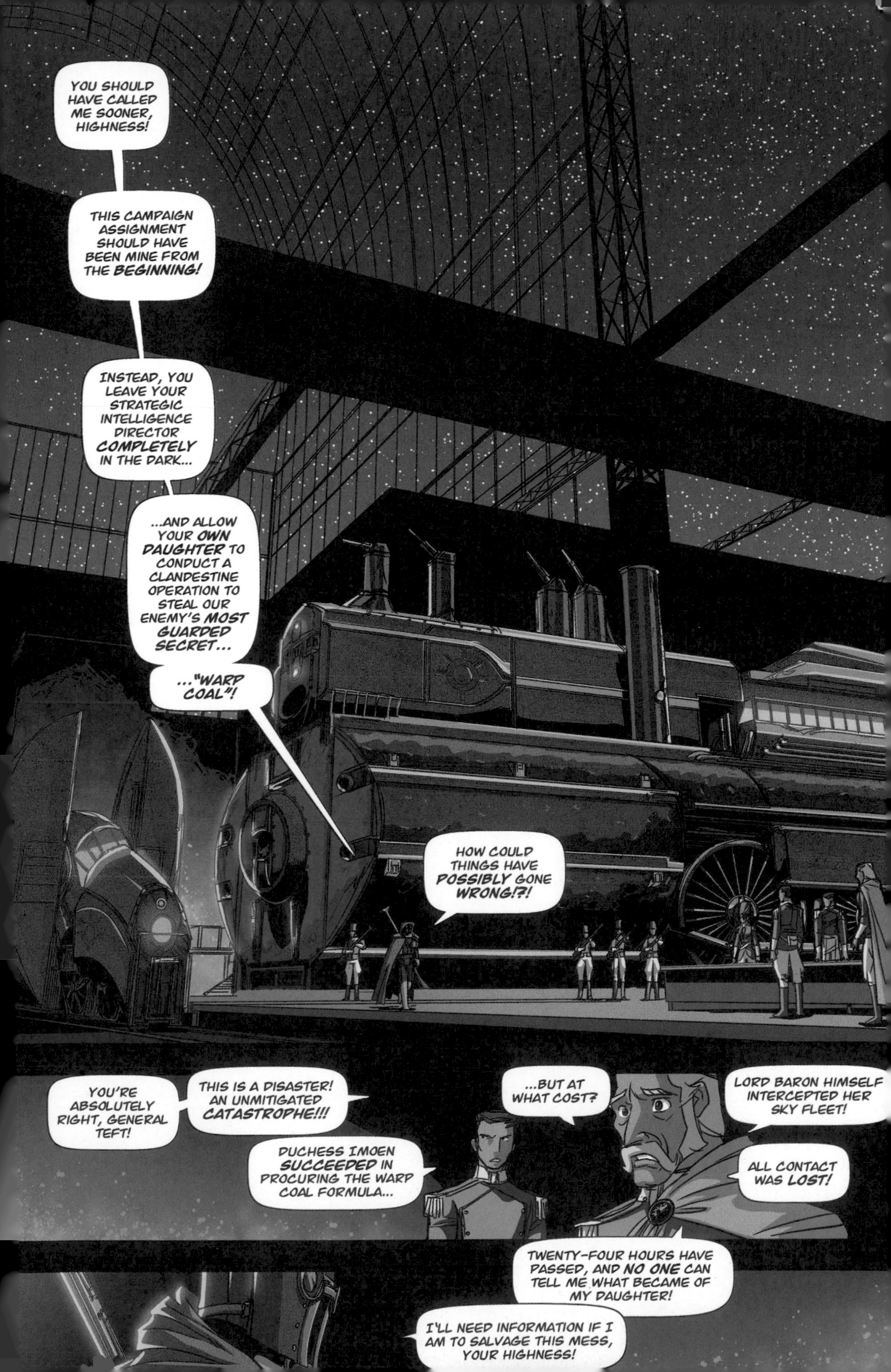
YOU SHOULD HAVE CALLED ME SOONER, HIGHNESS!
THIS CAMPAIGN ASSIGNMENT SHOULD HAVE BEEN MINE FROM THE BEGINNING!
INSTEAD, YOU LEAVE YOUR STRATEGIC INTELLIGENCE DIRECTOR COMPLETELY IN THE DARK...
...AND ALLOW YOUR OWN DAUGHTER TO CONDUCT A CLANDESTINE OPERATION TO STEAL OUR ENEMY'S MOST GUARDED SECRET...
..."WARP COAL"!
HOW COULD THINGS HAVE POSSIBLY GONE WRONG!?!
YOU'RE ABSOLUTELY RIGHT, GENERAL TEFT!
THIS IS A DISASTER! AN UNMITIGATED CATASTROPHE!!!
DUCHESS IMOEN SUCCEEDED IN PROCURING THE WARP COAL FORMULA...
...BUT AT WHAT COST?
LORD BARON HIMSELF INTERCEPTED HER SKY FLEET!
ALL CONTACT WAS LOST!
TWENTY-FOUR HOURS HAVE PASSED, AND NO ONE CAN TELL ME WHAT BECAME OF MY DAUGHTER!
I'LL NEED INFORMATION IF I AM TO SALVAGE THIS MESS, YOUR HIGHNESS!

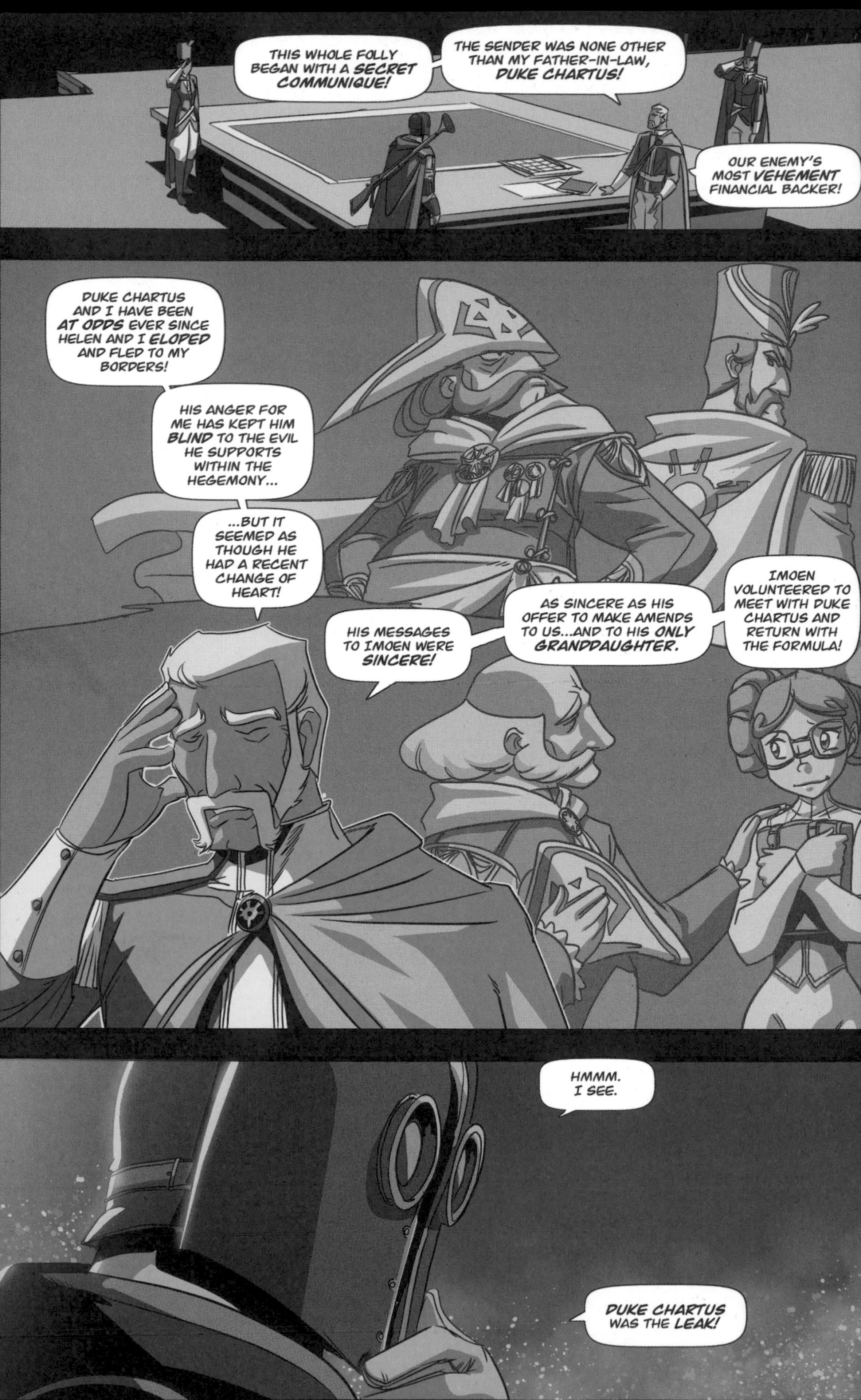
THIS WHOLE FOLLY BEGAN WITH A SECRET COMMUNIQUE!
THE SENDER WAS NONE OTHER THAN MY FATHER-IN-LAW, DUKE CHARTUS!
OUR ENEMY'S MOST VEHEMENT FINANCIAL BACKER!
DUKE CHARTUS AND I HAVE BEEN AT ODDS EVER SINCE HELEN AND I ELOPED AND FLED TO MY BORDERS!
HIS ANGER FOR ME HAS KEPT HIM BLIND TO THE EVIL HE SUPPORTS WITHIN THE HEGEMONY...
...BUT IT SEEMED AS THOUGH HE HAD A RECENT CHANGE OF HEART!
HIS MESSAGES TO IMOEN WERE SINCERE!
AS SINCERE AS HIS OFFER TO MAKE AMENDS TO US...AND TO HIS ONLY GRANDDAUGHTER.
IMOEN VOLUNTEERED TO MEET WITH DUKE CHARTUS AND RETURN WITH THE FORMULA!
HMMM. I SEE.
DUKE CHARTUS WAS THE LEAK!

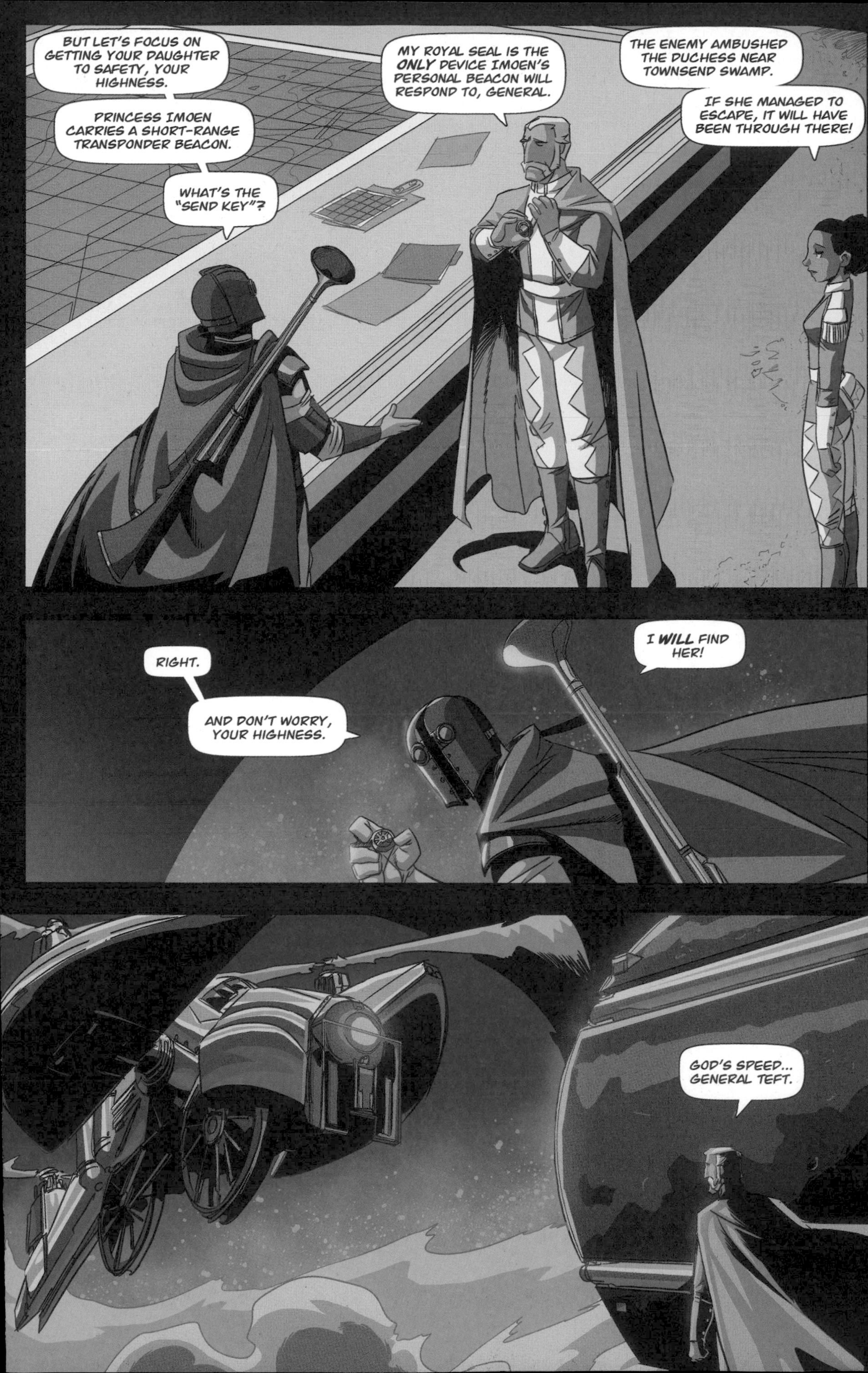

BUT LET'S FOCUS ON GETTING YOUR DAUGHTER TO SAFETY, YOUR HIGHNESS.
PRINCESS IMOEN CARRIES A SHORT-RANGE TRANSPONDER BEACON.
WHAT'S THE "SEND KEY"?
MY ROYAL SEAL IS THE ONLY DEVICE IMOEN'S PERSONAL BEACON WILL RESPOND TO, GENERAL.
THE ENEMY AMBUSHED THE DUCHESS NEAR TOWNSEND SWAMP.
IF SHE MANAGED TO ESCAPE, IT WILL HAVE BEEN THROUGH THERE!
RIGHT.
AND DON'T WORRY, YOUR HIGHNESS.
I WILL FIND HER!
GOD'S SPEED... GENERAL TEFT.

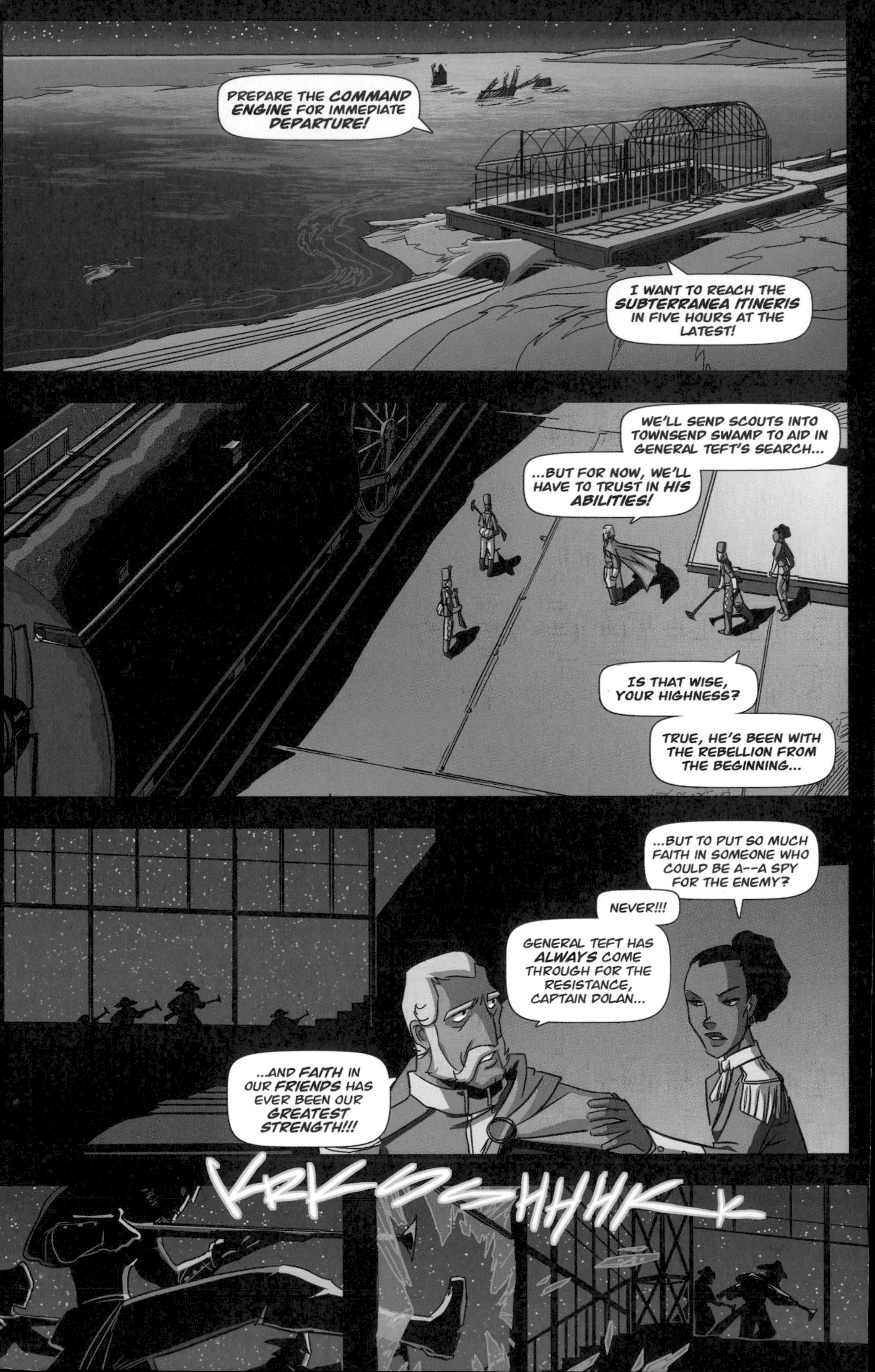
PREPARE THE COMMAND ENGINE FOR IMMEDIATE DEPARTURE!
I WANT TO REACH THE SUBTERRANEA ITINERIS IN FIVE HOURS AT THE LATEST!
WE'LL SEND SCOUTS INTO TOWNSEND SWAMP TO AID IN GENERAL TEFT'S SEARCH...
...BUT FOR NOW, WE'LL HAVE TO TRUST IN HIS ABILITIES!
IS THAT WISE, YOUR HIGHNESS?
TRUE, HE'S BEEN WITH THE REBELLION FROM THE BEGINNING...
...BUT TO PUT SO MUCH FAITH IN SOMEONE WHO COULD BE A--A SPY FOR THE ENEMY?
NEVER!!!
GENERAL TEFT HAS ALWAYS COME THROUGH FOR THE RESISTANCE, CAPTAIN DOLAN...
...AND FAITH IN OUR FRIENDS HAS EVER BEEN OUR GREATEST STRENGTH!!!
KRKSSHHHKK

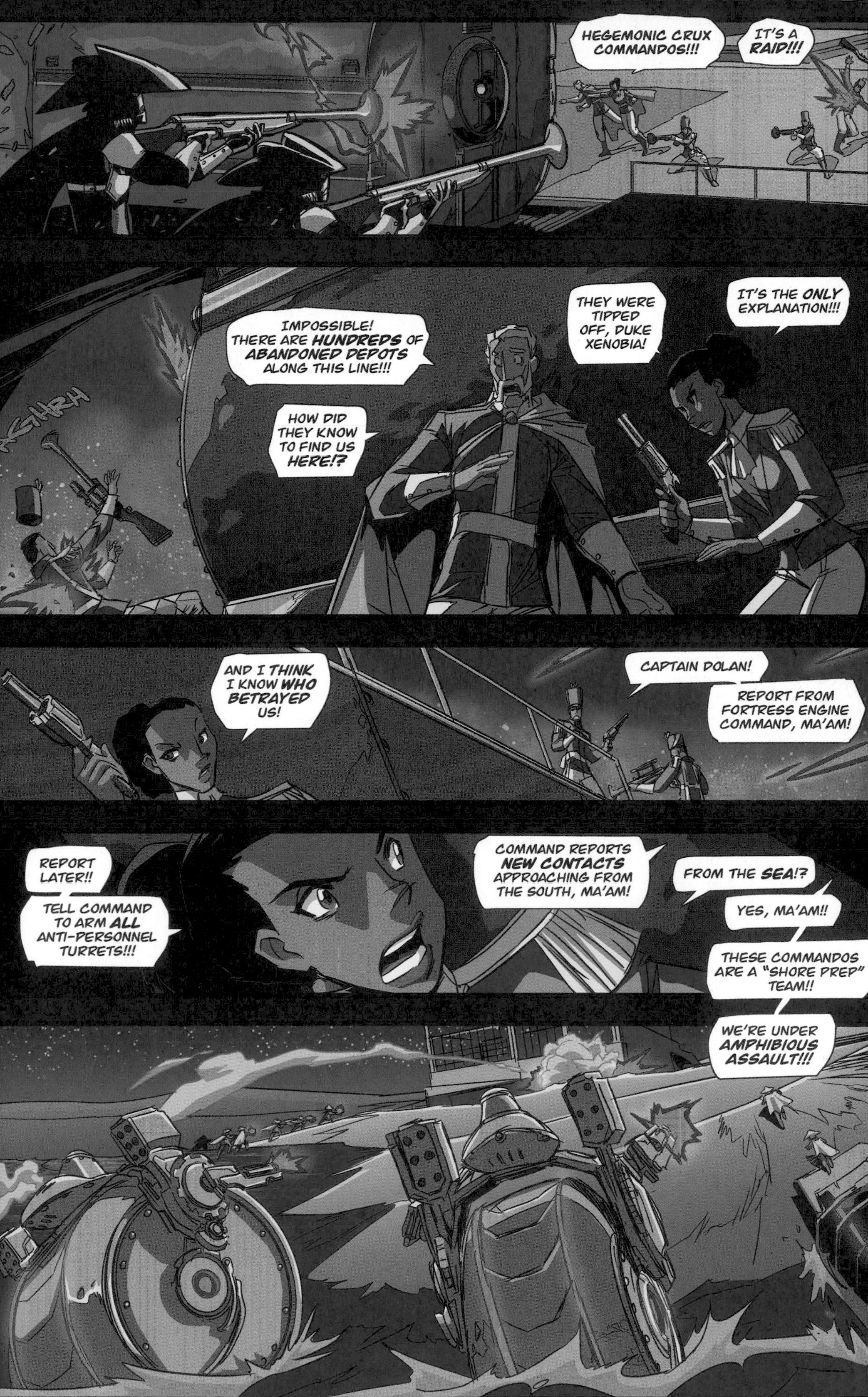
HEGEMONIC CRUX COMMANDOS!!!
IT'S A RAID!!!
IMPOSSIBLE! THERE ARE HUNDREDS OF ABANDONED DEPOTS ALONG THIS LINE!!!
HOW DID THEY KNOW TO FIND US HERE!?
THEY WERE TIPPED OFF, DUKE XENOBIA!
IT'S THE ONLY EXPLANATION!!!
AAGHRH
AND I THINK I KNOW WHO BETRAYED US!
CAPTAIN DOLAN!
REPORT FROM FORTRESS ENGINE COMMAND, MA'AM!
REPORT LATER!!
TELL COMMAND TO ARM ALL ANTI-PERSONNEL TURRETS!!!
COMMAND REPORTS NEW CONTACTS APPROACHING FROM THE SOUTH, MA'AM!
FROM THE SEA!?
YES, MA'AM!!
THESE COMMANDOS ARE A "SHORE PREP" TEAM!!
WE'RE UNDER AMPHIBIOUS ASSAULT!!!

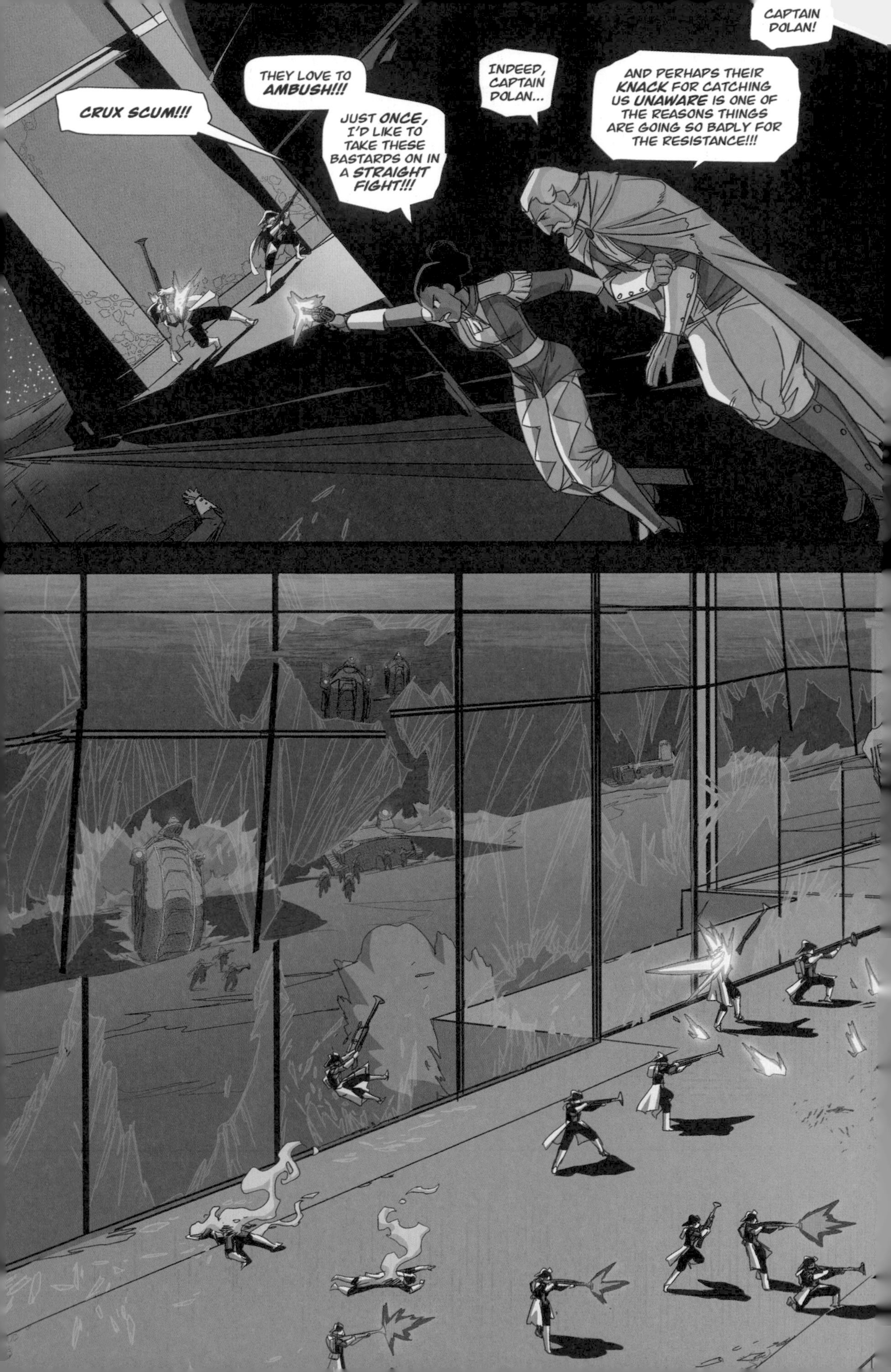
CRUX SCUM!!!
THEY LOVE TO AMBUSH!!!
JUST ONCE, I'D LIKE TO TAKE THESE BASTARDS ON IN A STRAIGHT FIGHT!!!
INDEED, CAPTAIN DOLAN...
AND PERHAPS THEIR KNACK FOR CATCHING US UNAWARE IS ONE OF THE REASONS THINGS ARE GOING SO BADLY FOR THE RESISTANCE!!!
CAPTAIN DOLAN!

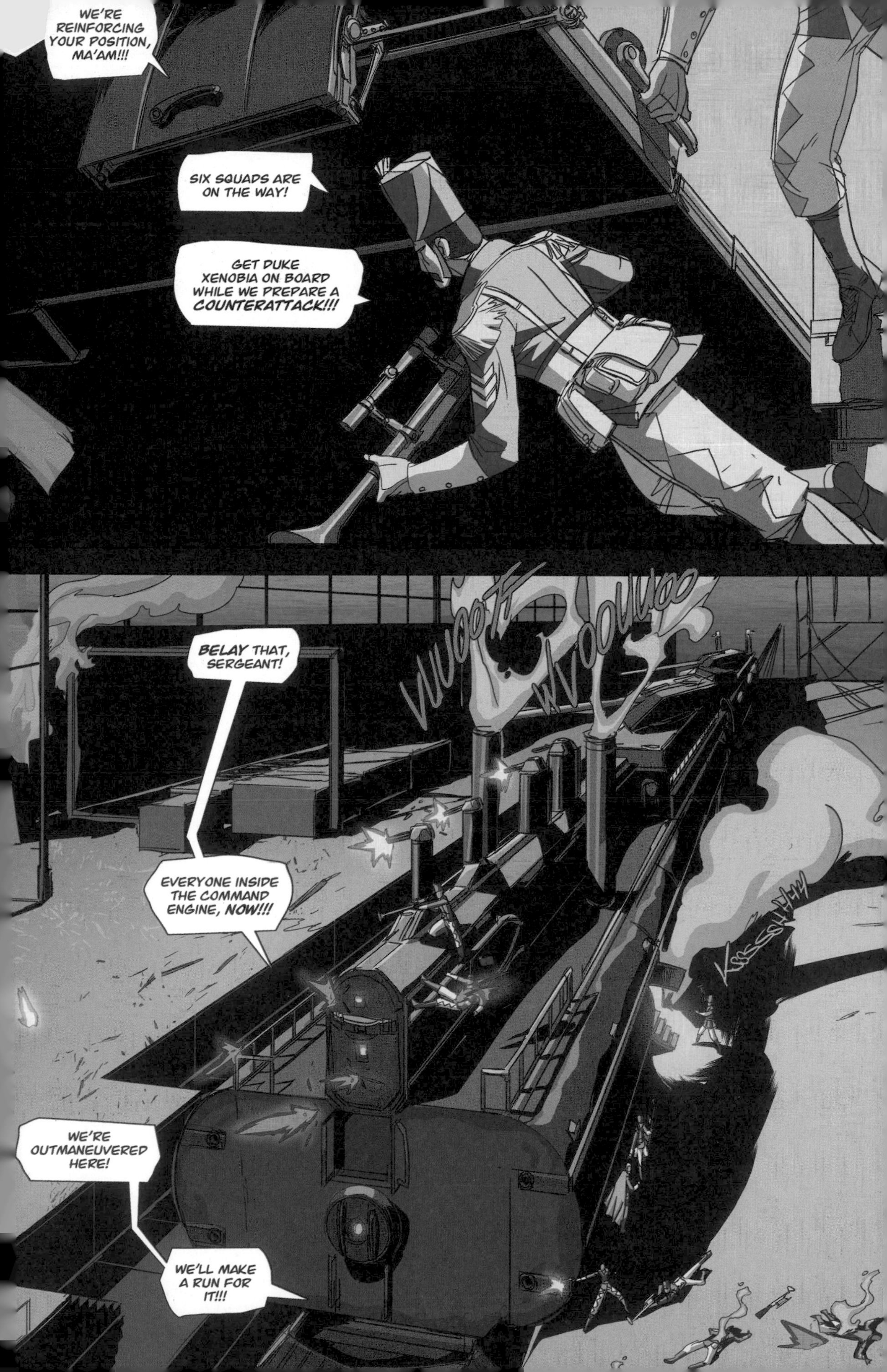
WE'RE REINFORCING YOUR POSITION, MA'AM!!!
SIX SQUADS ARE ON THE WAY!
GET DUKE XENOBIA ON BOARD WHILE WE PREPARE A COUNTERATTACK!!!
BELAY THAT, SERGEANT!
EVERYONE INSIDE THE COMMAND ENGINE, NOW!!!
WE'RE OUTMANEUVERED HERE!
WE'LL MAKE A RUN FOR IT!!!

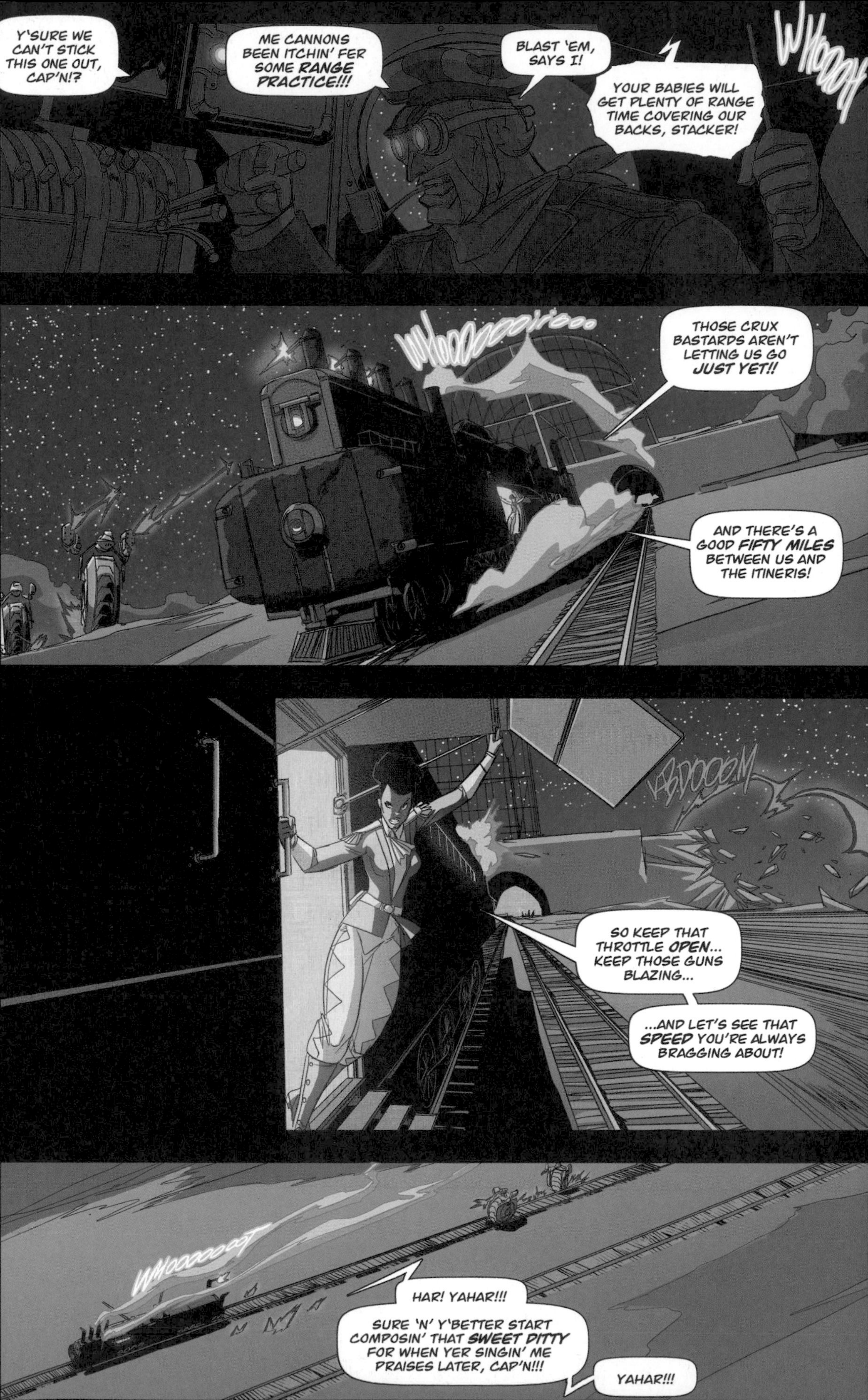
Y'SURE WE CAN'T STICK THIS ONE OUT, CAP'N!?
ME CANNONS BEEN ITCHIN' FER SOME RANGE PRACTICE!!!
BLAST 'EM, SAYS I!
YOUR BABIES WILL GET PLENTY OF RANGE TIME COVERING OUR BACKS, STACKER!
THOSE CRUX BASTARDS AREN'T LETTING US GO JUST YET!!
AND THERE'S A GOOD FIFTY MILES BETWEEN US AND THE ITINERIS!
VBDOOOM
SO KEEP THAT THROTTLE OPEN... KEEP THOSE GUNS BLAZING...
...AND LET'S SEE THAT SPEED YOU'RE ALWAYS BRAGGING ABOUT!
HAR! YAHAR!!!
SURE 'N' Y'BETTER START COMPOSIN' THAT SWEET DITTY FOR WHEN YER SINGIN' ME PRAISES LATER, CAP'N!!!
YAHAR!!!

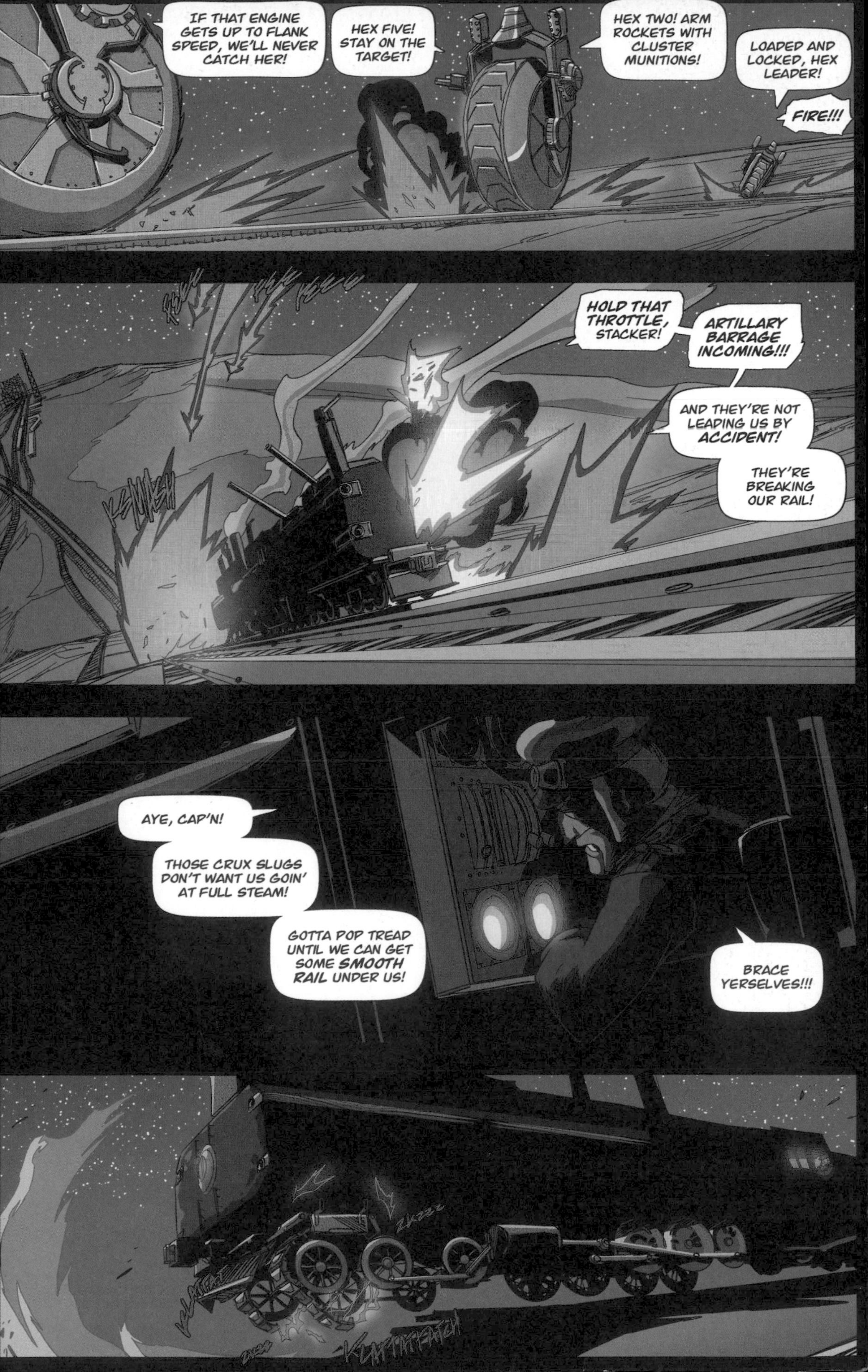
IF THAT ENGINE GETS UP TO FLANK SPEED, WE'LL NEVER CATCH HER!
HEX FIVE! STAY ON THE TARGET!
HEX TWO! ARM ROCKETS WITH CLUSTER MUNITIONS!
LOADED AND LOCKED, HEX LEADER!
FIRE!!!
HOLD THAT THROTTLE, STACKER!
ARTILLARY BARRAGE INCOMING!!!
AND THEY'RE NOT LEADING US BY ACCIDENT!
THEY'RE BREAKING OUR RAIL!
AYE, CAP'N!
THOSE CRUX SLUGS DON'T WANT US GOIN' AT FULL STEAM!
GOTTA POP TREAD UNTIL WE CAN GET SOME SMOOTH RAIL UNDER US!
BRACE YERSELVES!!!

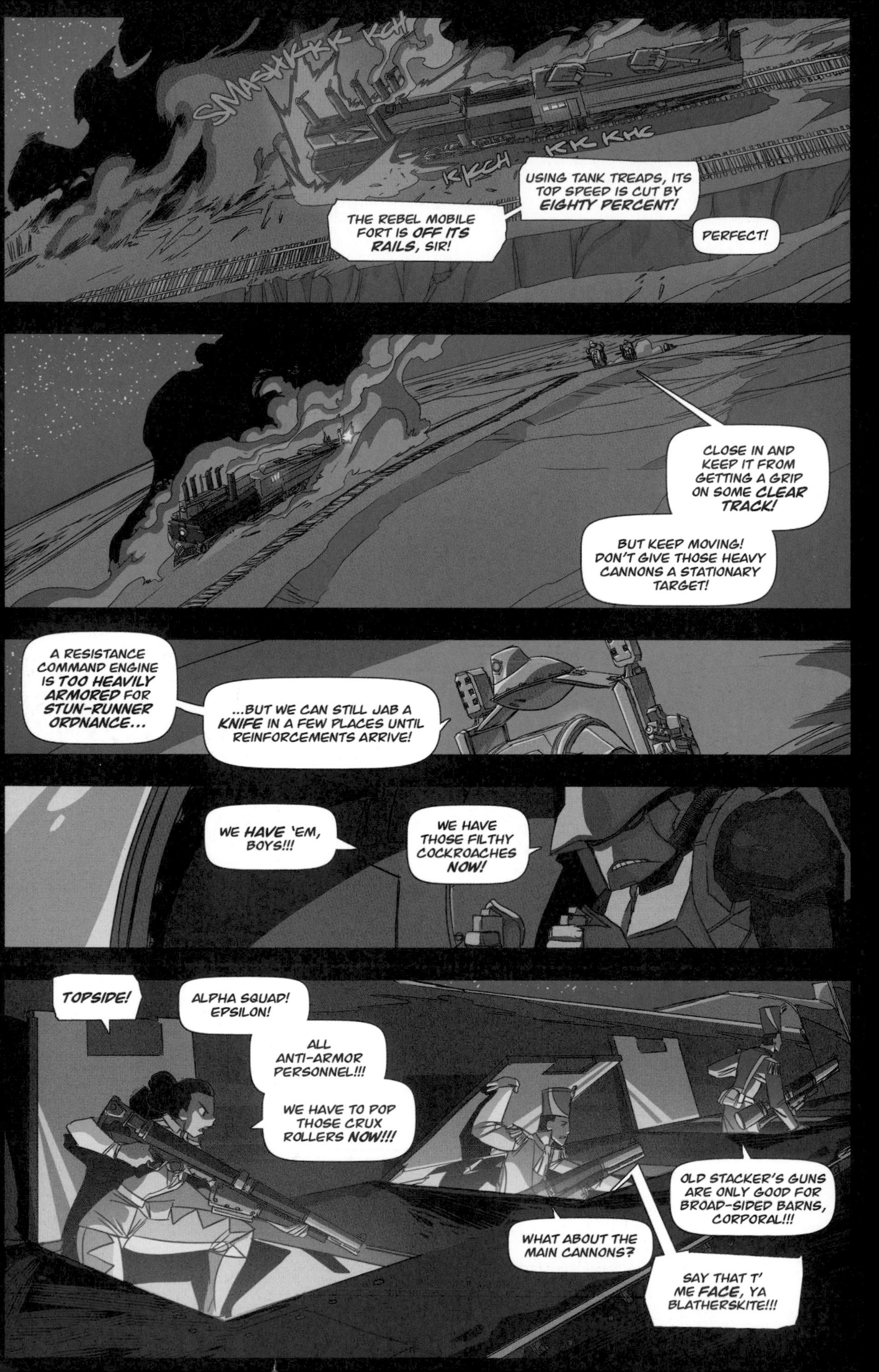
SMASHKKK KCH
KKCH KK KHC
THE REBEL MOBILE FORT IS OFF ITS RAILS, SIR!
USING TANK TREADS, ITS TOP SPEED IS CUT BY EIGHTY PERCENT!
PERFECT!
CLOSE IN AND KEEP IT FROM GETTING A GRIP ON SOME CLEAR TRACK!
BUT KEEP MOVING! DON'T GIVE THOSE HEAVY CANNONS A STATIONARY TARGET!
A RESISTANCE COMMAND ENGINE IS TOO HEAVILY ARMORED FOR STUN-RUNNER ORDNANCE...
...BUT WE CAN STILL JAB A KNIFE IN A FEW PLACES UNTIL REINFORCEMENTS ARRIVE!
WE HAVE 'EM, BOYS!!!
WE HAVE THOSE FILTHY COCKROACHES NOW!
TOPSIDE!
ALPHA SQUAD! EPSILON!
ALL ANTI-ARMOR PERSONNEL!!!
WE HAVE TO POP THOSE CRUX ROLLERS NOW!!!
OLD STACKER'S GUNS ARE ONLY GOOD FOR BROAD-SIDED BARNS, CORPORAL!!!
WHAT ABOUT THE MAIN CANNONS?
SAY THAT T' ME FACE, YA BLATHERSKITE!!!

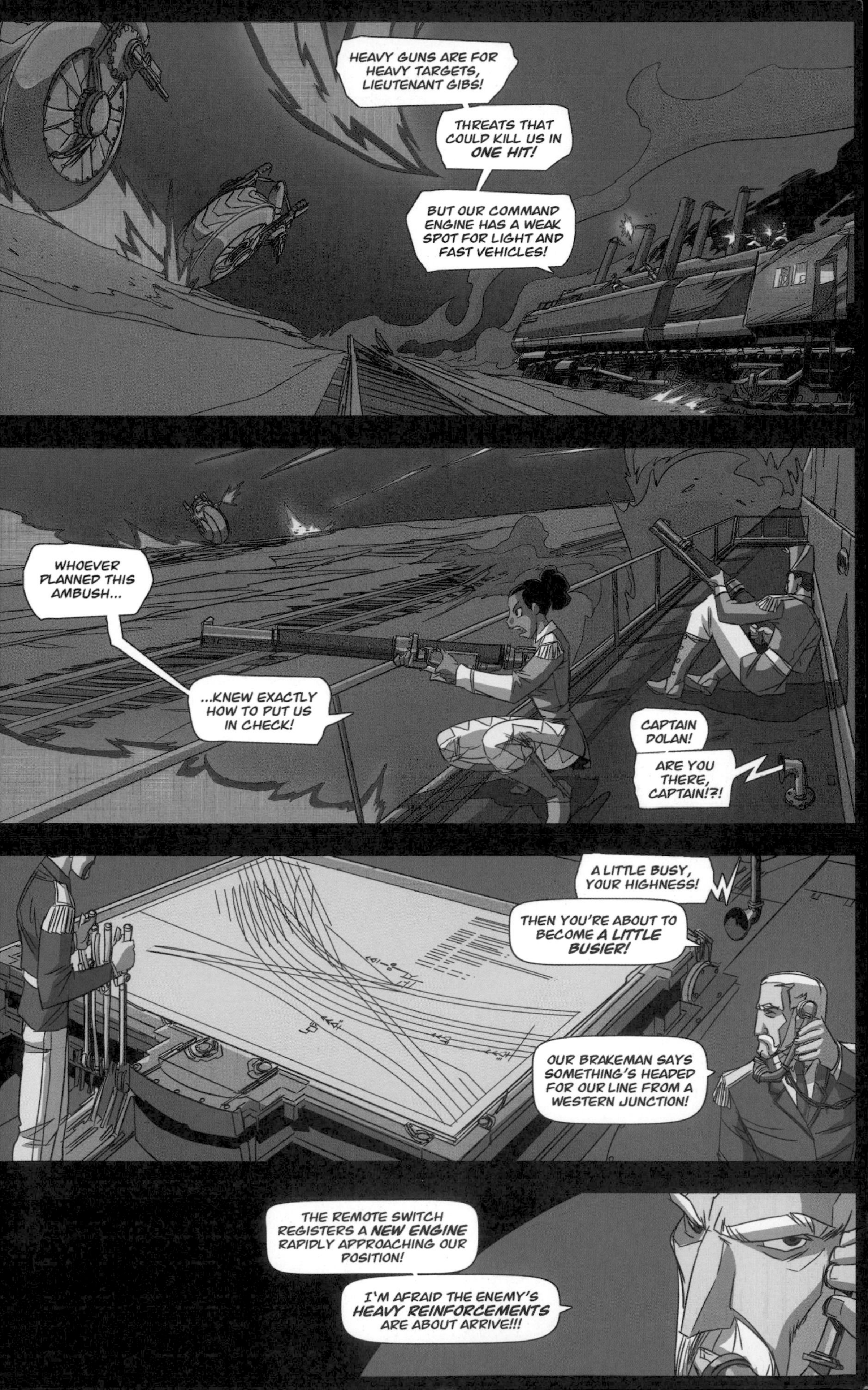
HEAVY GUNS ARE FOR HEAVY TARGETS, LIEUTENANT GIBS!
THREATS THAT COULD KILL US IN ONE HIT!
BUT OUR COMMAND ENGINE HAS A WEAK SPOT FOR LIGHT AND FAST VEHICLES!
WHOEVER PLANNED THIS AMBUSH...
...KNEW EXACTLY HOW TO PUT US IN CHECK!
CAPTAIN DOLAN!
ARE YOU THERE, CAPTAIN!?!
A LITTLE BUSY, YOUR HIGHNESS!
THEN YOU'RE ABOUT TO BECOME A LITTLE BUSIER!
OUR BRAKEMAN SAYS SOMETHING'S HEADED FOR OUR LINE FROM A WESTERN JUNCTION!
THE REMOTE SWITCH REGISTERS A NEW ENGINE RAPIDLY APPROACHING OUR POSITION!
I'M AFRAID THE ENEMY'S HEAVY REINFORCEMENTS ARE ABOUT ARRIVE!!!

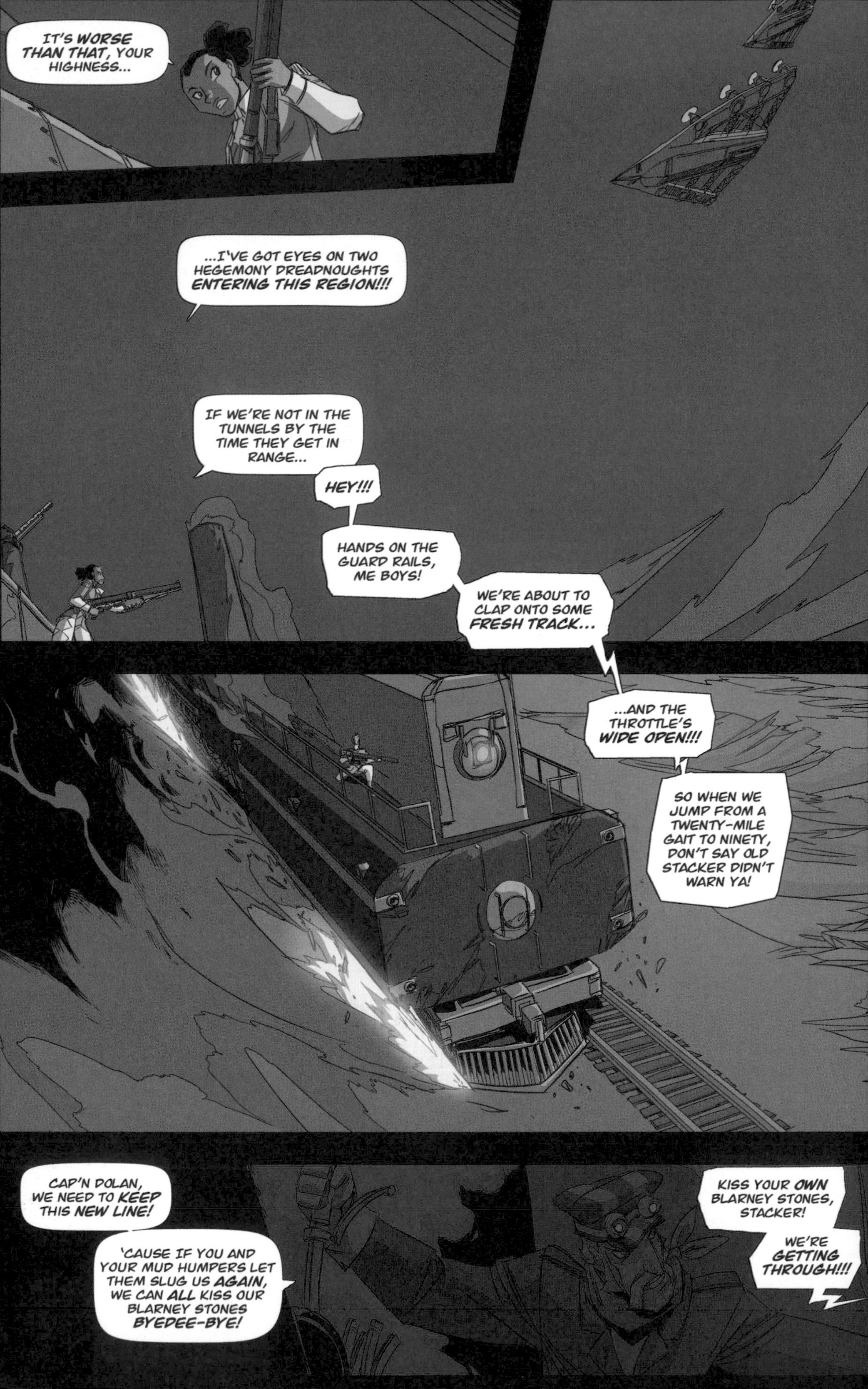
IT'S WORSE THAN THAT, YOUR HIGHNESS...
...I'VE GOT EYES ON TWO HEGEMONY DREADNOUGHTS ENTERING THIS REGION!!!
IF WE'RE NOT IN THE TUNNELS BY THE TIME THEY GET IN RANGE...
HEY!!!
HANDS ON THE GUARD RAILS, ME BOYS!
WE'RE ABOUT TO CLAP ONTO SOME FRESH TRACK...
...AND THE THROTTLE'S WIDE OPEN!!!
SO WHEN WE JUMP FROM A TWENTY-MILE GAIT TO NINETY, DON'T SAY OLD STACKER DIDN'T WARN YA!
CAP'N DOLAN, WE NEED TO KEEP THIS NEW LINE!
'CAUSE IF YOU AND YOUR MUD HUMPERS LET THEM SLUG US AGAIN, WE CAN ALL KISS OUR BLARNEY STONES BYEDEE-BYE!
KISS YOUR OWN BLARNEY STONES, STACKER!
WE'RE GETTING THROUGH!!!

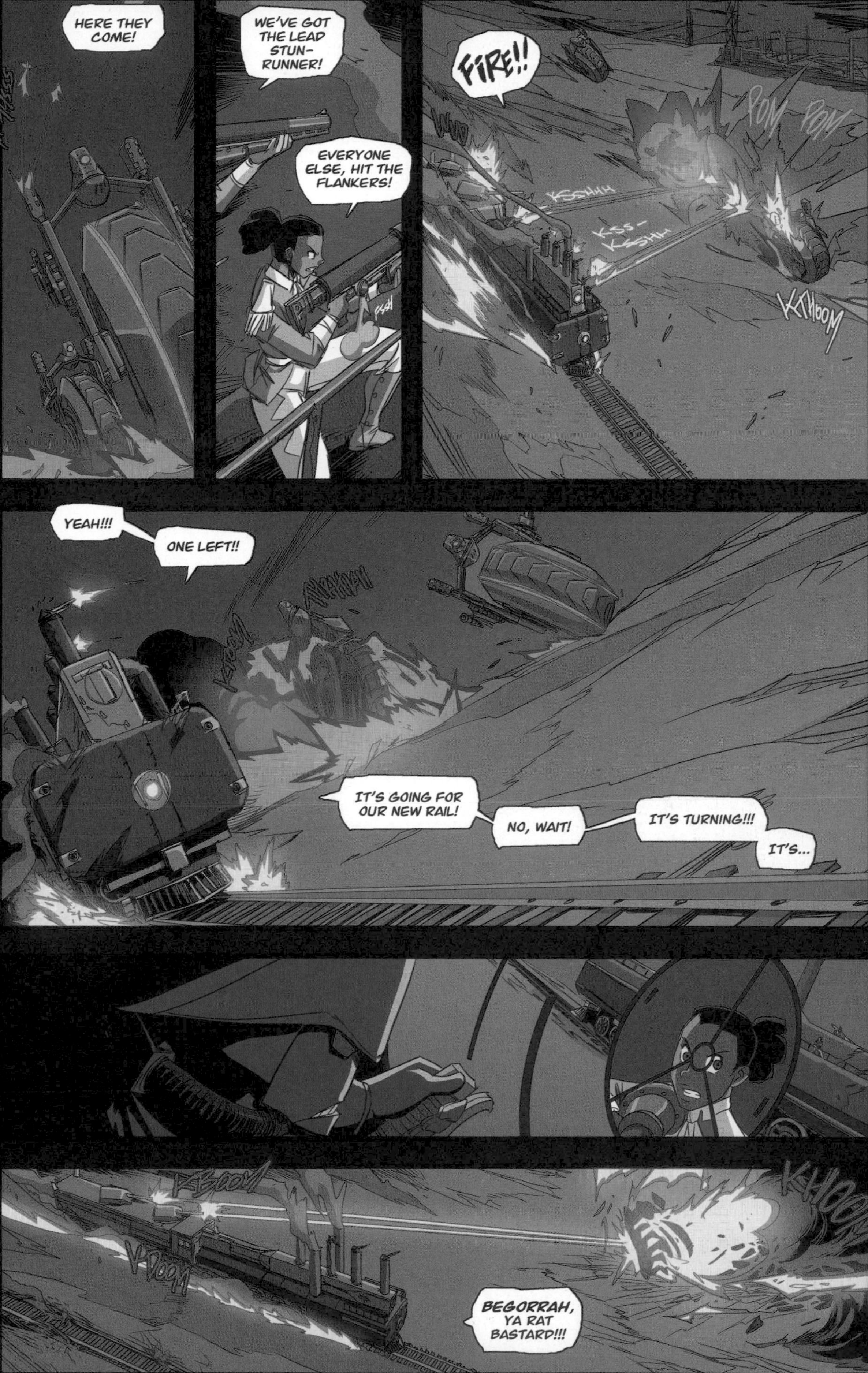
HERE THEY COME!
WE'VE GOT THE LEAD STUN-RUNNER!
EVERYONE ELSE, HIT THE FLANKERS!
FIRE!!
POM POM
KSSHHH
KSS-KSSHHH
KTHOOM
YEAH!!!
ONE LEFT!!
IT'S GOING FOR OUR NEW RAIL!
NO, WAIT!
IT'S TURNING!!!
IT'S...
KBOOM
VROOM
BEGORRAH, YA RAT BASTARD!!!

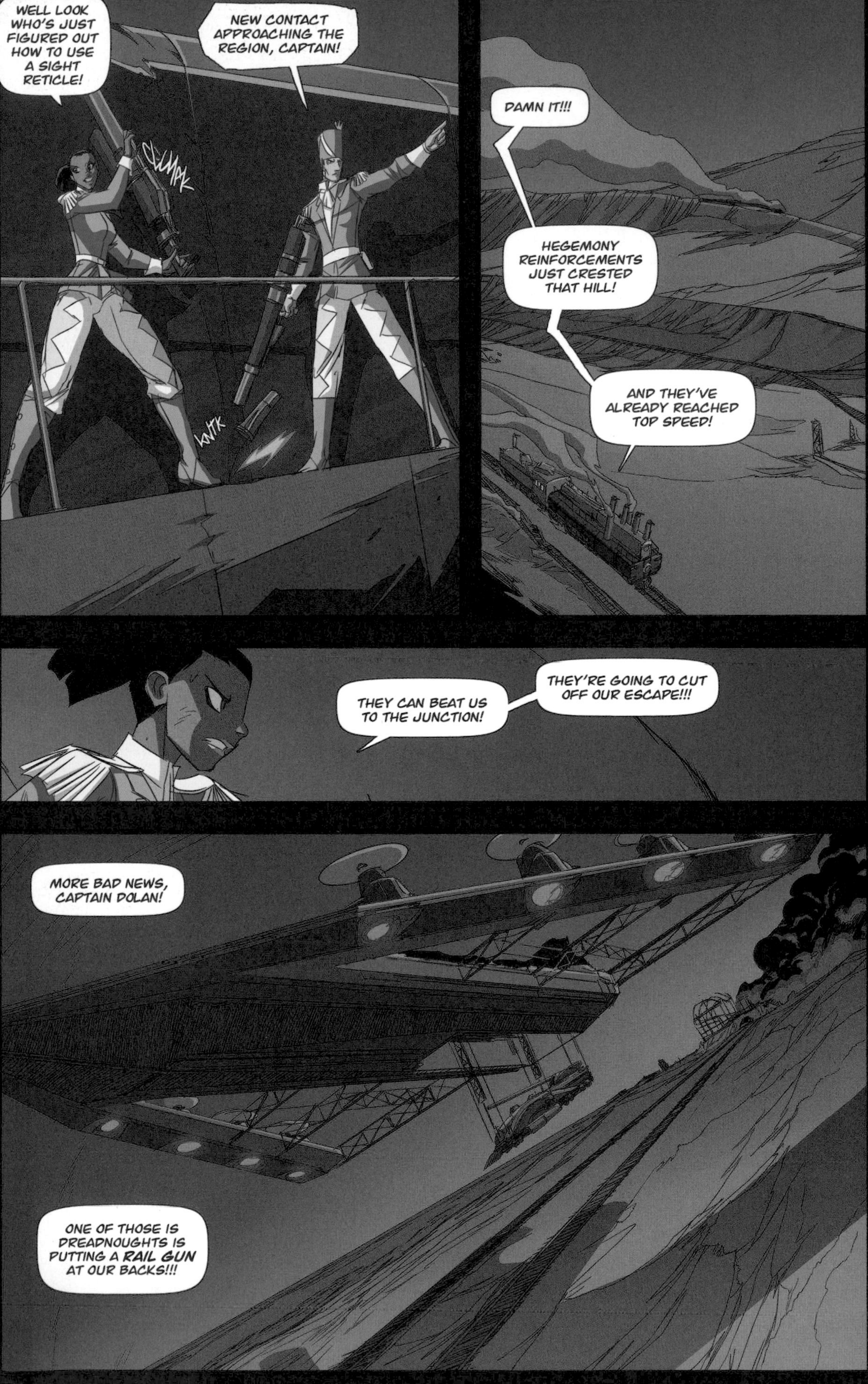
WELL LOOK WHO'S JUST FIGURED OUT HOW TO USE A SIGHT RETICLE!
NEW CONTACT APPROACHING THE REGION, CAPTAIN!
DAMN IT!!!
HEGEMONY REINFORCEMENTS JUST CRESTED THAT HILL!
AND THEY'VE ALREADY REACHED TOP SPEED!
THEY CAN BEAT US TO THE JUNCTION!
THEY'RE GOING TO CUT OFF OUR ESCAPE!!!
MORE BAD NEWS, CAPTAIN DOLAN!
ONE OF THOSE IS DREADNOUGHTS IS PUTTING A RAIL GUN AT OUR BACKS!!!

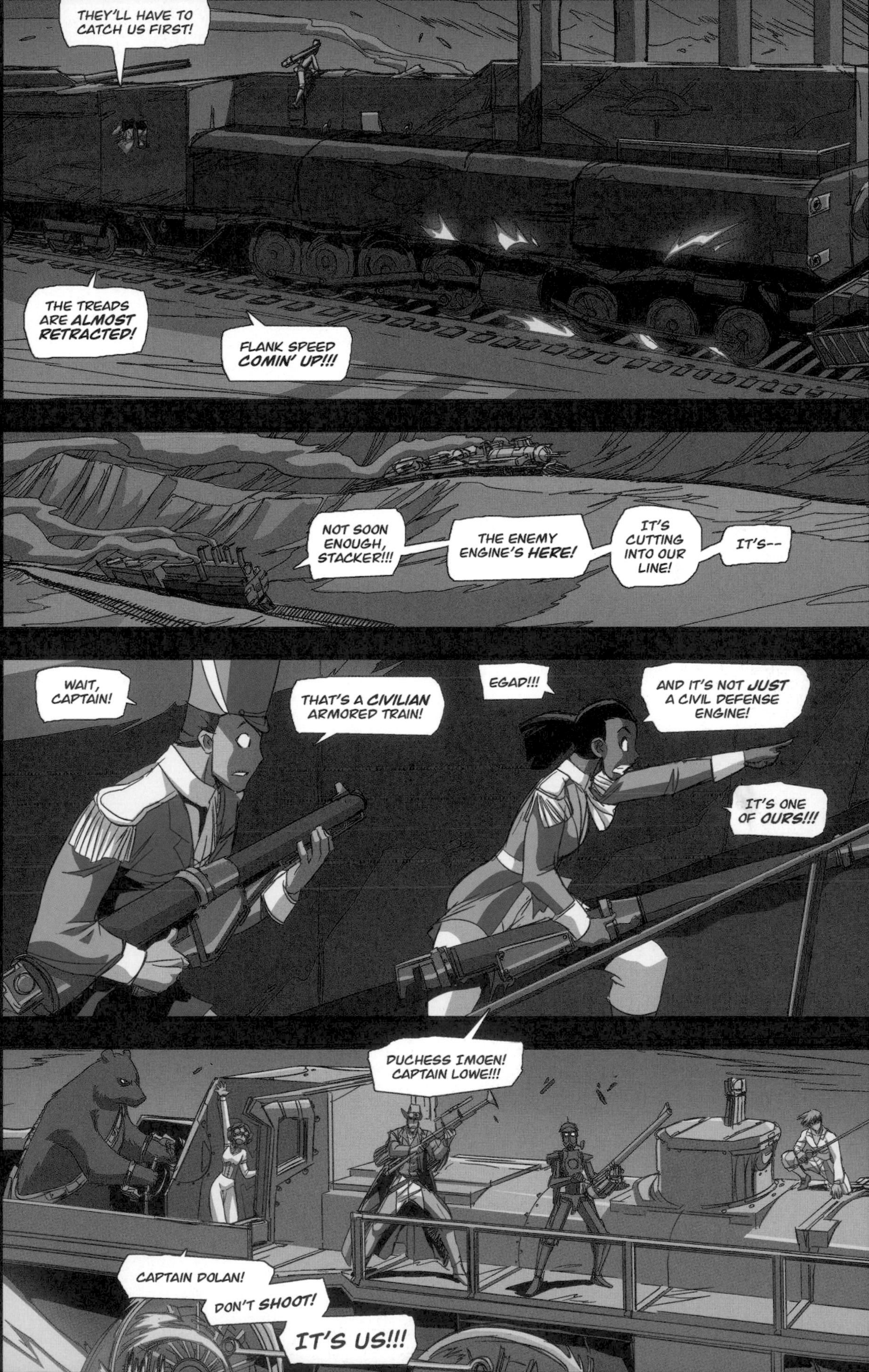
THEY'LL HAVE TO CATCH US FIRST!
THE TREADS ARE ALMOST RETRACTED!
FLANK SPEED COMIN' UP!!!
NOT SOON ENOUGH, STACKER!!!
THE ENEMY ENGINE'S HERE!
IT'S CUTTING INTO OUR LINE!
IT'S--
WAIT, CAPTAIN!
THAT'S A CIVILIAN ARMORED TRAIN!
EGAD!!!
AND IT'S NOT JUST A CIVIL DEFENSE ENGINE!
IT'S ONE OF OURS!!!
DUCHESS IMOEN! CAPTAIN LOWE!!!
CAPTAIN DOLAN!
DON'T SHOOT!
IT'S US!!!

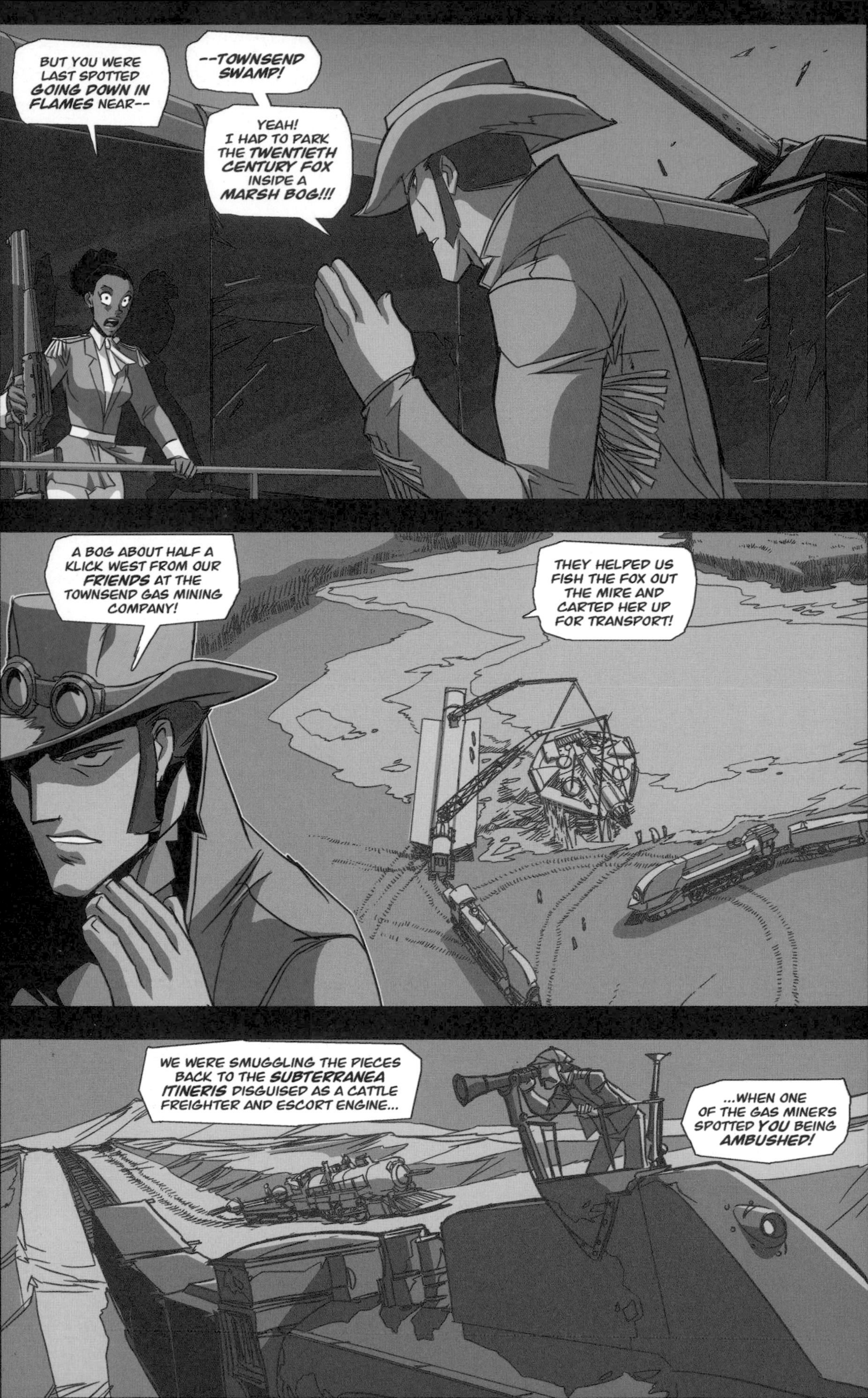
BUT YOU WERE LAST SPOTTED GOING DOWN IN FLAMES NEAR--
--TOWNSEND SWAMP!
YEAH! I HAD TO PARK THE TWENTIETH CENTURY FOX INSIDE A MARSH BOG!!!
A BOG ABOUT HALF A KLICK WEST FROM OUR FRIENDS AT THE TOWNSEND GAS MINING COMPANY!
THEY HELPED US FISH THE FOX OUT THE MIRE AND CARTED HER UP FOR TRANSPORT!
WE WERE SMUGGLING THE PIECES BACK TO THE SUBTERRANEA ITINERIS DISGUISED AS A CATTLE FREIGHTER AND ESCORT ENGINE...
...WHEN ONE OF THE GAS MINERS SPOTTED YOU BEING AMBUSHED!

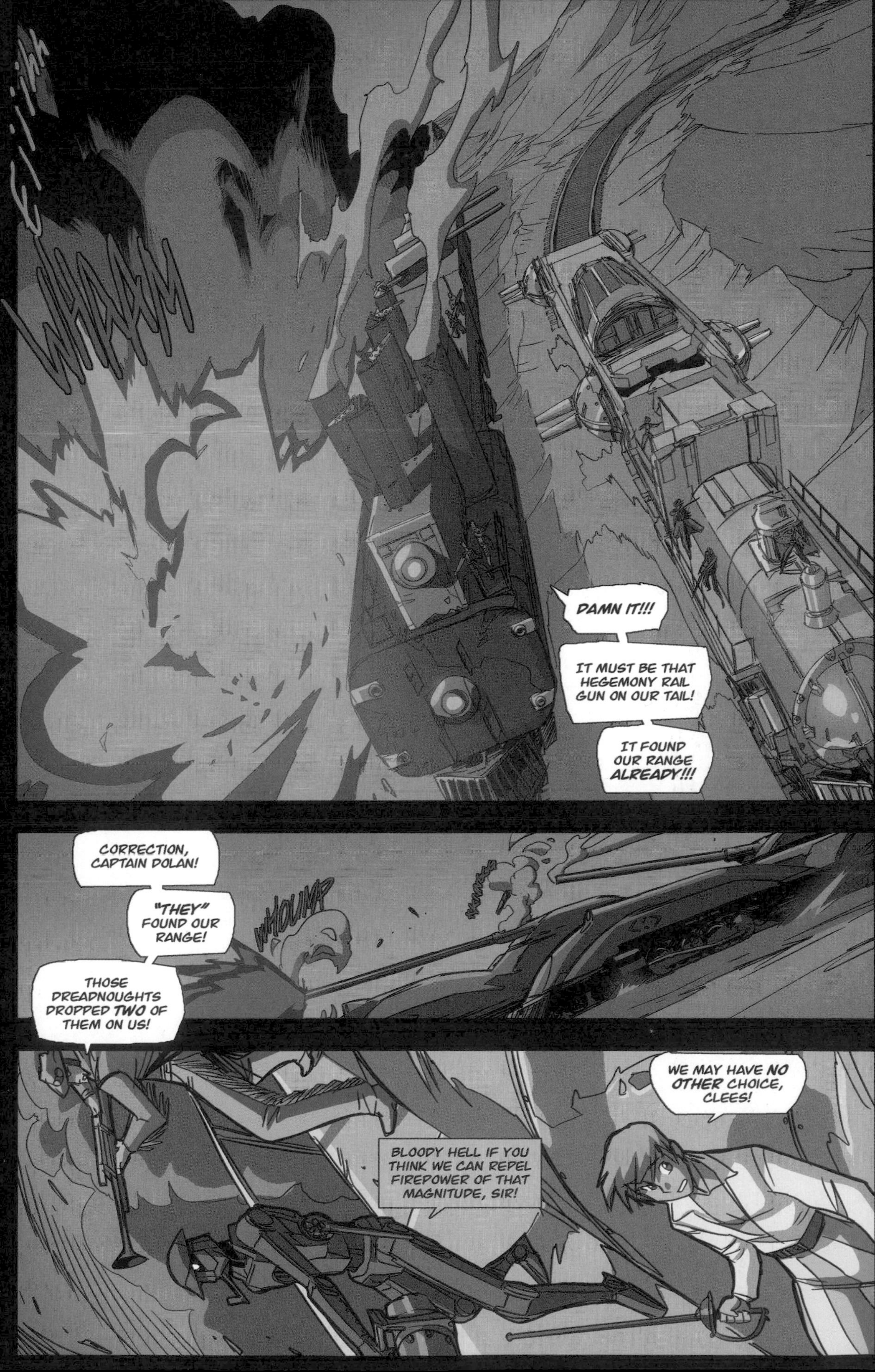
Eeiiiihh
WHAAM
DAMN IT!!!
IT MUST BE THAT HEGEMONY RAIL GUN ON OUR TAIL!
IT FOUND OUR RANGE **ALREADY**!!!
CORRECTION, CAPTAIN DOLAN!
"THEY" FOUND OUR RANGE!
THOSE DREADNOUGHTS DROPPED **TWO** OF THEM ON US!
WHOUMP
WE MAY HAVE **NO OTHER** CHOICE, CLEES!
BLOODY HELL IF YOU THINK WE CAN REPEL FIREPOWER OF THAT MAGNITUDE, SIR!

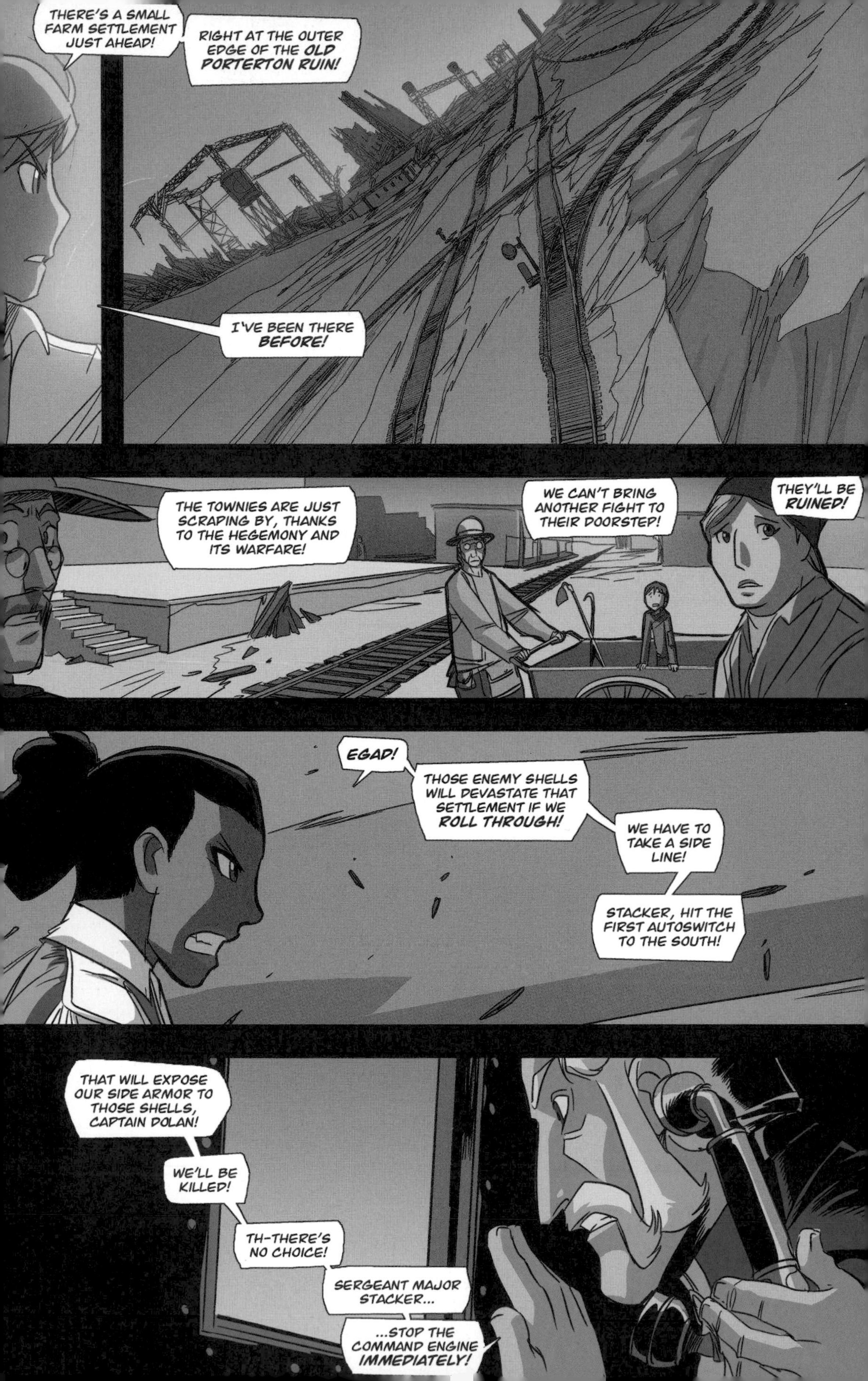
THERE'S A SMALL FARM SETTLEMENT JUST AHEAD!
RIGHT AT THE OUTER EDGE OF THE OLD PORTERTON RUIN!
I'VE BEEN THERE BEFORE!
THE TOWNIES ARE JUST SCRAPING BY, THANKS TO THE HEGEMONY AND ITS WARFARE!
WE CAN'T BRING ANOTHER FIGHT TO THEIR DOORSTEP!
THEY'LL BE RUINED!
EGAD!
THOSE ENEMY SHELLS WILL DEVASTATE THAT SETTLEMENT IF WE ROLL THROUGH!
WE HAVE TO TAKE A SIDE LINE!
STACKER, HIT THE FIRST AUTOSWITCH TO THE SOUTH!
THAT WILL EXPOSE OUR SIDE ARMOR TO THOSE SHELLS, CAPTAIN DOLAN!
WE'LL BE KILLED!
TH-THERE'S NO CHOICE!
SERGEANT MAJOR STACKER...
...STOP THE COMMAND ENGINE IMMEDIATELY!

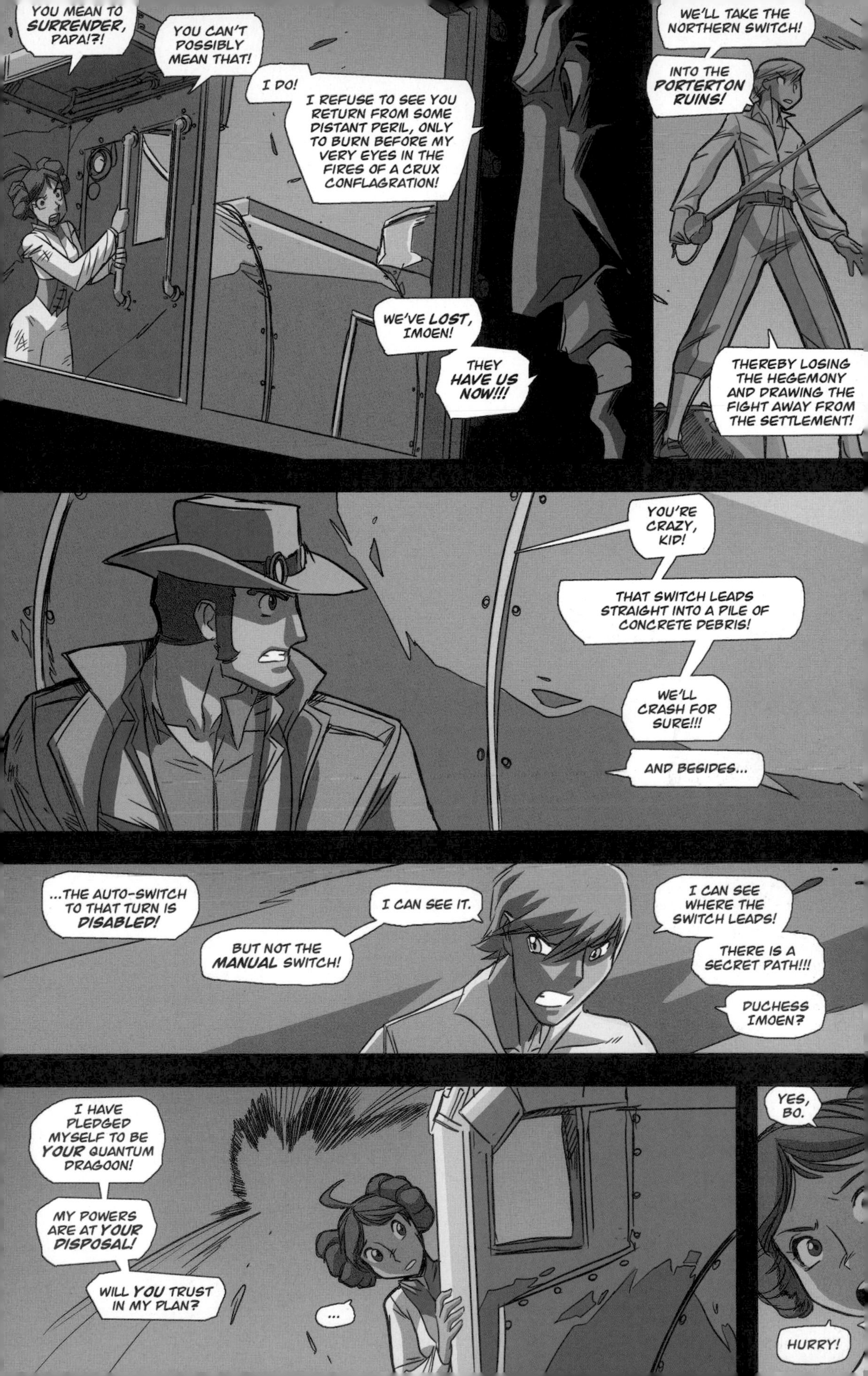

YOU MEAN TO SURRENDER, PAPA!?!
YOU CAN'T POSSIBLY MEAN THAT!
I DO!
I REFUSE TO SEE YOU RETURN FROM SOME DISTANT PERIL, ONLY TO BURN BEFORE MY VERY EYES IN THE FIRES OF A CRUX CONFLAGRATION!
WE'VE LOST, IMOEN!
THEY HAVE US NOW!!!
WE'LL TAKE THE NORTHERN SWITCH!
INTO THE PORTERTON RUINS!
THEREBY LOSING THE HEGEMONY AND DRAWING THE FIGHT AWAY FROM THE SETTLEMENT!
YOU'RE CRAZY, KID!
THAT SWITCH LEADS STRAIGHT INTO A PILE OF CONCRETE DEBRIS!
WE'LL CRASH FOR SURE!!!
AND BESIDES...
...THE AUTO-SWITCH TO THAT TURN IS DISABLED!
I CAN SEE IT.
BUT NOT THE MANUAL SWITCH!
I CAN SEE WHERE THE SWITCH LEADS!
THERE IS A SECRET PATH!!!
DUCHESS IMOEN?
I HAVE PLEDGED MYSELF TO BE YOUR QUANTUM DRAGOON!
MY POWERS ARE AT YOUR DISPOSAL!
WILL YOU TRUST IN MY PLAN?
...
YES, BO.
HURRY!

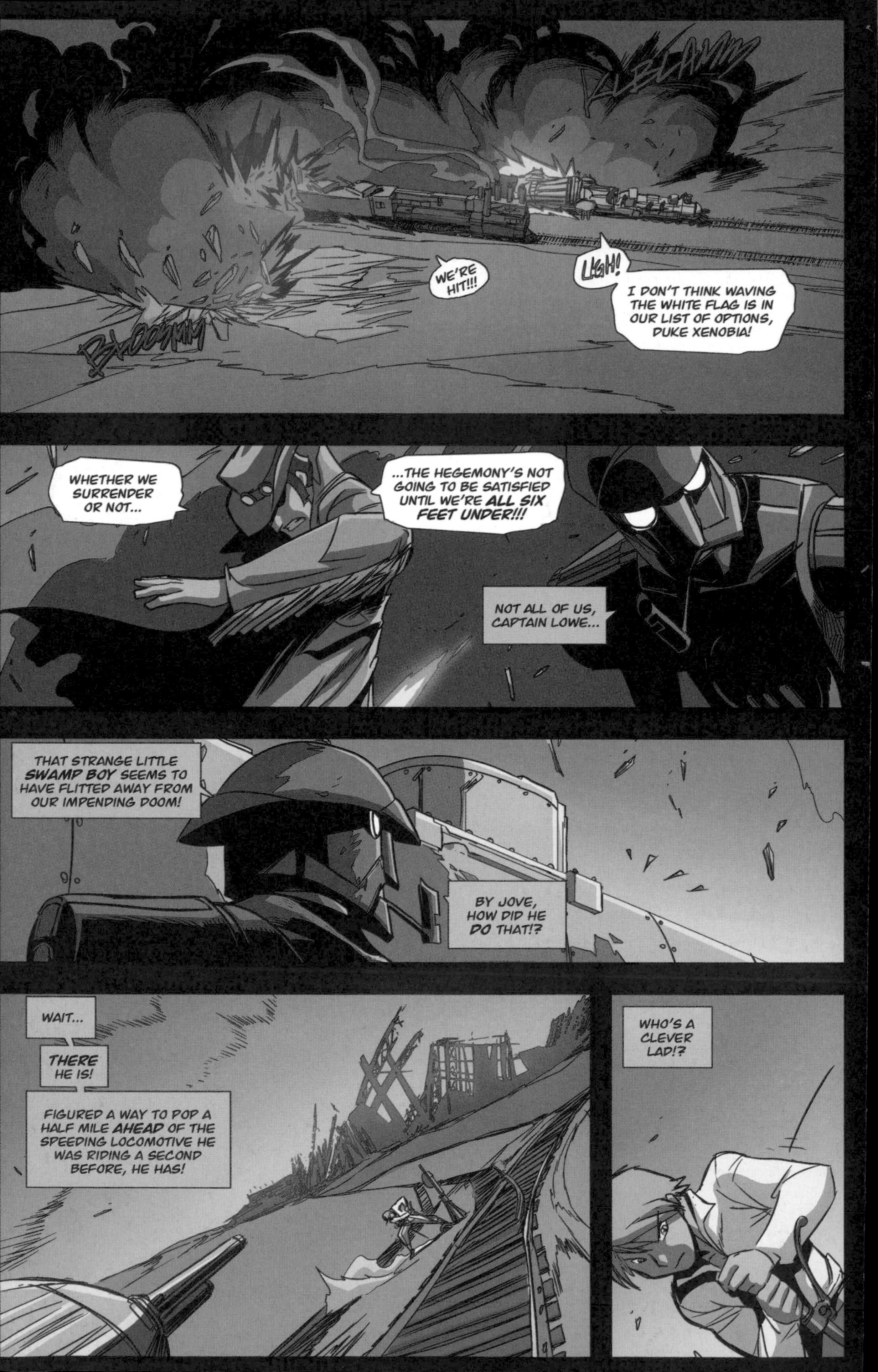

KABLAMM
WE'RE HIT!!!
UGH!
I DON'T THINK WAVING THE WHITE FLAG IS IN OUR LIST OF OPTIONS, DUKE XENOBIA!
BLOOSHH
WHETHER WE SURRENDER OR NOT...
...THE HEGEMONY'S NOT GOING TO BE SATISFIED UNTIL WE'RE ALL SIX FEET UNDER!!!
NOT ALL OF US, CAPTAIN LOWE...
THAT STRANGE LITTLE SWAMP BOY SEEMS TO HAVE FLITTED AWAY FROM OUR IMPENDING DOOM!
BY JOVE, HOW DID HE DO THAT!?
WAIT...
THERE HE IS!
FIGURED A WAY TO POP A HALF MILE AHEAD OF THE SPEEDING LOCOMOTIVE HE WAS RIDING A SECOND BEFORE, HE HAS!
WHO'S A CLEVER LAD!?

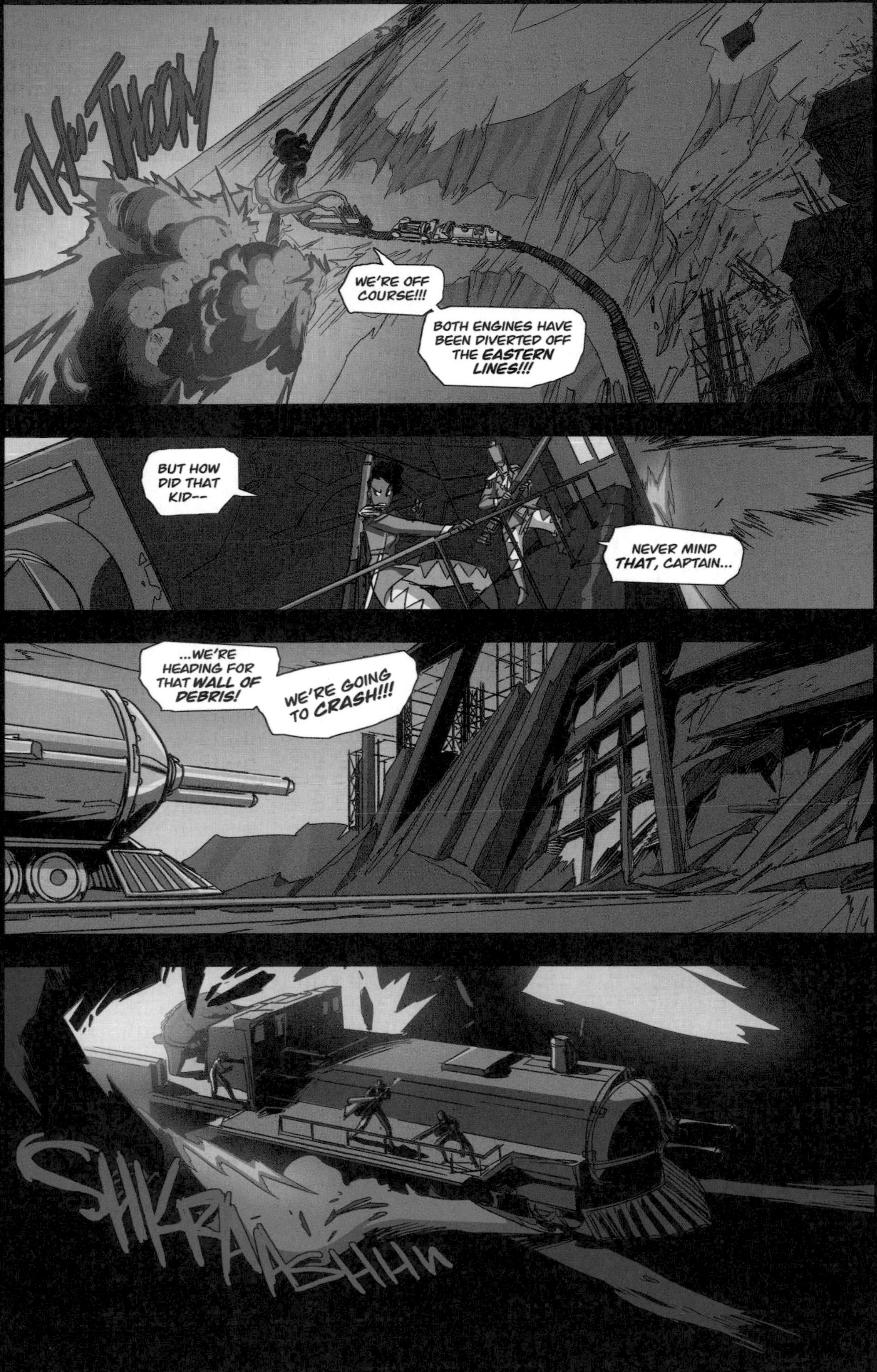

THU-THOOM
WE'RE OFF COURSE!!!
BOTH ENGINES HAVE BEEN DIVERTED OFF THE EASTERN LINES!!!
BUT HOW DID THAT KID--
NEVER MIND THAT, CAPTAIN...
...WE'RE HEADING FOR THAT WALL OF DEBRIS!
WE'RE GOING TO CRASH!!!
SHKRAASHHH

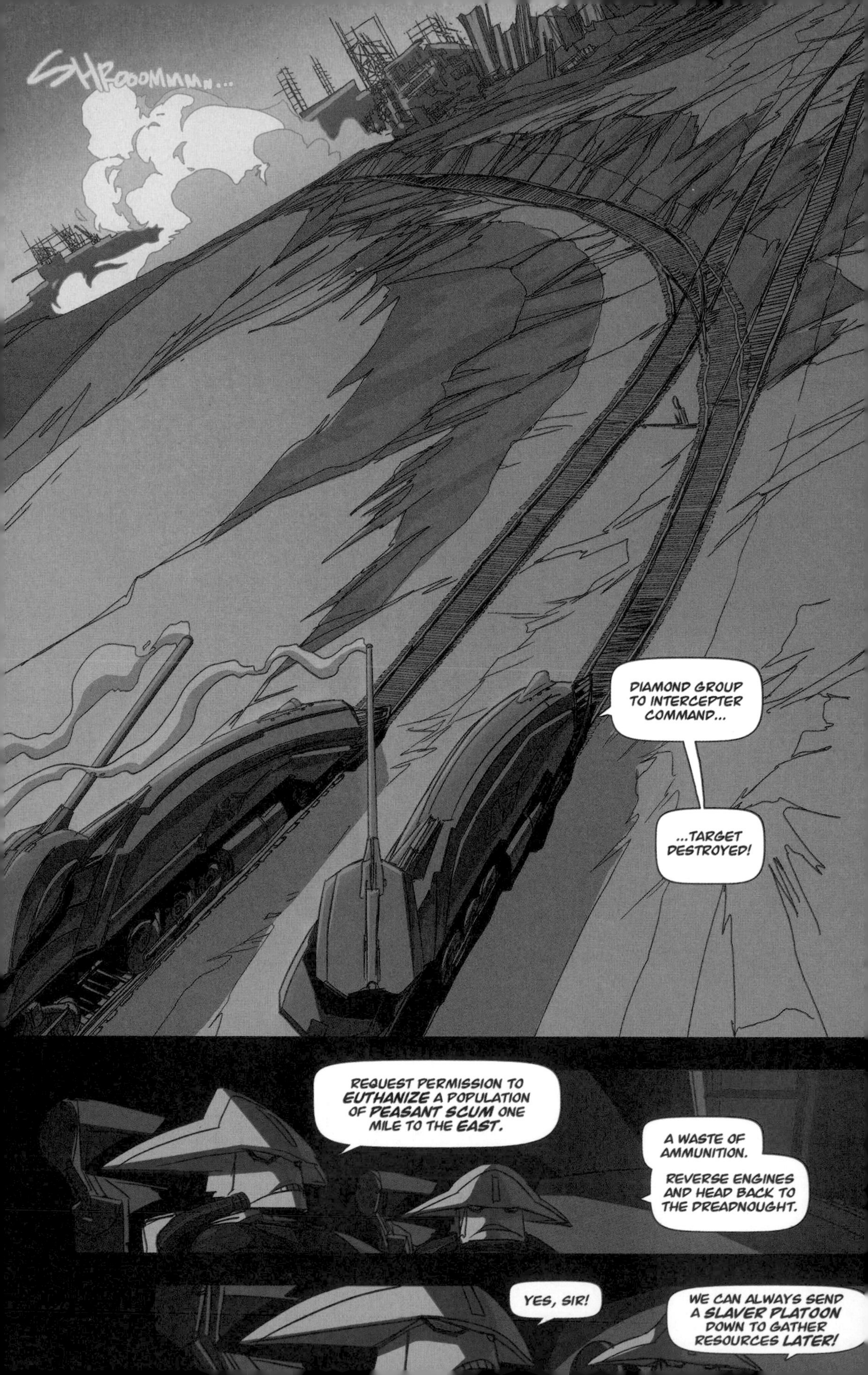
SHROOOMMMN...
DIAMOND GROUP TO INTERCEPTER COMMAND...
...TARGET DESTROYED!
REQUEST PERMISSION TO EUTHANIZE A POPULATION OF PEASANT SCUM ONE MILE TO THE EAST.
A WASTE OF AMMUNITION.
REVERSE ENGINES AND HEAD BACK TO THE DREADNOUGHT.
YES, SIR!
WE CAN ALWAYS SEND A SLAVER PLATOON DOWN TO GATHER RESOURCES LATER!

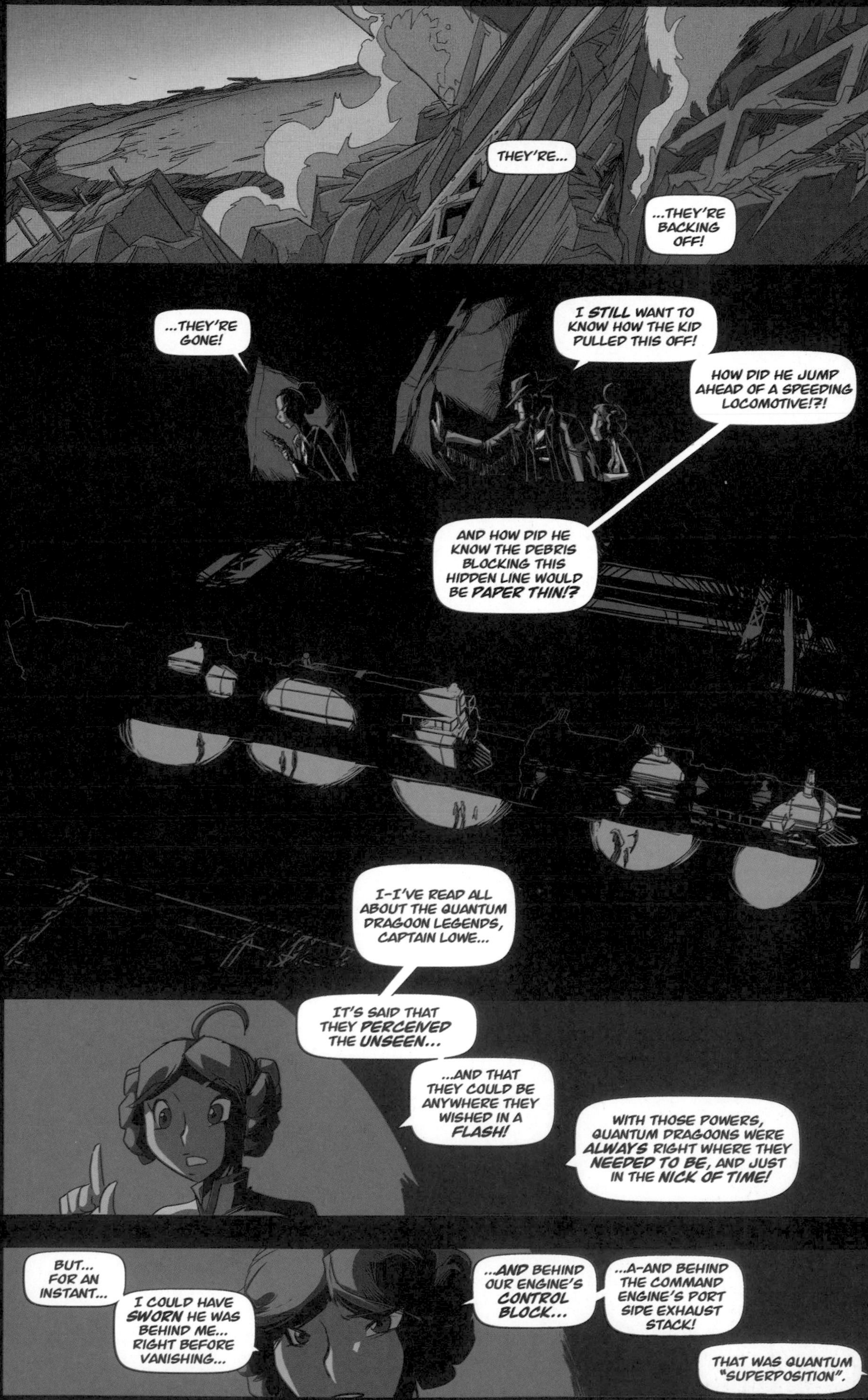
THEY'RE...
...THEY'RE BACKING OFF!
...THEY'RE GONE!
I STILL WANT TO KNOW HOW THE KID PULLED THIS OFF!
HOW DID HE JUMP AHEAD OF A SPEEDING LOCOMOTIVE!?!
AND HOW DID HE KNOW THE DEBRIS BLOCKING THIS HIDDEN LINE WOULD BE PAPER THIN!?
I-I'VE READ ALL ABOUT THE QUANTUM DRAGOON LEGENDS, CAPTAIN LOWE...
IT'S SAID THAT THEY PERCEIVED THE UNSEEN...
...AND THAT THEY COULD BE ANYWHERE THEY WISHED IN A FLASH!
WITH THOSE POWERS, QUANTUM DRAGOONS WERE ALWAYS RIGHT WHERE THEY NEEDED TO BE, AND JUST IN THE NICK OF TIME!
BUT... FOR AN INSTANT...
I COULD HAVE SWORN HE WAS BEHIND ME... RIGHT BEFORE VANISHING...
...AND BEHIND OUR ENGINE'S CONTROL BLOCK...
...A-AND BEHIND THE COMMAND ENGINE'S PORT SIDE EXHAUST STACK!
THAT WAS QUANTUM "SUPERPOSITION".

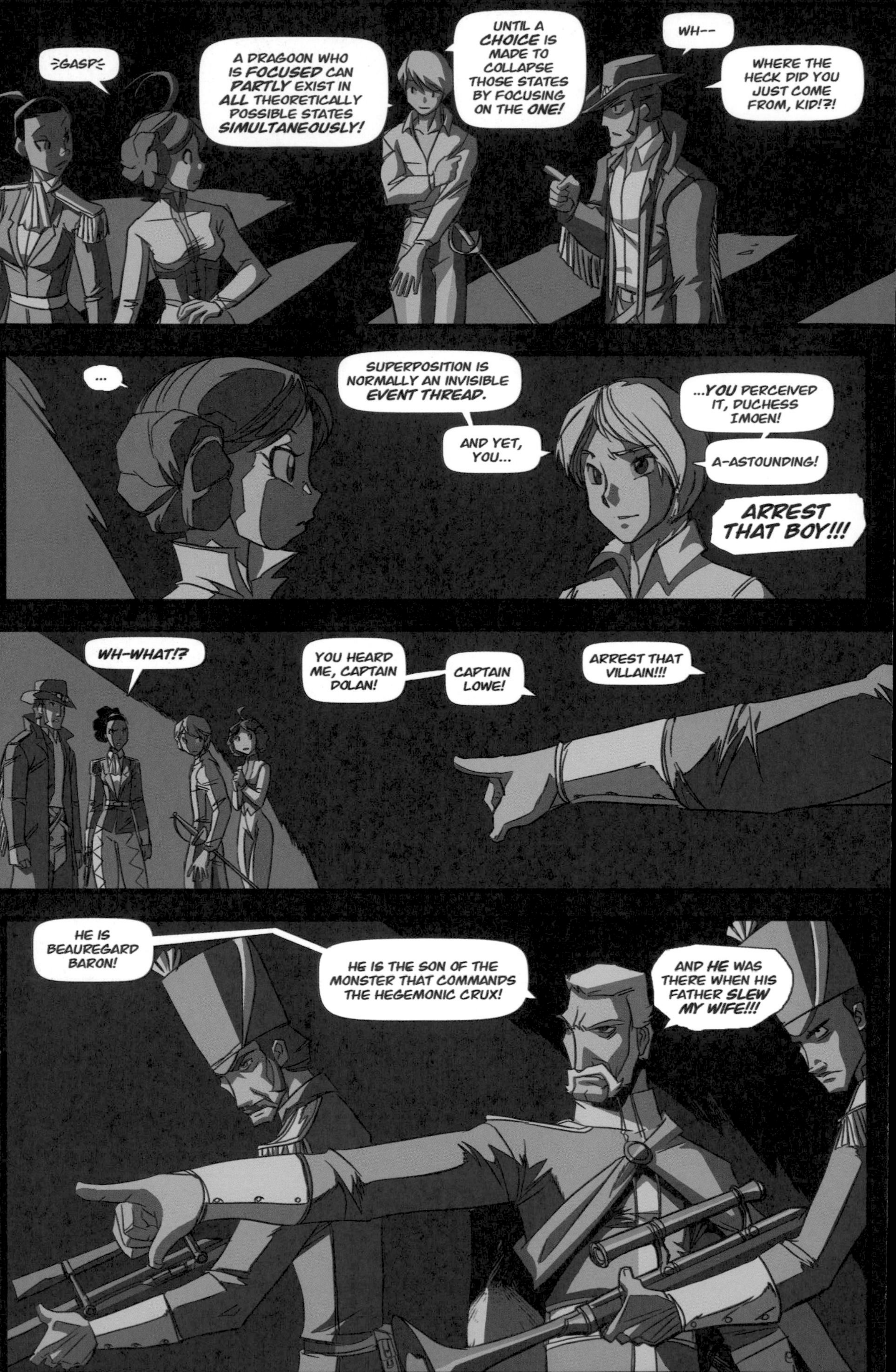

⋡GASP⋠
A DRAGOON WHO IS FOCUSED CAN PARTLY EXIST IN ALL THEORETICALLY POSSIBLE STATES SIMULTANEOUSLY!
UNTIL A CHOICE IS MADE TO COLLAPSE THOSE STATES BY FOCUSING ON THE ONE!
WH--
WHERE THE HECK DID YOU JUST COME FROM, KID!?!
...
SUPERPOSITION IS NORMALLY AN INVISIBLE EVENT THREAD.
AND YET, YOU...
...YOU PERCEIVED IT, DUCHESS IMOEN!
A-ASTOUNDING!
ARREST THAT BOY!!!
WH-WHAT!?
YOU HEARD ME, CAPTAIN DOLAN!
CAPTAIN LOWE!
ARREST THAT VILLAIN!!!
HE IS BEAUREGARD BARON!
HE IS THE SON OF THE MONSTER THAT COMMANDS THE HEGEMONIC CRUX!
AND HE WAS THERE WHEN HIS FATHER SLEW MY WIFE!!!

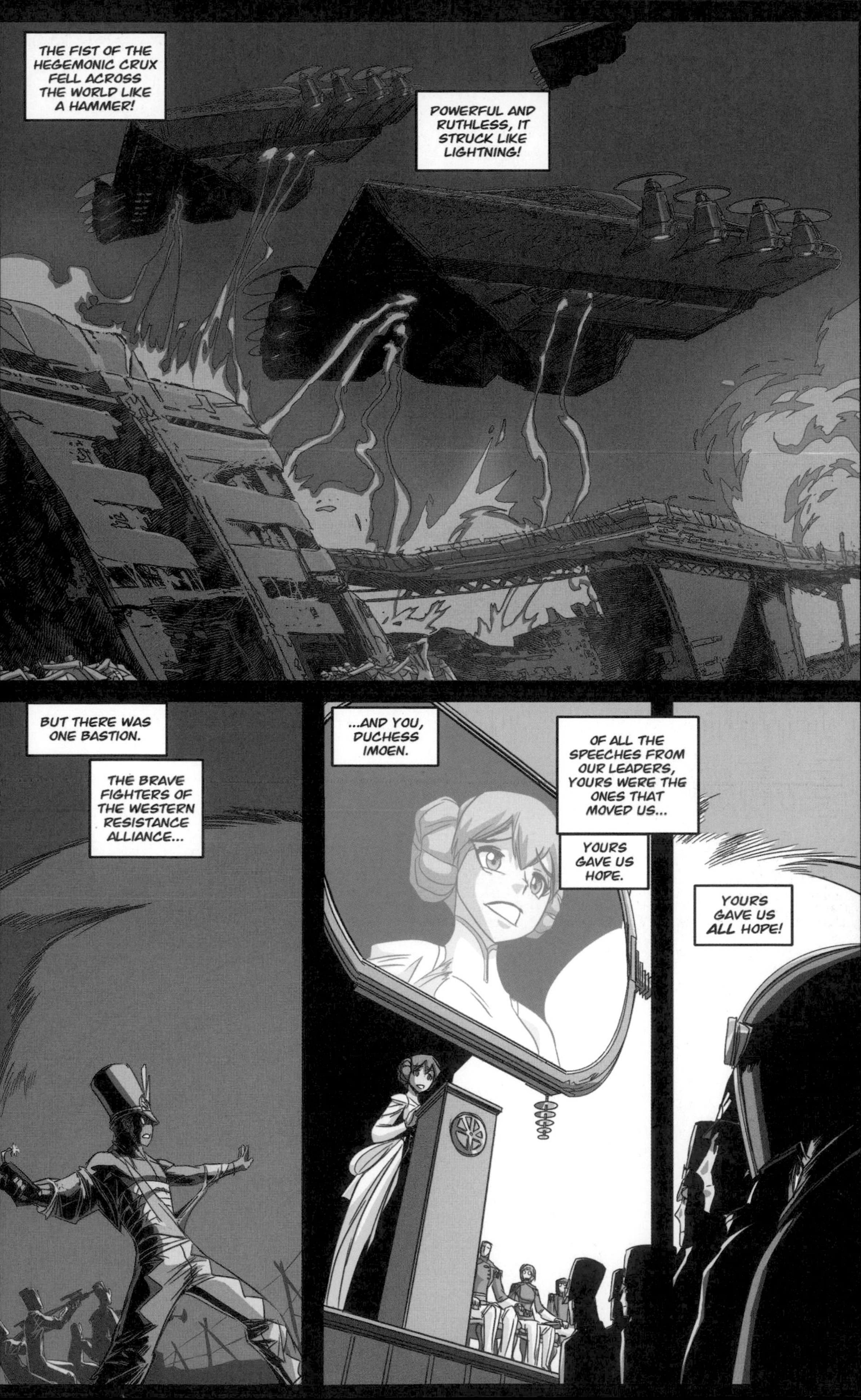
THE FIST OF THE HEGEMONIC CRUX FELL ACROSS THE WORLD LIKE A HAMMER!
POWERFUL AND RUTHLESS, IT STRUCK LIKE LIGHTNING!
BUT THERE WAS ONE BASTION.
THE BRAVE FIGHTERS OF THE WESTERN RESISTANCE ALLIANCE...
...AND YOU, DUCHESS IMOEN.
OF ALL THE SPEECHES FROM OUR LEADERS, YOURS WERE THE ONES THAT MOVED US...
YOURS GAVE US HOPE.
YOURS GAVE US ALL HOPE!

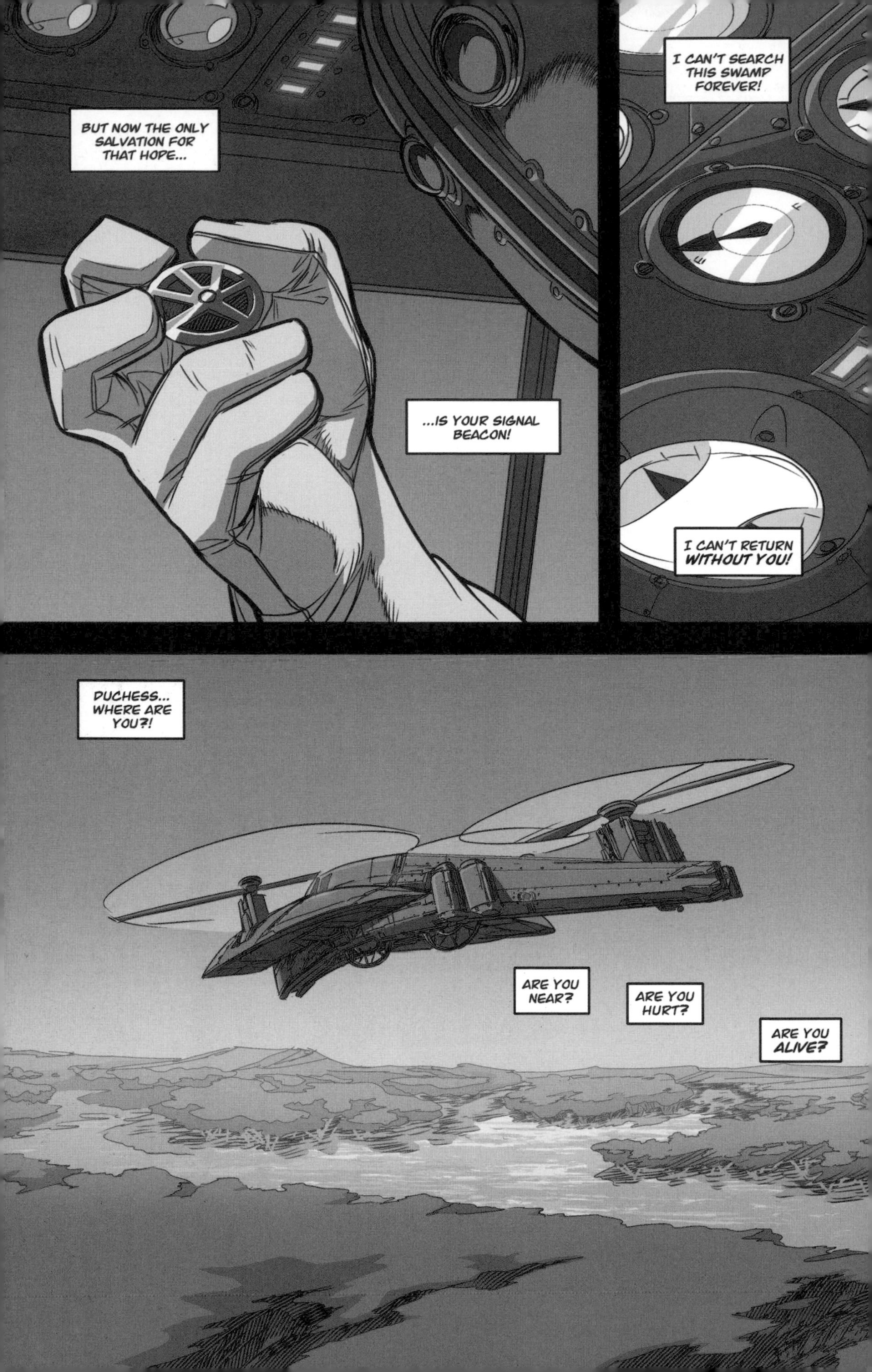
BUT NOW THE ONLY SALVATION FOR THAT HOPE...
...IS YOUR SIGNAL BEACON!
I CAN'T SEARCH THIS SWAMP FOREVER!
I CAN'T RETURN WITHOUT YOU!
DUCHESS... WHERE ARE YOU?!
ARE YOU NEAR?
ARE YOU HURT?
ARE YOU ALIVE?

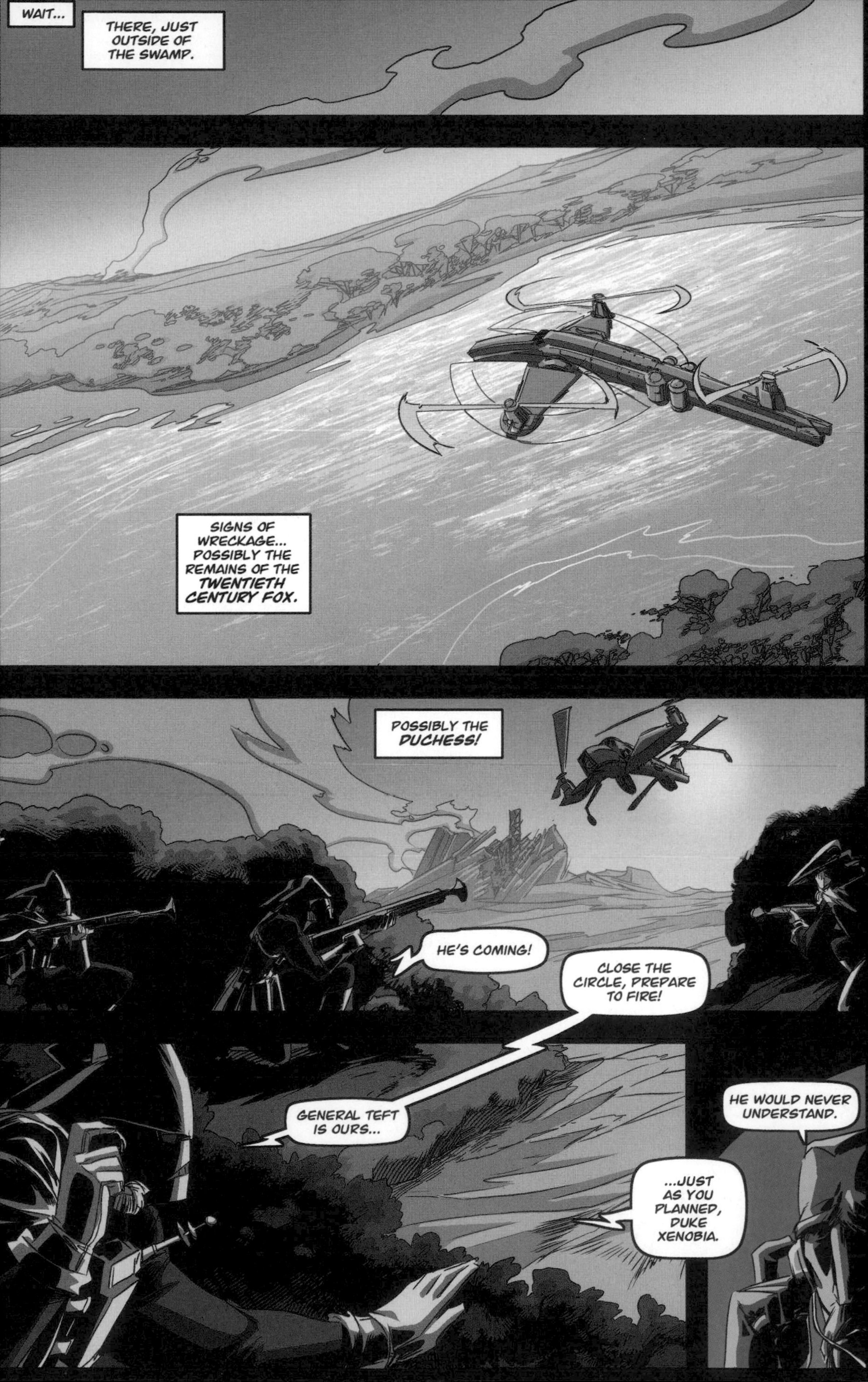
WAIT...
THERE, JUST OUTSIDE OF THE SWAMP.
SIGNS OF WRECKAGE... POSSIBLY THE REMAINS OF THE TWENTIETH CENTURY FOX.
POSSIBLY THE DUCHESS!
HE'S COMING!
CLOSE THE CIRCLE, PREPARE TO FIRE!
GENERAL TEFT IS OURS...
...JUST AS YOU PLANNED, DUKE XENOBIA.
HE WOULD NEVER UNDERSTAND.

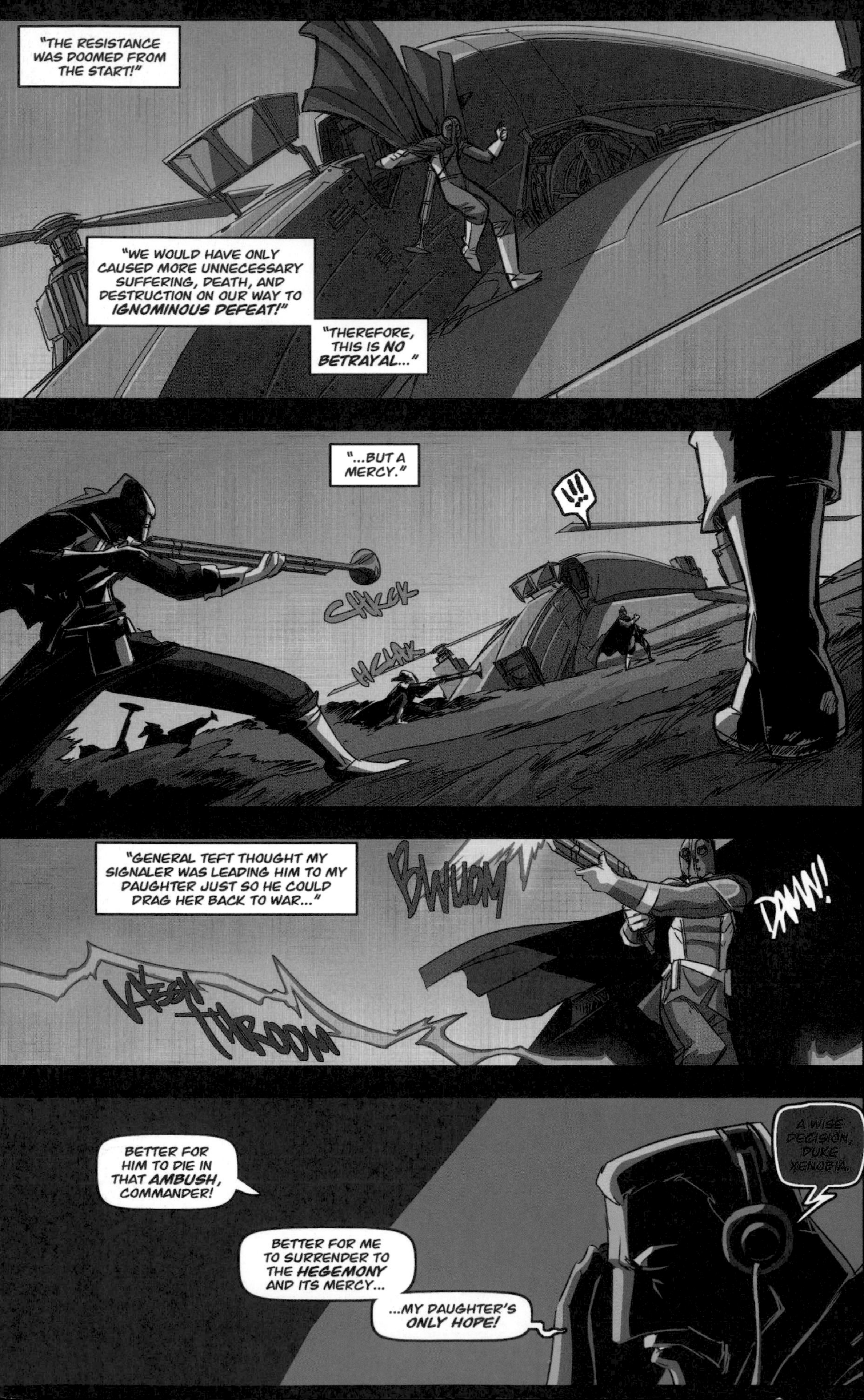
"THE RESISTANCE WAS DOOMED FROM THE START!"
"WE WOULD HAVE ONLY CAUSED MORE UNNECESSARY SUFFERING, DEATH, AND DESTRUCTION ON OUR WAY TO IGNOMINOUS DEFEAT!"
"THEREFORE, THIS IS NO BETRAYAL..."
"...BUT A MERCY."
"GENERAL TEFT THOUGHT MY SIGNALER WAS LEADING HIM TO MY DAUGHTER JUST SO HE COULD DRAG HER BACK TO WAR..."
THROOM
BETTER FOR HIM TO DIE IN THAT AMBUSH, COMMANDER!
A WISE DECISION, DUKE XENOBIA.
BETTER FOR ME TO SURRENDER TO THE HEGEMONY AND ITS MERCY...
...MY DAUGHTER'S ONLY HOPE!

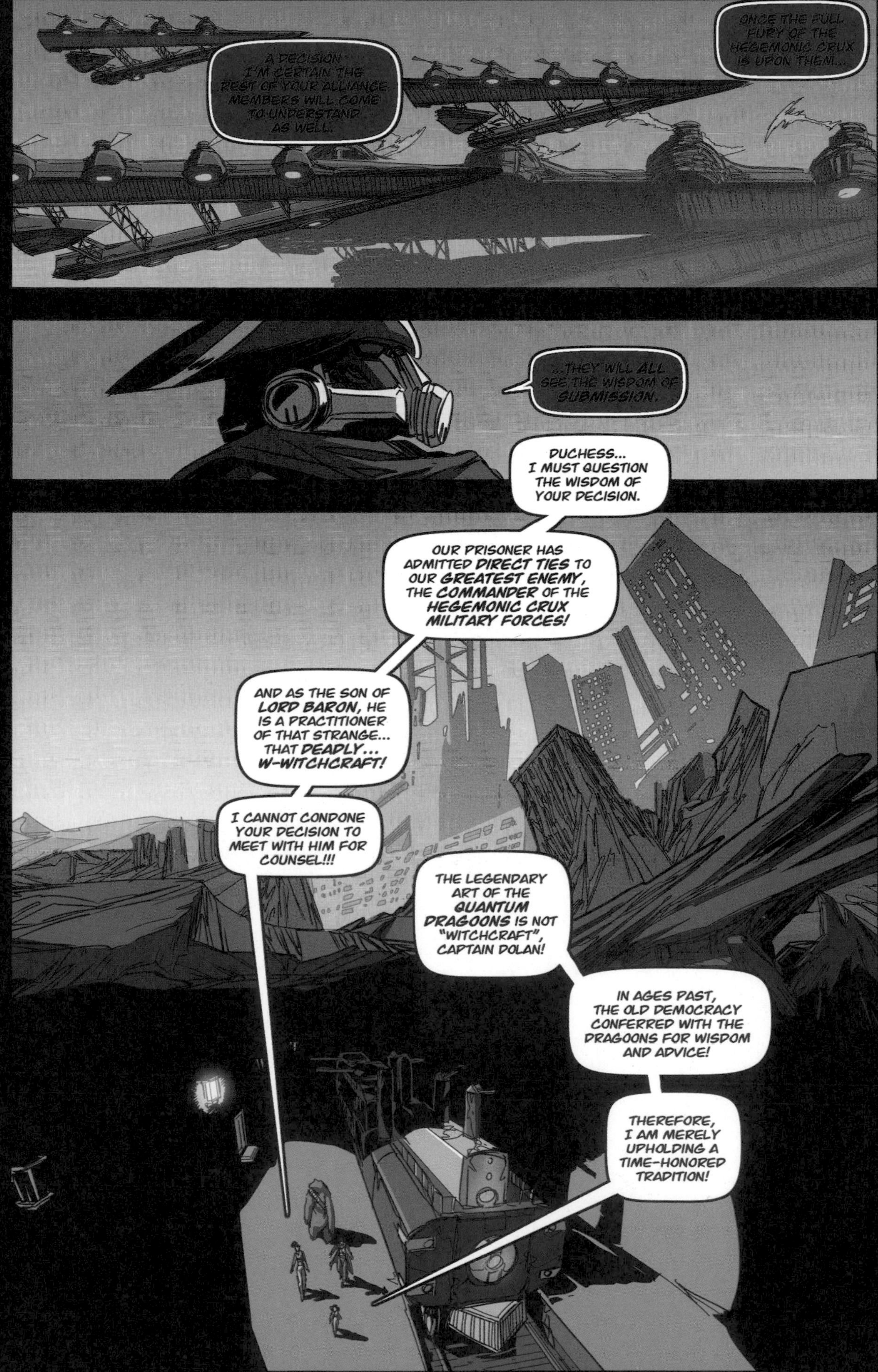
A DECISION I'M CERTAIN THE REST OF YOUR ALLIANCE MEMBERS WILL COME TO UNDERSTAND AS WELL.
ONCE THE FULL FURY OF THE HEGEMONIC CRUX IS UPON THEM...
...THEY WILL ALL SEE THE WISDOM OF SUBMISSION.
DUCHESS... I MUST QUESTION THE WISDOM OF YOUR DECISION.
OUR PRISONER HAS ADMITTED DIRECT TIES TO OUR GREATEST ENEMY, THE COMMANDER OF THE HEGEMONIC CRUX MILITARY FORCES!
AND AS THE SON OF LORD BARON, HE IS A PRACTITIONER OF THAT STRANGE... THAT DEADLY... W-WITCHCRAFT!
I CANNOT CONDONE YOUR DECISION TO MEET WITH HIM FOR COUNSEL!!!
THE LEGENDARY ART OF THE QUANTUM DRAGOONS IS NOT "WITCHCRAFT", CAPTAIN DOLAN!
IN AGES PAST, THE OLD DEMOCRACY CONFERRED WITH THE DRAGOONS FOR WISDOM AND ADVICE!
THEREFORE, I AM MERELY UPHOLDING A TIME-HONORED TRADITION!

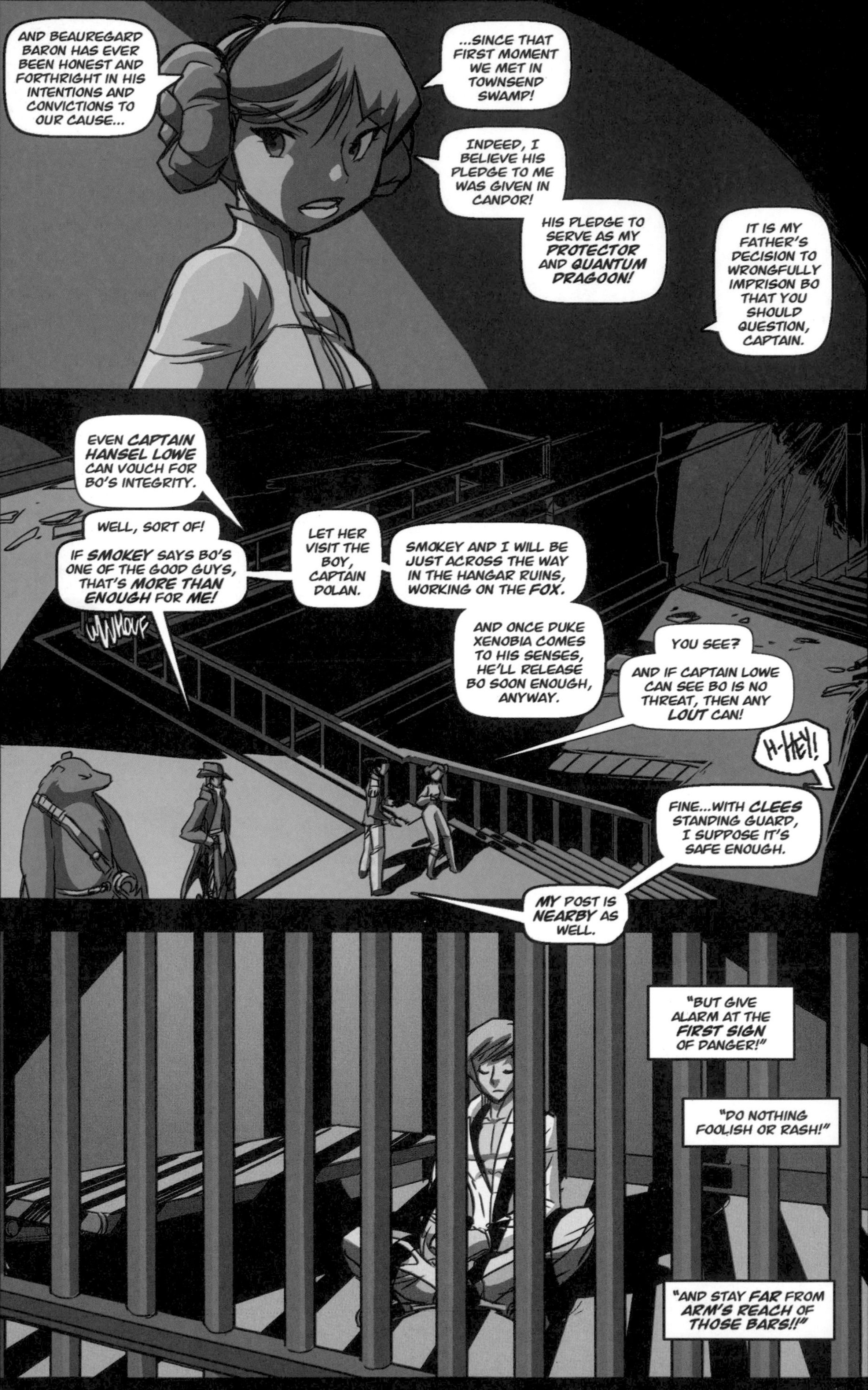
AND BEAUREGARD BARON HAS EVER BEEN HONEST AND FORTHRIGHT IN HIS INTENTIONS AND CONVICTIONS TO OUR CAUSE...
...SINCE THAT FIRST MOMENT WE MET IN TOWNSEND SWAMP!
INDEED, I BELIEVE HIS PLEDGE TO ME WAS GIVEN IN CANDOR!
HIS PLEDGE TO SERVE AS MY PROTECTOR AND QUANTUM DRAGOON!
IT IS MY FATHER'S DECISION TO WRONGFULLY IMPRISON BO THAT YOU SHOULD QUESTION, CAPTAIN.
EVEN CAPTAIN HANSEL LOWE CAN VOUCH FOR BO'S INTEGRITY.
WELL, SORT OF!
IF SMOKEY SAYS BO'S ONE OF THE GOOD GUYS, THAT'S MORE THAN ENOUGH FOR ME!
WWHOUF
LET HER VISIT THE BOY, CAPTAIN DOLAN.
SMOKEY AND I WILL BE JUST ACROSS THE WAY IN THE HANGAR RUINS, WORKING ON THE FOX.
AND ONCE DUKE XENOBIA COMES TO HIS SENSES, HE'LL RELEASE BO SOON ENOUGH, ANYWAY.
YOU SEE?
AND IF CAPTAIN LOWE CAN SEE BO IS NO THREAT, THEN ANY LOUT CAN!
H-HEY!
FINE...WITH CLEES STANDING GUARD, I SUPPOSE IT'S SAFE ENOUGH.
MY POST IS NEARBY AS WELL.
"BUT GIVE ALARM AT THE FIRST SIGN OF DANGER!"
"DO NOTHING FOOLISH OR RASH!"
"AND STAY FAR FROM ARM'S REACH OF THOSE BARS!!"

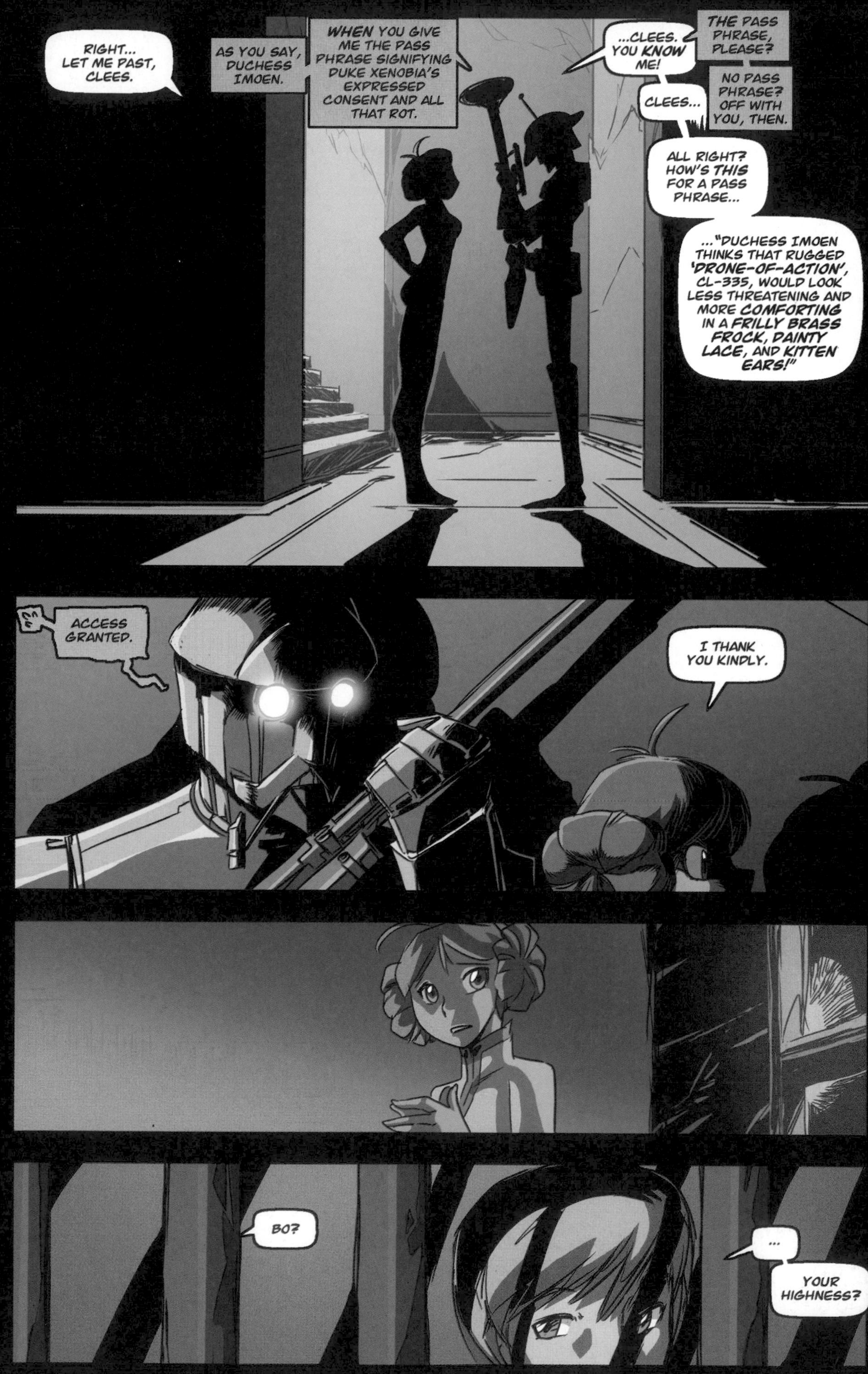
RIGHT... LET ME PAST, CLEES.
AS YOU SAY, DUCHESS IMOEN.
WHEN YOU GIVE ME THE PASS PHRASE SIGNIFYING DUKE XENOBIA'S EXPRESSED CONSENT AND ALL THAT ROT.
...CLEES. YOU KNOW ME!
THE PASS PHRASE, PLEASE?
CLEES...
NO PASS PHRASE? OFF WITH YOU, THEN.
ALL RIGHT? HOW'S THIS FOR A PASS PHRASE...
..."DUCHESS IMOEN THINKS THAT RUGGED 'DRONE-OF-ACTION', CL-335, WOULD LOOK LESS THREATENING AND MORE COMFORTING IN A FRILLY BRASS FROCK, DAINTY LACE, AND KITTEN EARS!"
ACCESS GRANTED.
I THANK YOU KINDLY.
BO?
...
YOUR HIGHNESS?

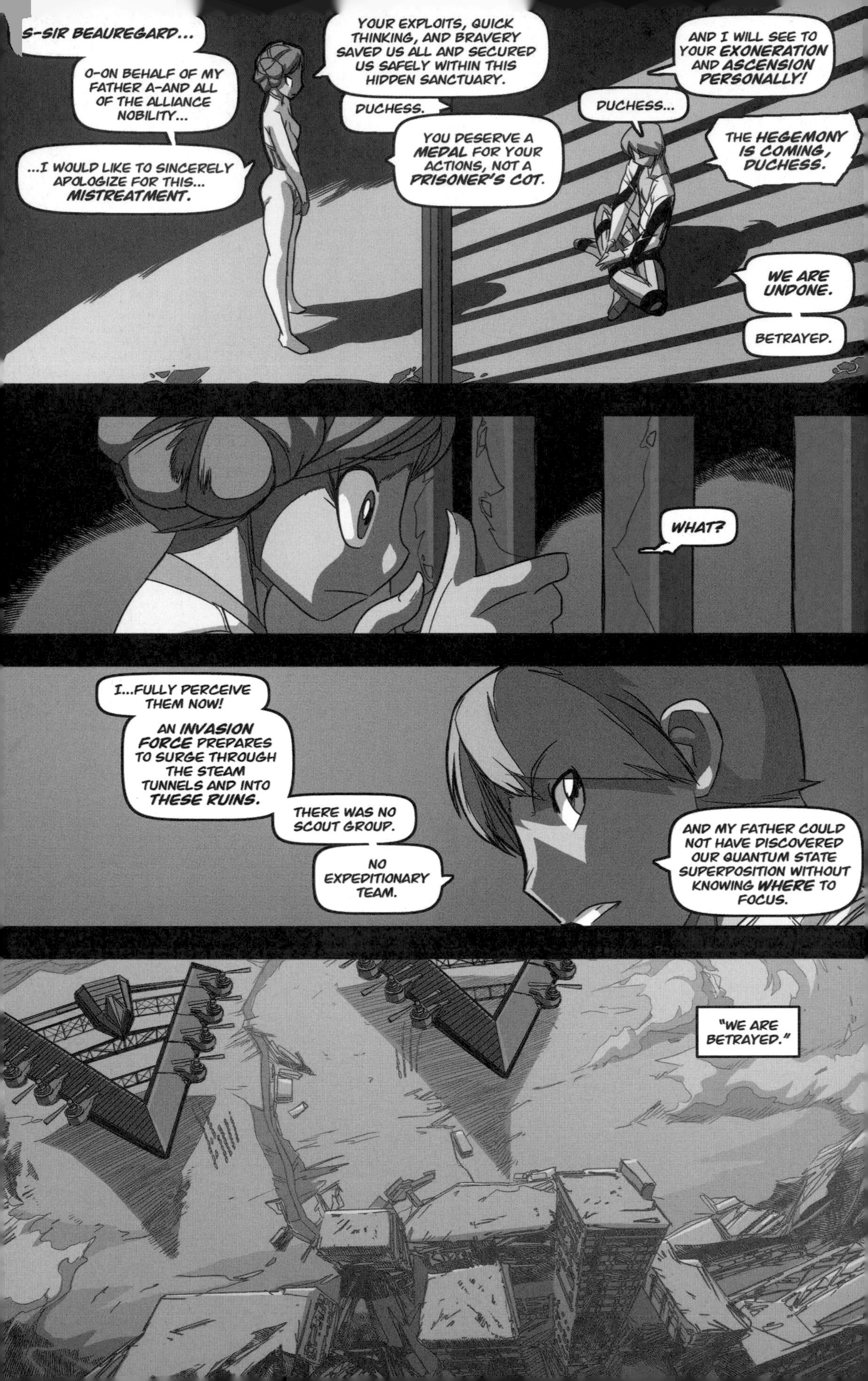
S-SIR BEAUREGARD...
O-ON BEHALF OF MY FATHER A-AND ALL OF THE ALLIANCE NOBILITY...
...I WOULD LIKE TO SINCERELY APOLOGIZE FOR THIS... MISTREATMENT.
YOUR EXPLOITS, QUICK THINKING, AND BRAVERY SAVED US ALL AND SECURED US SAFELY WITHIN THIS HIDDEN SANCTUARY.
DUCHESS.
YOU DESERVE A MEDAL FOR YOUR ACTIONS, NOT A PRISONER'S COT.
AND I WILL SEE TO YOUR EXONERATION AND ASCENSION PERSONALLY!
DUCHESS...
THE HEGEMONY IS COMING, DUCHESS.
WE ARE UNDONE.
BETRAYED.
WHAT?
I...FULLY PERCEIVE THEM NOW!
AN INVASION FORCE PREPARES TO SURGE THROUGH THE STEAM TUNNELS AND INTO THESE RUINS.
THERE WAS NO SCOUT GROUP.
NO EXPEDITIONARY TEAM.
AND MY FATHER COULD NOT HAVE DISCOVERED OUR QUANTUM STATE SUPERPOSITION WITHOUT KNOWING WHERE TO FOCUS.
"WE ARE BETRAYED."

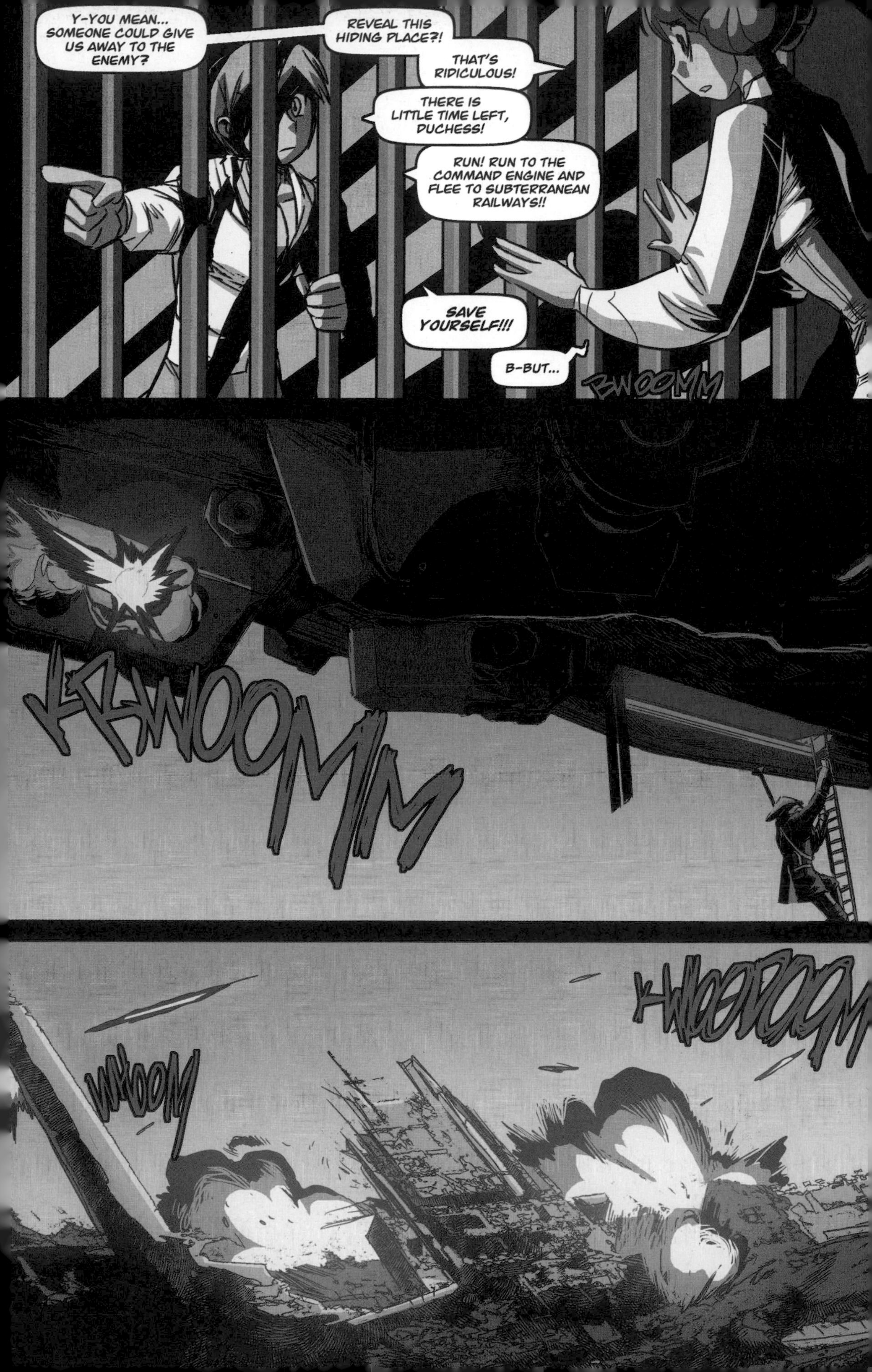
Y-YOU MEAN... SOMEONE COULD GIVE US AWAY TO THE ENEMY?
REVEAL THIS HIDING PLACE?!
THAT'S RIDICULOUS!
THERE IS LITTLE TIME LEFT, DUCHESS!
RUN! RUN TO THE COMMAND ENGINE AND FLEE TO SUBTERRANEAN RAILWAYS!!
SAVE YOURSELF!!!
B-BUT...
BWOOMM
KRWOOMM

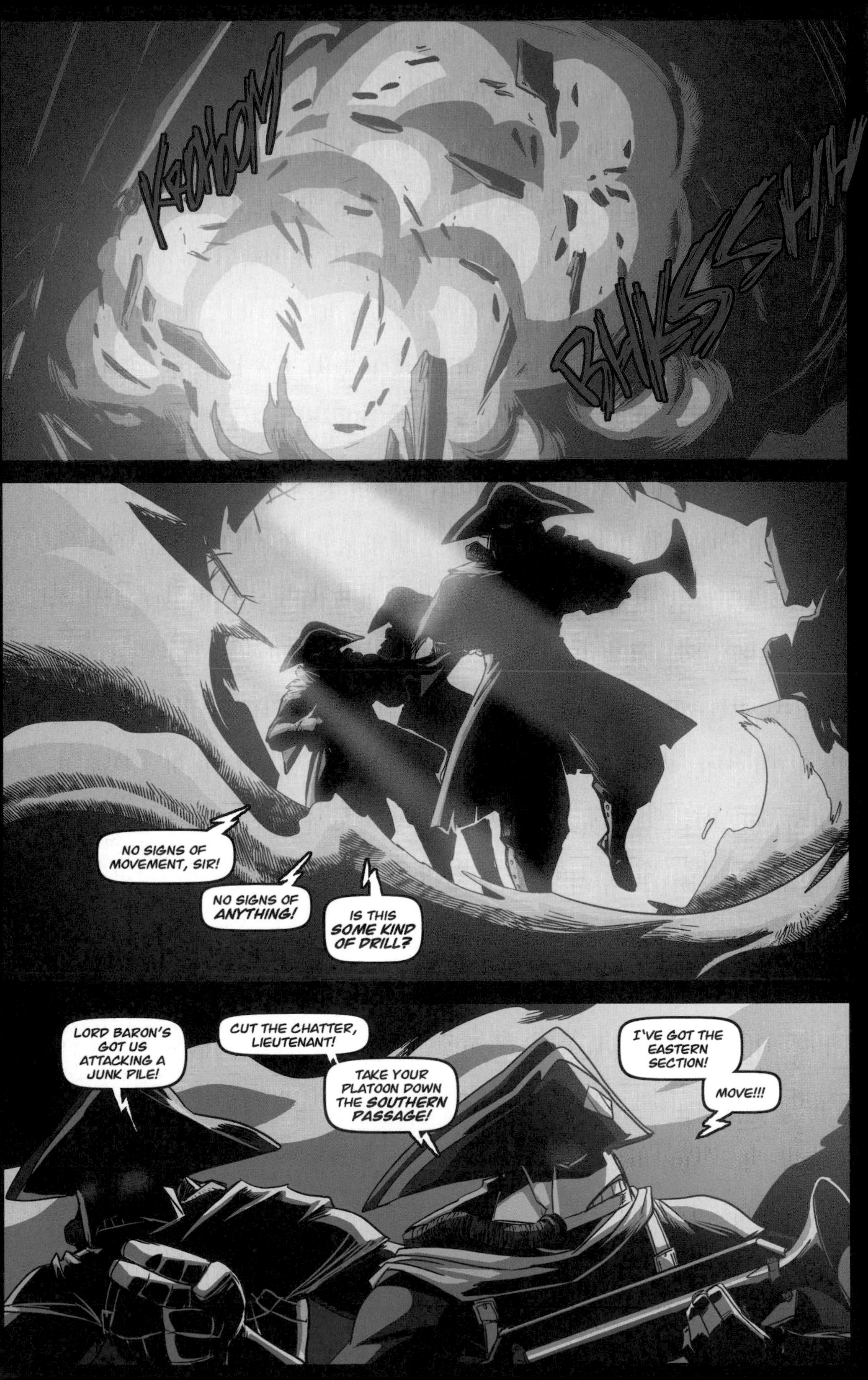
KRAHOOM
BKKSSHH
NO SIGNS OF MOVEMENT, SIR!
NO SIGNS OF ANYTHING!
IS THIS SOME KIND OF DRILL?
LORD BARON'S GOT US ATTACKING A JUNK PILE!
CUT THE CHATTER, LIEUTENANT!
TAKE YOUR PLATOON DOWN THE SOUTHERN PASSAGE!
I'VE GOT THE EASTERN SECTION!
MOVE!!!

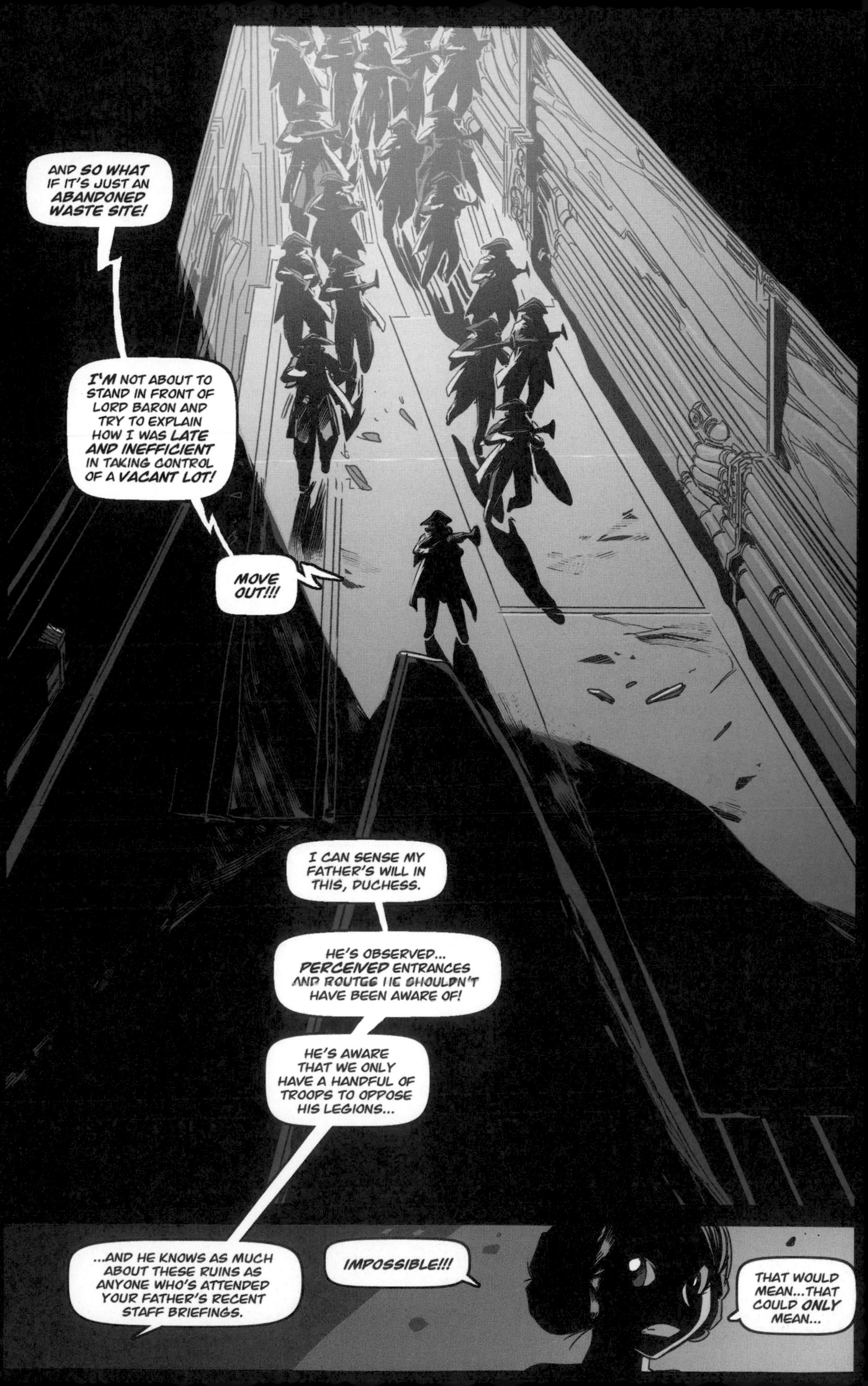
AND SO WHAT IF IT'S JUST AN ABANDONED WASTE SITE!
I'M NOT ABOUT TO STAND IN FRONT OF LORD BARON AND TRY TO EXPLAIN HOW I WAS LATE AND INEFFICIENT IN TAKING CONTROL OF A VACANT LOT!
MOVE OUT!!!
I CAN SENSE MY FATHER'S WILL IN THIS, DUCHESS.
HE'S OBSERVED... PERCEIVED ENTRANCES AND ROUTES HE SHOULDN'T HAVE BEEN AWARE OF!
HE'S AWARE THAT WE ONLY HAVE A HANDFUL OF TROOPS TO OPPOSE HIS LEGIONS...
...AND HE KNOWS AS MUCH ABOUT THESE RUINS AS ANYONE WHO'S ATTENDED YOUR FATHER'S RECENT STAFF BRIEFINGS.
IMPOSSIBLE!!!
THAT WOULD MEAN...THAT COULD ONLY MEAN...

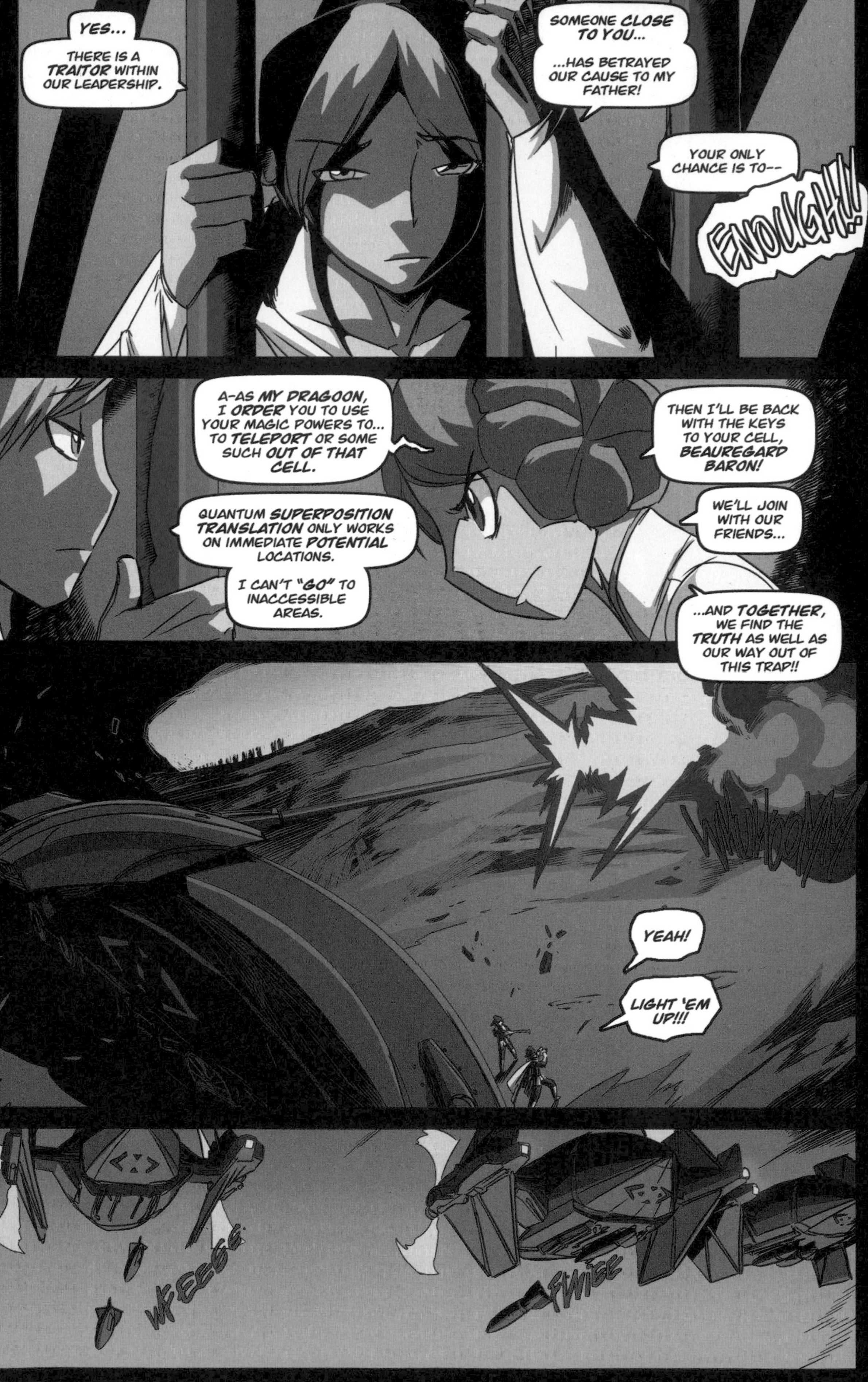

YES...
THERE IS A TRAITOR WITHIN OUR LEADERSHIP.
SOMEONE CLOSE TO YOU...
...HAS BETRAYED OUR CAUSE TO MY FATHER!
YOUR ONLY CHANCE IS TO--
ENOUGH!!
A-AS MY DRAGOON, I ORDER YOU TO USE YOUR MAGIC POWERS TO... TO TELEPORT OR SOME SUCH OUT OF THAT CELL.
QUANTUM SUPERPOSITION TRANSLATION ONLY WORKS ON IMMEDIATE POTENTIAL LOCATIONS.
I CAN'T "GO" TO INACCESSIBLE AREAS.
THEN I'LL BE BACK WITH THE KEYS TO YOUR CELL, BEAUREGARD BARON!
WE'LL JOIN WITH OUR FRIENDS...
...AND TOGETHER, WE FIND THE TRUTH AS WELL AS OUR WAY OUT OF THIS TRAP!!
WHUMBOOMM!
YEAH!
LIGHT 'EM UP!!!
WFEEEEE
FWIEE

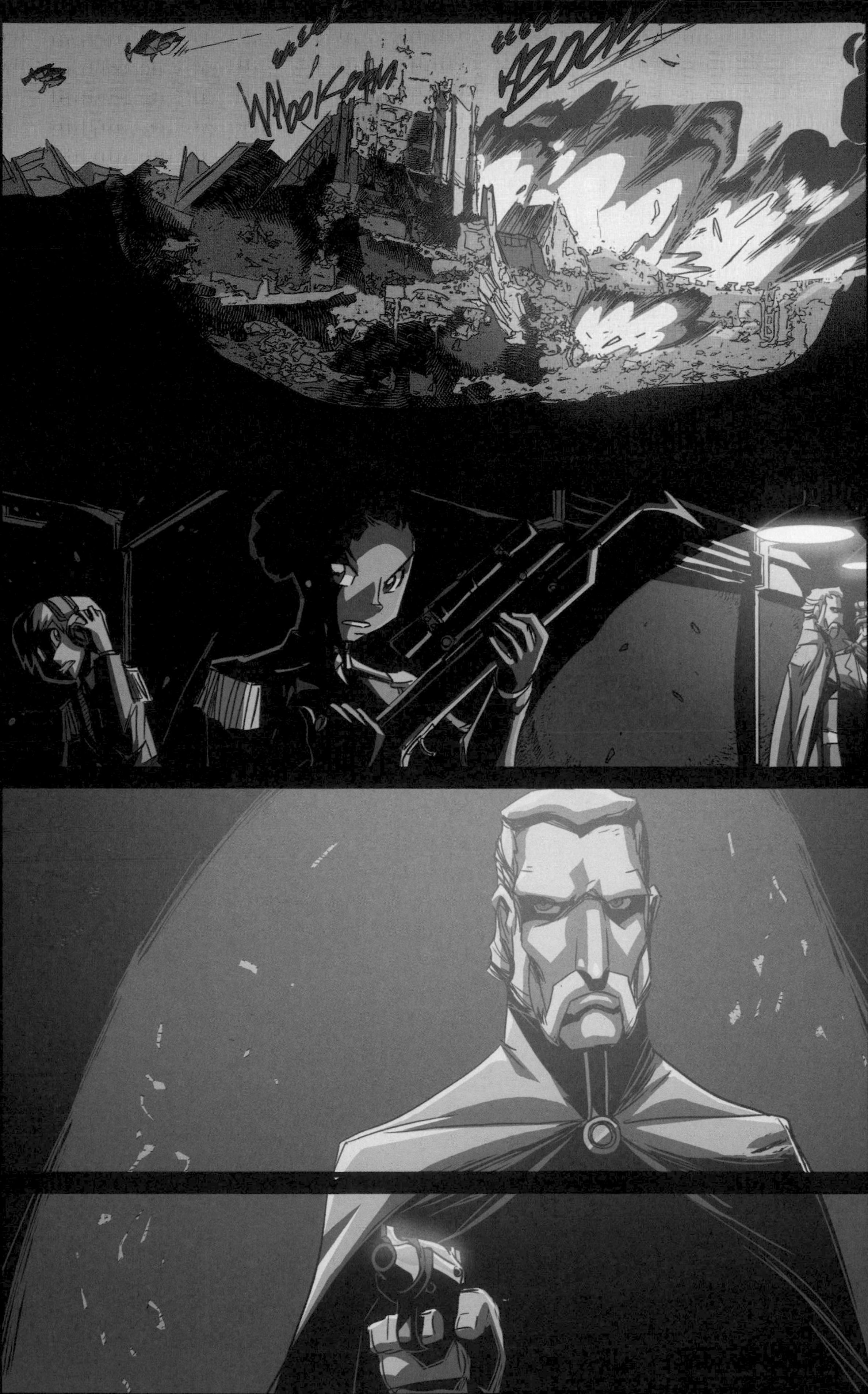
WHOOKOOM
BOOM

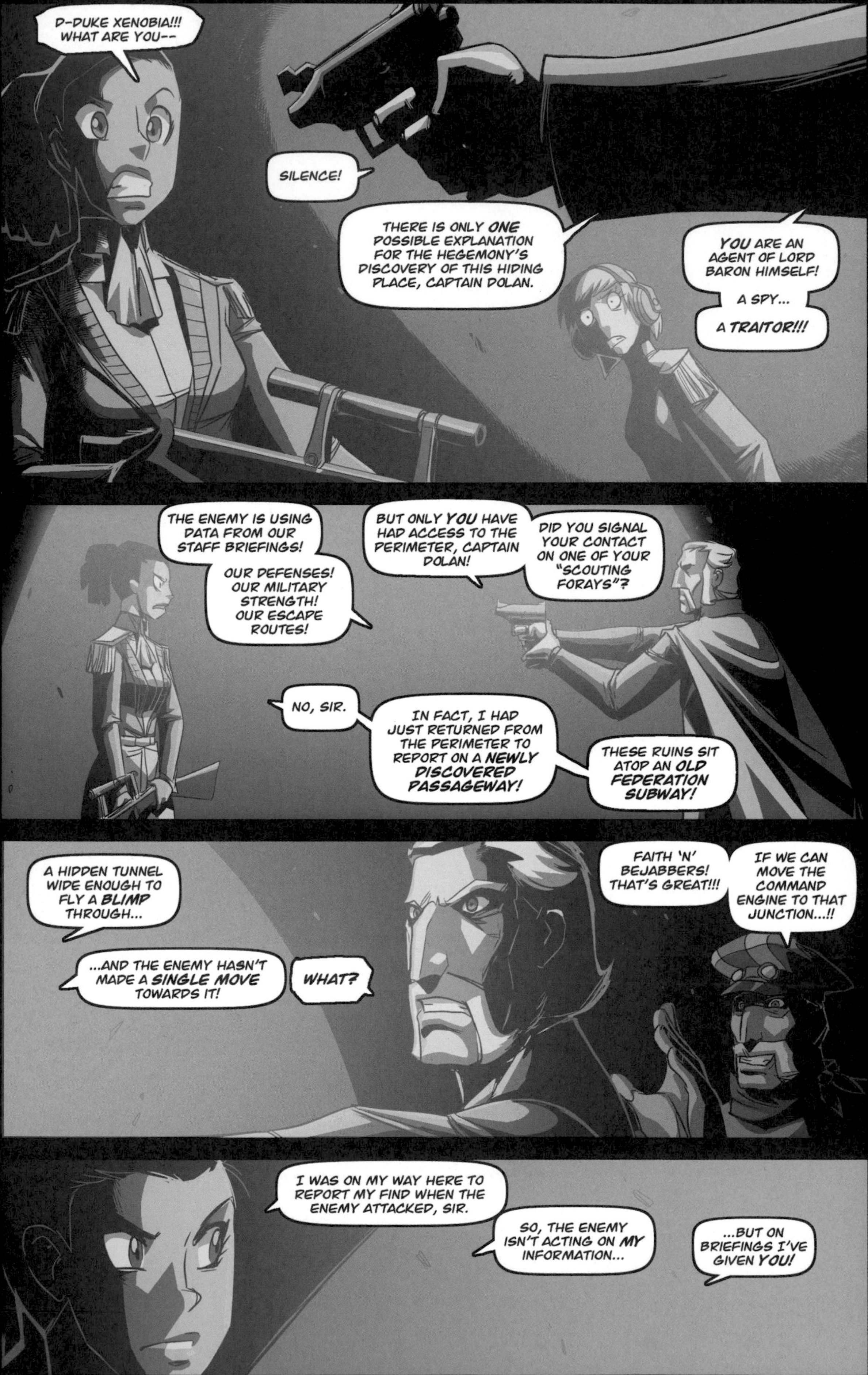
D-DUKE XENOBIA!!! WHAT ARE YOU--
SILENCE!
THERE IS ONLY ONE POSSIBLE EXPLANATION FOR THE HEGEMONY'S DISCOVERY OF THIS HIDING PLACE, CAPTAIN DOLAN.
YOU ARE AN AGENT OF LORD BARON HIMSELF!
A SPY...
A TRAITOR!!!
THE ENEMY IS USING DATA FROM OUR STAFF BRIEFINGS!
OUR DEFENSES! OUR MILITARY STRENGTH! OUR ESCAPE ROUTES!
BUT ONLY YOU HAVE HAD ACCESS TO THE PERIMETER, CAPTAIN DOLAN!
DID YOU SIGNAL YOUR CONTACT ON ONE OF YOUR "SCOUTING FORAYS"?
NO, SIR.
IN FACT, I HAD JUST RETURNED FROM THE PERIMETER TO REPORT ON A NEWLY DISCOVERED PASSAGEWAY!
THESE RUINS SIT ATOP AN OLD FEDERATION SUBWAY!
A HIDDEN TUNNEL WIDE ENOUGH TO FLY A BLIMP THROUGH...
...AND THE ENEMY HASN'T MADE A SINGLE MOVE TOWARDS IT!
WHAT?
FAITH 'N' BEJABBERS! THAT'S GREAT!!!
IF WE CAN MOVE THE COMMAND ENGINE TO THAT JUNCTION...!!
I WAS ON MY WAY HERE TO REPORT MY FIND WHEN THE ENEMY ATTACKED, SIR.
SO, THE ENEMY ISN'T ACTING ON MY INFORMATION...
...BUT ON BRIEFINGS I'VE GIVEN YOU!

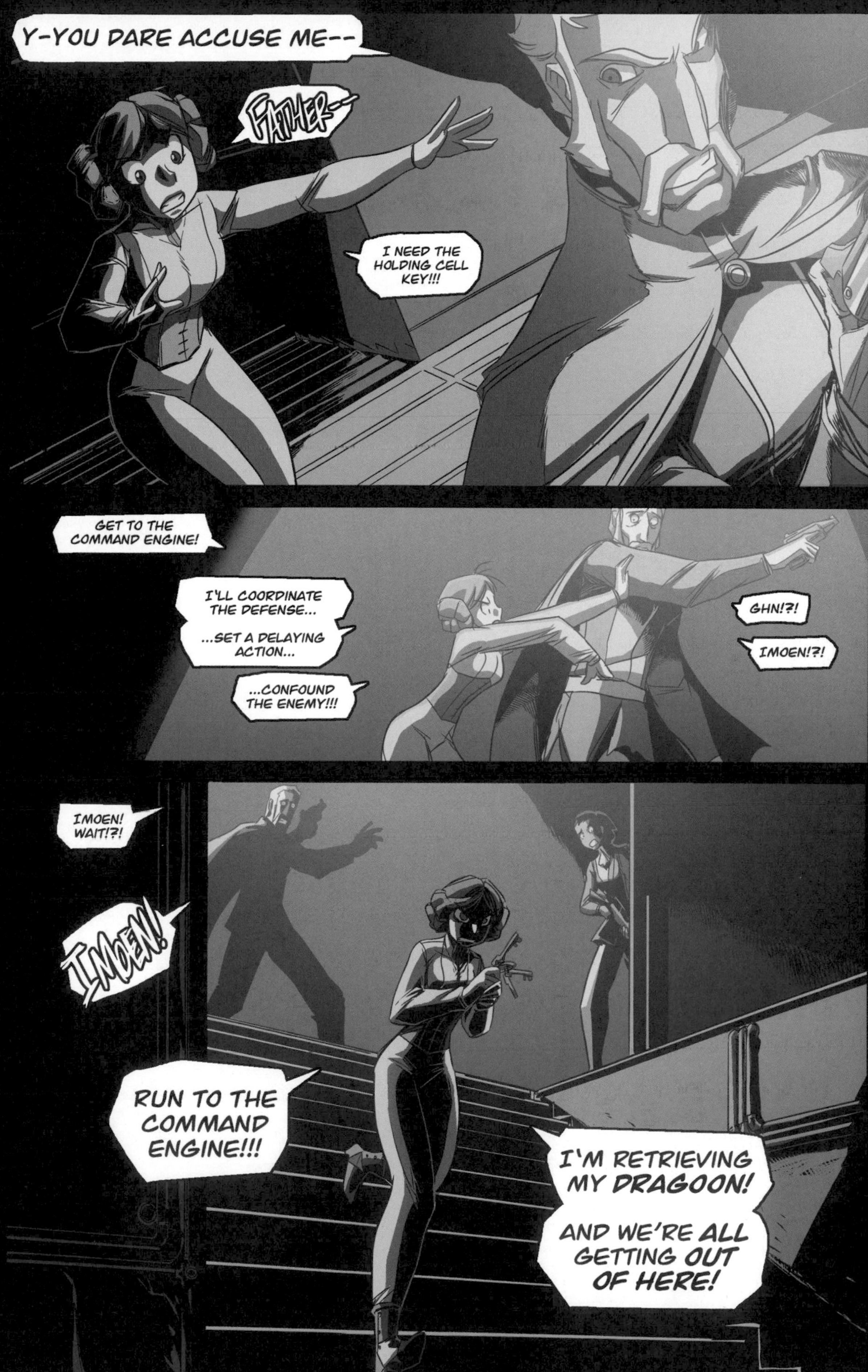

Y-YOU DARE ACCUSE ME--
FATHER--
I NEED THE HOLDING CELL KEY!!!
GET TO THE COMMAND ENGINE!
I'LL COORDINATE THE DEFENSE...
...SET A DELAYING ACTION...
...CONFOUND THE ENEMY!!!
GHN!?!
IMOEN!?!
IMOEN! WAIT!?!
IMOEN!
RUN TO THE COMMAND ENGINE!!!
I'M RETRIEVING MY DRAGOON!
AND WE'RE ALL GETTING OUT OF HERE!

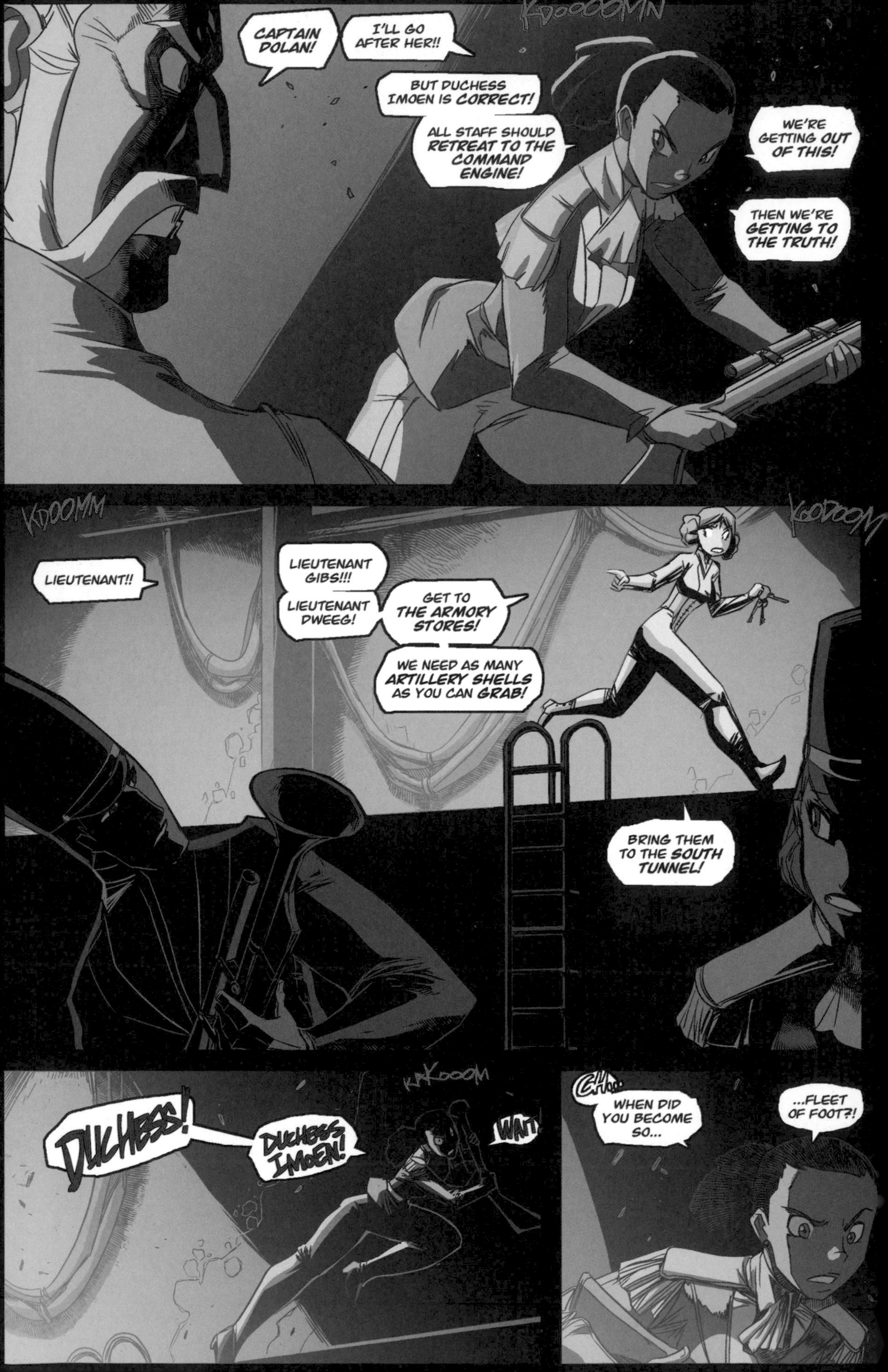
KDOOOOMN
CAPTAIN DOLAN!
I'LL GO AFTER HER!!
BUT DUCHESS IMOEN IS CORRECT!
ALL STAFF SHOULD RETREAT TO THE COMMAND ENGINE!
WE'RE GETTING OUT OF THIS!
THEN WE'RE GETTING TO THE TRUTH!
KDOOMM
KDOOM
LIEUTENANT!!
LIEUTENANT GIBS!!!
LIEUTENANT DWEEG!
GET TO THE ARMORY STORES!
WE NEED AS MANY ARTILLERY SHELLS AS YOU CAN GRAB!
BRING THEM TO THE SOUTH TUNNEL!
KAKOOOM
DUCHESS!
DUCHESS IMOEN!
WAIT
WHEN DID YOU BECOME SO...
...FLEET OF FOOT?!

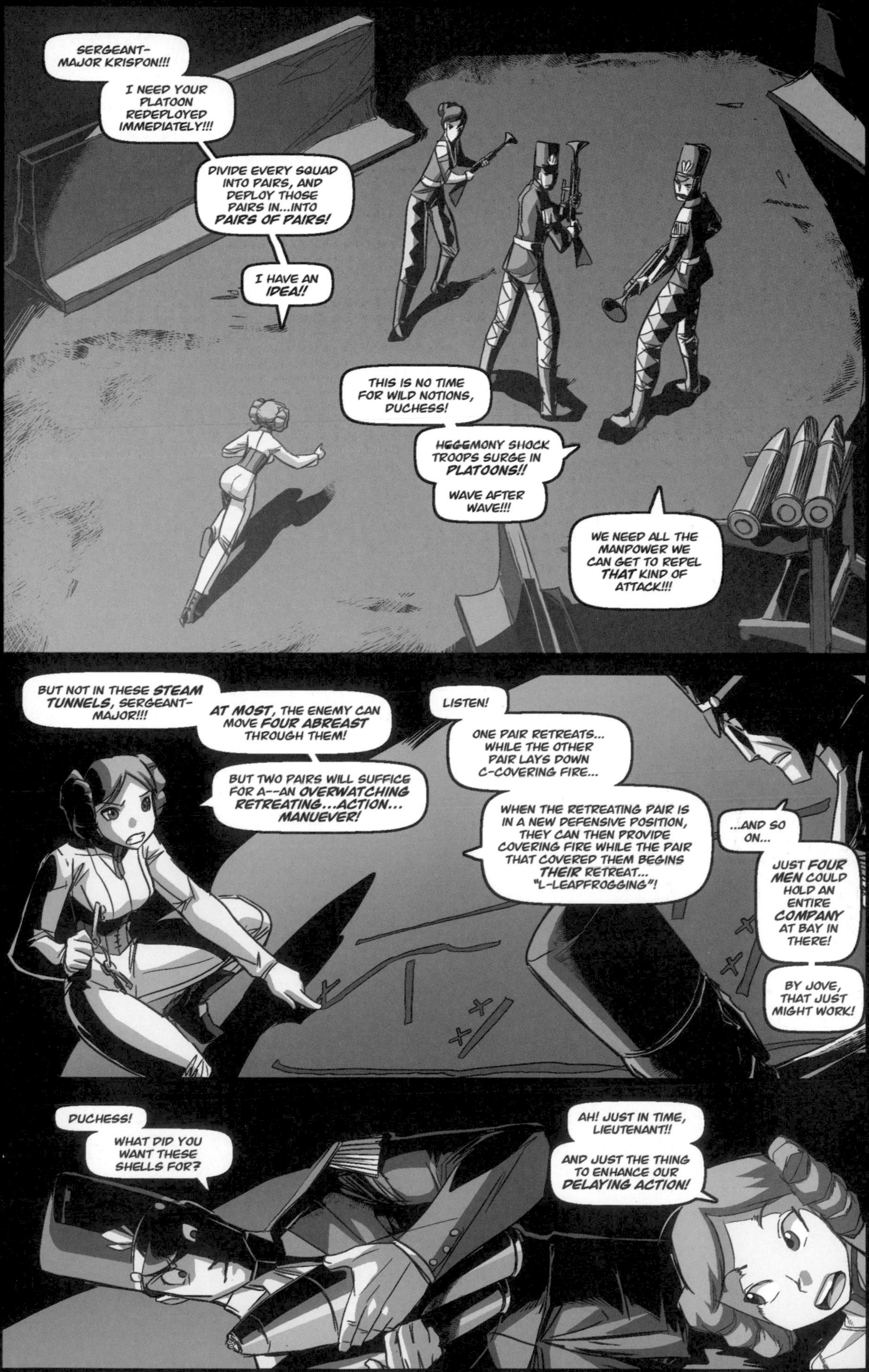
SERGEANT-MAJOR KRISPON!!!
I NEED YOUR PLATOON REDEPLOYED IMMEDIATELY!!!
DIVIDE EVERY SQUAD INTO PAIRS, AND DEPLOY THOSE PAIRS IN...INTO PAIRS OF PAIRS!
I HAVE AN IDEA!!
THIS IS NO TIME FOR WILD NOTIONS, DUCHESS!
HEGGEMONY SHOCK TROOPS SURGE IN PLATOONS!!
WAVE AFTER WAVE!!!
WE NEED ALL THE MANPOWER WE CAN GET TO REPEL THAT KIND OF ATTACK!!!
BUT NOT IN THESE STEAM TUNNELS, SERGEANT-MAJOR!!!
AT MOST, THE ENEMY CAN MOVE FOUR ABREAST THROUGH THEM!
BUT TWO PAIRS WILL SUFFICE FOR A--AN OVERWATCHING RETREATING...ACTION...MANUEVER!
LISTEN!
ONE PAIR RETREATS... WHILE THE OTHER PAIR LAYS DOWN C-COVERING FIRE...
WHEN THE RETREATING PAIR IS IN A NEW DEFENSIVE POSITION, THEY CAN THEN PROVIDE COVERING FIRE WHILE THE PAIR THAT COVERED THEM BEGINS THEIR RETREAT... "L-LEAPFROGGING"!
...AND SO ON...
JUST FOUR MEN COULD HOLD AN ENTIRE COMPANY AT BAY IN THERE!
BY JOVE, THAT JUST MIGHT WORK!
DUCHESS!
WHAT DID YOU WANT THESE SHELLS FOR?
AH! JUST IN TIME, LIEUTENANT!!
AND JUST THE THING TO ENHANCE OUR DELAYING ACTION!

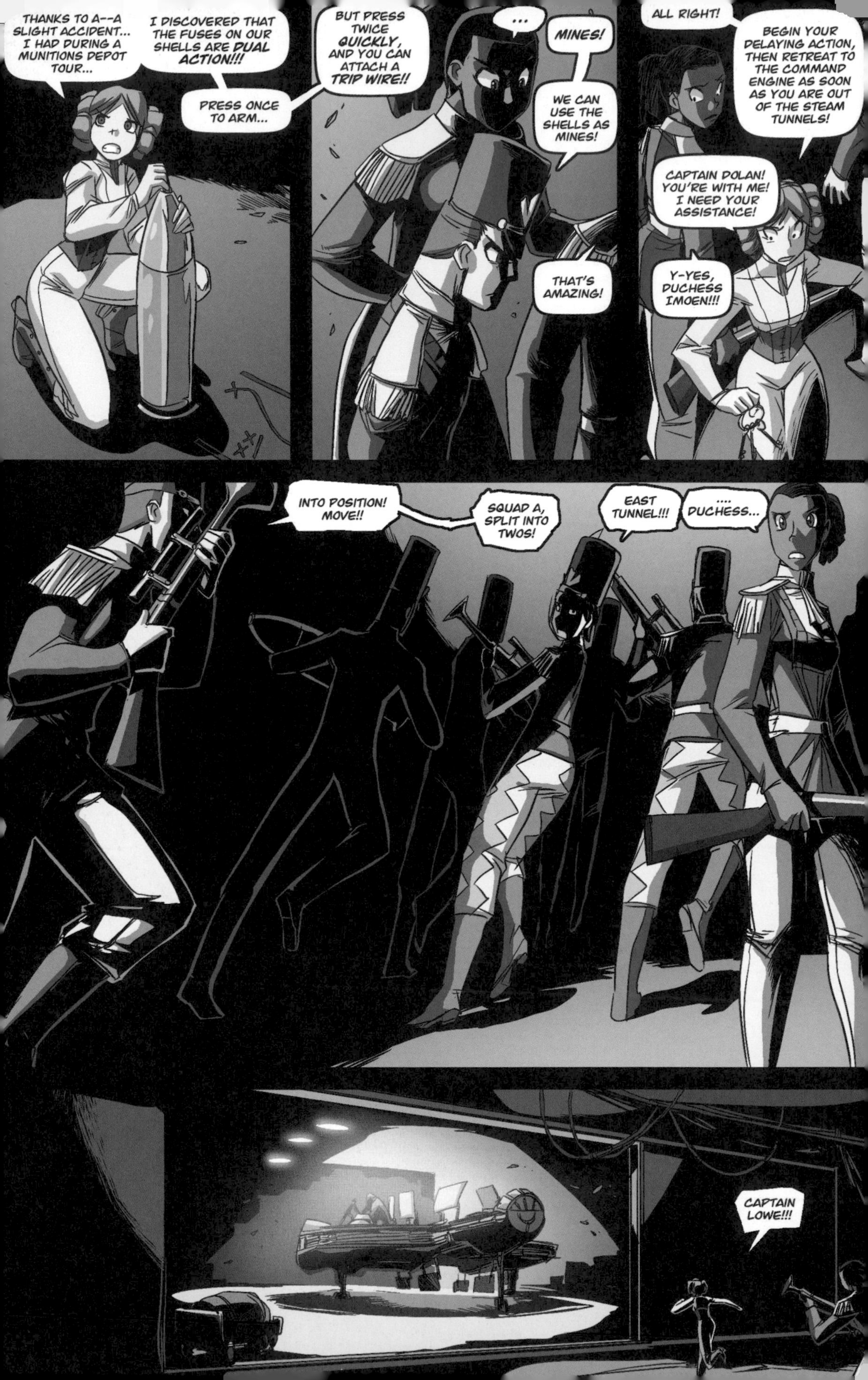
THANKS TO A--A SLIGHT ACCIDENT... I HAD DURING A MUNITIONS DEPOT TOUR...
I DISCOVERED THAT THE FUSES ON OUR SHELLS ARE DUAL ACTION!!!
PRESS ONCE TO ARM...
BUT PRESS TWICE QUICKLY, AND YOU CAN ATTACH A TRIP WIRE!!
...
MINES!
WE CAN USE THE SHELLS AS MINES!
THAT'S AMAZING!
ALL RIGHT!
BEGIN YOUR DELAYING ACTION, THEN RETREAT TO THE COMMAND ENGINE AS SOON AS YOU ARE OUT OF THE STEAM TUNNELS!
CAPTAIN DOLAN! YOU'RE WITH ME! I NEED YOUR ASSISTANCE!
Y-YES, DUCHESS IMOEN!!!
INTO POSITION! MOVE!!
SQUAD A, SPLIT INTO TWOS!
EAST TUNNEL!!!
.... DUCHESS...
CAPTAIN LOWE!!!

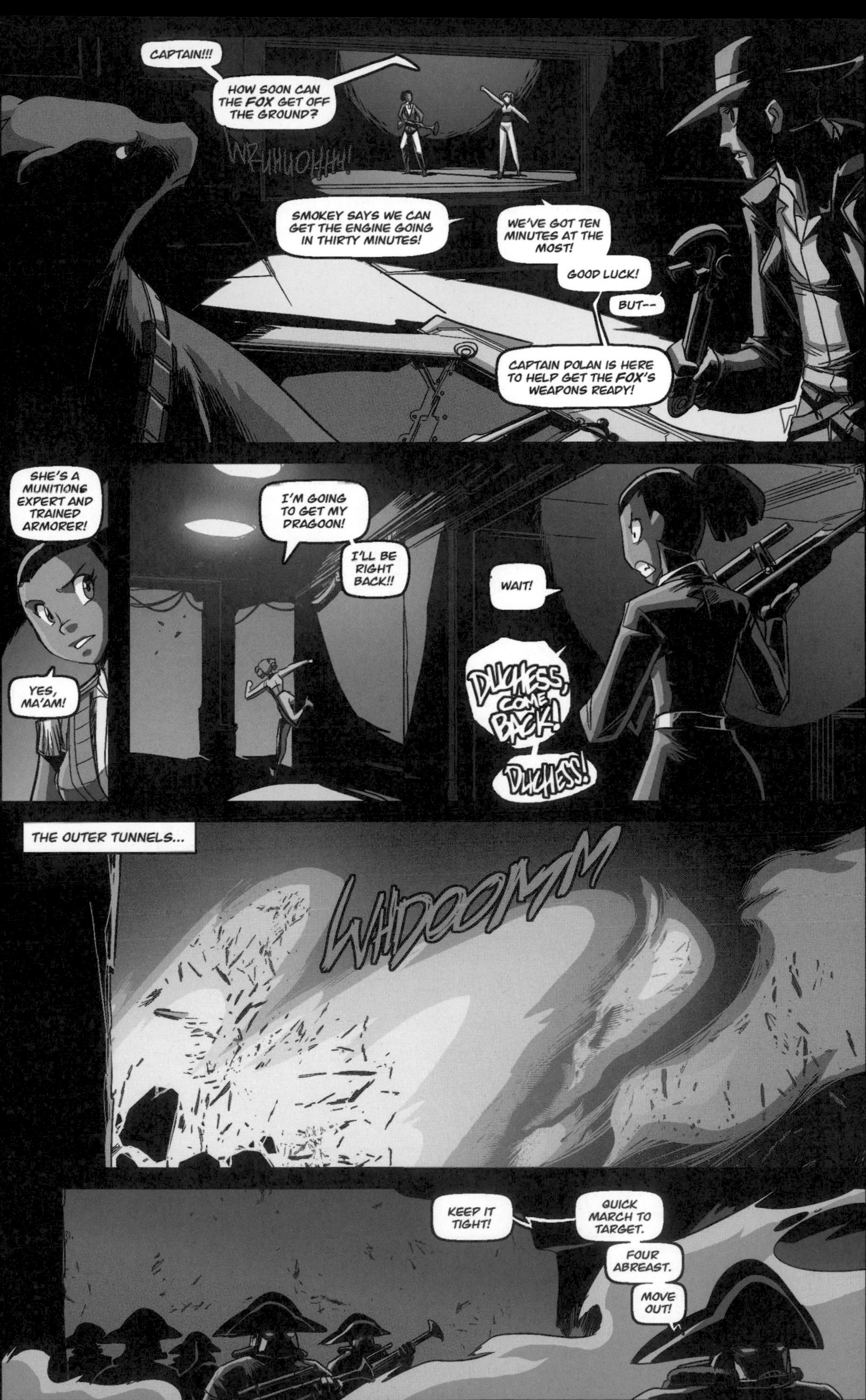
CAPTAIN!!!
HOW SOON CAN THE FOX GET OFF THE GROUND?
WRUHHOHHH!
SMOKEY SAYS WE CAN GET THE ENGINE GOING IN THIRTY MINUTES!
WE'VE GOT TEN MINUTES AT THE MOST!
GOOD LUCK!
BUT--
CAPTAIN DOLAN IS HERE TO HELP GET THE FOX'S WEAPONS READY!
SHE'S A MUNITIONS EXPERT AND TRAINED ARMORER!
YES, MA'AM!
I'M GOING TO GET MY DRAGOON!
I'LL BE RIGHT BACK!!
WAIT!
DUCHESS, COME BACK!
DUCHESS!
THE OUTER TUNNELS...
WHOOOMM
KEEP IT TIGHT!
QUICK MARCH TO TARGET.
FOUR ABREAST.
MOVE OUT!

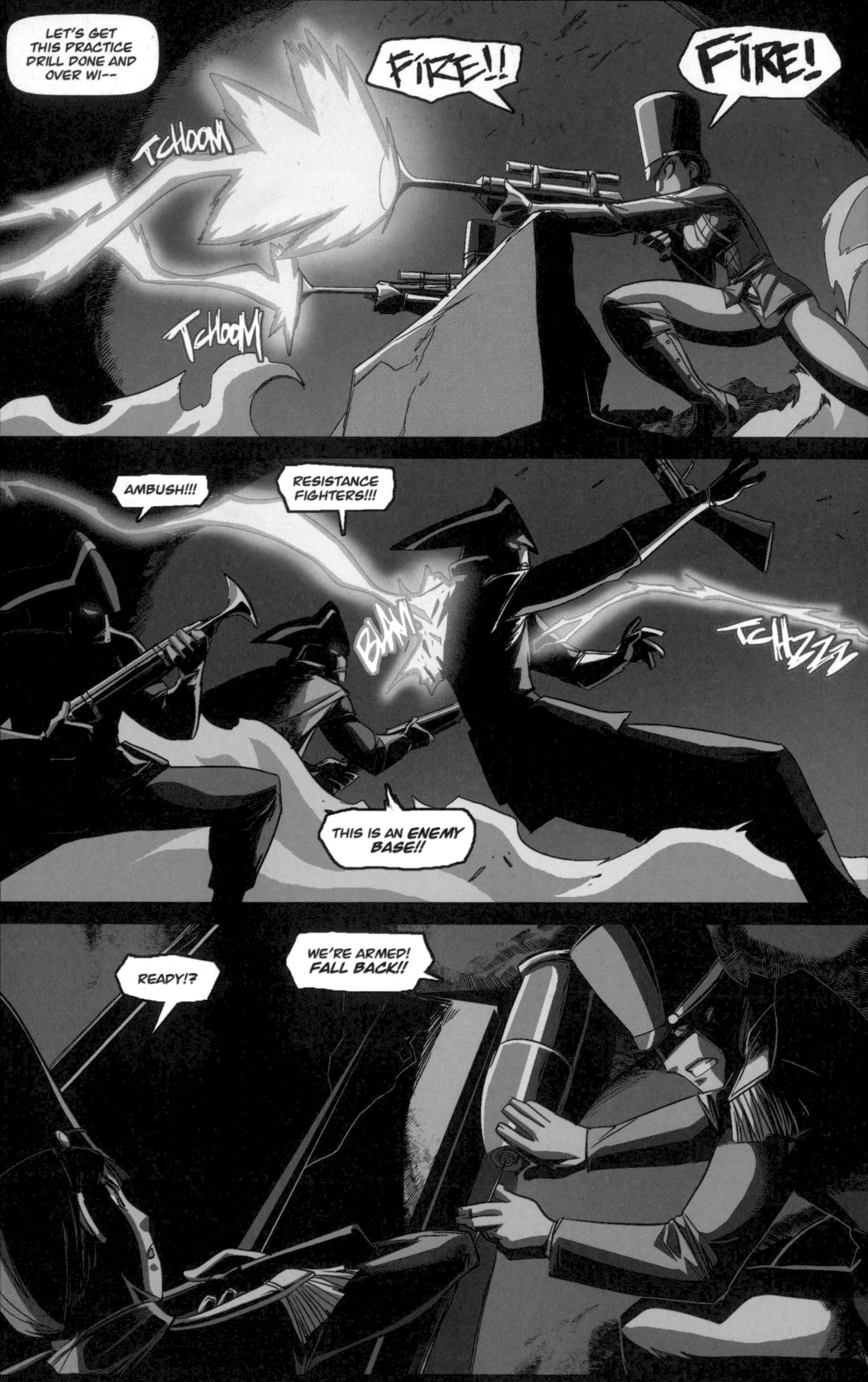
LET'S GET THIS PRACTICE DRILL DONE AND OVER WI--
FIRE!!
FIRE!
TCHOOM
TCHOOM
AMBUSH!!!
RESISTANCE FIGHTERS!!!
BLAM
TCHZZZZ
THIS IS AN ENEMY BASE!!
READY!?
WE'RE ARMED! FALL BACK!!

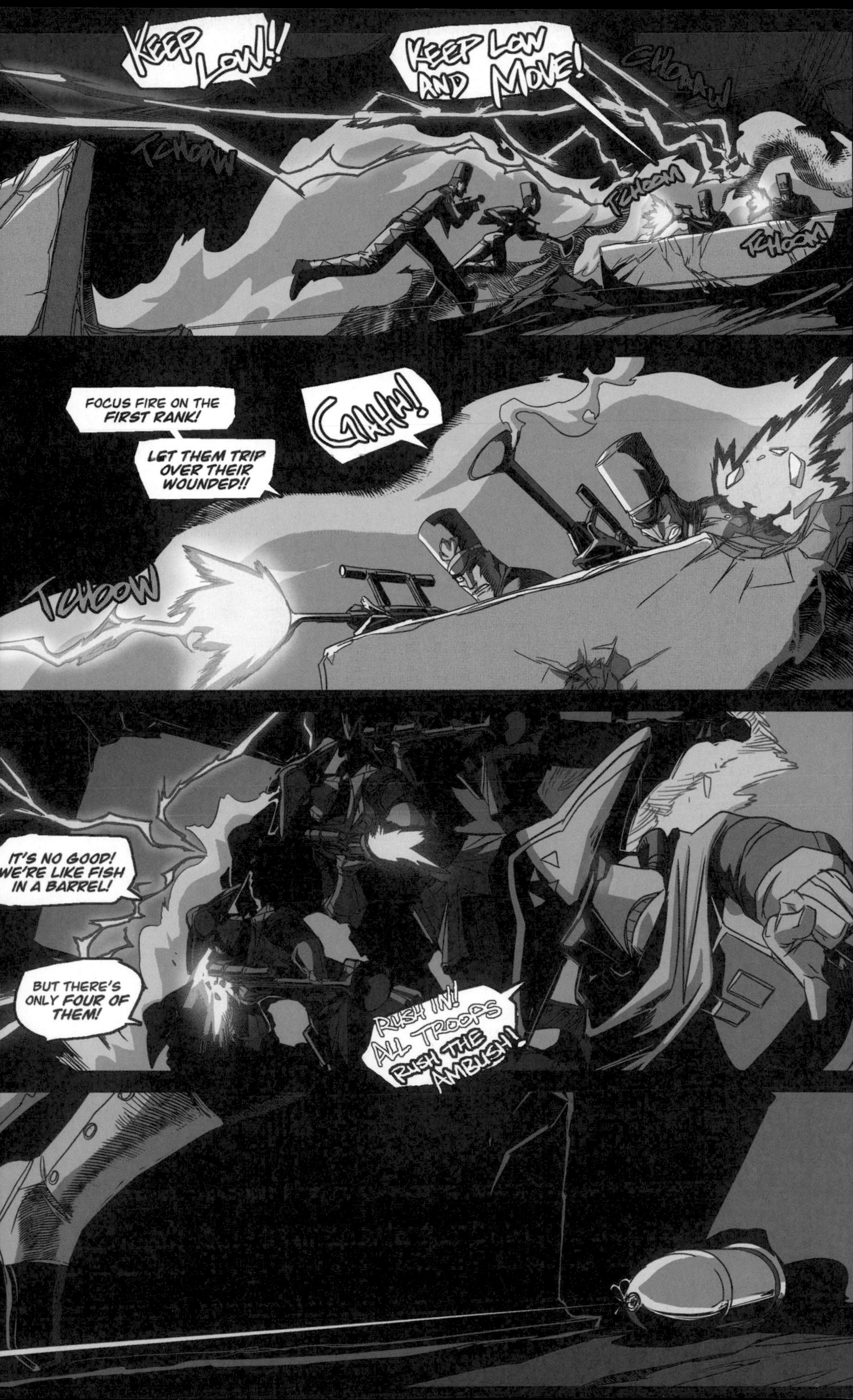
KEEP LOW!!
KEEP LOW AND MOVE!
CHOWAW
TCHOOOW
TCHOOM
TCHOOM
FOCUS FIRE ON THE FIRST RANK!
LET THEM TRIP OVER THEIR WOUNDED!!
GAHH!
TCHOOW
IT'S NO GOOD! WE'RE LIKE FISH IN A BARREL!
BUT THERE'S ONLY FOUR OF THEM!
RUSH IN! ALL TROOPS RUSH THE AMBUSH!

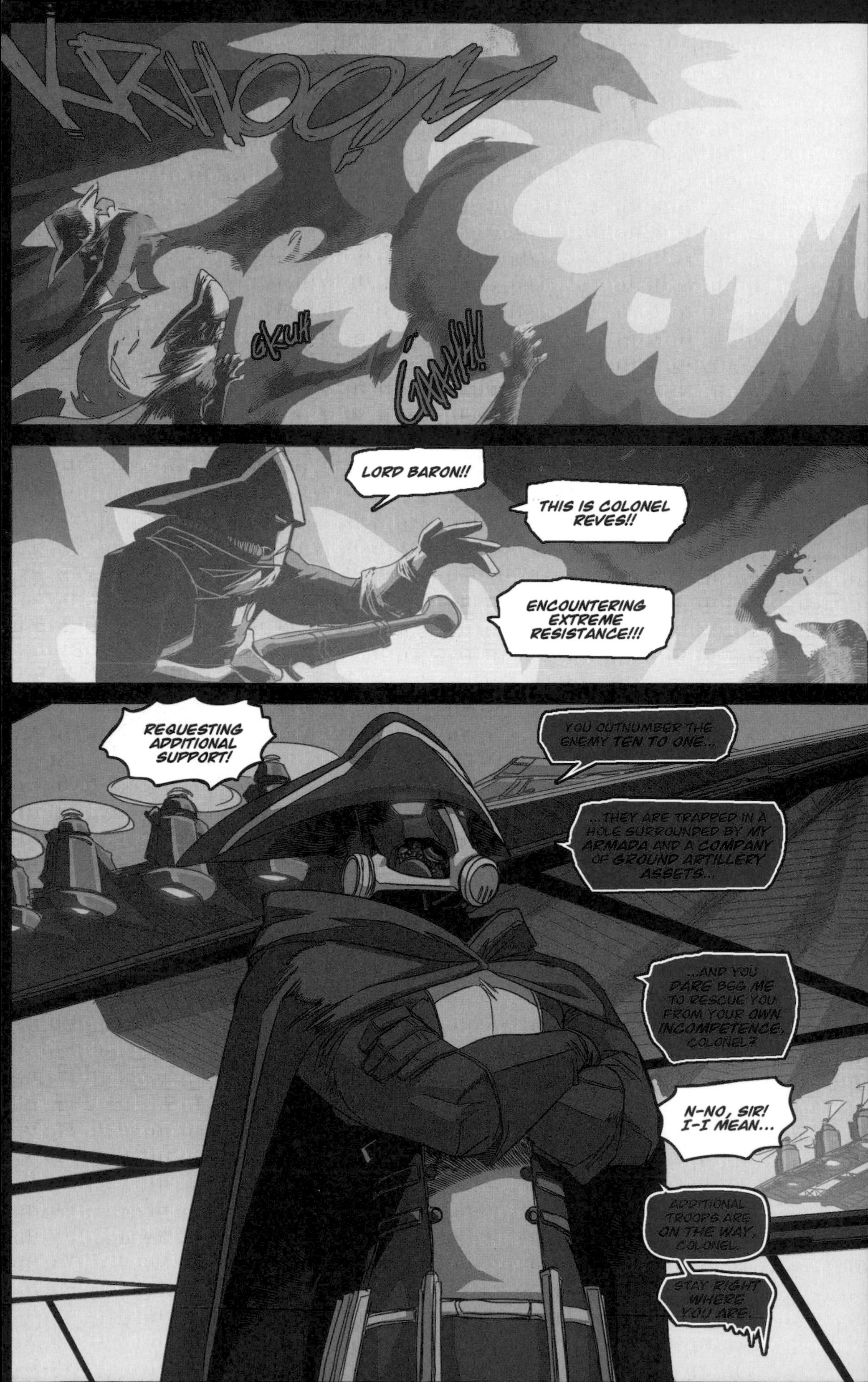
KRHOOM
LORD BARON!!
THIS IS COLONEL REVES!!
ENCOUNTERING EXTREME RESISTANCE!!!
REQUESTING ADDITIONAL SUPPORT!
YOU OUTNUMBER THE ENEMY TEN TO ONE...
...THEY ARE TRAPPED IN A HOLE SURROUNDED BY MY ARMADA AND A COMPANY OF GROUND ARTILLERY ASSETS...
...AND YOU DARE BEG ME TO RESCUE YOU FROM YOUR OWN INCOMPETENCE, COLONEL?
N-NO, SIR! I-I MEAN...
ADDITIONAL TROOPS ARE ON THE WAY, COLONEL.
STAY RIGHT WHERE YOU ARE.

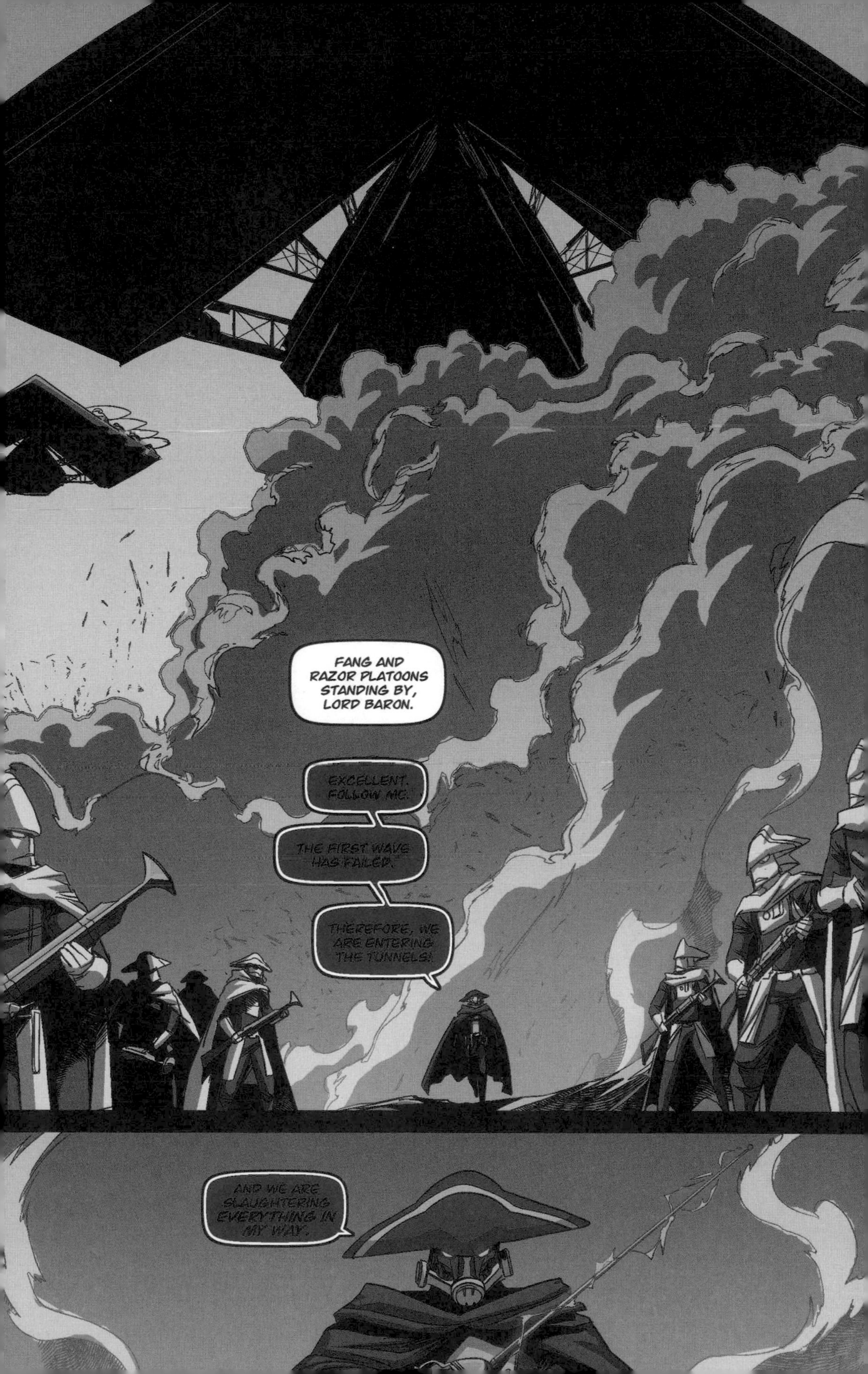
FANG AND RAZOR PLATOONS STANDING BY, LORD BARON.
EXCELLENT. FOLLOW ME.
THE FIRST WAVE HAS FAILED.
THEREFORE, WE ARE ENTERING THE TUNNELS!
AND WE ARE SLAUGHTERING EVERYTHING IN MY WAY.

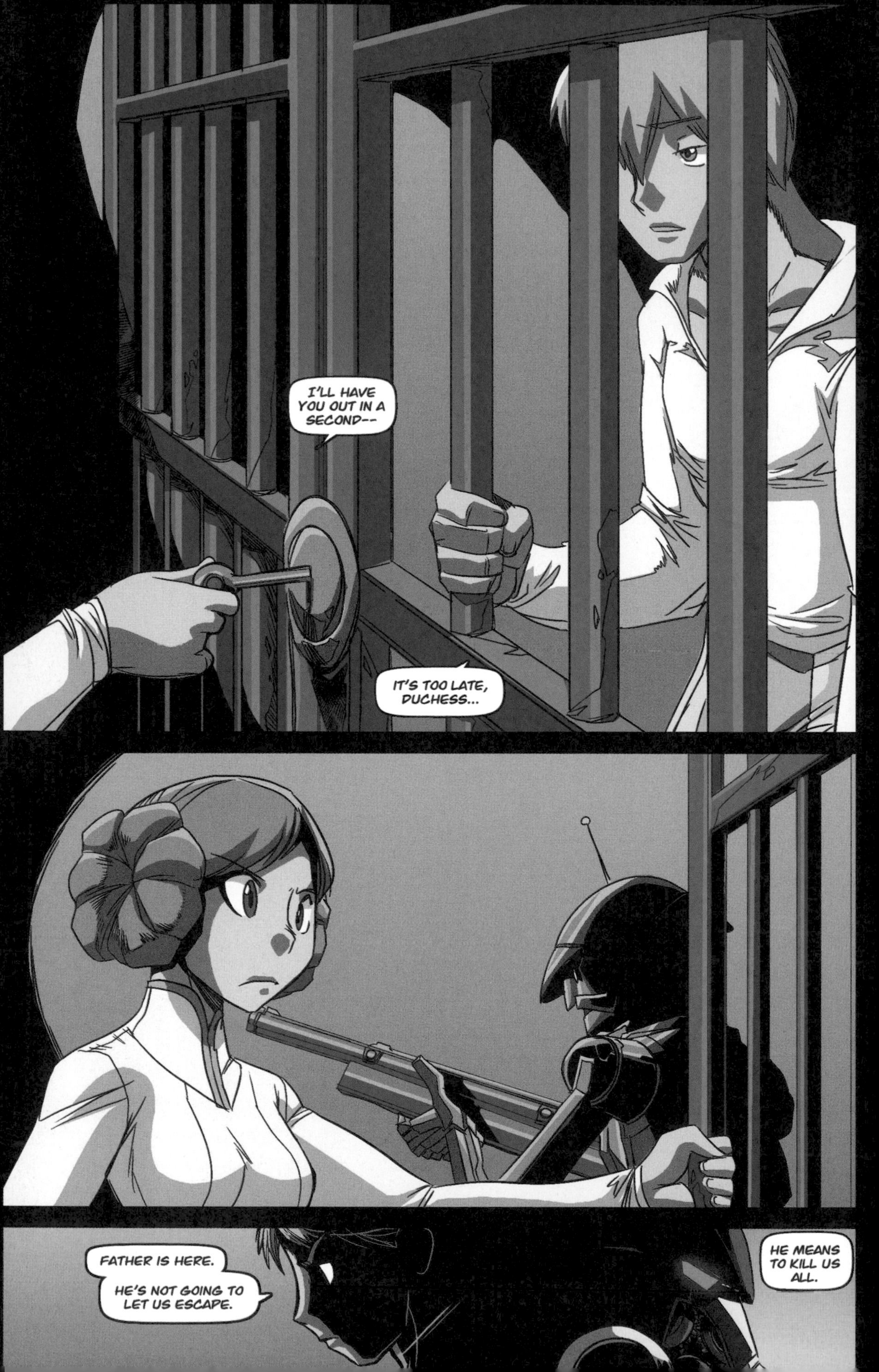
I'LL HAVE YOU OUT IN A SECOND--
IT'S TOO LATE, DUCHESS...
FATHER IS HERE.
HE'S NOT GOING TO LET US ESCAPE.
HE MEANS TO KILL US ALL.

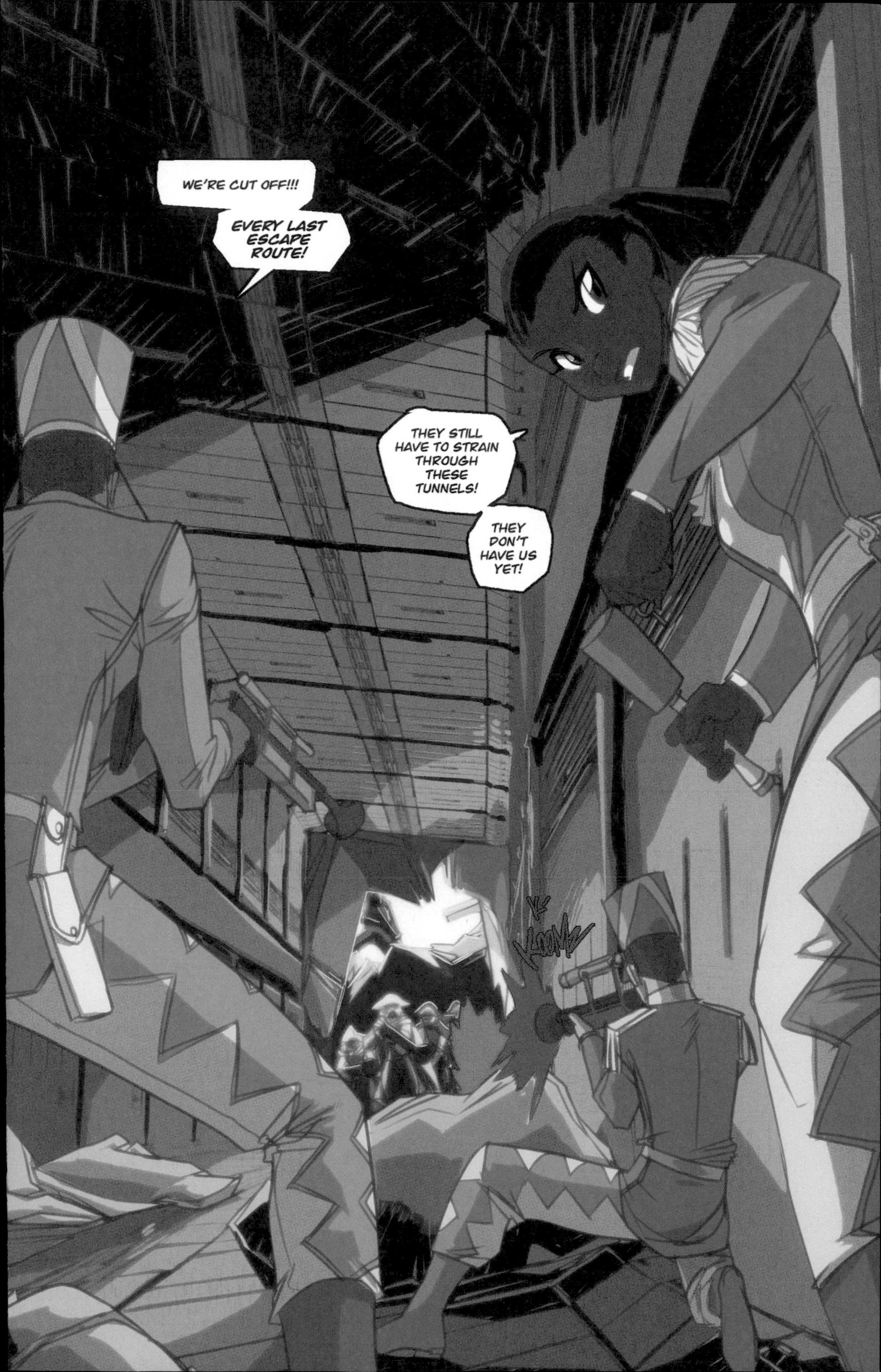
WE'RE CUT OFF!!!
EVERY LAST ESCAPE ROUTE!
THEY STILL HAVE TO STRAIN THROUGH THESE TUNNELS!
THEY DON'T HAVE US YET!

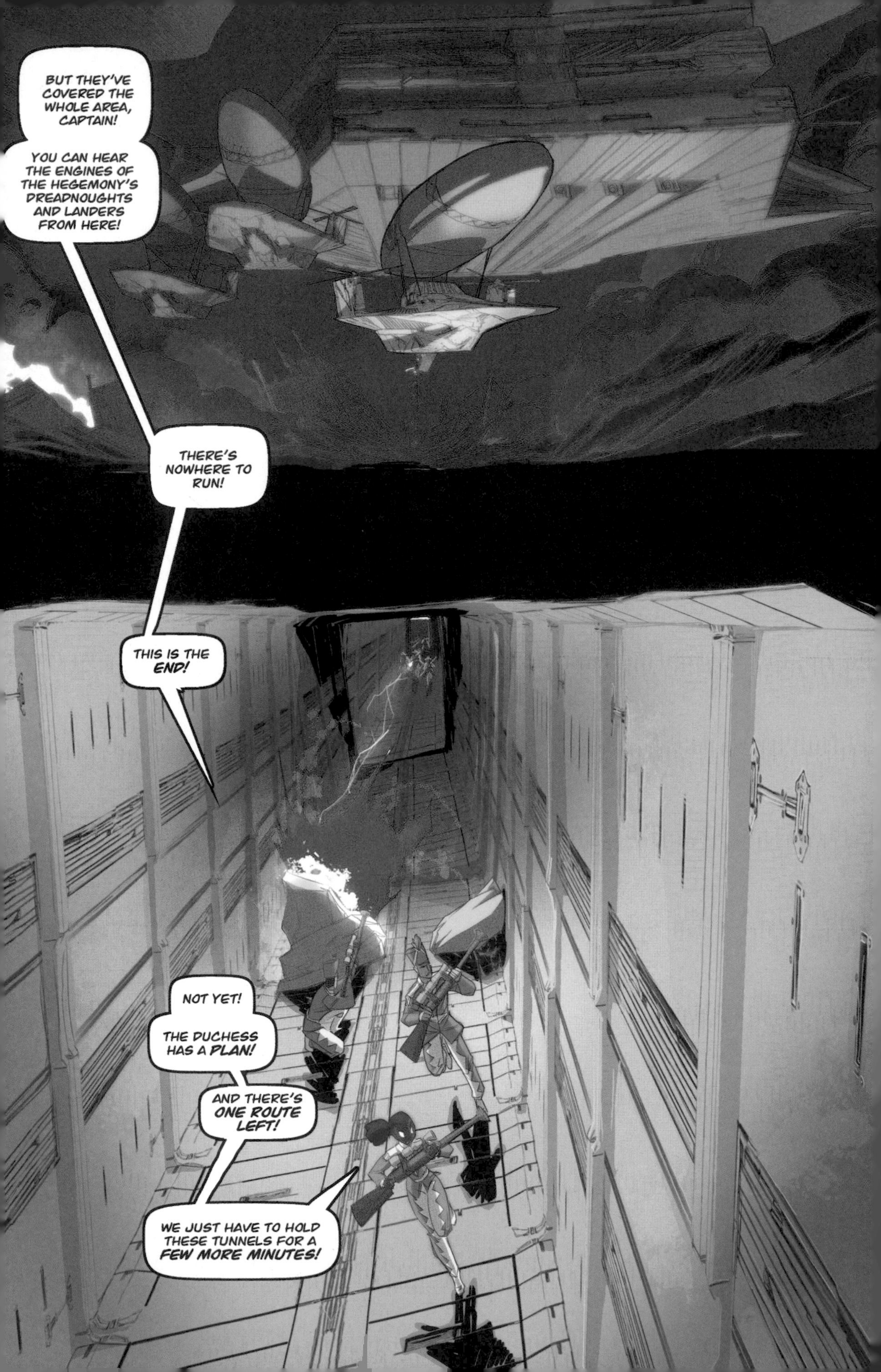
BUT THEY'VE COVERED THE WHOLE AREA, CAPTAIN!
YOU CAN HEAR THE ENGINES OF THE HEGEMONY'S DREADNOUGHTS AND LANDERS FROM HERE!
THERE'S NOWHERE TO RUN!
THIS IS THE END!
NOT YET!
THE DUCHESS HAS A PLAN!
AND THERE'S ONE ROUTE LEFT!
WE JUST HAVE TO HOLD THESE TUNNELS FOR A FEW MORE MINUTES!

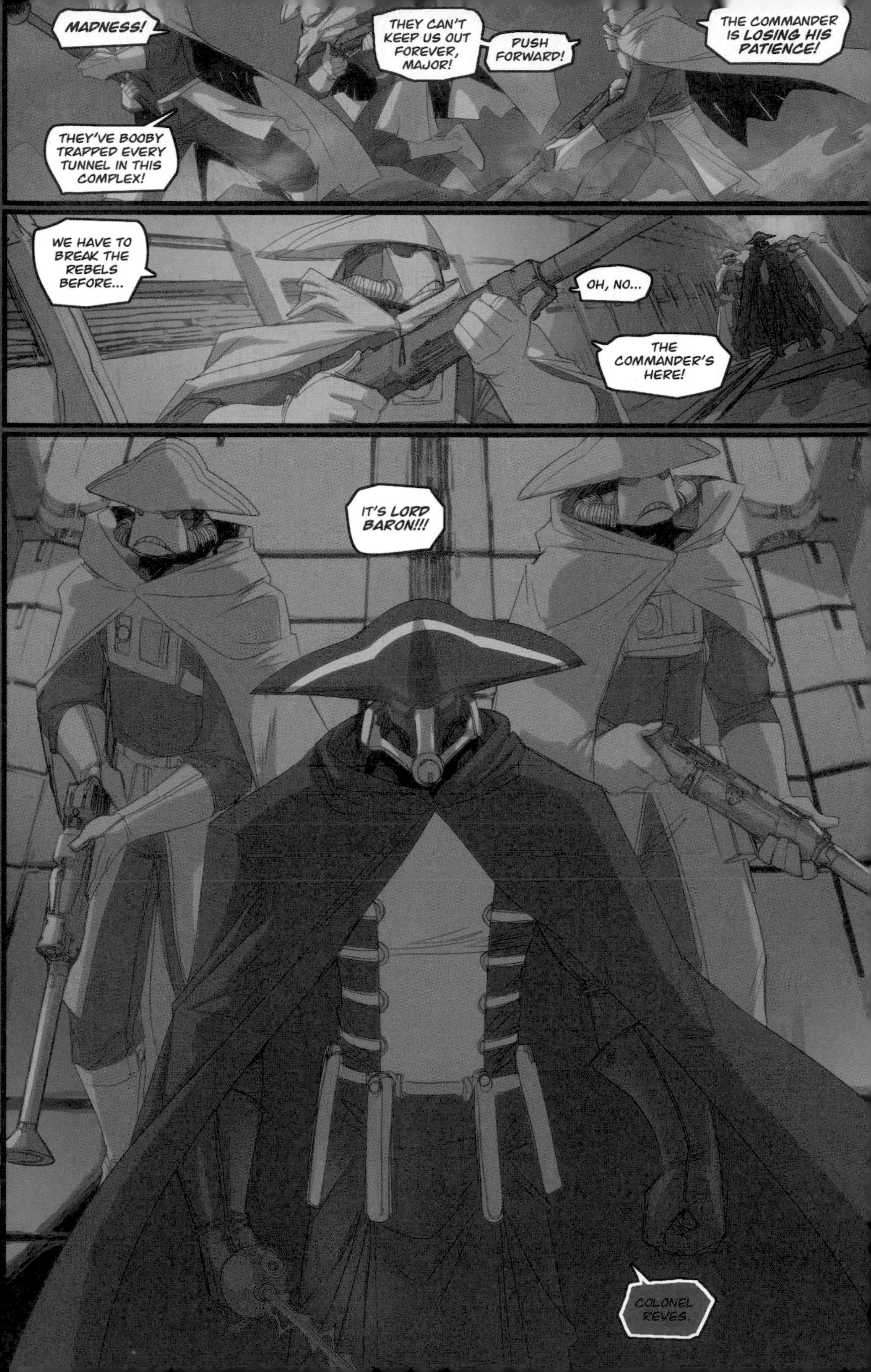
MADNESS!
THEY CAN'T KEEP US OUT FOREVER, MAJOR!
PUSH FORWARD!
THE COMMANDER IS LOSING HIS PATIENCE!
THEY'VE BOOBY TRAPPED EVERY TUNNEL IN THIS COMPLEX!
WE HAVE TO BREAK THE REBELS BEFORE...
OH, NO...
THE COMMANDER'S HERE!
IT'S LORD BARON!!!
COLONEL REVES.

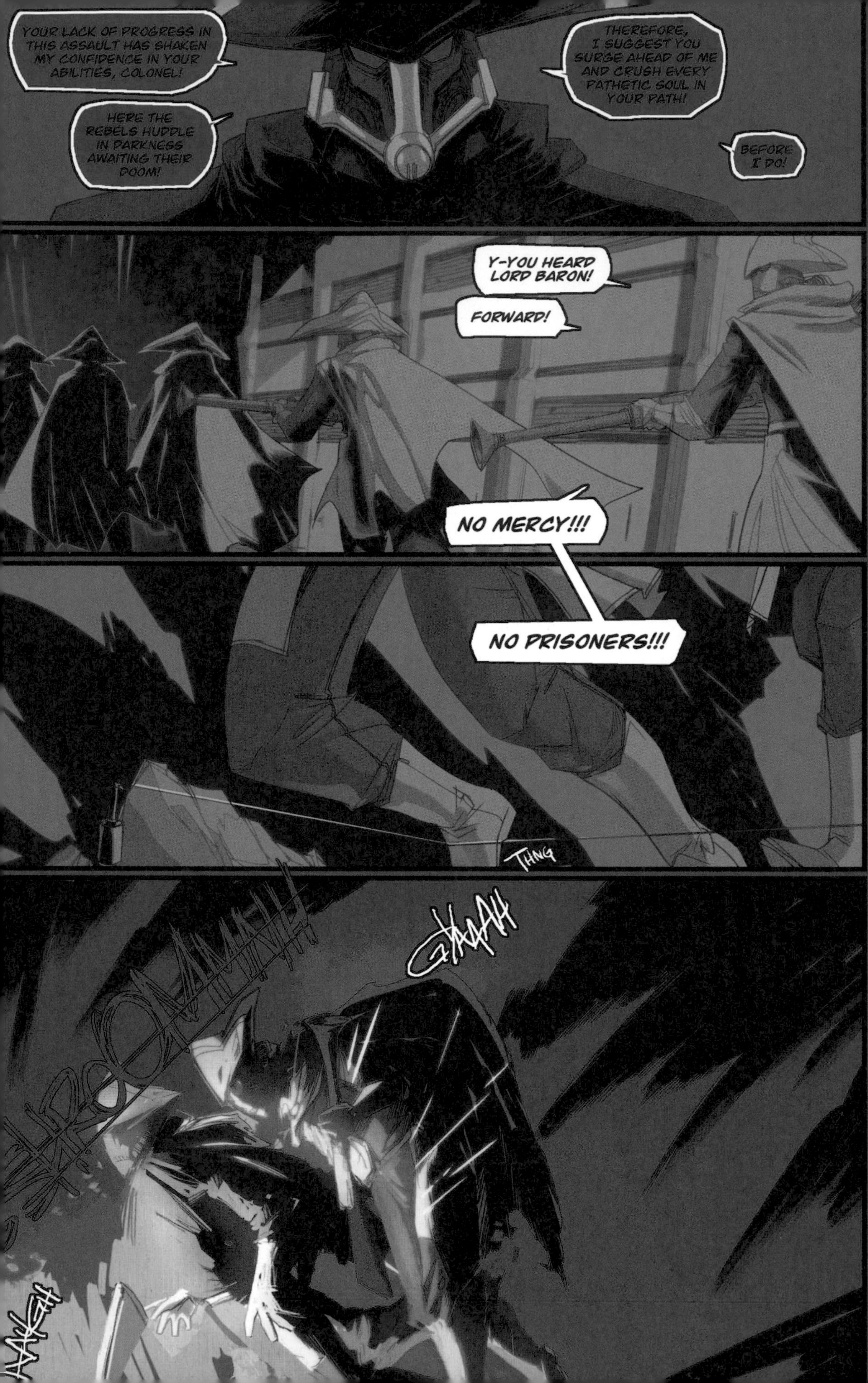
YOUR LACK OF PROGRESS IN THIS ASSAULT HAS SHAKEN MY CONFIDENCE IN YOUR ABILITIES, COLONEL!
HERE THE REBELS HUDDLE IN DARKNESS AWAITING THEIR DOOM!
THEREFORE, I SUGGEST YOU SURGE AHEAD OF ME AND CRUSH EVERY PATHETIC SOUL IN YOUR PATH!
BEFORE I DO!
Y-YOU HEARD LORD BARON!
FORWARD!
NO MERCY!!!
NO PRISONERS!!!
THNG

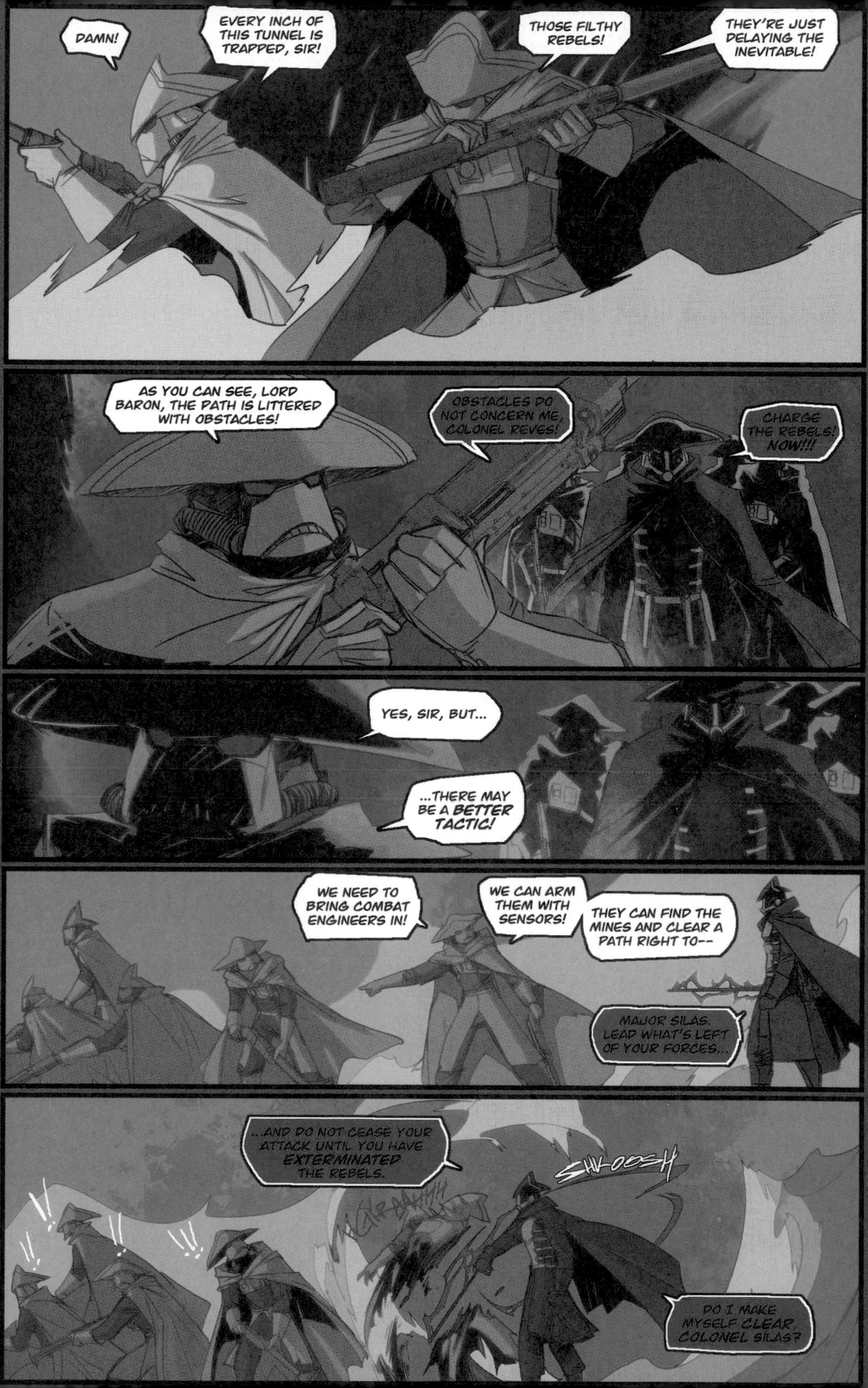
DAMN!
EVERY INCH OF THIS TUNNEL IS TRAPPED, SIR!
THOSE FILTHY REBELS!
THEY'RE JUST DELAYING THE INEVITABLE!
AS YOU CAN SEE, LORD BARON, THE PATH IS LITTERED WITH OBSTACLES!
OBSTACLES DO NOT CONCERN ME, COLONEL REVES!
CHARGE THE REBELS! NOW!!!
YES, SIR, BUT...
...THERE MAY BE A BETTER TACTIC!
WE NEED TO BRING COMBAT ENGINEERS IN!
WE CAN ARM THEM WITH SENSORS!
THEY CAN FIND THE MINES AND CLEAR A PATH RIGHT TO--
MAJOR SILAS. LEAD WHAT'S LEFT OF YOUR FORCES...
...AND DO NOT CEASE YOUR ATTACK UNTIL YOU HAVE EXTERMINATED THE REBELS.
SHLOOSH
DO I MAKE MYSELF CLEAR, COLONEL SILAS?

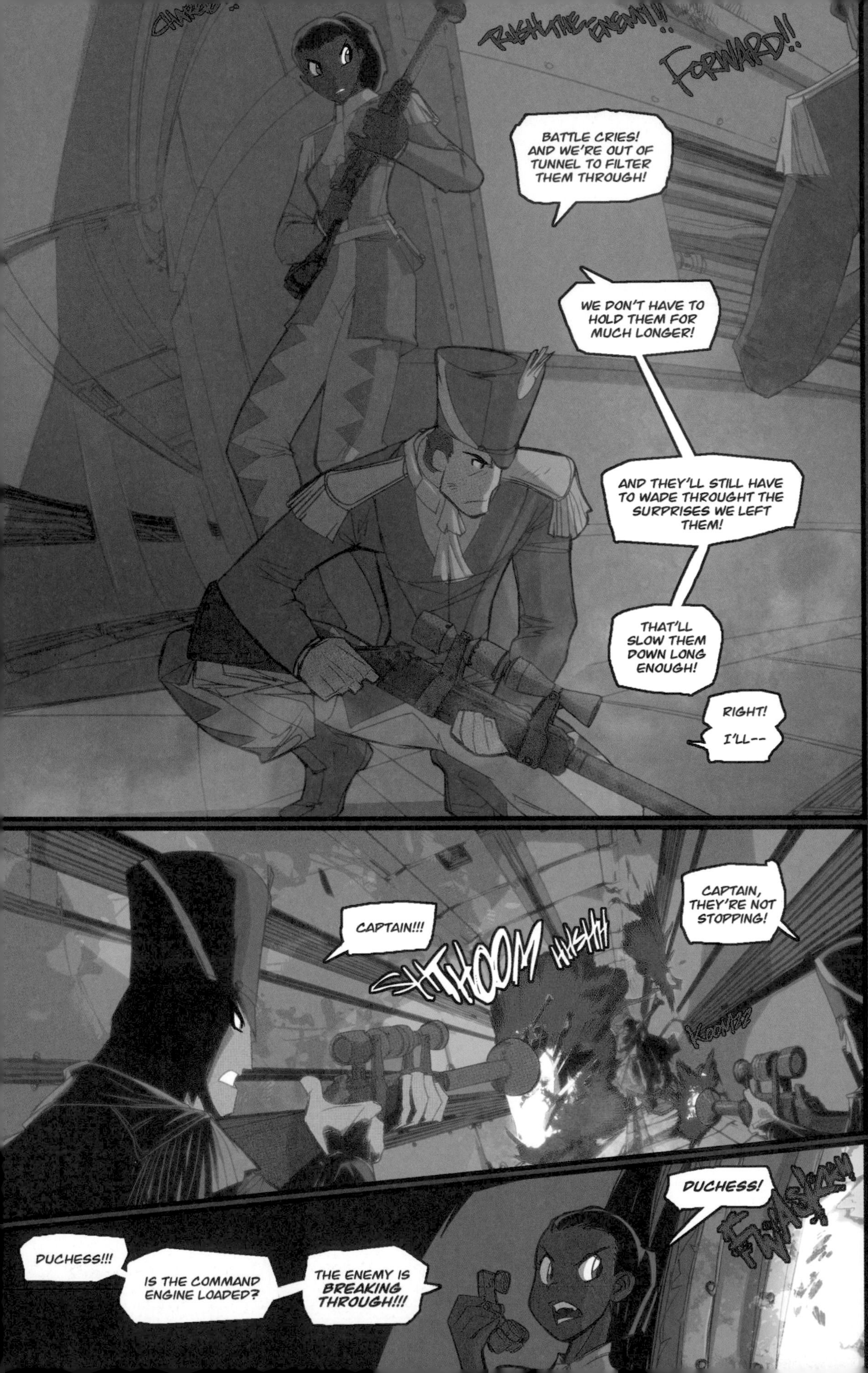
RUSH THE ENEMY!!
FORWARD!!
BATTLE CRIES! AND WE'RE OUT OF TUNNEL TO FILTER THEM THROUGH!
WE DON'T HAVE TO HOLD THEM FOR MUCH LONGER!
AND THEY'LL STILL HAVE TO WADE THROUGHT THE SURPRISES WE LEFT THEM!
THAT'LL SLOW THEM DOWN LONG ENOUGH!
RIGHT!
I'LL--
CAPTAIN!!!
CAPTAIN, THEY'RE NOT STOPPING!
DUCHESS!
DUCHESS!!!
IS THE COMMAND ENGINE LOADED?
THE ENEMY IS BREAKING THROUGH!!!

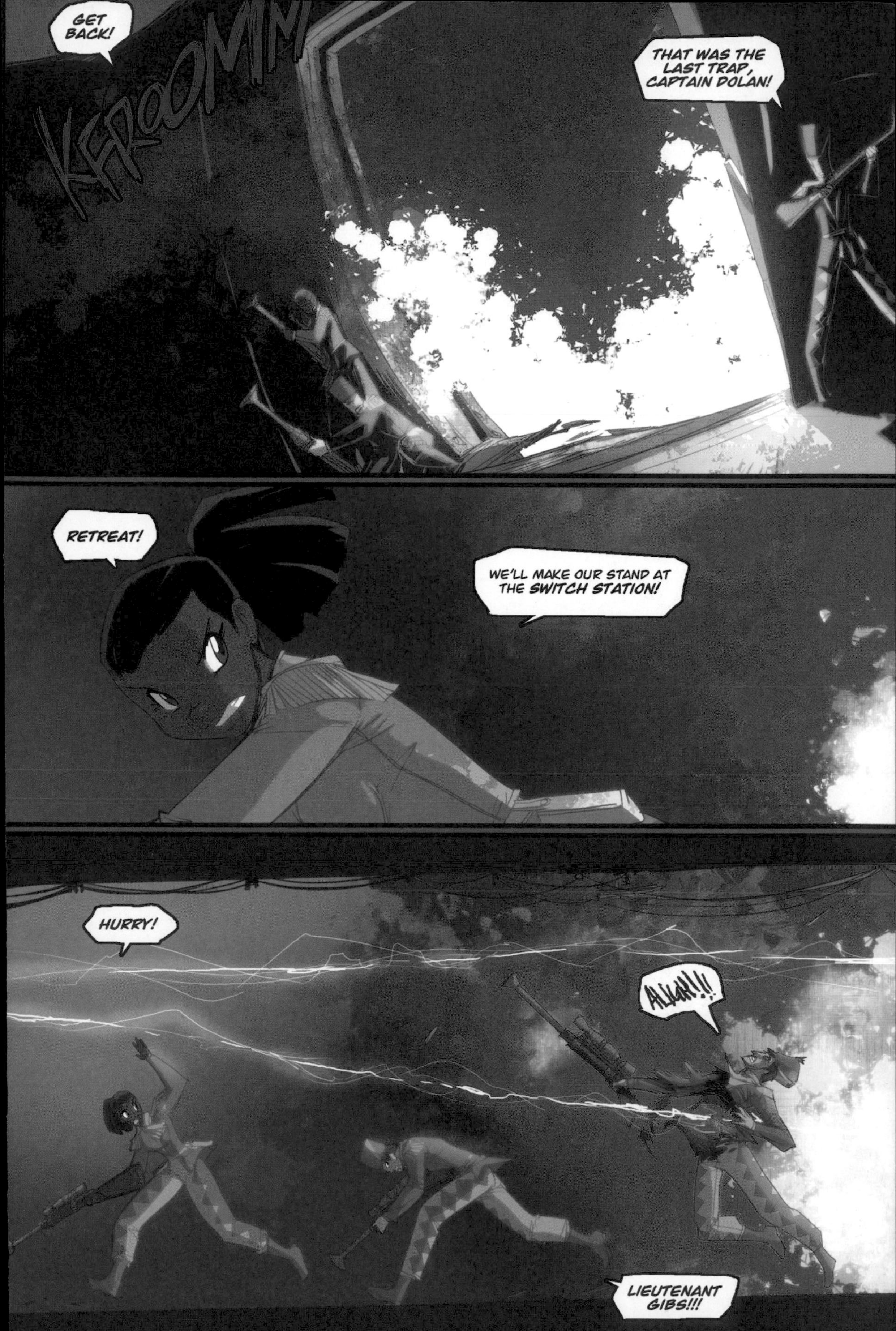
GET BACK!
KFROOMM
THAT WAS THE LAST TRAP, CAPTAIN DOLAN!
RETREAT!
WE'LL MAKE OUR STAND AT THE SWITCH STATION!
HURRY!
ALKK!!!
LIEUTENANT GIBS!!!

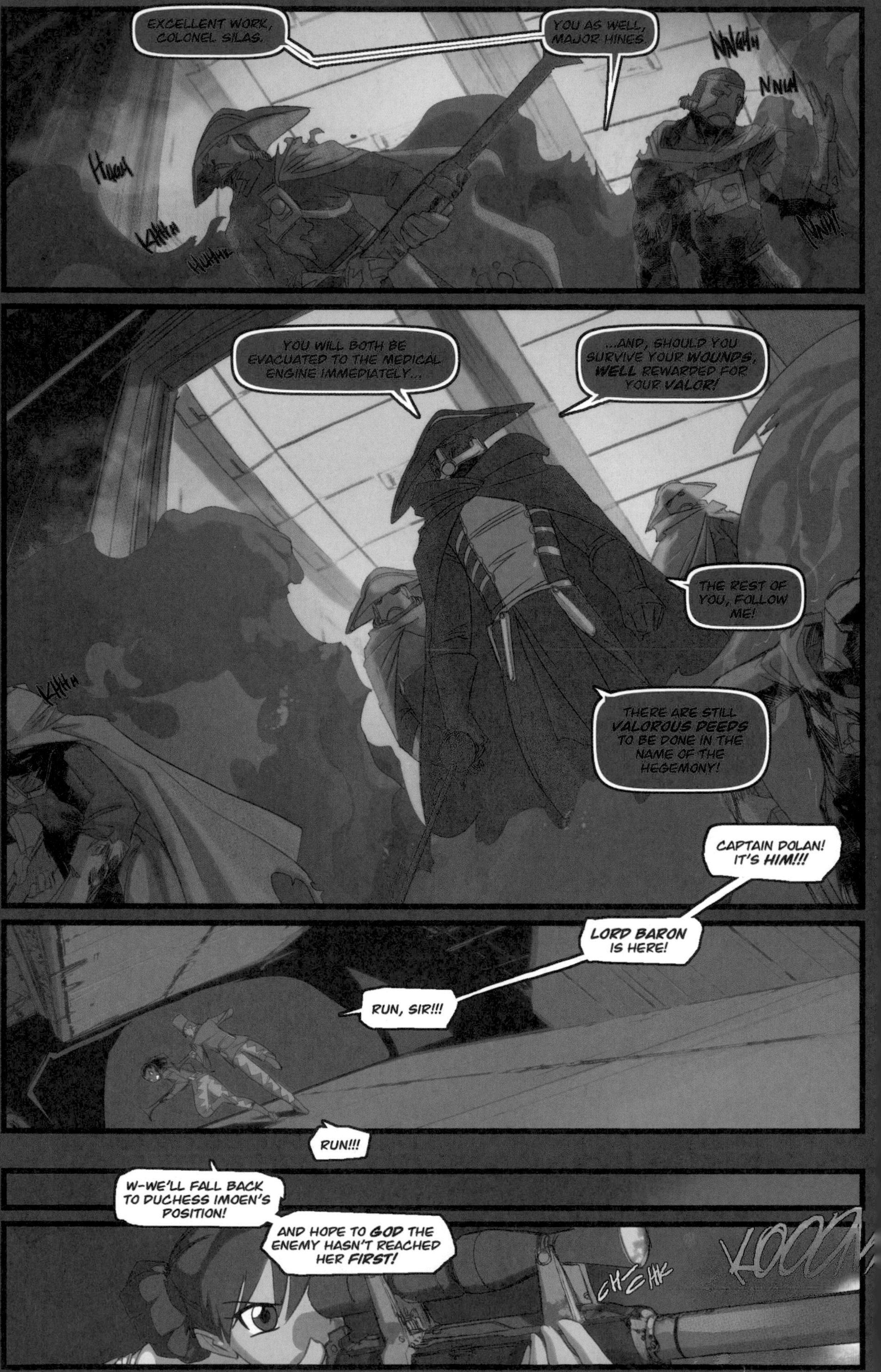
EXCELLENT WORK, COLONEL SILAS.
YOU AS WELL, MAJOR HINES.
YOU WILL BOTH BE EVACUATED TO THE MEDICAL ENGINE IMMEDIATELY...
...AND, SHOULD YOU SURVIVE YOUR WOUNDS, WELL REWARDED FOR YOUR VALOR!
THE REST OF YOU, FOLLOW ME!
THERE ARE STILL VALOROUS DEEDS TO BE DONE IN THE NAME OF THE HEGEMONY!
CAPTAIN DOLAN! IT'S HIM!!!
LORD BARON IS HERE!
RUN, SIR!!!
RUN!!!
W-WE'LL FALL BACK TO DUCHESS IMOEN'S POSITION!
AND HOPE TO GOD THE ENEMY HASN'T REACHED HER FIRST!

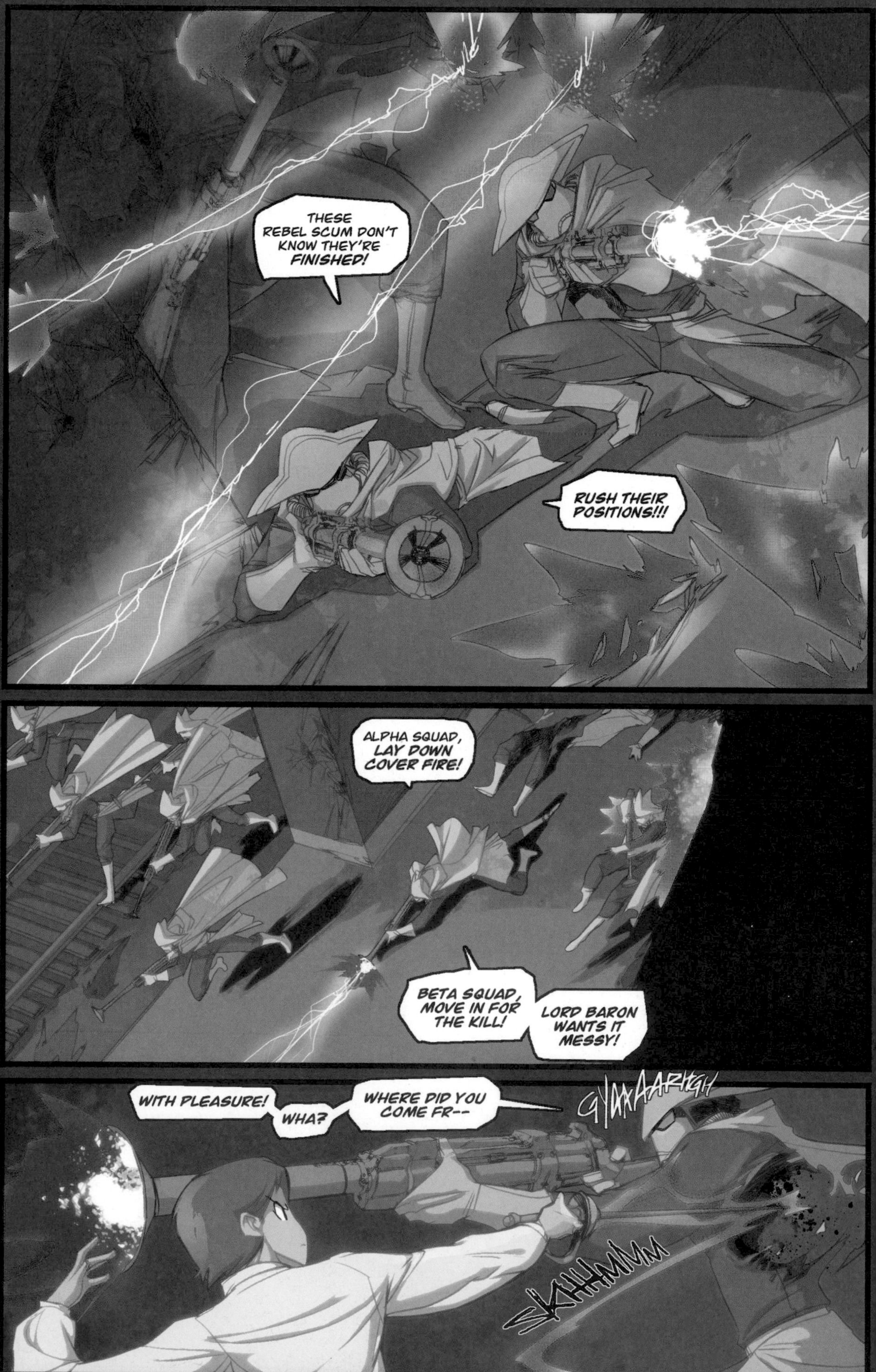
THESE REBEL SCUM DON'T KNOW THEY'RE FINISHED!
RUSH THEIR POSITIONS!!!
ALPHA SQUAD, LAY DOWN COVER FIRE!
BETA SQUAD, MOVE IN FOR THE KILL!
LORD BARON WANTS IT MESSY!
WITH PLEASURE!
WHA?
WHERE DID YOU COME FR--
GYAAAARHGH
SKHHMMM

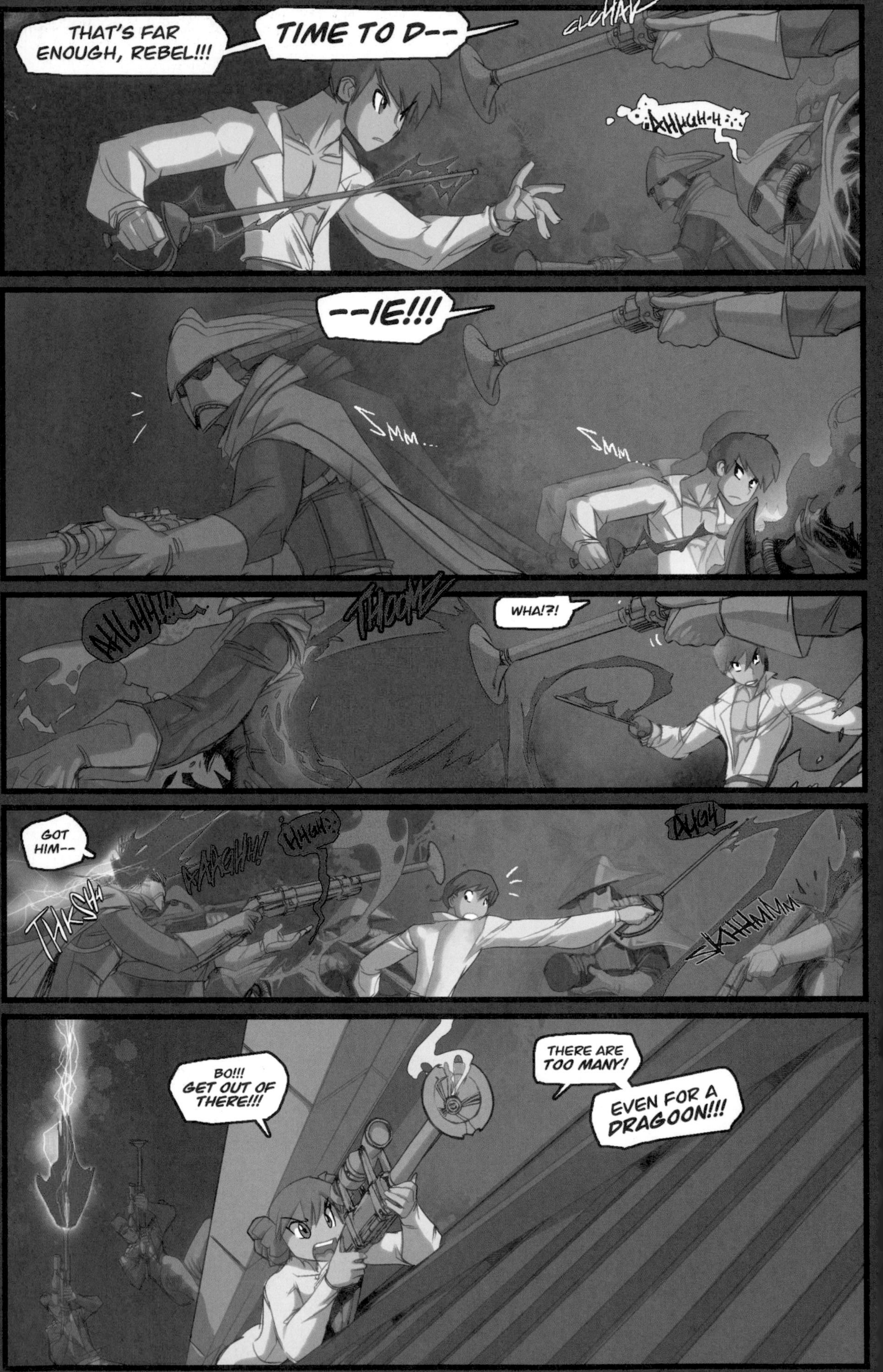
THAT'S FAR ENOUGH, REBEL!!!
TIME TO D--
AHHUGH-H
--IE!!!
SMM...
SMM...
THOOMZ
WHA!?!
GOT HIM--
THKSH
AARGHH!!
DUGH
BO!!! GET OUT OF THERE!!!
THERE ARE TOO MANY!
EVEN FOR A DRAGOON!!!

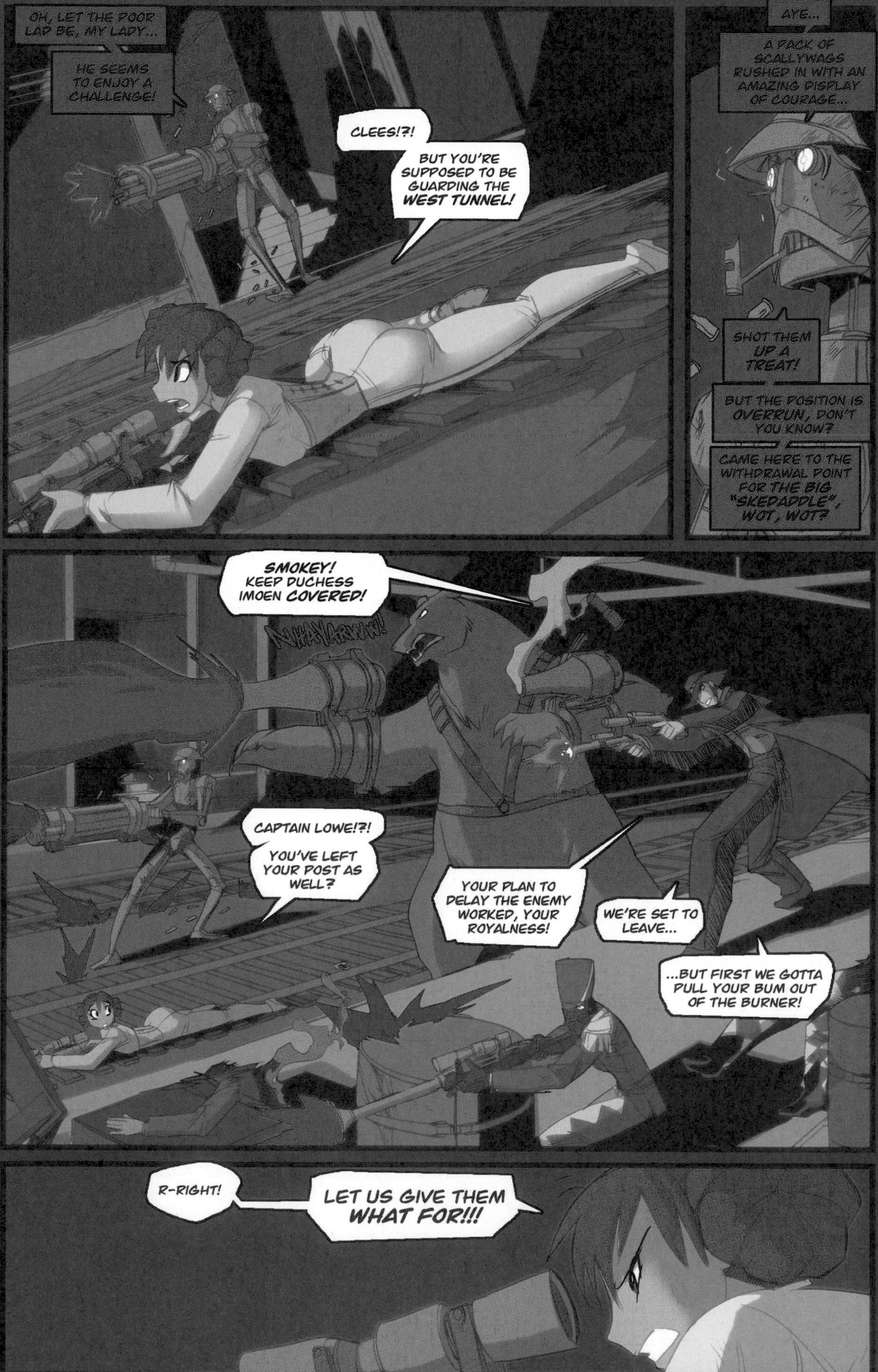
OH, LET THE POOR LAD BE, MY LADY...
HE SEEMS TO ENJOY A CHALLENGE!
CLEES!?!
BUT YOU'RE SUPPOSED TO BE GUARDING THE WEST TUNNEL!
AYE...
A PACK OF SCALLYWAGS RUSHED IN WITH AN AMAZING DISPLAY OF COURAGE...
SHOT THEM UP A TREAT!
BUT THE POSITION IS OVERRUN, DON'T YOU KNOW?
CAME HERE TO THE WITHDRAWAL POINT FOR THE BIG "SKEDADDLE", WOT, WOT?
SMOKEY! KEEP DUCHESS IMOEN COVERED!
NHAYARWW!
CAPTAIN LOWE!?!
YOU'VE LEFT YOUR POST AS WELL?
YOUR PLAN TO DELAY THE ENEMY WORKED, YOUR ROYALNESS!
WE'RE SET TO LEAVE...
...BUT FIRST WE GOTTA PULL YOUR BUM OUT OF THE BURNER!
R-RIGHT!
LET US GIVE THEM WHAT FOR!!!

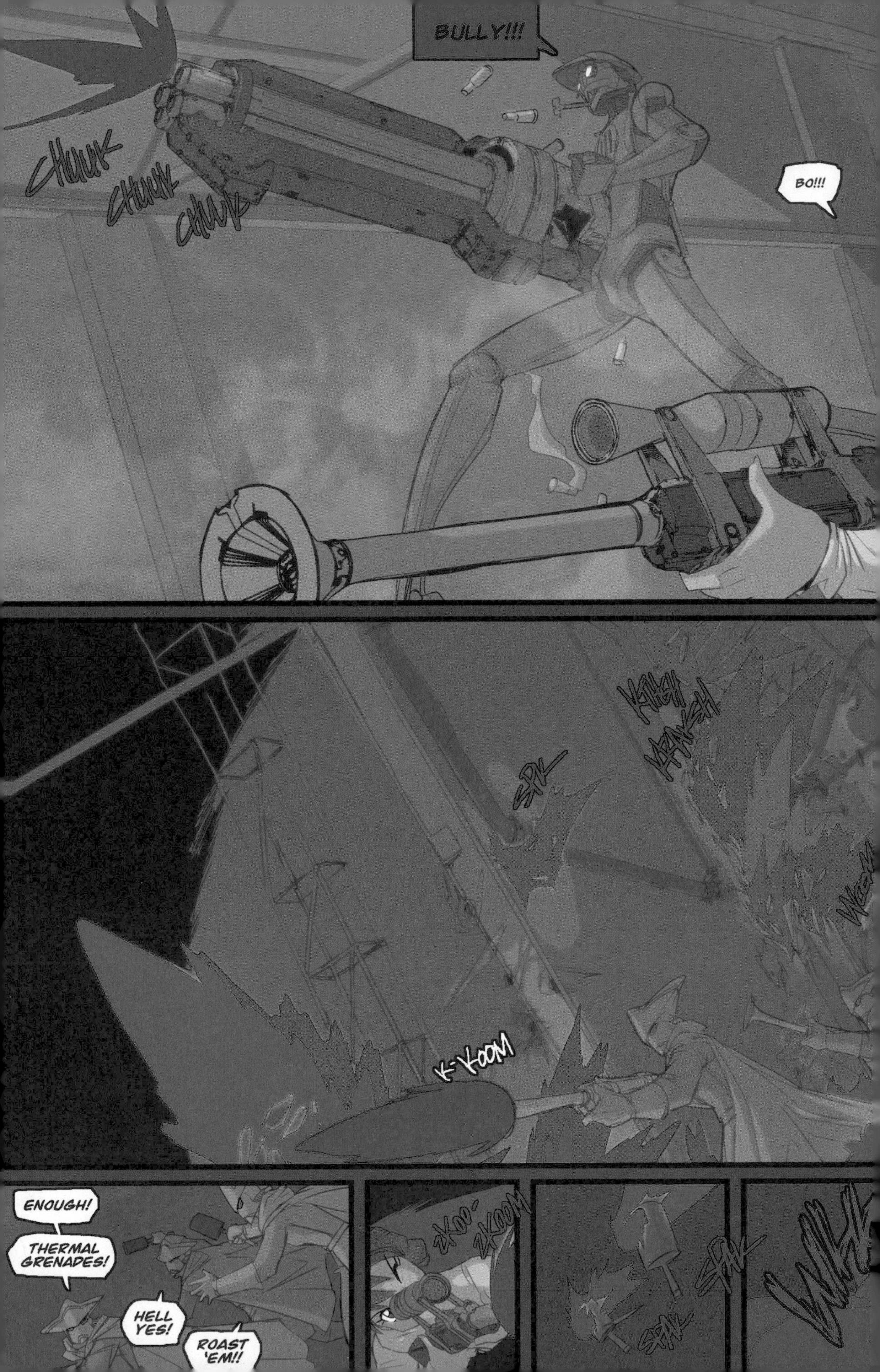
BULLY!!!
CHUNK
CHUNK
CHUNK
BO!!!
K-KOOM
ENOUGH!
THERMAL GRENADES!
HELL YES!
ROAST 'EM!!
ZKOO-
ZKOOM
SPAK
SPAK

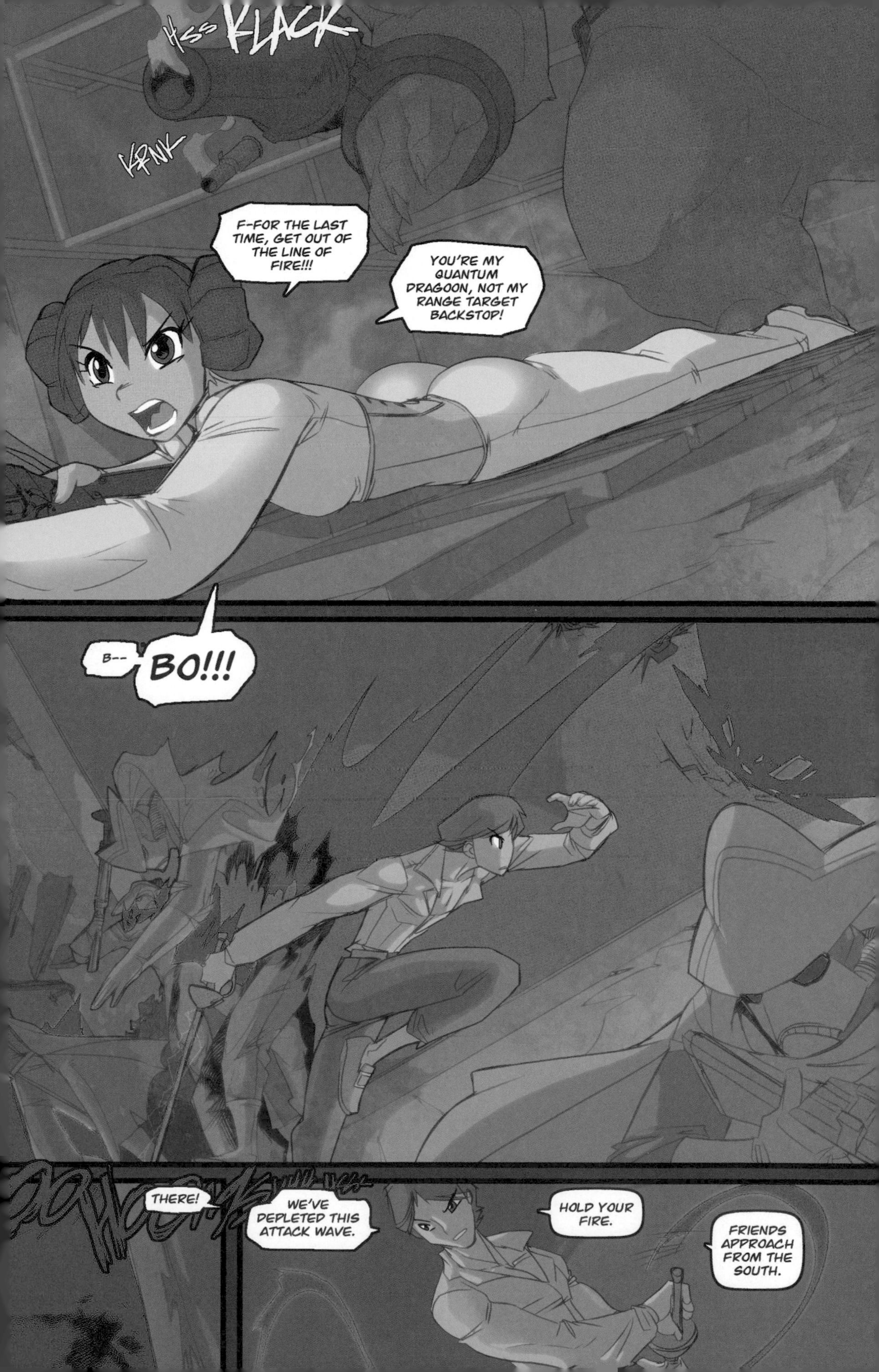

HSS KLACK
KRNK
F-FOR THE LAST TIME, GET OUT OF THE LINE OF FIRE!!!
YOU'RE MY QUANTUM DRAGOON, NOT MY RANGE TARGET BACKSTOP!
B--
BO!!!
THERE!
WE'VE DEPLETED THIS ATTACK WAVE.
HOLD YOUR FIRE.
FRIENDS APPROACH FROM THE SOUTH.

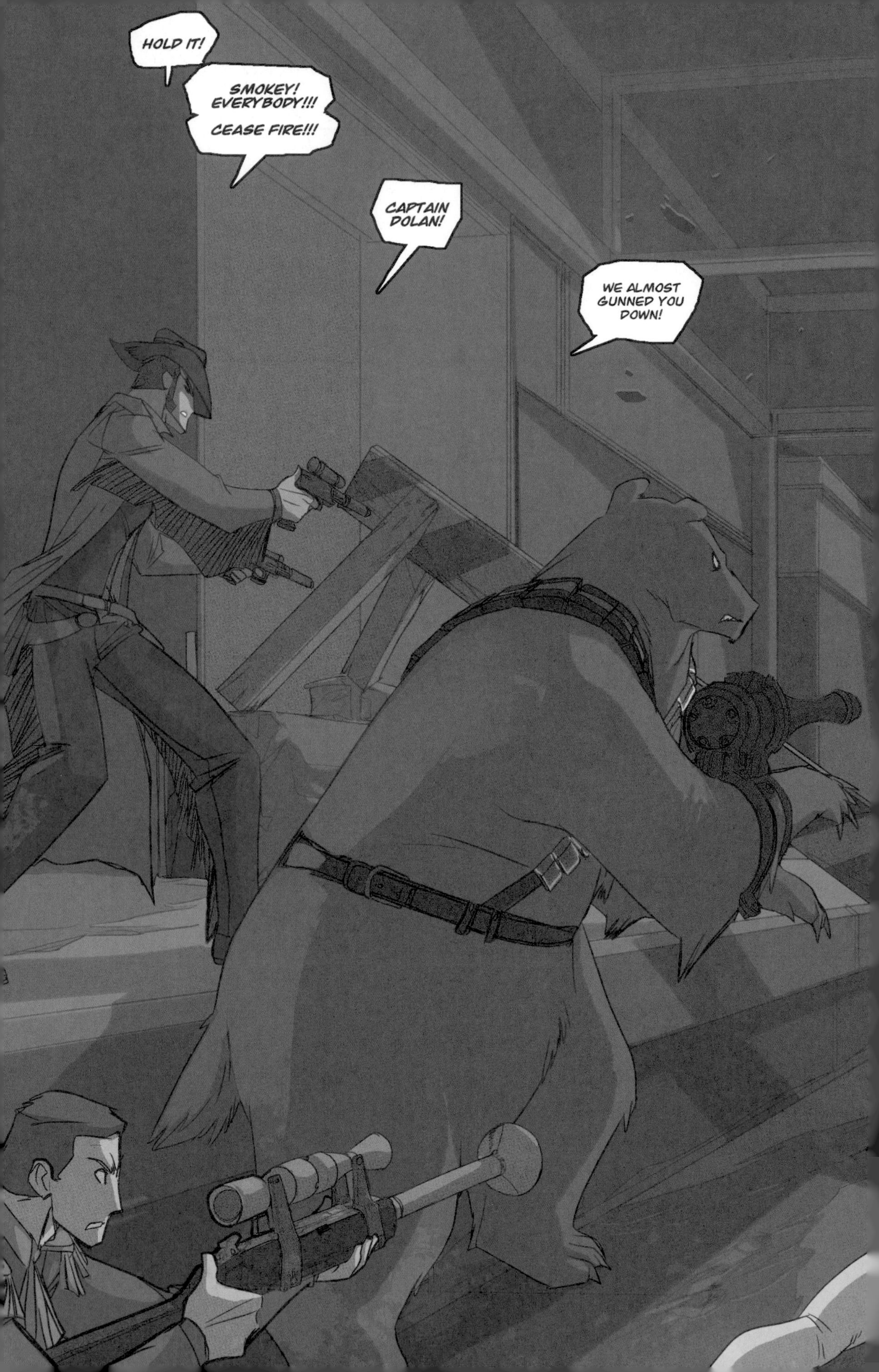
HOLD IT!
SMOKEY! EVERYBODY!!!
CEASE FIRE!!!
CAPTAIN DOLAN!
WE ALMOST GUNNED YOU DOWN!

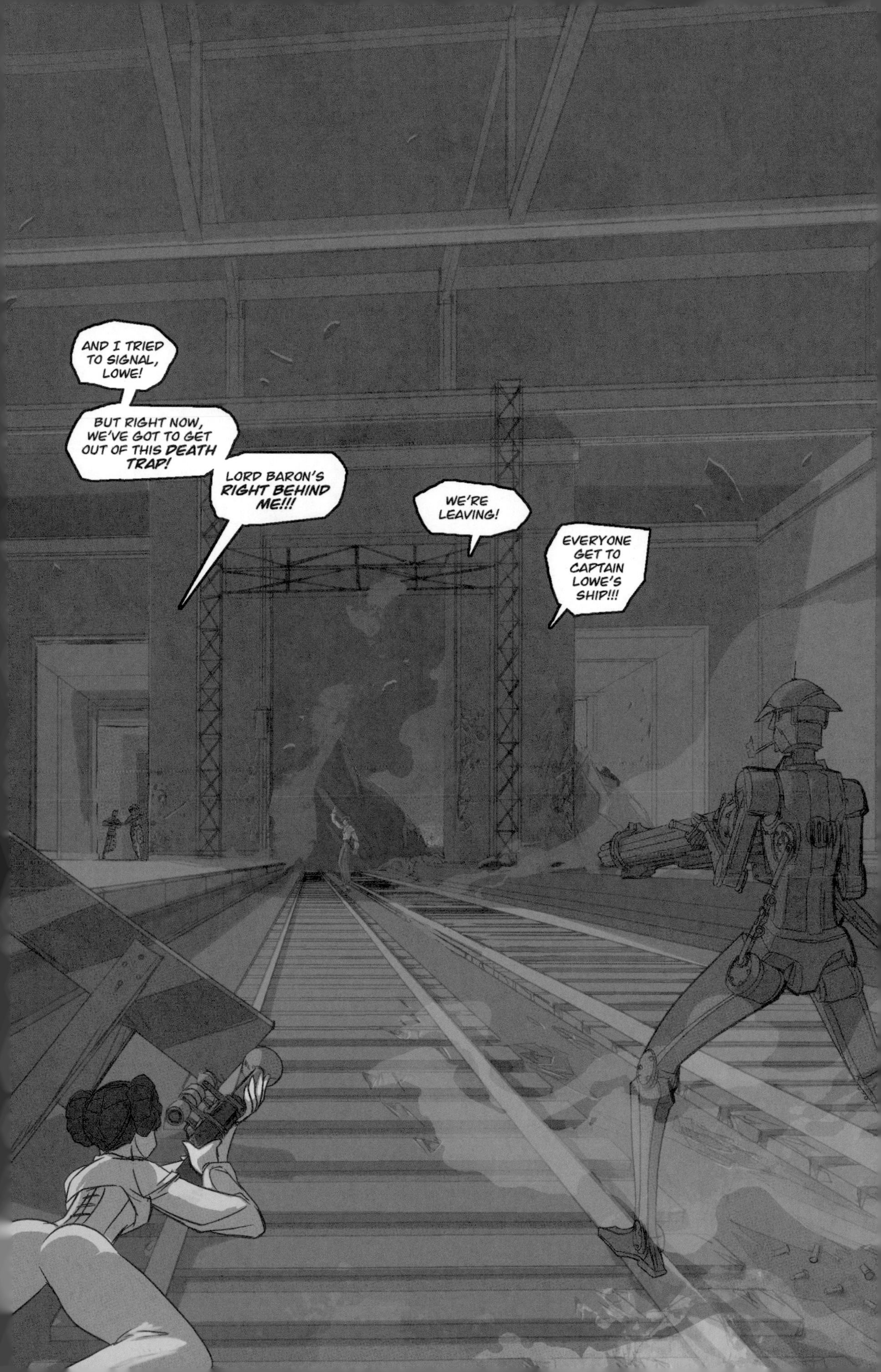
AND I TRIED TO SIGNAL, LOWE!
BUT RIGHT NOW, WE'VE GOT TO GET OUT OF THIS DEATH TRAP!
LORD BARON'S RIGHT BEHIND ME!!!
WE'RE LEAVING!
EVERYONE GET TO CAPTAIN LOWE'S SHIP!!!

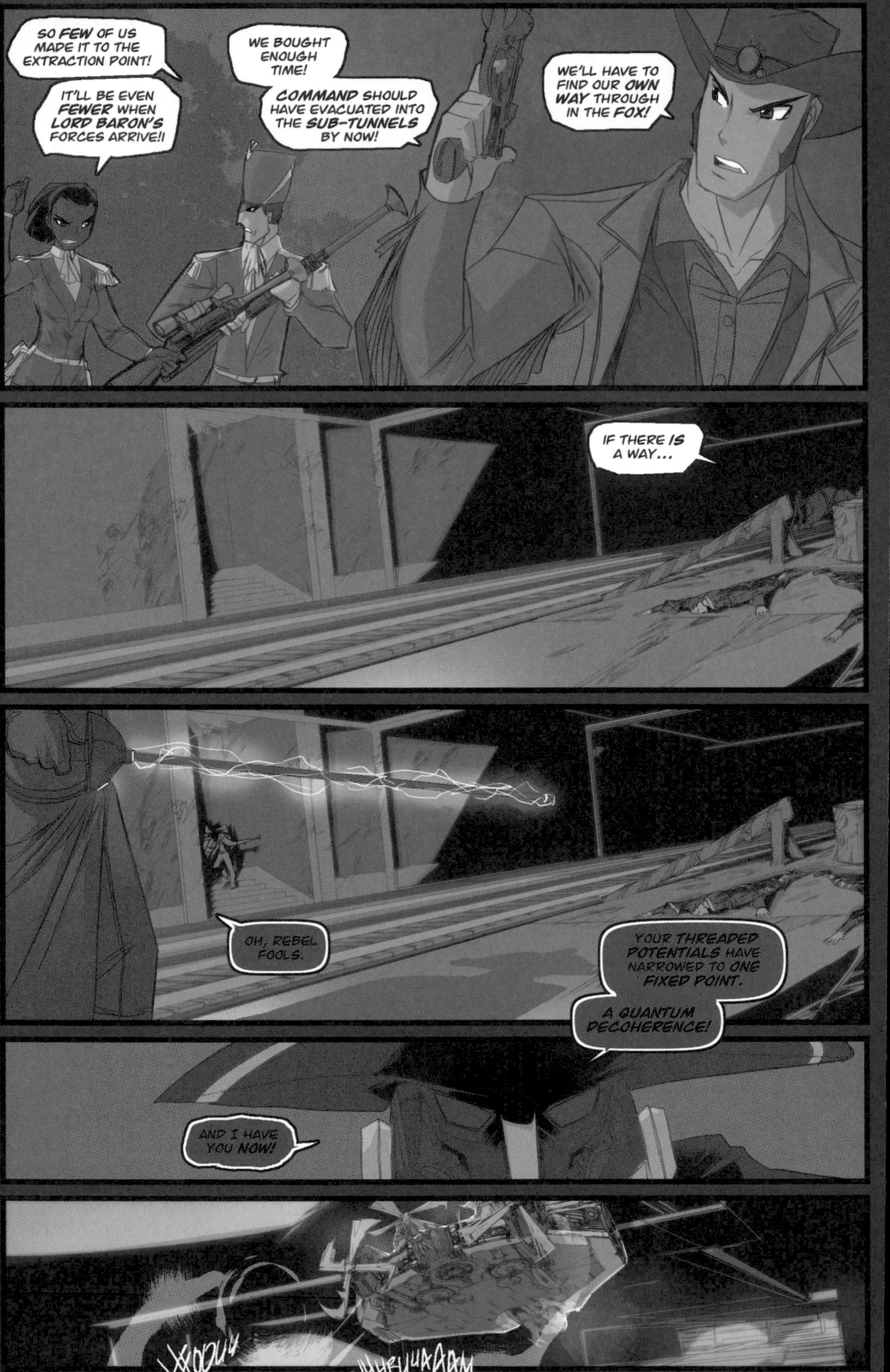
SO FEW OF US MADE IT TO THE EXTRACTION POINT!
IT'LL BE EVEN FEWER WHEN LORD BARON'S FORCES ARRIVE!!
WE BOUGHT ENOUGH TIME!
COMMAND SHOULD HAVE EVACUATED INTO THE SUB-TUNNELS BY NOW!
WE'LL HAVE TO FIND OUR OWN WAY THROUGH IN THE FOX!
IF THERE IS A WAY...
OH, REBEL FOOLS.
YOUR THREADED POTENTIALS HAVE NARROWED TO ONE FIXED POINT.
A QUANTUM DECOHERENCE!
AND I HAVE YOU NOW!

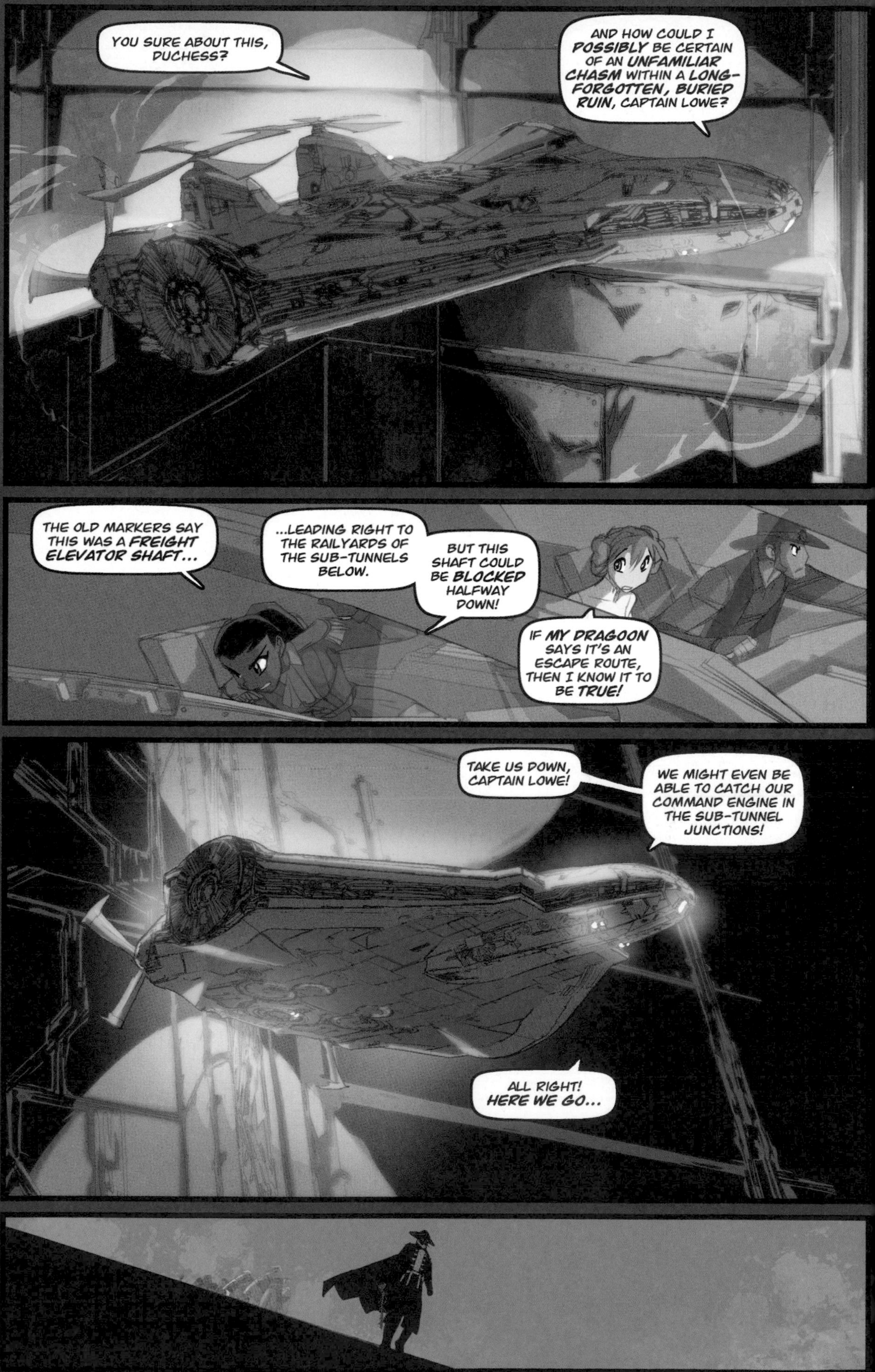
YOU SURE ABOUT THIS, DUCHESS?
AND HOW COULD I POSSIBLY BE CERTAIN OF AN UNFAMILIAR CHASM WITHIN A LONG-FORGOTTEN, BURIED RUIN, CAPTAIN LOWE?
THE OLD MARKERS SAY THIS WAS A FREIGHT ELEVATOR SHAFT...
...LEADING RIGHT TO THE RAILYARDS OF THE SUB-TUNNELS BELOW.
BUT THIS SHAFT COULD BE BLOCKED HALFWAY DOWN!
IF MY DRAGOON SAYS IT'S AN ESCAPE ROUTE, THEN I KNOW IT TO BE TRUE!
TAKE US DOWN, CAPTAIN LOWE!
WE MIGHT EVEN BE ABLE TO CATCH OUR COMMAND ENGINE IN THE SUB-TUNNEL JUNCTIONS!
ALL RIGHT! HERE WE GO...

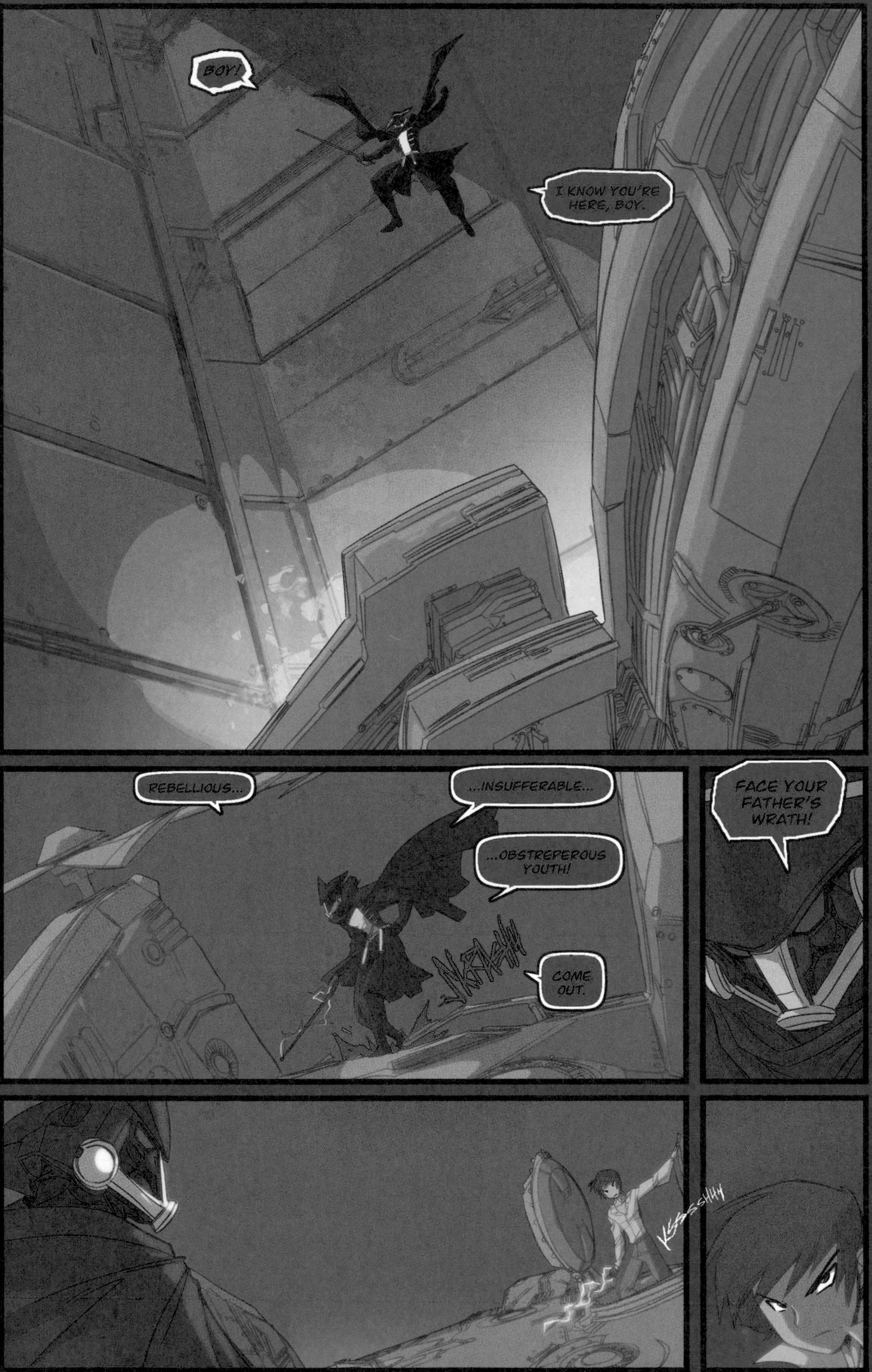
BOY!
I KNOW YOU'RE HERE, BOY.
REBELLIOUS...
...INSUFFERABLE...
...OBSTREPEROUS YOUTH!
COME OUT.
FACE YOUR FATHER'S WRATH!
KSSSSHHH

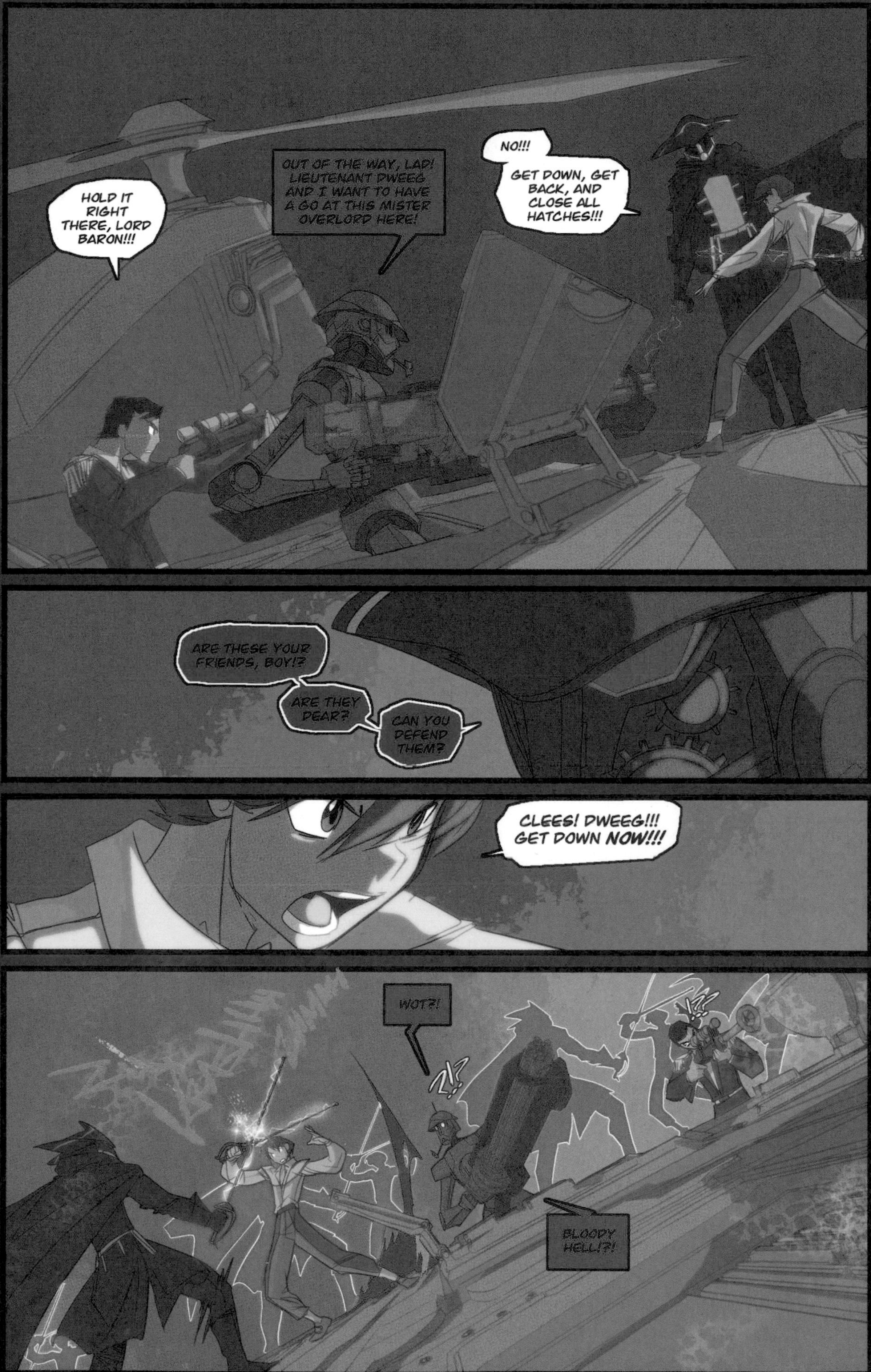
HOLD IT RIGHT THERE, LORD BARON!!!
OUT OF THE WAY, LAD! LIEUTENANT DWEEG AND I WANT TO HAVE A GO AT THIS MISTER OVERLORD HERE!
NO!!!
GET DOWN, GET BACK, AND CLOSE ALL HATCHES!!!
ARE THESE YOUR FRIENDS, BOY!?
ARE THEY DEAR?
CAN YOU DEFEND THEM?
CLEES! DWEEG!!! GET DOWN NOW!!!
WOT?!
BLOODY HELL!?!

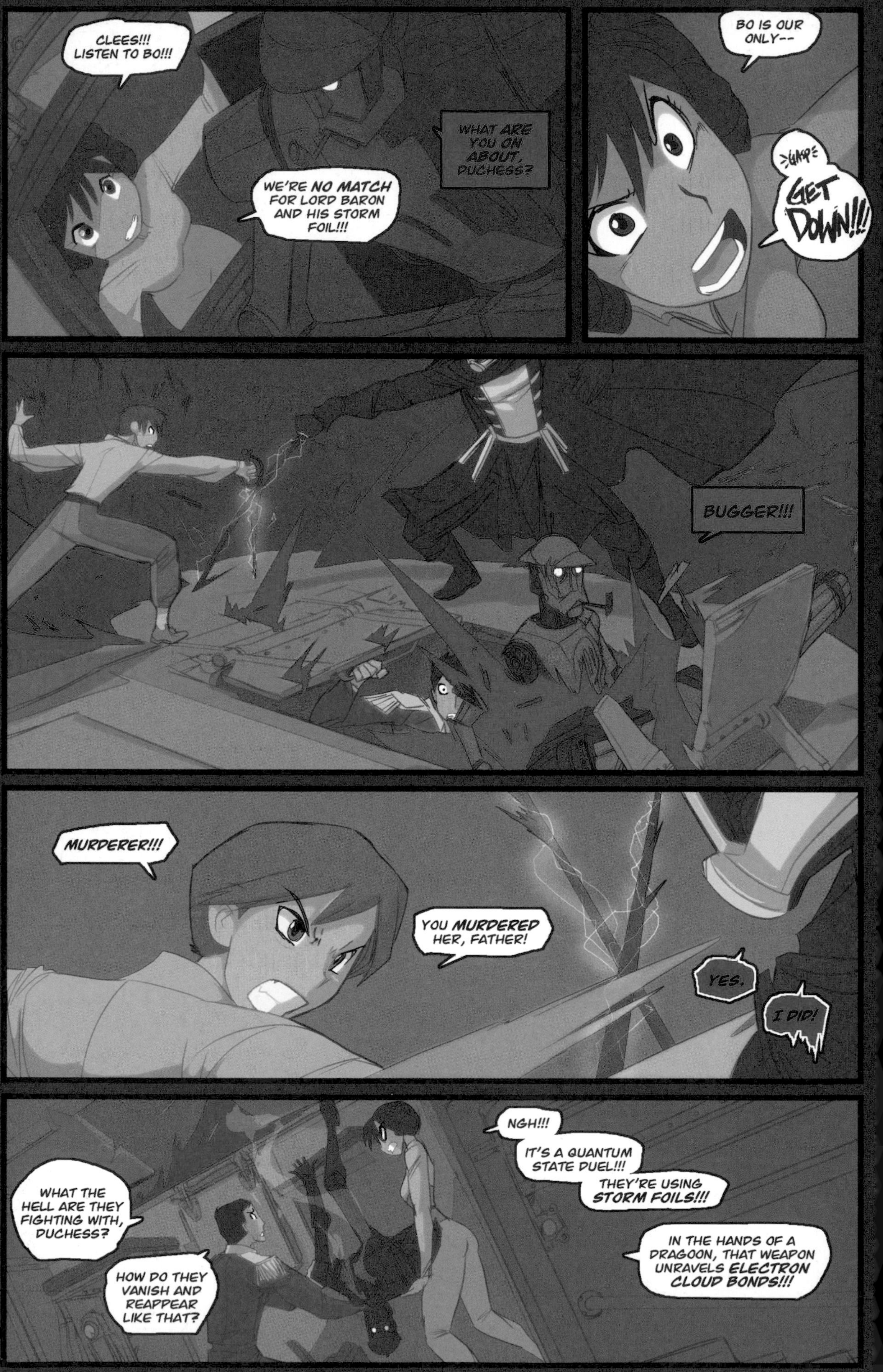
CLEES!!! LISTEN TO BO!!!
WE'RE NO MATCH FOR LORD BARON AND HIS STORM FOIL!!!
WHAT ARE YOU ON ABOUT, DUCHESS?
BO IS OUR ONLY--
GASP
GET DOWN!!!
BUGGER!!!
MURDERER!!!
YOU MURDERED HER, FATHER!
YES.
I DID!
NGH!!!
IT'S A QUANTUM STATE DUEL!!!
THEY'RE USING STORM FOILS!!!
WHAT THE HELL ARE THEY FIGHTING WITH, DUCHESS?
IN THE HANDS OF A DRAGOON, THAT WEAPON UNRAVELS ELECTRON CLOUD BONDS!!!
HOW DO THEY VANISH AND REAPPEAR LIKE THAT?

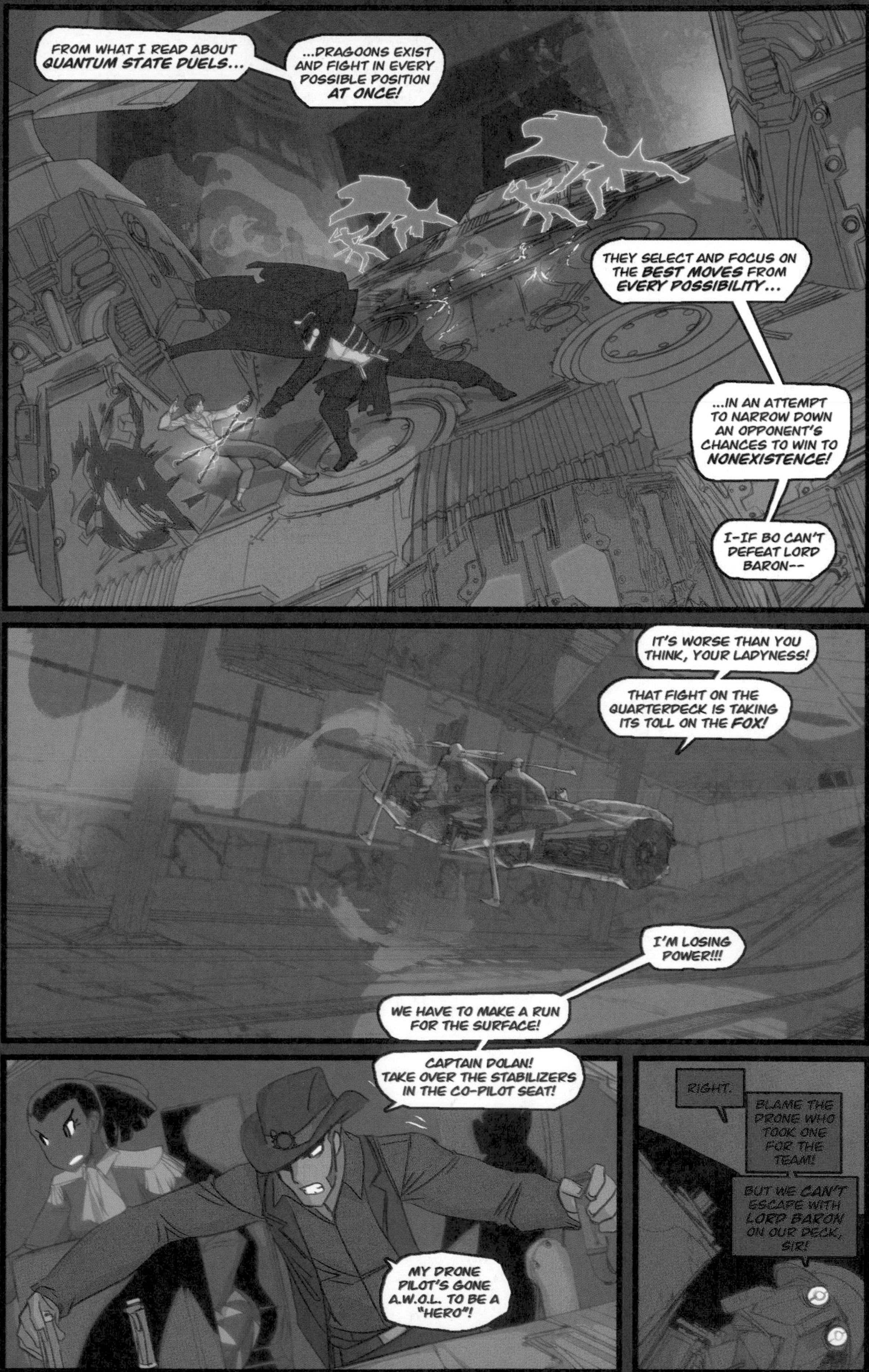
FROM WHAT I READ ABOUT QUANTUM STATE DUELS...
...DRAGOONS EXIST AND FIGHT IN EVERY POSSIBLE POSITION AT ONCE!
THEY SELECT AND FOCUS ON THE BEST MOVES FROM EVERY POSSIBILITY...
...IN AN ATTEMPT TO NARROW DOWN AN OPPONENT'S CHANCES TO WIN TO NONEXISTENCE!
I-IF BO CAN'T DEFEAT LORD BARON--
IT'S WORSE THAN YOU THINK, YOUR LADYNESS!
THAT FIGHT ON THE QUARTERDECK IS TAKING ITS TOLL ON THE FOX!
I'M LOSING POWER!!!
WE HAVE TO MAKE A RUN FOR THE SURFACE!
CAPTAIN DOLAN! TAKE OVER THE STABILIZERS IN THE CO-PILOT SEAT!
MY DRONE PILOT'S GONE A.W.O.L. TO BE A "HERO"!
RIGHT.
BLAME THE DRONE WHO TOOK ONE FOR THE TEAM!
BUT WE CAN'T ESCAPE WITH LORD BARON ON OUR DECK, SIR!

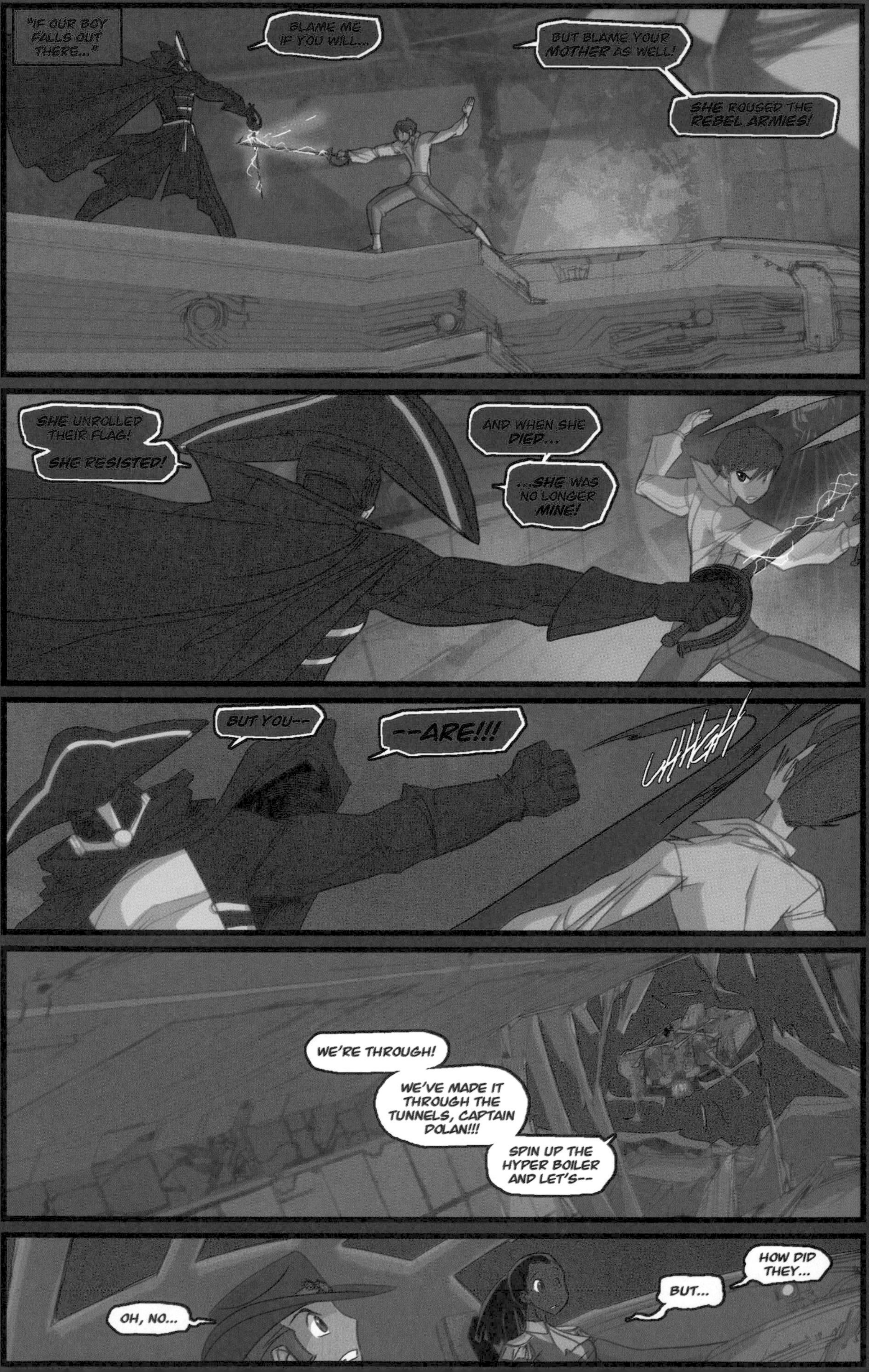
"IF OUR BOY FALLS OUT THERE..."
BLAME ME IF YOU WILL...
BUT BLAME YOUR MOTHER AS WELL!
SHE ROUSED THE REBEL ARMIES!
SHE UNROLLED THEIR FLAG! SHE RESISTED!
AND WHEN SHE DIED...
...SHE WAS NO LONGER MINE!
BUT YOU--
--ARE!!!
UHHGH
WE'RE THROUGH!
WE'VE MADE IT THROUGH THE TUNNELS, CAPTAIN DOLAN!!!
SPIN UP THE HYPER BOILER AND LET'S--
OH, NO...
BUT...
HOW DID THEY...

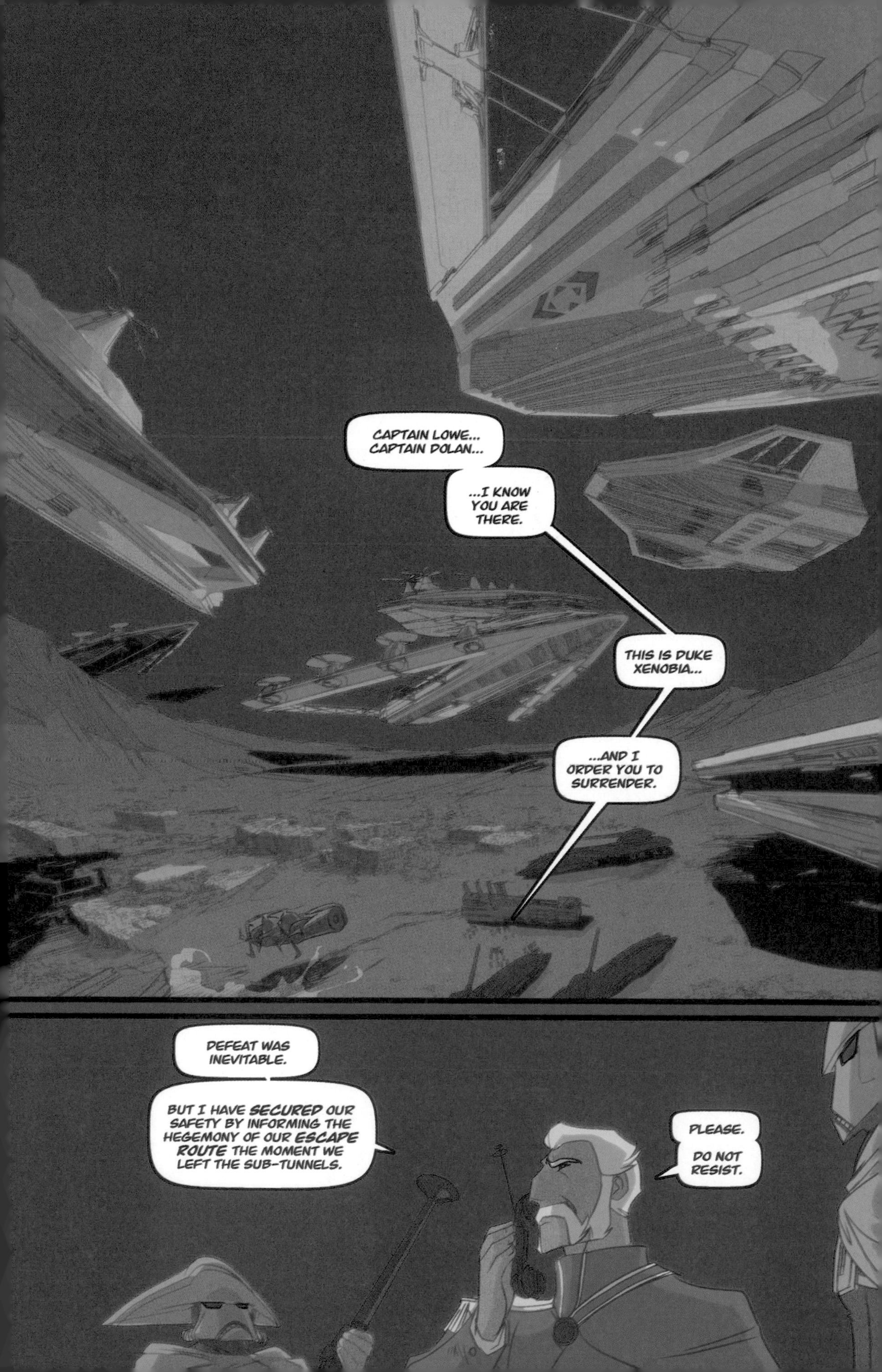
CAPTAIN LOWE... CAPTAIN DOLAN...
...I KNOW YOU ARE THERE.
THIS IS DUKE XENOBIA...
...AND I ORDER YOU TO SURRENDER.
DEFEAT WAS INEVITABLE.
BUT I HAVE SECURED OUR SAFETY BY INFORMING THE HEGEMONY OF OUR ESCAPE ROUTE THE MOMENT WE LEFT THE SUB-TUNNELS.
PLEASE.
DO NOT RESIST.

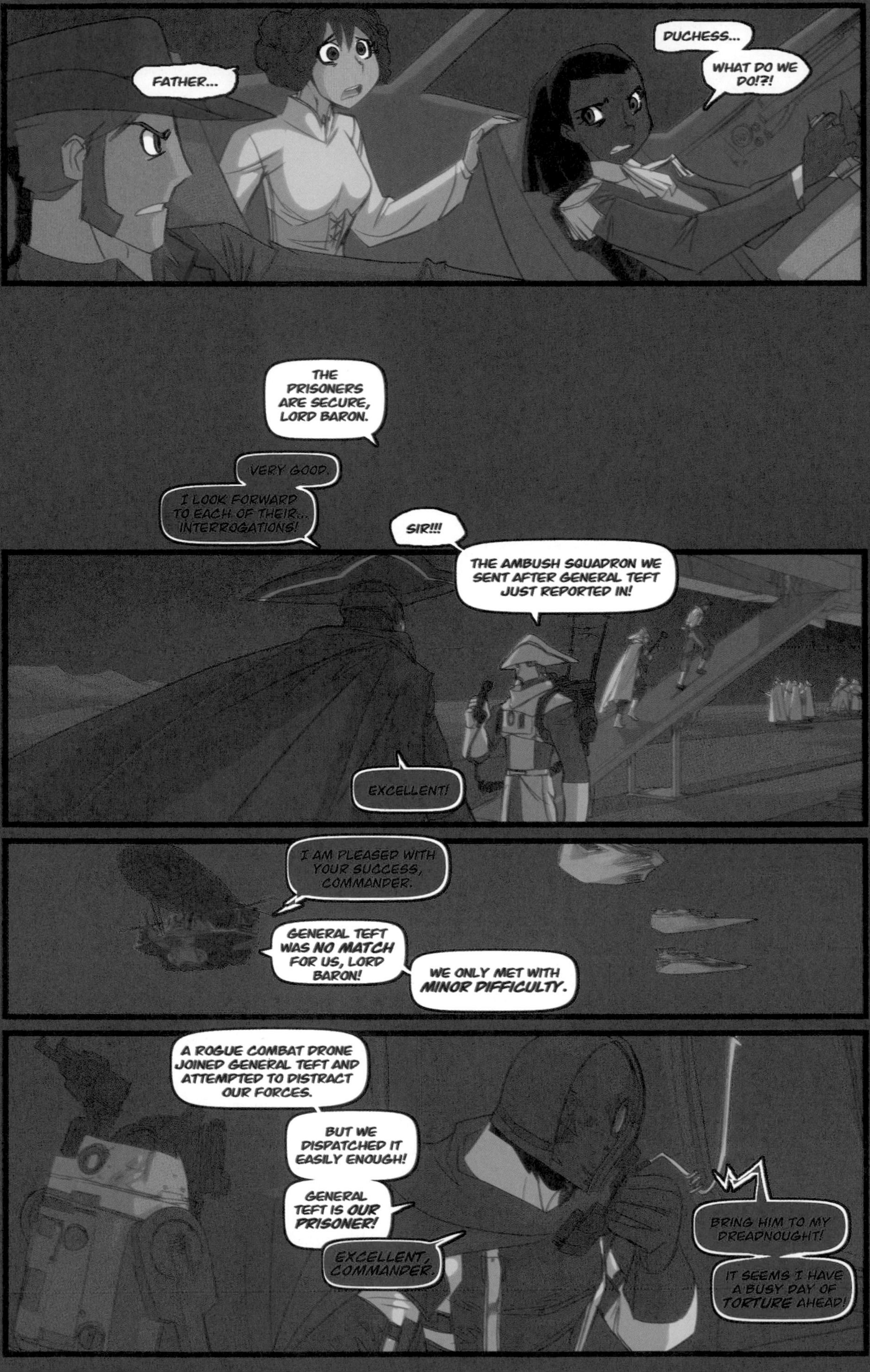
FATHER...
DUCHESS...
WHAT DO WE DO!?!
THE PRISONERS ARE SECURE, LORD BARON.
VERY GOOD.
I LOOK FORWARD TO EACH OF THEIR... INTERROGATIONS!
SIR!!!
THE AMBUSH SQUADRON WE SENT AFTER GENERAL TEFT JUST REPORTED IN!
EXCELLENT!
I AM PLEASED WITH YOUR SUCCESS, COMMANDER.
GENERAL TEFT WAS NO MATCH FOR US, LORD BARON!
WE ONLY MET WITH MINOR DIFFICULTY.
A ROGUE COMBAT DRONE JOINED GENERAL TEFT AND ATTEMPTED TO DISTRACT OUR FORCES.
BUT WE DISPATCHED IT EASILY ENOUGH!
GENERAL TEFT IS OUR PRISONER!
EXCELLENT, COMMANDER.
BRING HIM TO MY DREADNOUGHT!
IT SEEMS I HAVE A BUSY DAY OF TORTURE AHEAD!

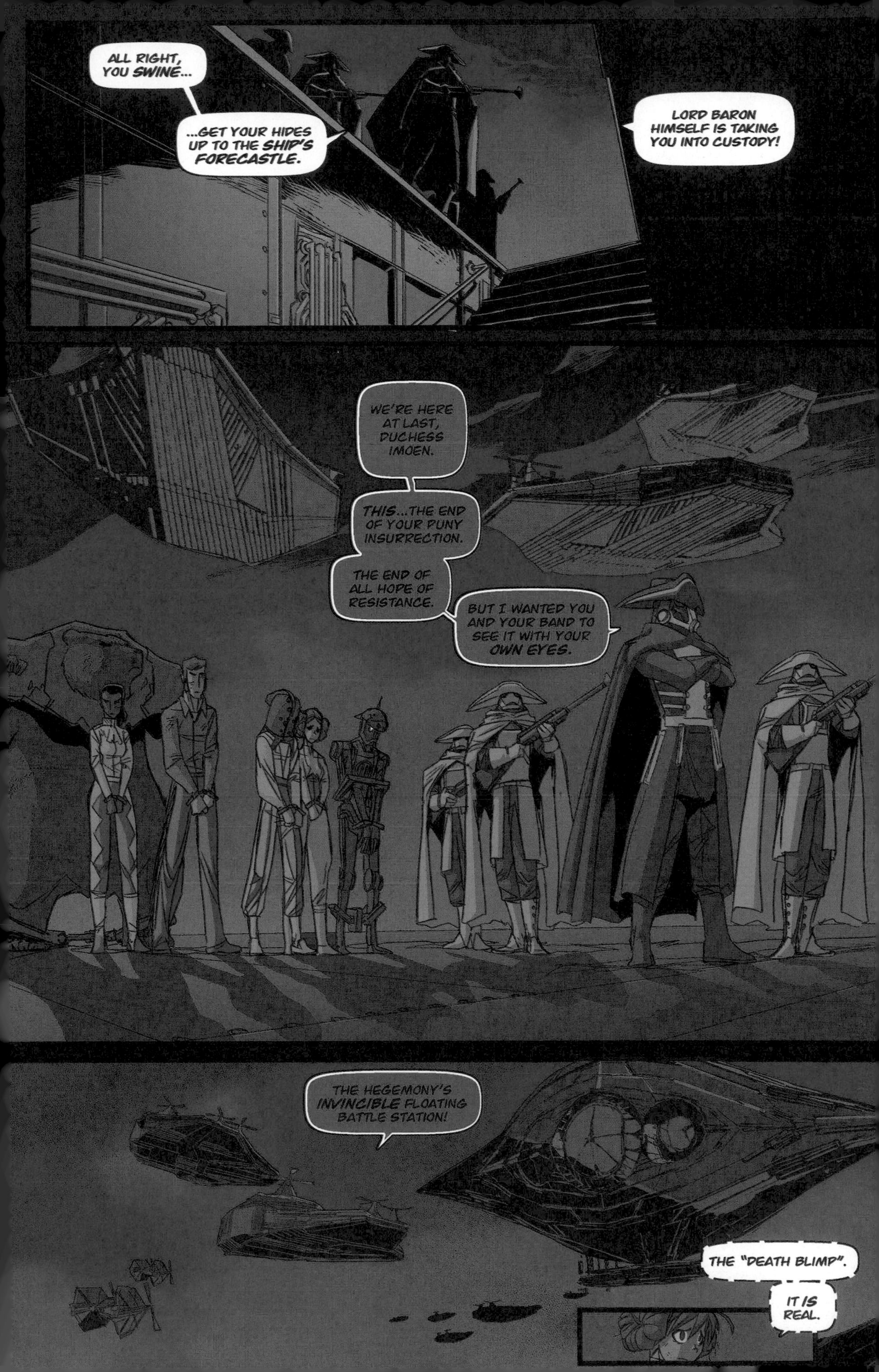
ALL RIGHT, YOU SWINE...
...GET YOUR HIDES UP TO THE SHIP'S FORECASTLE.
LORD BARON HIMSELF IS TAKING YOU INTO CUSTODY!
WE'RE HERE AT LAST, DUCHESS IMOEN.
THIS...THE END OF YOUR PUNY INSURRECTION.
THE END OF ALL HOPE OF RESISTANCE.
BUT I WANTED YOU AND YOUR BAND TO SEE IT WITH YOUR OWN EYES.
THE HEGEMONY'S INVINCIBLE FLOATING BATTLE STATION!
THE "DEATH BLIMP".
IT IS REAL.

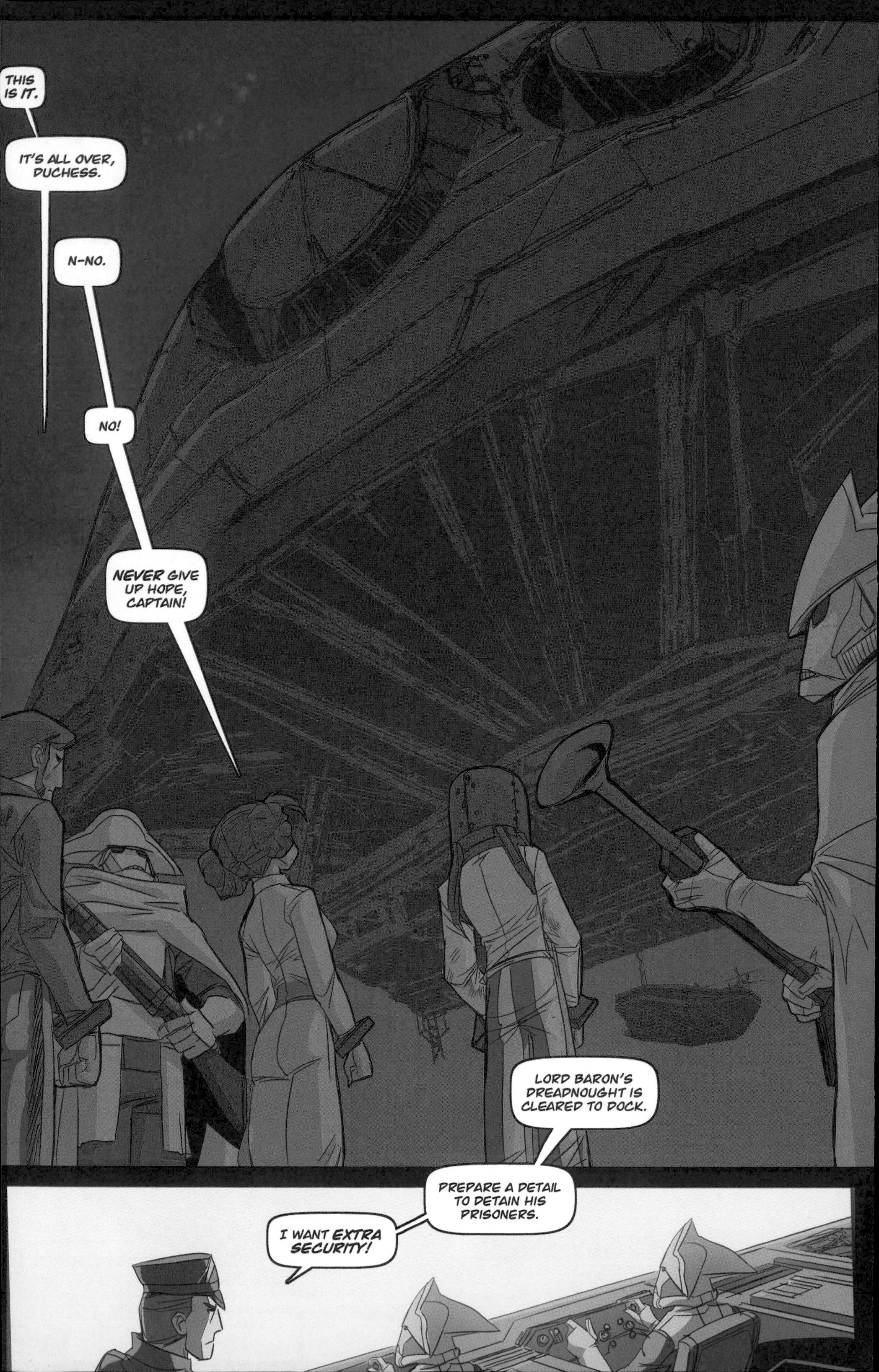
THIS IS IT.
IT'S ALL OVER, DUCHESS.
N-NO.
NO!
NEVER GIVE UP HOPE, CAPTAIN!
LORD BARON'S DREADNOUGHT IS CLEARED TO DOCK.
PREPARE A DETAIL TO DETAIN HIS PRISONERS.
I WANT EXTRA SECURITY!

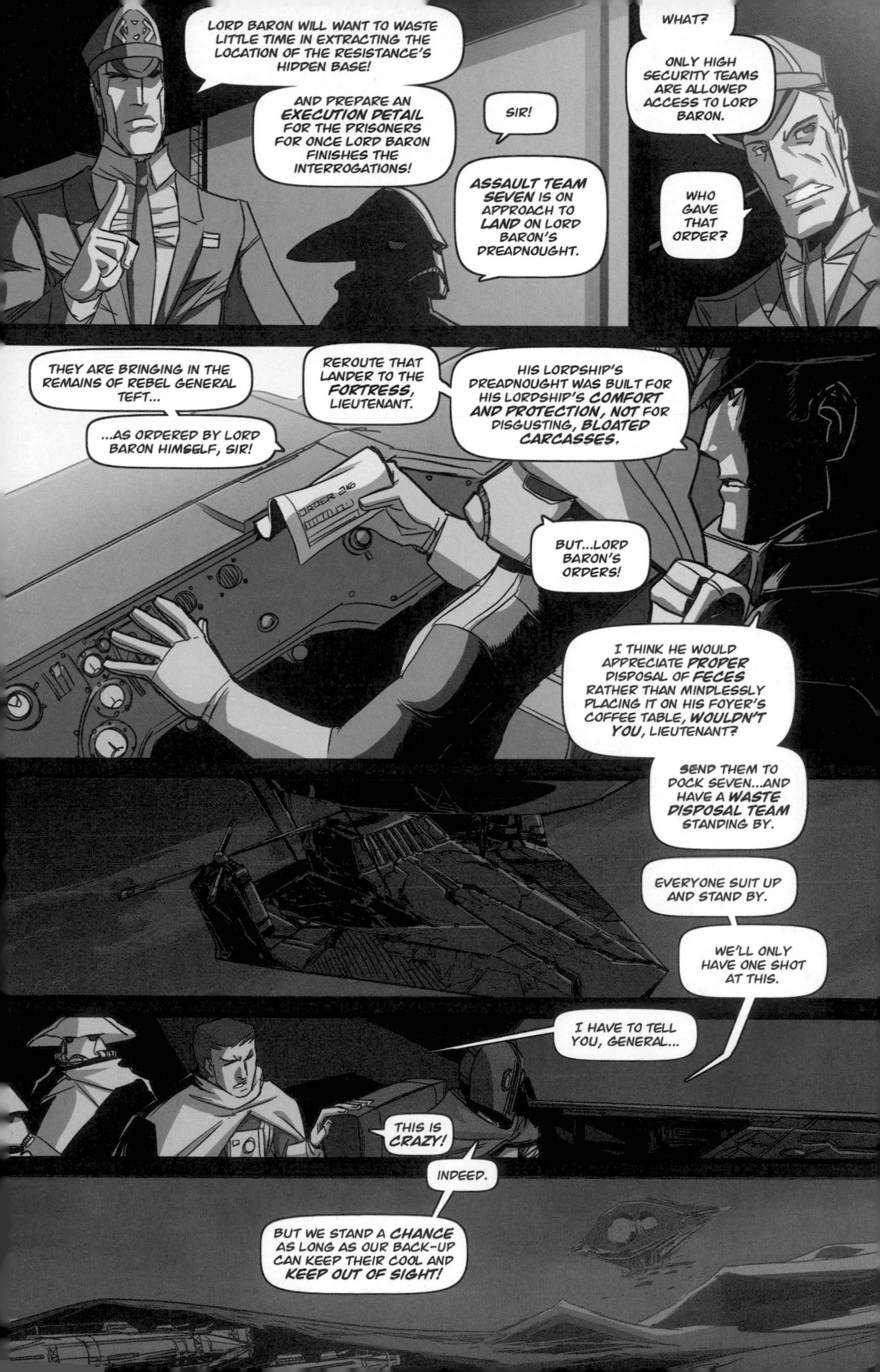
LORD BARON WILL WANT TO WASTE LITTLE TIME IN EXTRACTING THE LOCATION OF THE RESISTANCE'S HIDDEN BASE!
AND PREPARE AN EXECUTION DETAIL FOR THE PRISONERS FOR ONCE LORD BARON FINISHES THE INTERROGATIONS!
SIR!
ASSAULT TEAM SEVEN IS ON APPROACH TO LAND ON LORD BARON'S DREADNOUGHT.
WHAT?
ONLY HIGH SECURITY TEAMS ARE ALLOWED ACCESS TO LORD BARON.
WHO GAVE THAT ORDER?
THEY ARE BRINGING IN THE REMAINS OF REBEL GENERAL TEFT...
...AS ORDERED BY LORD BARON HIMSELF, SIR!
REROUTE THAT LANDER TO THE FORTRESS, LIEUTENANT.
HIS LORDSHIP'S DREADNOUGHT WAS BUILT FOR HIS LORDSHIP'S COMFORT AND PROTECTION, NOT FOR DISGUSTING, BLOATED CARCASSES.
ORDER 216
BUT...LORD BARON'S ORDERS!
I THINK HE WOULD APPRECIATE PROPER DISPOSAL OF FECES RATHER THAN MINDLESSLY PLACING IT ON HIS FOYER'S COFFEE TABLE, WOULDN'T YOU, LIEUTENANT?
SEND THEM TO DOCK SEVEN...AND HAVE A WASTE DISPOSAL TEAM STANDING BY.
EVERYONE SUIT UP AND STAND BY.
WE'LL ONLY HAVE ONE SHOT AT THIS.
I HAVE TO TELL YOU, GENERAL...
THIS IS CRAZY!
INDEED.
BUT WE STAND A CHANCE AS LONG AS OUR BACK-UP CAN KEEP THEIR COOL AND KEEP OUT OF SIGHT!

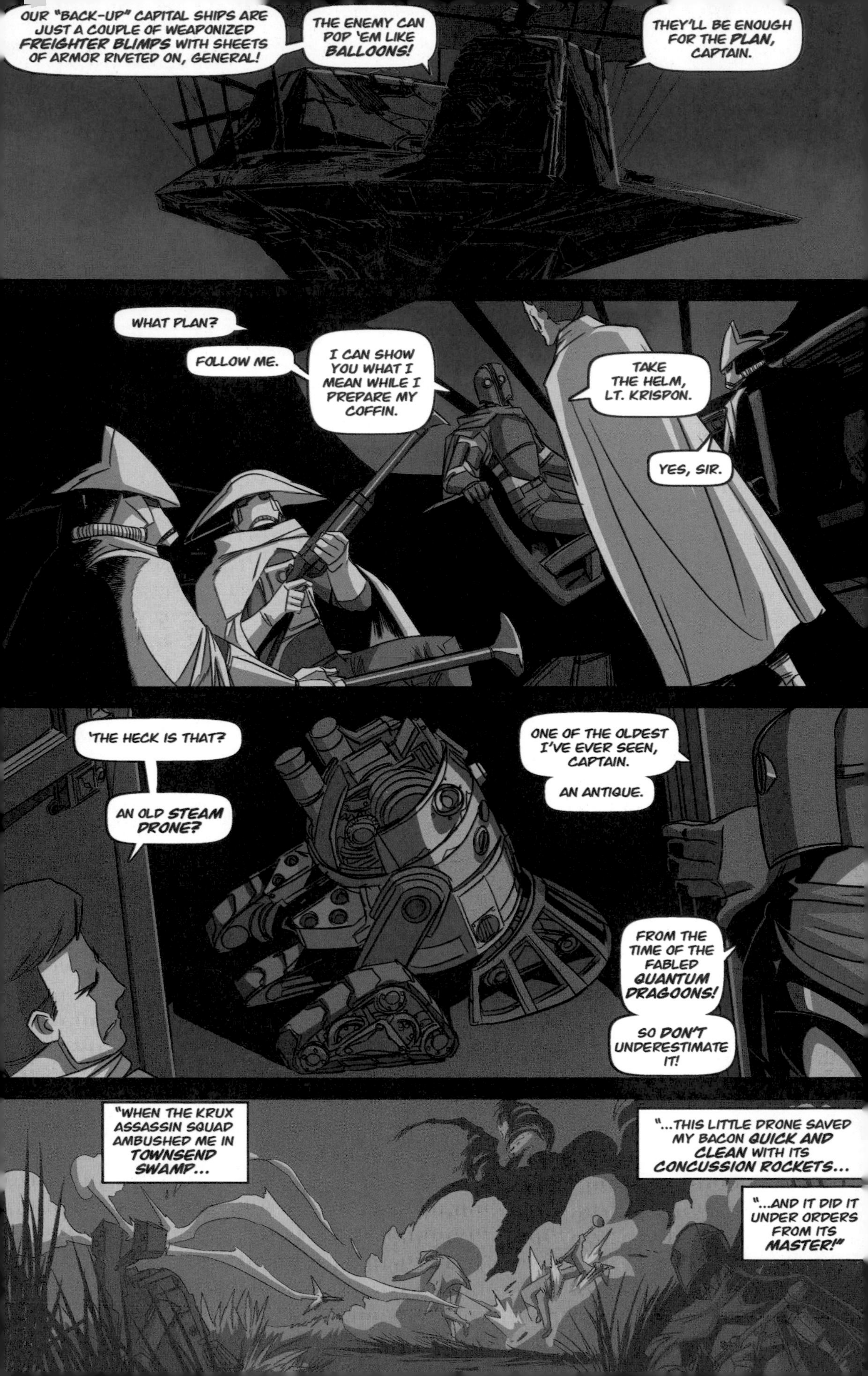
OUR "BACK-UP" CAPITAL SHIPS ARE JUST A COUPLE OF WEAPONIZED FREIGHTER BLIMPS WITH SHEETS OF ARMOR RIVETED ON, GENERAL!
THE ENEMY CAN POP 'EM LIKE BALLOONS!
THEY'LL BE ENOUGH FOR THE PLAN, CAPTAIN.
WHAT PLAN?
FOLLOW ME.
I CAN SHOW YOU WHAT I MEAN WHILE I PREPARE MY COFFIN.
TAKE THE HELM, LT. KRISPON.
YES, SIR.
'THE HECK IS THAT?
AN OLD STEAM DRONE?
ONE OF THE OLDEST I'VE EVER SEEN, CAPTAIN.
AN ANTIQUE.
FROM THE TIME OF THE FABLED QUANTUM DRAGOONS!
SO DON'T UNDERESTIMATE IT!
"WHEN THE KRUX ASSASSIN SQUAD AMBUSHED ME IN TOWNSEND SWAMP...
"...THIS LITTLE DRONE SAVED MY BACON QUICK AND CLEAN WITH ITS CONCUSSION ROCKETS...
"...AND IT DID IT UNDER ORDERS FROM ITS MASTER!"

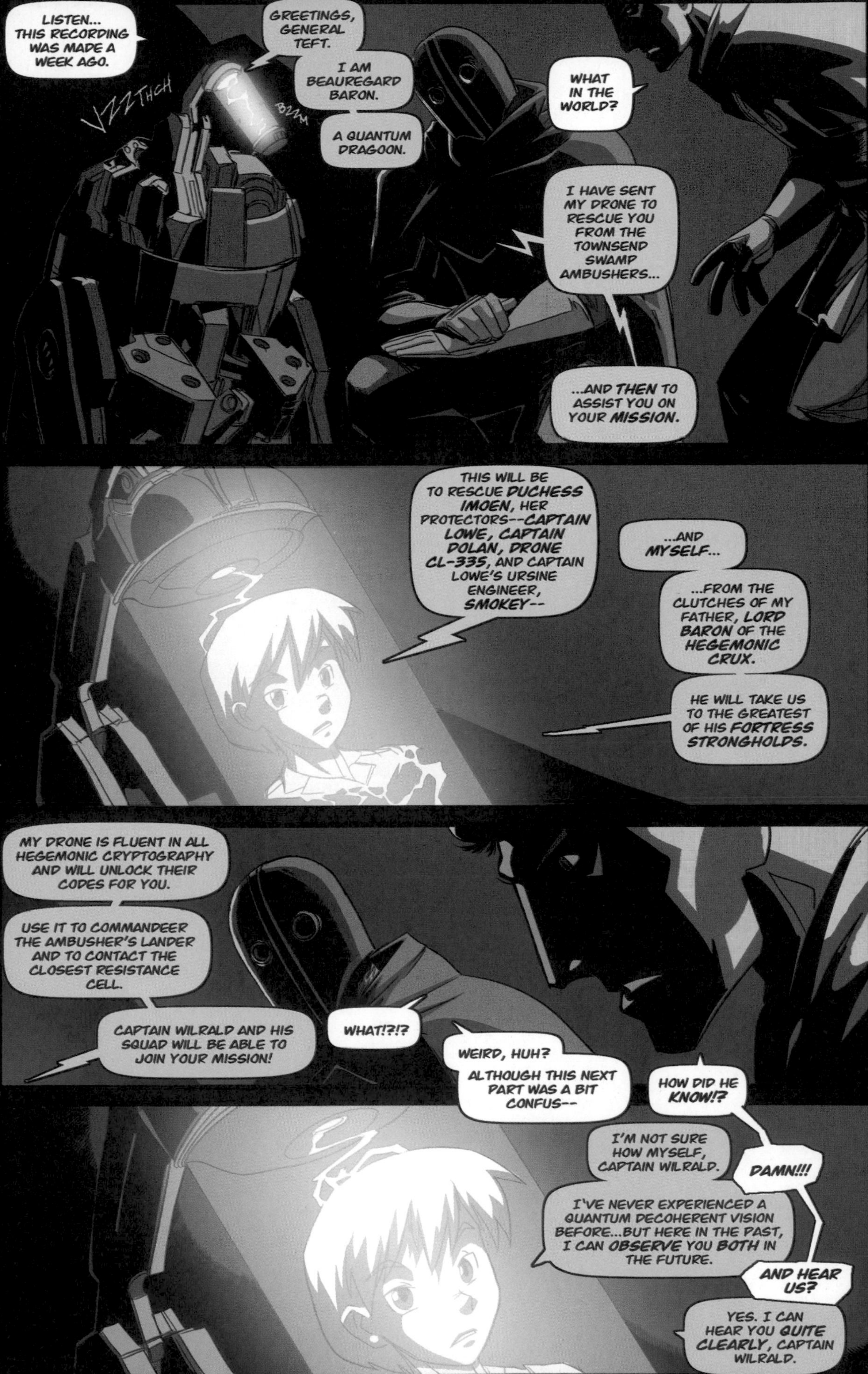
LISTEN... THIS RECORDING WAS MADE A WEEK AGO.
GREETINGS, GENERAL TEFT.
I AM BEAUREGARD BARON.
A QUANTUM DRAGOON.
VZZTHCH
BZZM
WHAT IN THE WORLD?
I HAVE SENT MY DRONE TO RESCUE YOU FROM THE TOWNSEND SWAMP AMBUSHERS...
...AND THEN TO ASSIST YOU ON YOUR MISSION.
THIS WILL BE TO RESCUE DUCHESS IMOEN, HER PROTECTORS--CAPTAIN LOWE, CAPTAIN DOLAN, DRONE CL-335, AND CAPTAIN LOWE'S URSINE ENGINEER, SMOKEY--
...AND MYSELF...
...FROM THE CLUTCHES OF MY FATHER, LORD BARON OF THE HEGEMONIC CRUX.
HE WILL TAKE US TO THE GREATEST OF HIS FORTRESS STRONGHOLDS.
MY DRONE IS FLUENT IN ALL HEGEMONIC CRYPTOGRAPHY AND WILL UNLOCK THEIR CODES FOR YOU.
USE IT TO COMMANDEER THE AMBUSHER'S LANDER AND TO CONTACT THE CLOSEST RESISTANCE CELL.
CAPTAIN WILRALD AND HIS SQUAD WILL BE ABLE TO JOIN YOUR MISSION!
WHAT!?!?
WEIRD, HUH?
ALTHOUGH THIS NEXT PART WAS A BIT CONFUS--
HOW DID HE KNOW!?
I'M NOT SURE HOW MYSELF, CAPTAIN WILRALD.
DAMN!!!
I'VE NEVER EXPERIENCED A QUANTUM DECOHERENT VISION BEFORE...BUT HERE IN THE PAST, I CAN OBSERVE YOU BOTH IN THE FUTURE.
AND HEAR US?
YES. I CAN HEAR YOU QUITE CLEARLY, CAPTAIN WILRALD.

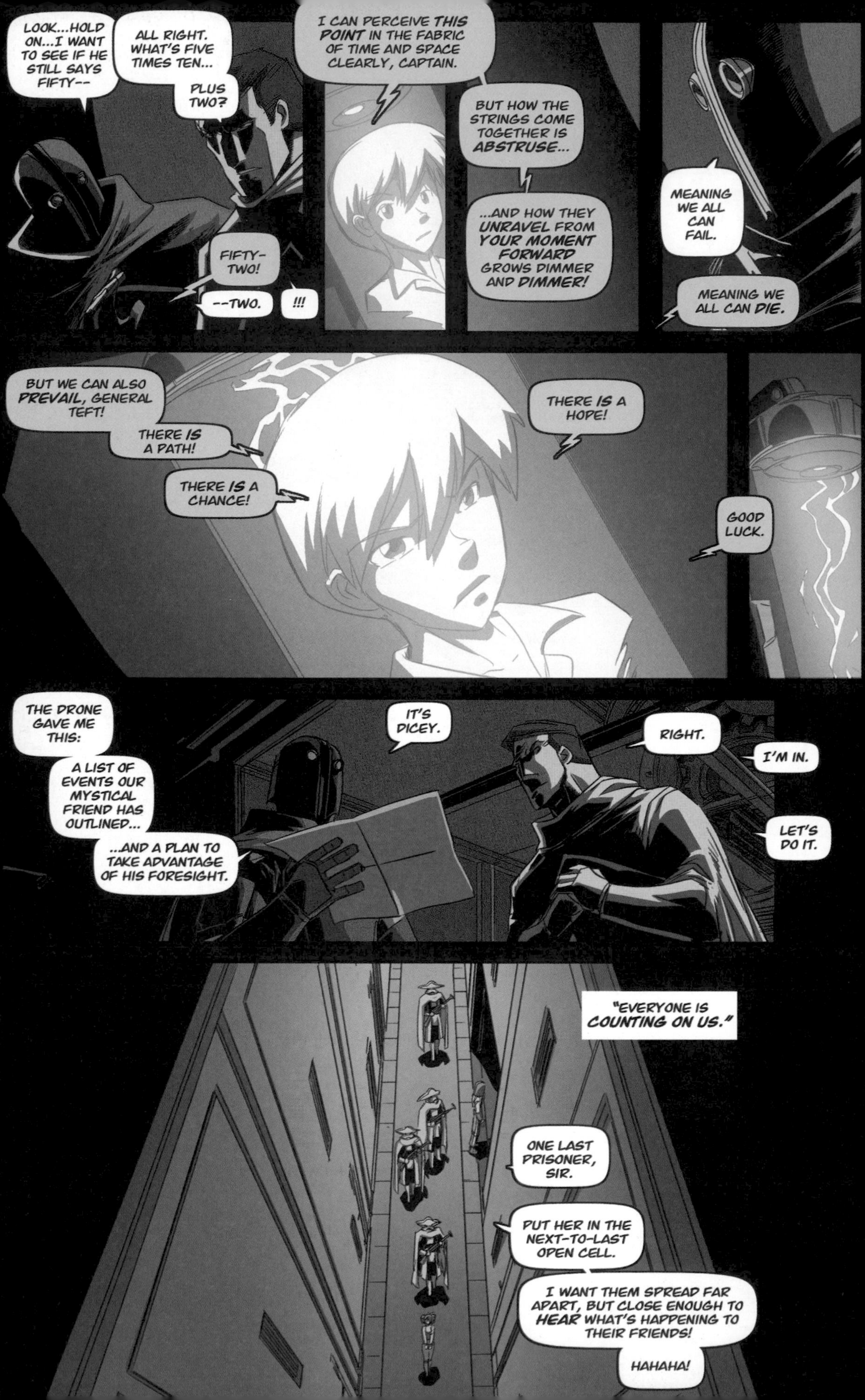
LOOK...HOLD ON...I WANT TO SEE IF HE STILL SAYS FIFTY--
ALL RIGHT. WHAT'S FIVE TIMES TEN...
PLUS TWO?
FIFTY-TWO!
--TWO.
!!!
I CAN PERCEIVE THIS POINT IN THE FABRIC OF TIME AND SPACE CLEARLY, CAPTAIN.
BUT HOW THE STRINGS COME TOGETHER IS ABSTRUSE...
...AND HOW THEY UNRAVEL FROM YOUR MOMENT FORWARD GROWS DIMMER AND DIMMER!
MEANING WE ALL CAN FAIL.
MEANING WE ALL CAN DIE.
BUT WE CAN ALSO PREVAIL, GENERAL TEFT!
THERE IS A PATH!
THERE IS A CHANCE!
THERE IS A HOPE!
GOOD LUCK.
THE DRONE GAVE ME THIS:
A LIST OF EVENTS OUR MYSTICAL FRIEND HAS OUTLINED...
...AND A PLAN TO TAKE ADVANTAGE OF HIS FORESIGHT.
IT'S DICEY.
RIGHT.
I'M IN.
LET'S DO IT.
"EVERYONE IS COUNTING ON US."
ONE LAST PRISONER, SIR.
PUT HER IN THE NEXT-TO-LAST OPEN CELL.
I WANT THEM SPREAD FAR APART, BUT CLOSE ENOUGH TO HEAR WHAT'S HAPPENING TO THEIR FRIENDS!
HAHAHA!

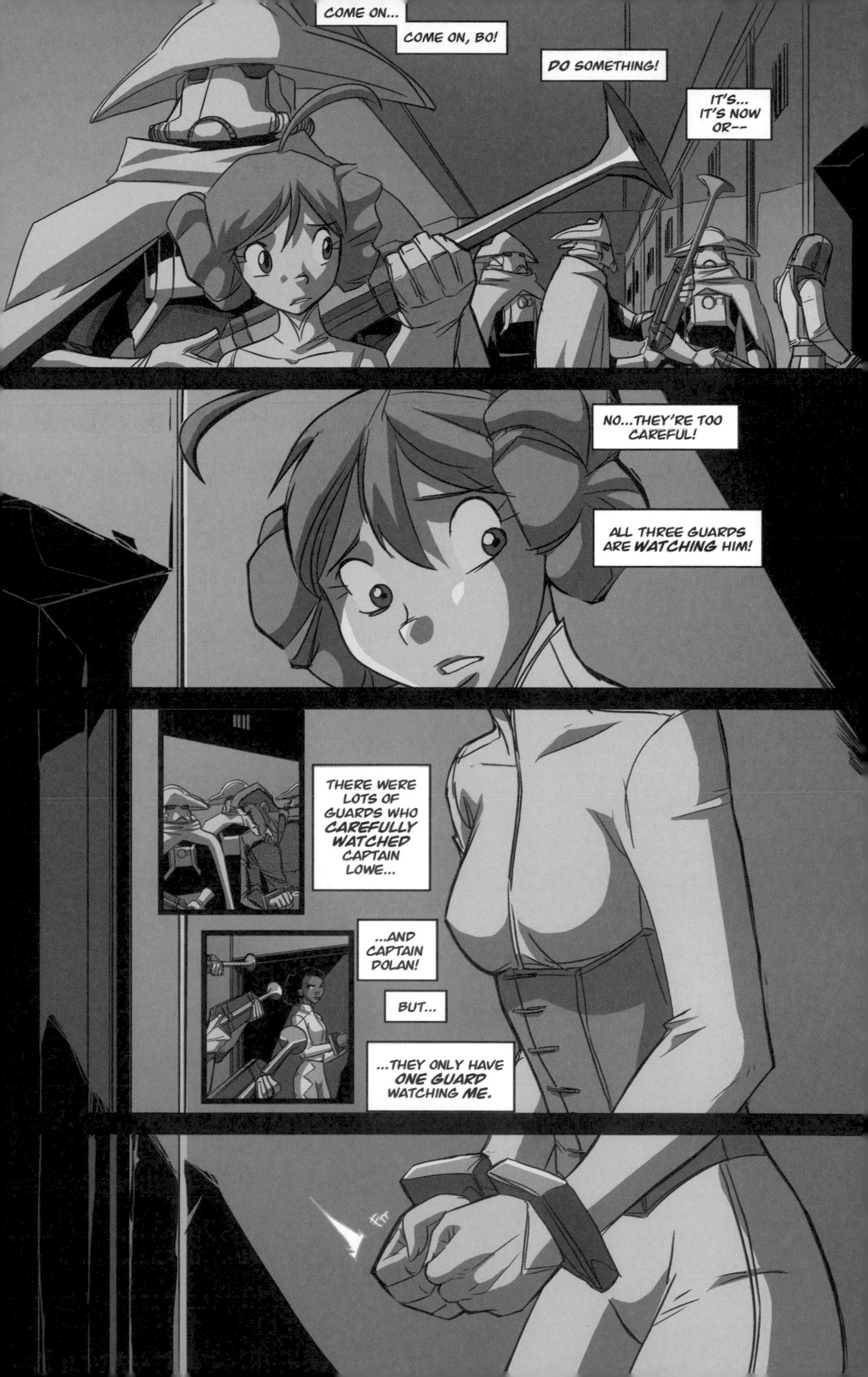
COME ON...
COME ON, BO!
DO SOMETHING!
IT'S... IT'S NOW OR--
NO...THEY'RE TOO CAREFUL!
ALL THREE GUARDS ARE WATCHING HIM!
THERE WERE LOTS OF GUARDS WHO CAREFULLY WATCHED CAPTAIN LOWE...
...AND CAPTAIN DOLAN!
BUT...
...THEY ONLY HAVE ONE GUARD WATCHING ME.

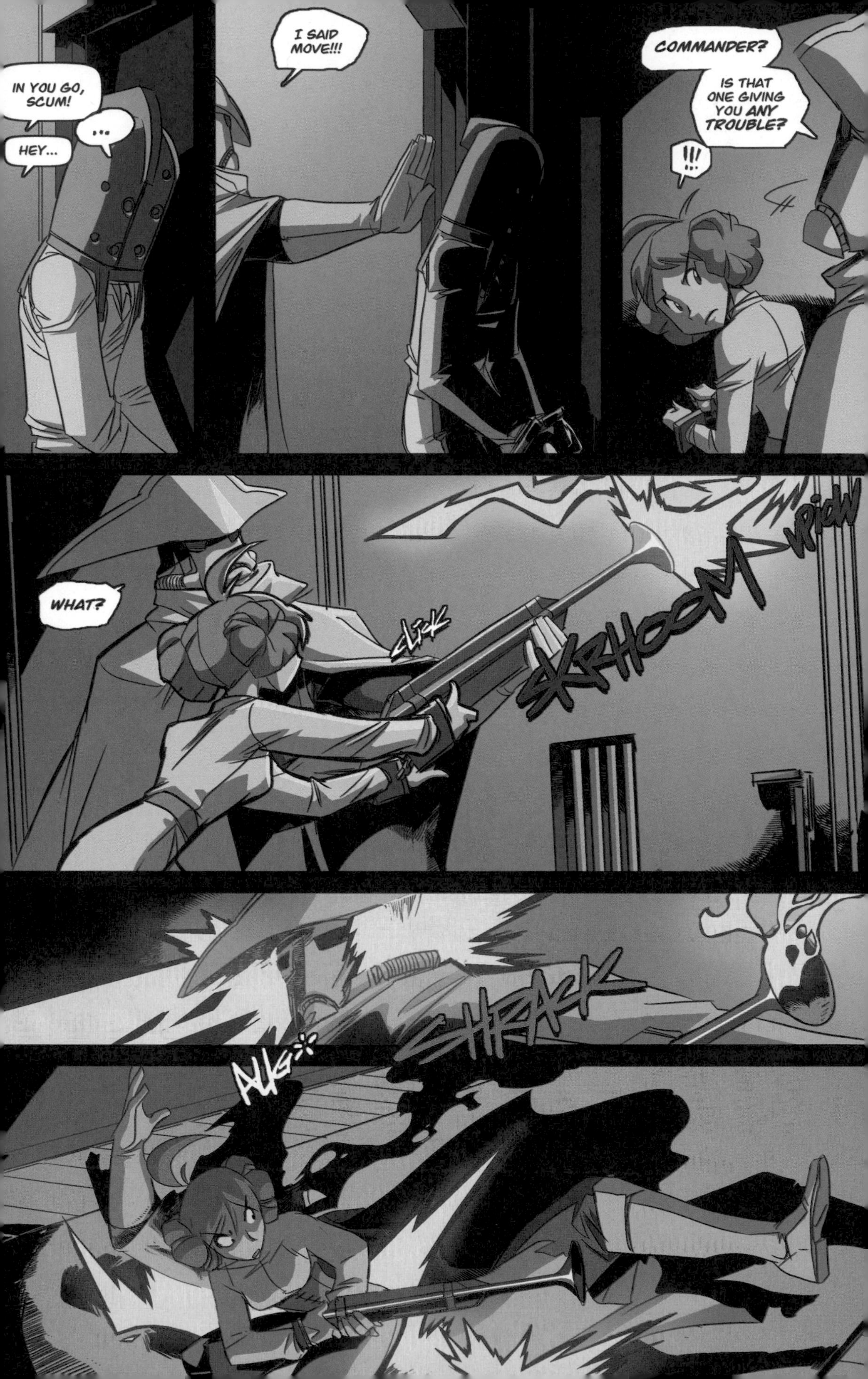
IN YOU GO, SCUM!
...
HEY...
I SAID MOVE!!!
COMMANDER?
IS THAT ONE GIVING YOU ANY TROUBLE?
!!!
WHAT?
CLICK
SKRHOOM
VPIEW
SHRAKK
AUG*!

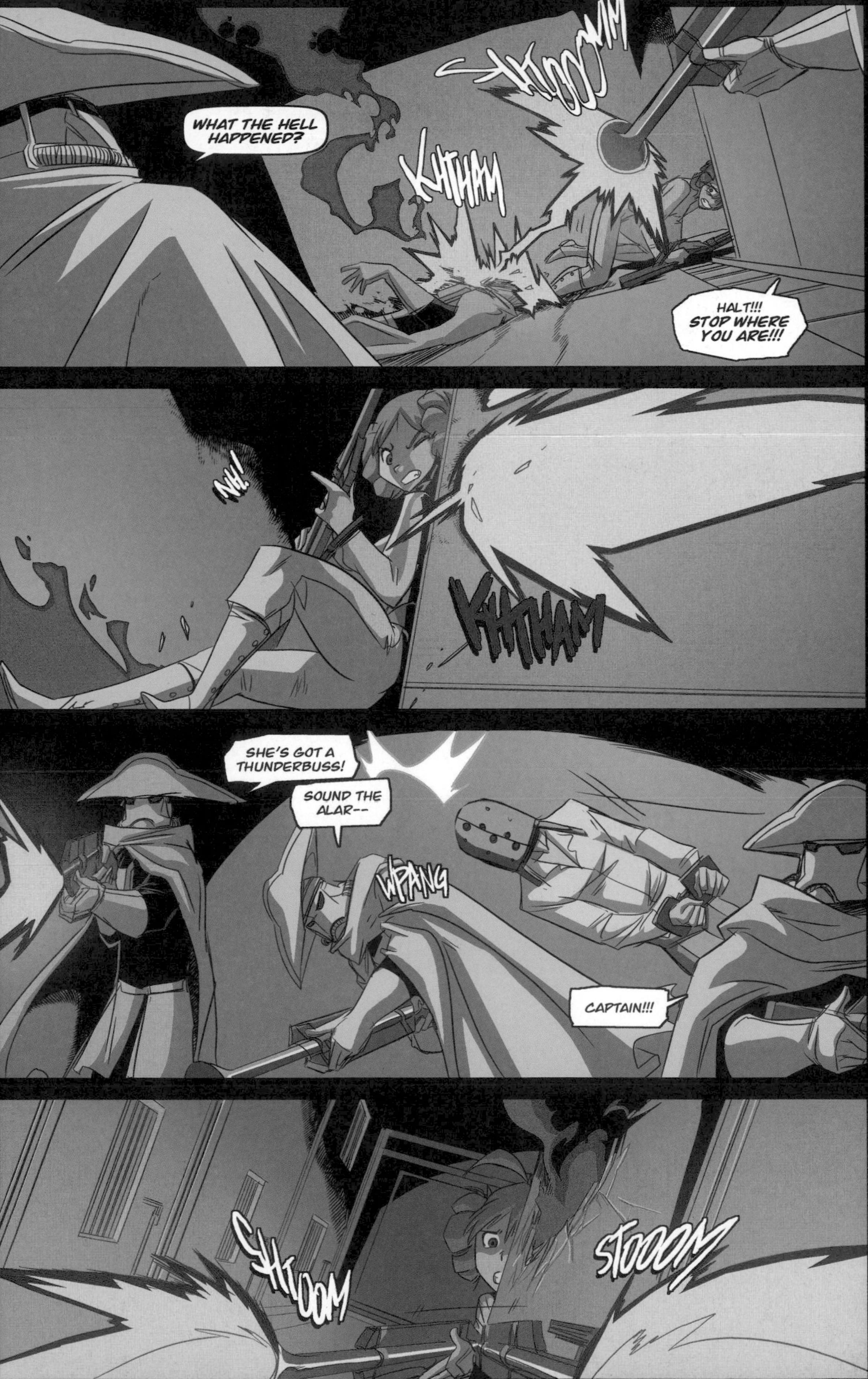
STOOOOM
WHAT THE HELL HAPPENED?
KHTHAM
HALT!!! STOP WHERE YOU ARE!!!
NH!
KHTHAM
SHE'S GOT A THUNDERBUSS!
SOUND THE ALAR--
WPANG
CAPTAIN!!!
SHTOOM
STOOOM

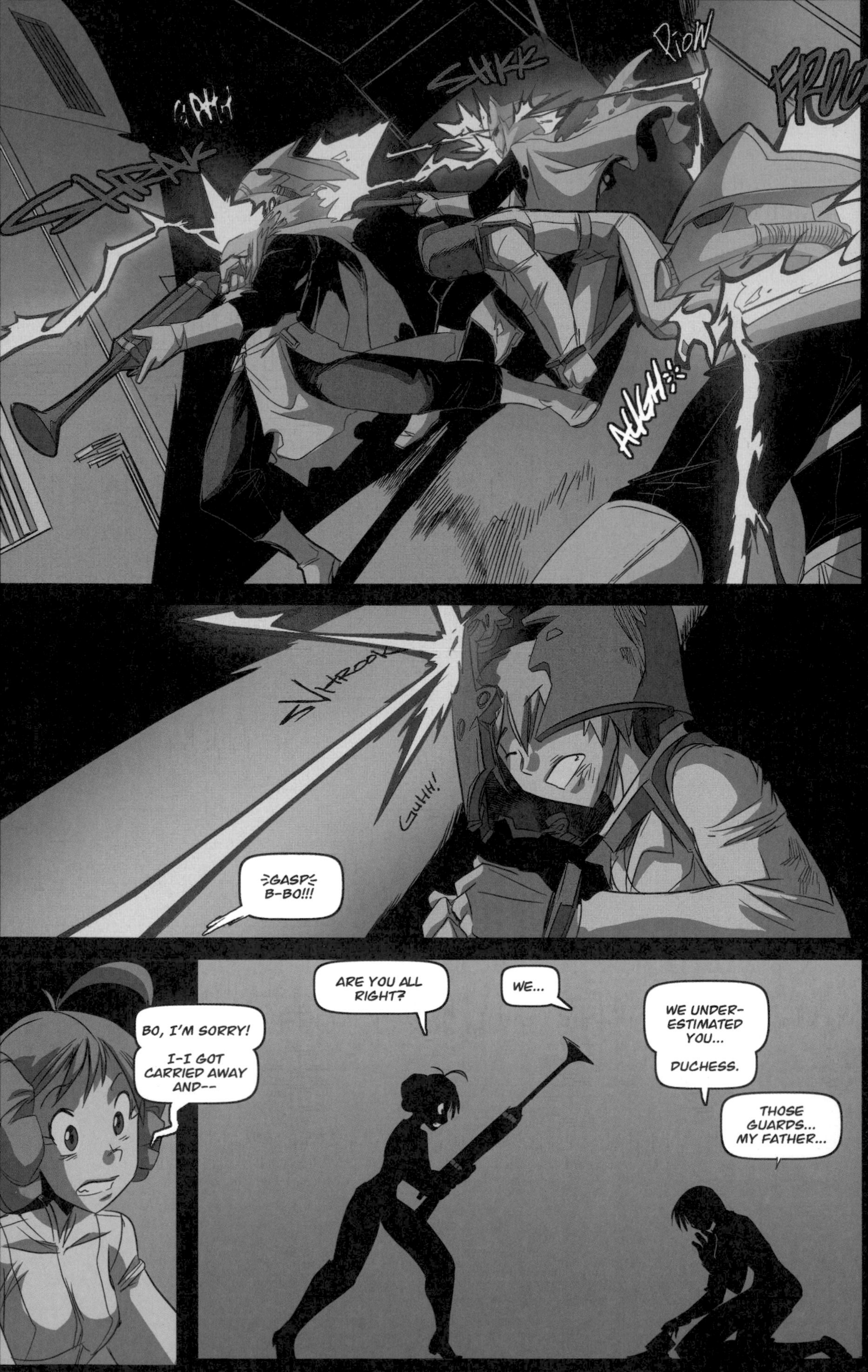

GAH
CHRAK
SHKK
PIOW
FROOS
AUGH
SVHROOK
GUHH!
GASP
B-BO!!!
BO, I'M SORRY!
I-I GOT CARRIED AWAY AND--
ARE YOU ALL RIGHT?
WE...
WE UNDER-ESTIMATED YOU...
DUCHESS.
THOSE GUARDS... MY FATHER...

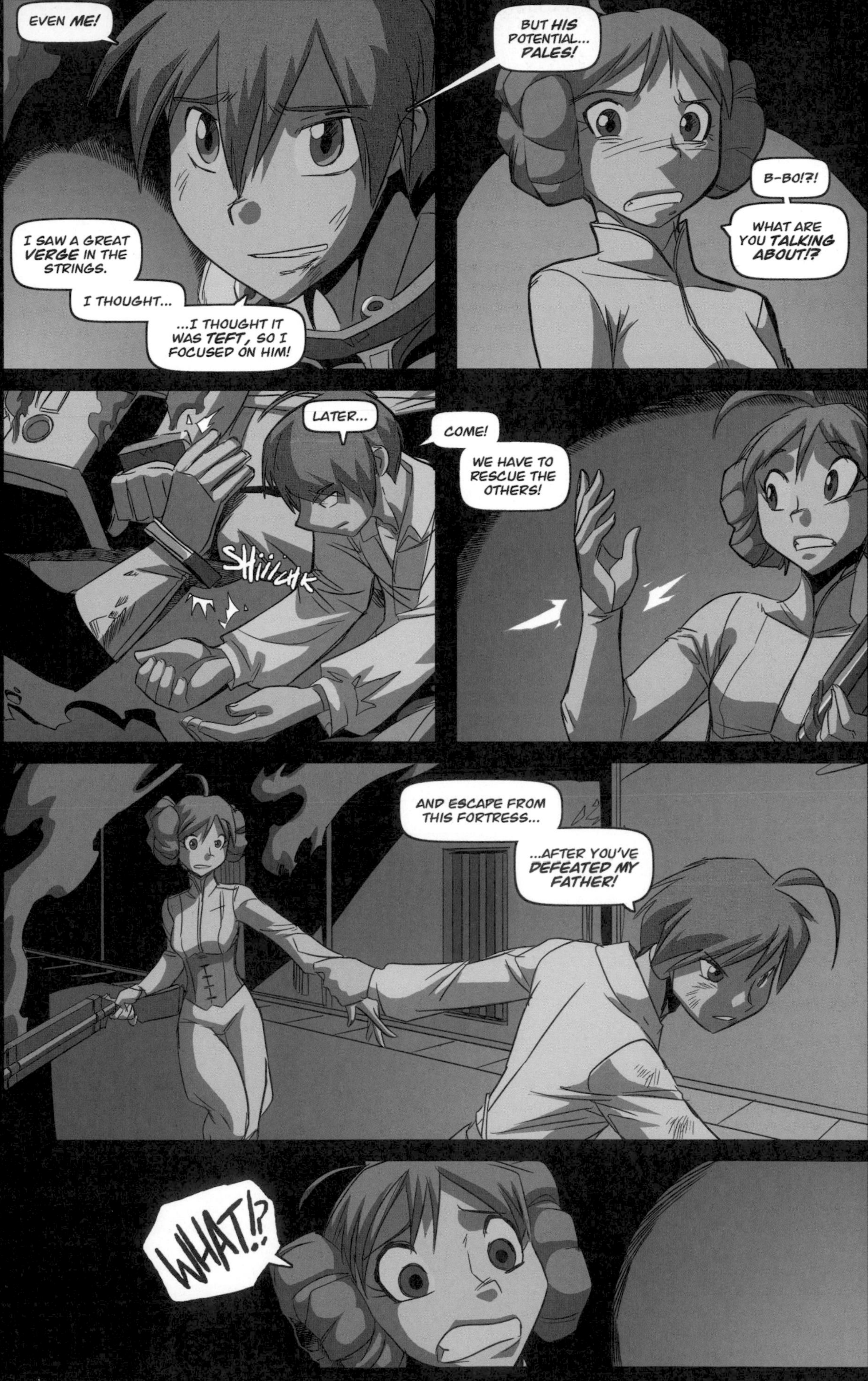
EVEN ME!
I SAW A GREAT VERGE IN THE STRINGS.
I THOUGHT...
...I THOUGHT IT WAS TEFT, SO I FOCUSED ON HIM!
BUT HIS POTENTIAL... PALES!
B-BO!?!
WHAT ARE YOU TALKING ABOUT!?
LATER...
SHIIICHK
COME!
WE HAVE TO RESCUE THE OTHERS!
AND ESCAPE FROM THIS FORTRESS...
...AFTER YOU'VE DEFEATED MY FATHER!
WHAT!?

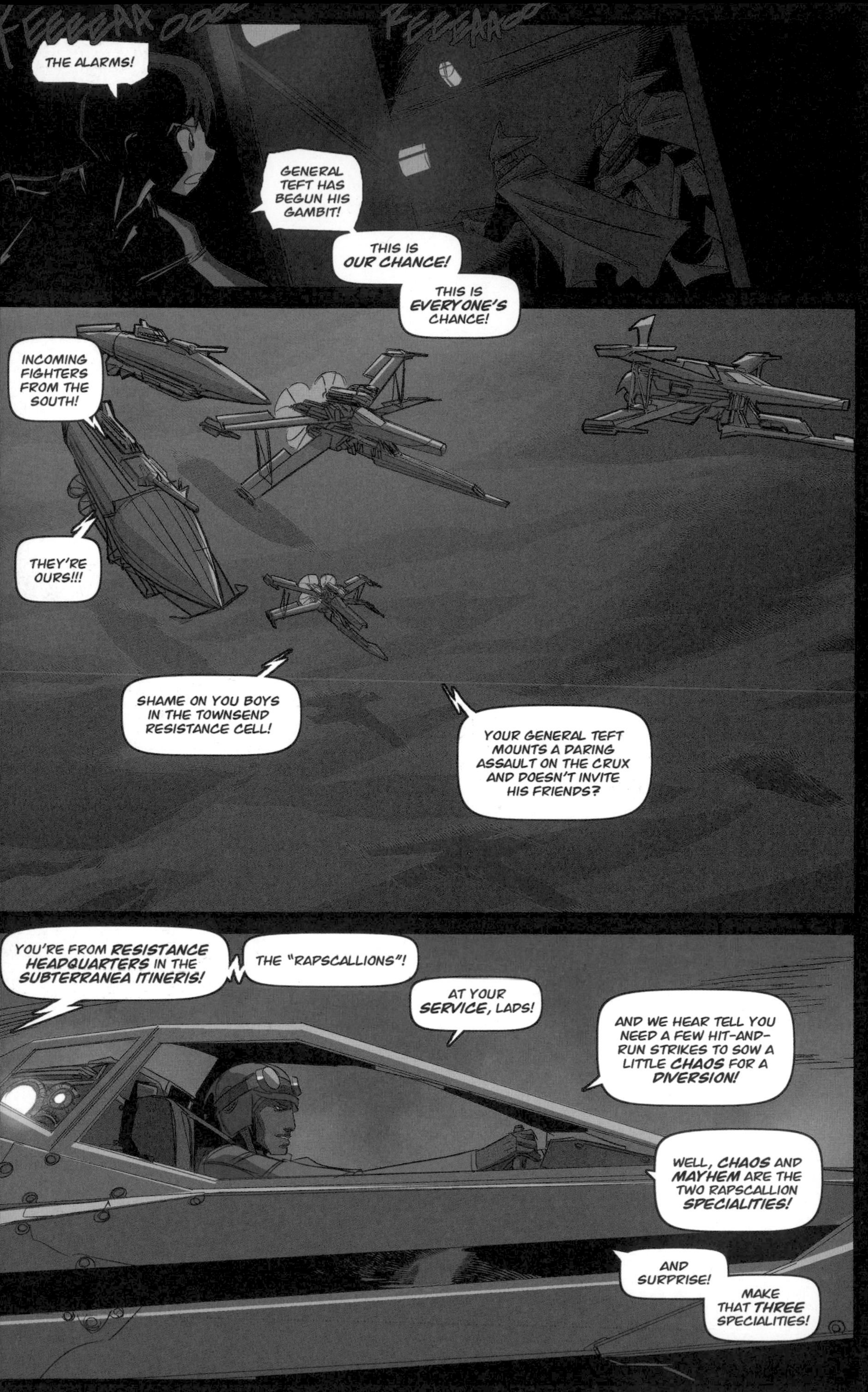
FEEEAA OOOO
FEEEAAOO
THE ALARMS!
GENERAL TEFT HAS BEGUN HIS GAMBIT!
THIS IS OUR CHANCE!
THIS IS EVERYONE'S CHANCE!
INCOMING FIGHTERS FROM THE SOUTH!
THEY'RE OURS!!!
SHAME ON YOU BOYS IN THE TOWNSEND RESISTANCE CELL!
YOUR GENERAL TEFT MOUNTS A DARING ASSAULT ON THE CRUX AND DOESN'T INVITE HIS FRIENDS?
YOU'RE FROM RESISTANCE HEADQUARTERS IN THE SUBTERRANEA ITINERIS!
THE "RAPSCALLIONS"!
AT YOUR SERVICE, LADS!
AND WE HEAR TELL YOU NEED A FEW HIT-AND-RUN STRIKES TO SOW A LITTLE CHAOS FOR A DIVERSION!
WELL, CHAOS AND MAYHEM ARE THE TWO RAPSCALLION SPECIALITIES!
AND SURPRISE!
MAKE THAT THREE SPECIALITIES!

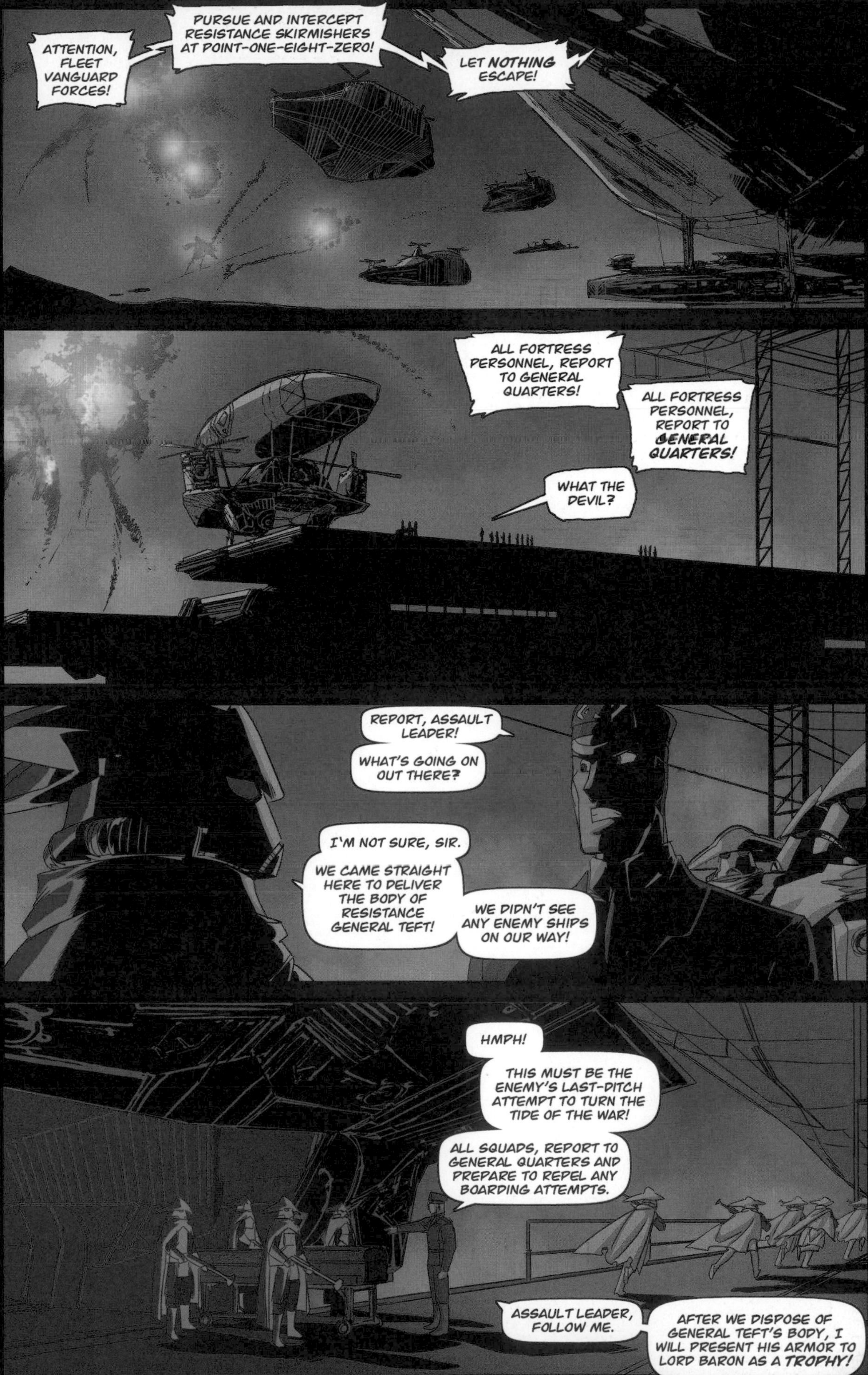
ATTENTION, FLEET VANGUARD FORCES!
PURSUE AND INTERCEPT RESISTANCE SKIRMISHERS AT POINT-ONE-EIGHT-ZERO!
LET NOTHING ESCAPE!
ALL FORTRESS PERSONNEL, REPORT TO GENERAL QUARTERS!
ALL FORTRESS PERSONNEL, REPORT TO GENERAL QUARTERS!
WHAT THE DEVIL?
REPORT, ASSAULT LEADER!
WHAT'S GOING ON OUT THERE?
I'M NOT SURE, SIR.
WE CAME STRAIGHT HERE TO DELIVER THE BODY OF RESISTANCE GENERAL TEFT!
WE DIDN'T SEE ANY ENEMY SHIPS ON OUR WAY!
HMPH!
THIS MUST BE THE ENEMY'S LAST-DITCH ATTEMPT TO TURN THE TIDE OF THE WAR!
ALL SQUADS, REPORT TO GENERAL QUARTERS AND PREPARE TO REPEL ANY BOARDING ATTEMPTS.
ASSAULT LEADER, FOLLOW ME.
AFTER WE DISPOSE OF GENERAL TEFT'S BODY, I WILL PRESENT HIS ARMOR TO LORD BARON AS A TROPHY!

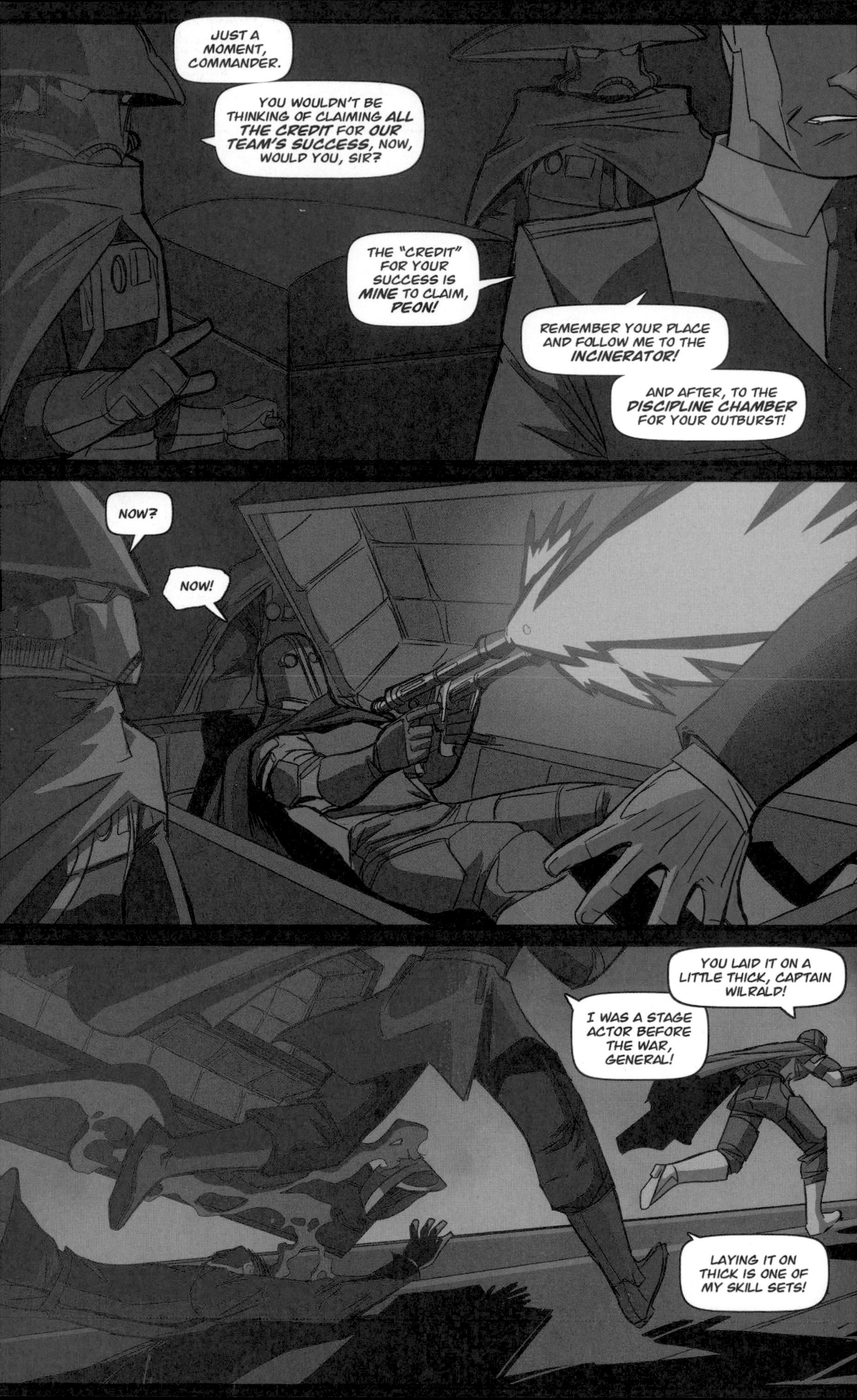
JUST A MOMENT, COMMANDER.
YOU WOULDN'T BE THINKING OF CLAIMING ALL THE CREDIT FOR OUR TEAM'S SUCCESS, NOW, WOULD YOU, SIR?
THE "CREDIT" FOR YOUR SUCCESS IS MINE TO CLAIM, PEON!
REMEMBER YOUR PLACE AND FOLLOW ME TO THE INCINERATOR!
AND AFTER, TO THE DISCIPLINE CHAMBER FOR YOUR OUTBURST!
NOW?
NOW!
YOU LAID IT ON A LITTLE THICK, CAPTAIN WILRALD!
I WAS A STAGE ACTOR BEFORE THE WAR, GENERAL!
LAYING IT ON THICK IS ONE OF MY SKILL SETS!

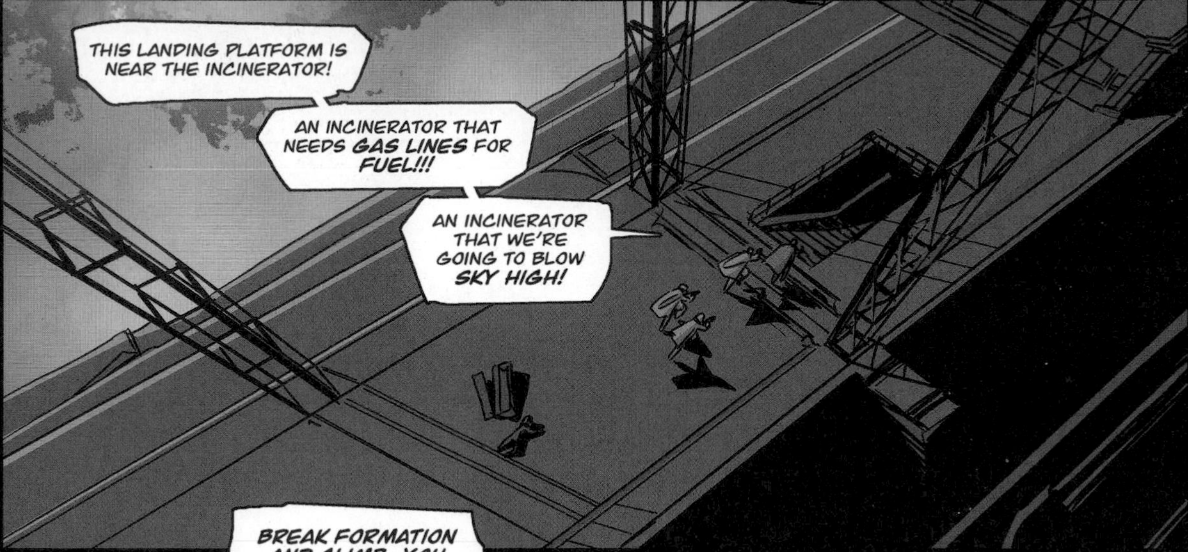
THIS LANDING PLATFORM IS NEAR THE INCINERATOR!
AN INCINERATOR THAT NEEDS GAS LINES FOR FUEL!!!
AN INCINERATOR THAT WE'RE GOING TO BLOW SKY HIGH!

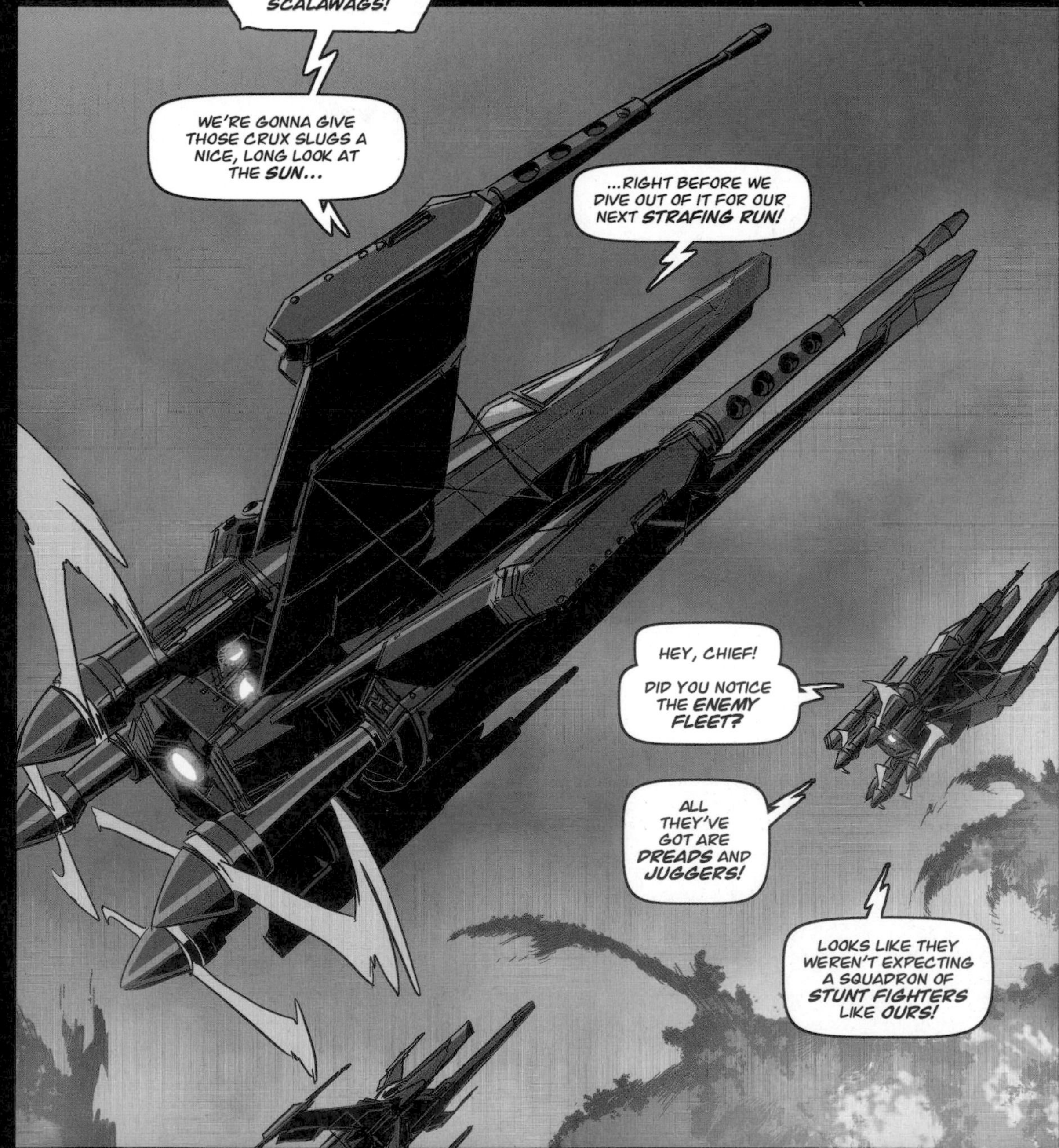
BREAK FORMATION AND CLIMB, YOU SCALAWAGS!
WE'RE GONNA GIVE THOSE CRUX SLUGS A NICE, LONG LOOK AT THE SUN...
...RIGHT BEFORE WE DIVE OUT OF IT FOR OUR NEXT STRAFING RUN!
HEY, CHIEF!
DID YOU NOTICE THE ENEMY FLEET?
ALL THEY'VE GOT ARE DREADS AND JUGGERS!
LOOKS LIKE THEY WEREN'T EXPECTING A SQUADRON OF STUNT FIGHTERS LIKE OURS!

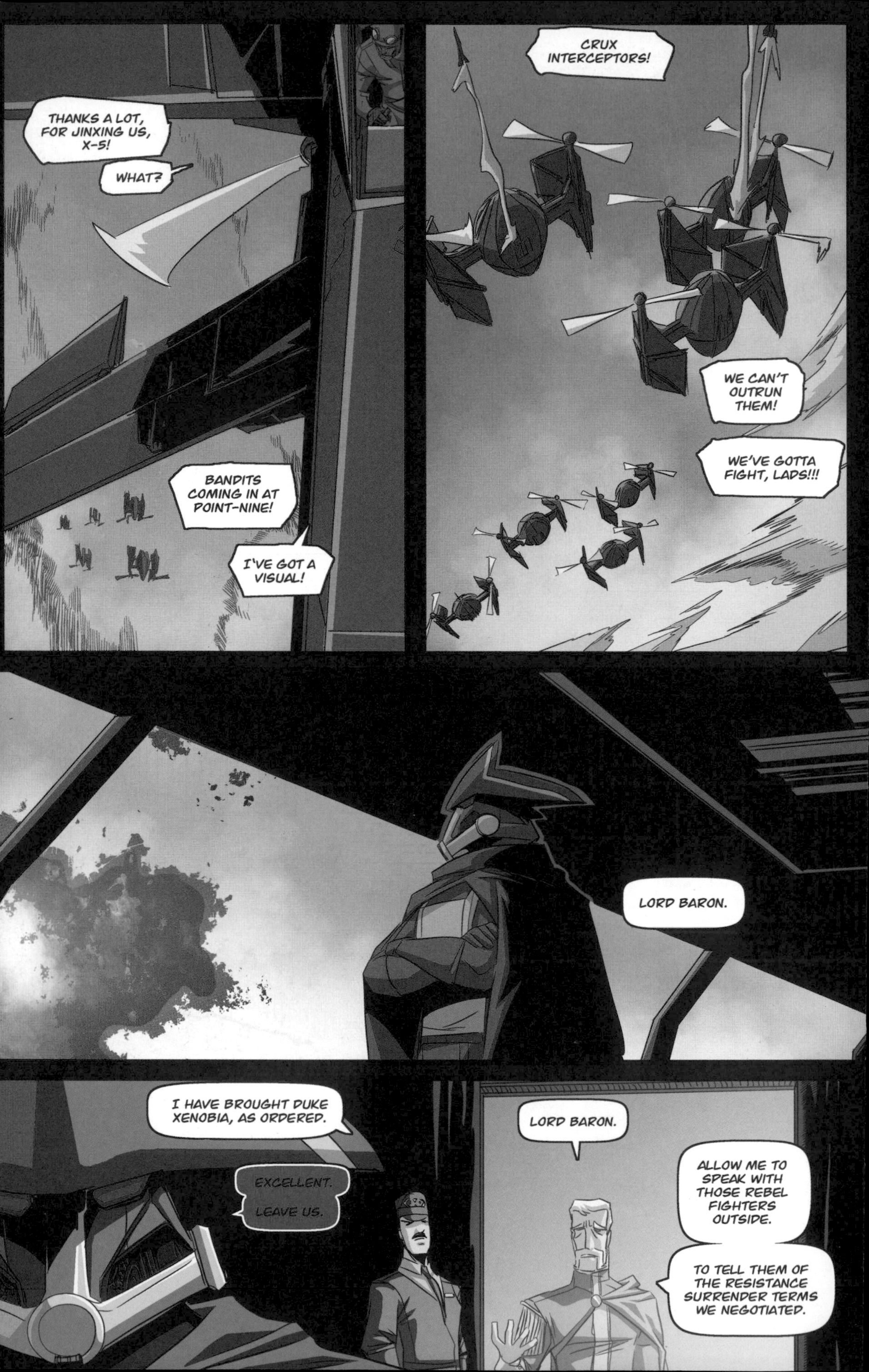
THANKS A LOT, FOR JINXING US, X-5!
WHAT?
BANDITS COMING IN AT POINT-NINE!
I'VE GOT A VISUAL!
CRUX INTERCEPTORS!
WE CAN'T OUTRUN THEM!
WE'VE GOTTA FIGHT, LADS!!!
LORD BARON.
I HAVE BROUGHT DUKE XENOBIA, AS ORDERED.
EXCELLENT.
LEAVE US.
LORD BARON.
ALLOW ME TO SPEAK WITH THOSE REBEL FIGHTERS OUTSIDE.
TO TELL THEM OF THE RESISTANCE SURRENDER TERMS WE NEGOTIATED.

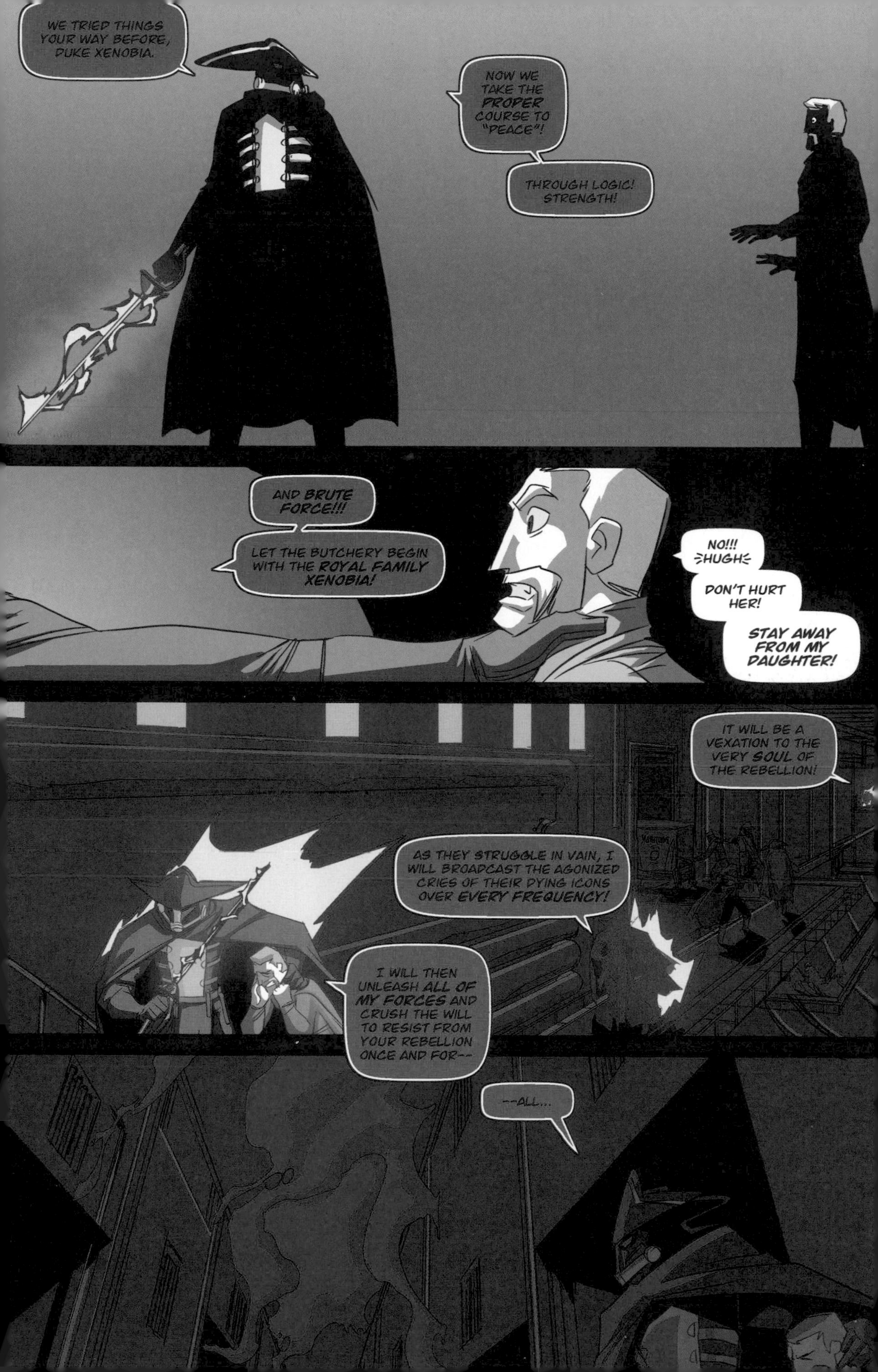
WE TRIED THINGS YOUR WAY BEFORE, DUKE XENOBIA.
NOW WE TAKE THE PROPER COURSE TO "PEACE"!
THROUGH LOGIC! STRENGTH!
AND BRUTE FORCE!!!
LET THE BUTCHERY BEGIN WITH THE ROYAL FAMILY XENOBIA!
NO!!! HUGH
DON'T HURT HER!
STAY AWAY FROM MY DAUGHTER!
IT WILL BE A VEXATION TO THE VERY SOUL OF THE REBELLION!
AS THEY STRUGGLE IN VAIN, I WILL BROADCAST THE AGONIZED CRIES OF THEIR DYING ICONS OVER EVERY FREQUENCY!
I WILL THEN UNLEASH ALL OF MY FORCES AND CRUSH THE WILL TO RESIST FROM YOUR REBELLION ONCE AND FOR--
--ALL...

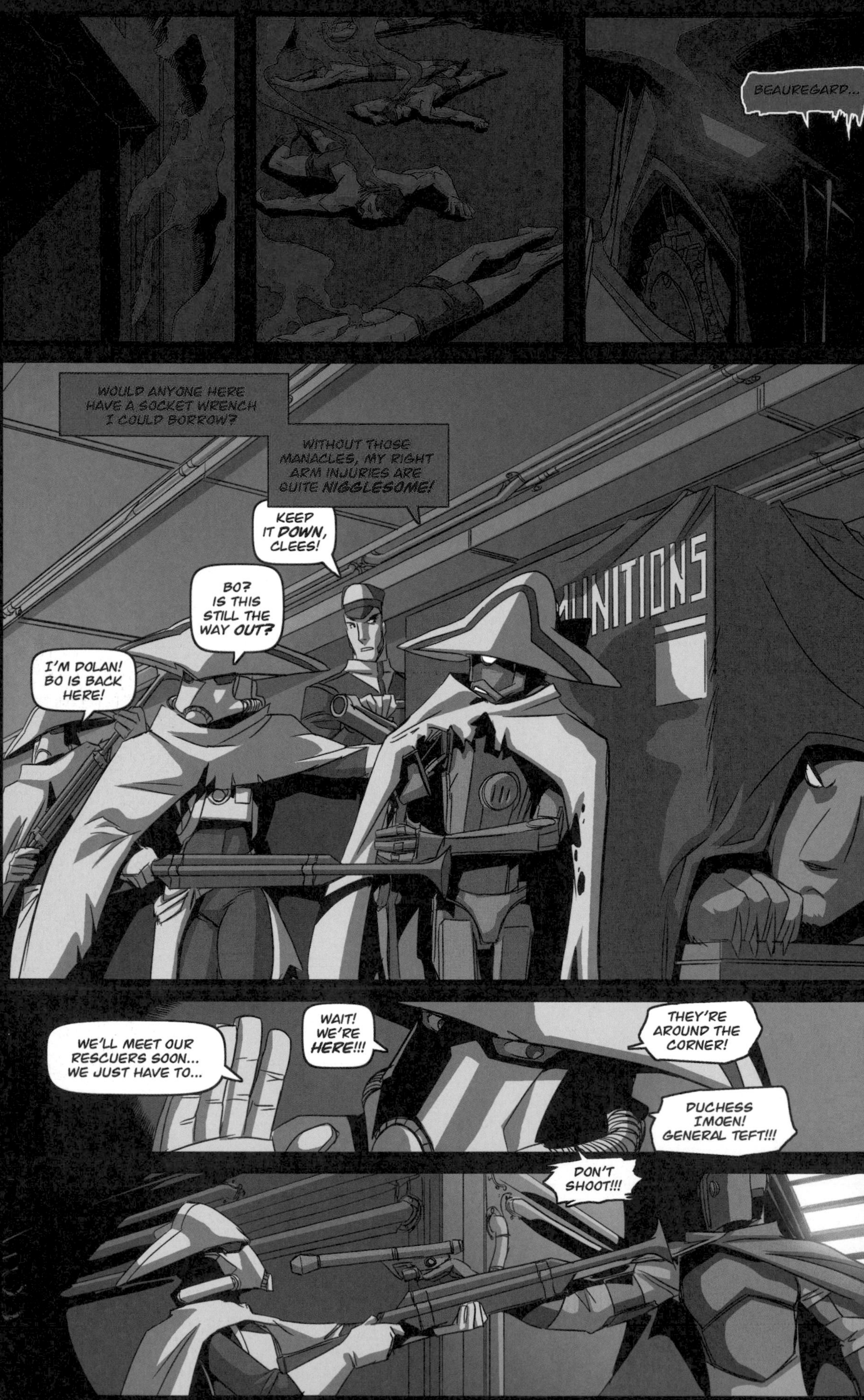
BEAUREGARD...
WOULD ANYONE HERE HAVE A SOCKET WRENCH I COULD BORROW?
WITHOUT THOSE MANACLES, MY RIGHT ARM INJURIES ARE QUITE NIGGLESOME!
KEEP IT DOWN, CLEES!
BO? IS THIS STILL THE WAY OUT?
I'M DOLAN! BO IS BACK HERE!
MUNITIONS
WE'LL MEET OUR RESCUERS SOON... WE JUST HAVE TO...
WAIT! WE'RE HERE!!!
THEY'RE AROUND THE CORNER!
DUCHESS IMOEN! GENERAL TEFT!!!
DON'T SHOOT!!!

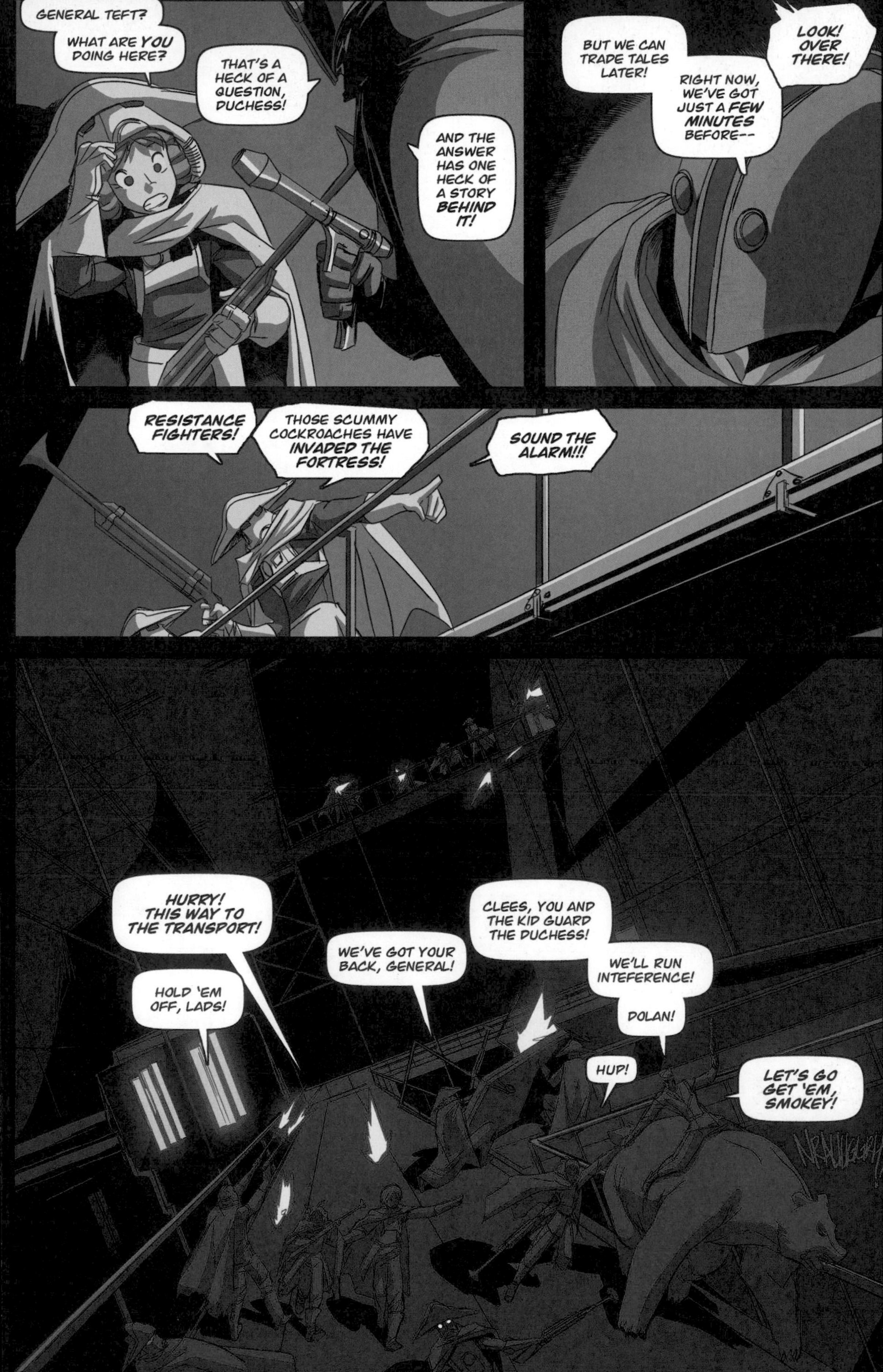
GENERAL TEFT?
WHAT ARE YOU DOING HERE?
THAT'S A HECK OF A QUESTION, DUCHESS!
AND THE ANSWER HAS ONE HECK OF A STORY BEHIND IT!
BUT WE CAN TRADE TALES LATER!
RIGHT NOW, WE'VE GOT JUST A FEW MINUTES BEFORE--
LOOK! OVER THERE!
RESISTANCE FIGHTERS!
THOSE SCUMMY COCKROACHES HAVE INVADED THE FORTRESS!
SOUND THE ALARM!!!
HURRY! THIS WAY TO THE TRANSPORT!
HOLD 'EM OFF, LADS!
WE'VE GOT YOUR BACK, GENERAL!
CLEES, YOU AND THE KID GUARD THE DUCHESS!
WE'LL RUN INTEFERENCE!
DOLAN!
HUP!
LET'S GO GET 'EM, SMOKEY!
NRAWGRH

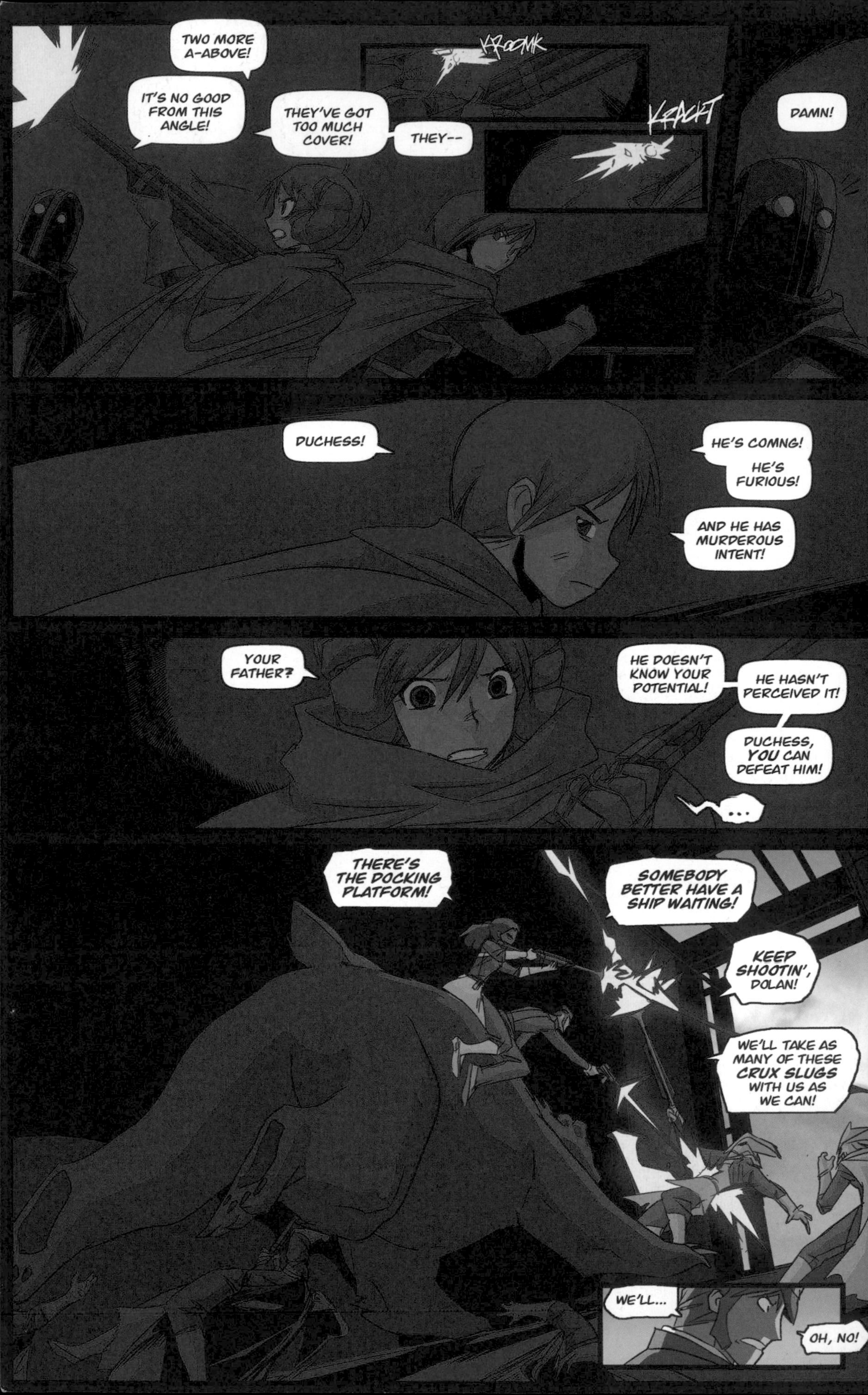
TWO MORE A-ABOVE!
IT'S NO GOOD FROM THIS ANGLE!
THEY'VE GOT TOO MUCH COVER!
THEY--
KROOMK
KRACKT
DAMN!
DUCHESS!
HE'S COMNG!
HE'S FURIOUS!
AND HE HAS MURDEROUS INTENT!
YOUR FATHER?
HE DOESN'T KNOW YOUR POTENTIAL!
HE HASN'T PERCEIVED IT!
DUCHESS, YOU CAN DEFEAT HIM!
...
THERE'S THE DOCKING PLATFORM!
SOMEBODY BETTER HAVE A SHIP WAITING!
KEEP SHOOTIN', DOLAN!
WE'LL TAKE AS MANY OF THESE CRUX SLUGS WITH US AS WE CAN!
WE'LL...
OH, NO!

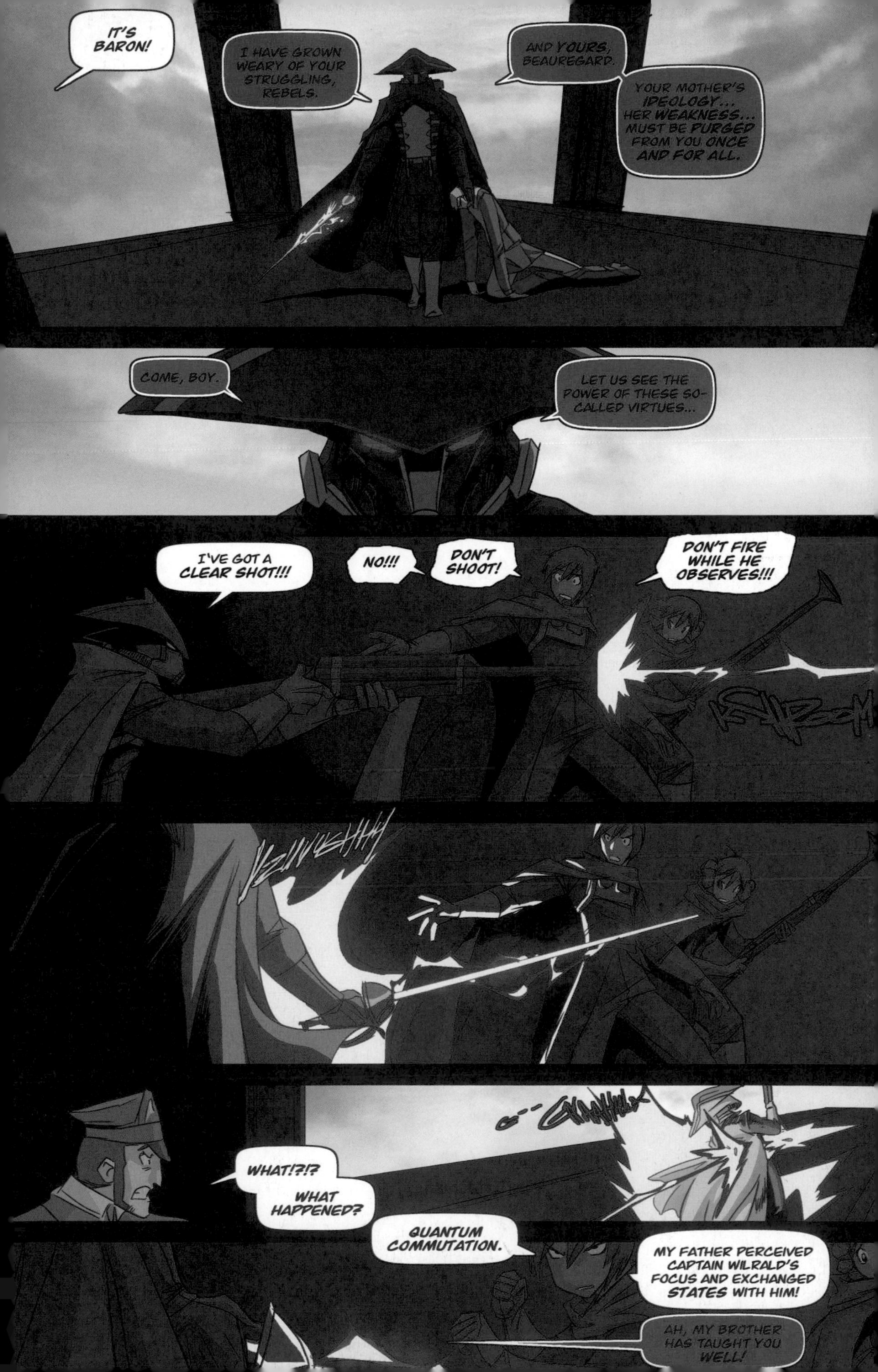

IT'S BARON!
I HAVE GROWN WEARY OF YOUR STRUGGLING, REBELS.
AND YOURS, BEAUREGARD.
YOUR MOTHER'S IDEOLOGY... HER WEAKNESS... MUST BE PURGED FROM YOU ONCE AND FOR ALL.
COME, BOY.
LET US SEE THE POWER OF THESE SO-CALLED VIRTUES...
I'VE GOT A CLEAR SHOT!!!
NO!!!
DON'T SHOOT!
DON'T FIRE WHILE HE OBSERVES!!!
WHAT!?!?
WHAT HAPPENED?
QUANTUM COMMUTATION.
MY FATHER PERCEIVED CAPTAIN WILRALD'S FOCUS AND EXCHANGED STATES WITH HIM!
AH, MY BROTHER HAS TAUGHT YOU WELL!

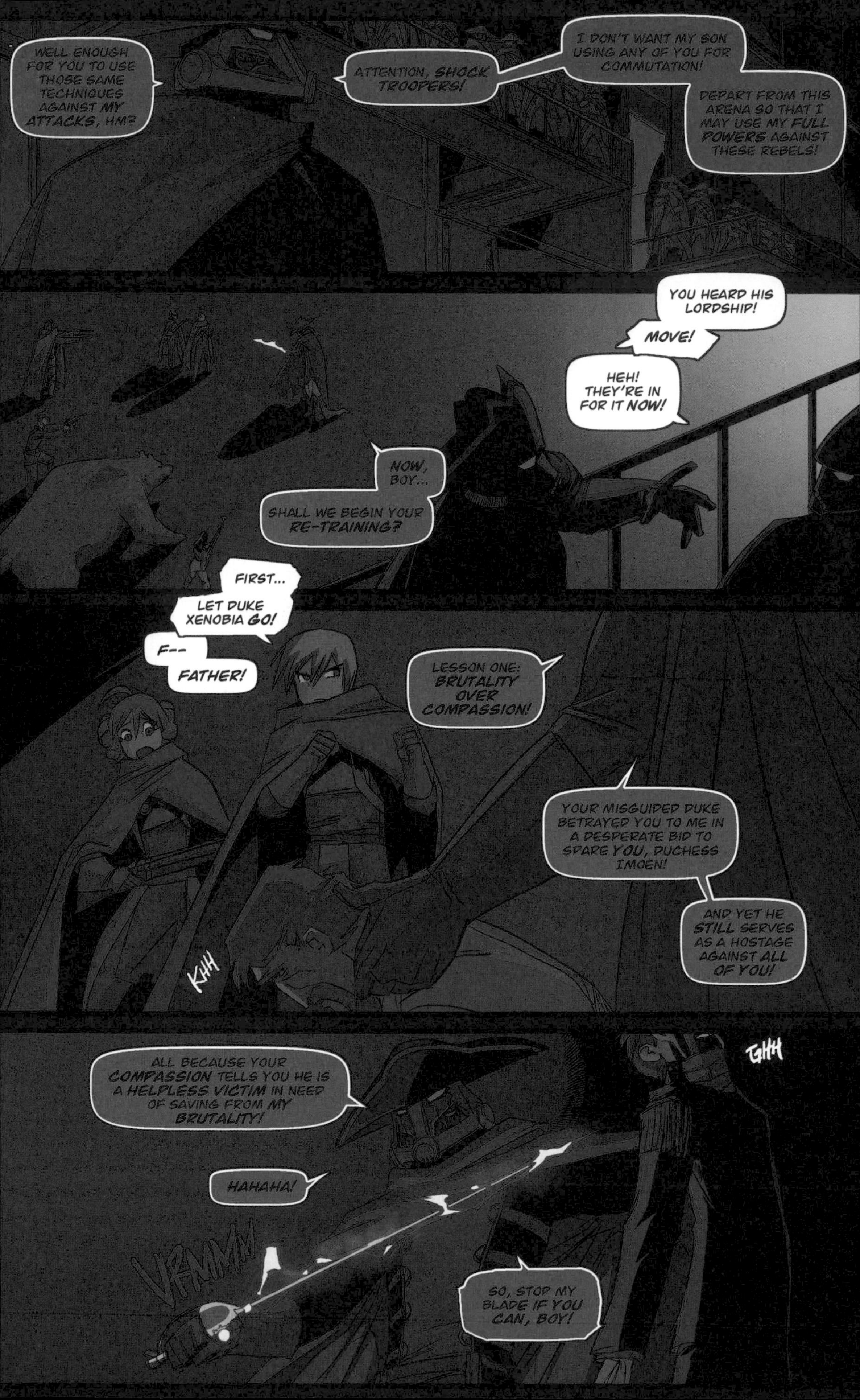
WELL ENOUGH FOR YOU TO USE THOSE SAME TECHNIQUES AGAINST MY ATTACKS, HM?
ATTENTION, SHOCK TROOPERS!
I DON'T WANT MY SON USING ANY OF YOU FOR COMMUTATION!
DEPART FROM THIS ARENA SO THAT I MAY USE MY FULL POWERS AGAINST THESE REBELS!
YOU HEARD HIS LORDSHIP!
MOVE!
HEH! THEY'RE IN FOR IT NOW!
NOW, BOY...
SHALL WE BEGIN YOUR RE-TRAINING?
FIRST...
LET DUKE XENOBIA GO!
F--
FATHER!
LESSON ONE: BRUTALITY OVER COMPASSION!
YOUR MISGUIDED DUKE BETRAYED YOU TO ME IN A DESPERATE BID TO SPARE YOU, DUCHESS IMOEN!
AND YET HE STILL SERVES AS A HOSTAGE AGAINST ALL OF YOU!
KHH
GHH
ALL BECAUSE YOUR COMPASSION TELLS YOU HE IS A HELPLESS VICTIM IN NEED OF SAVING FROM MY BRUTALITY!
HAHAHA!
VRMMM
SO, STOP MY BLADE IF YOU CAN, BOY!

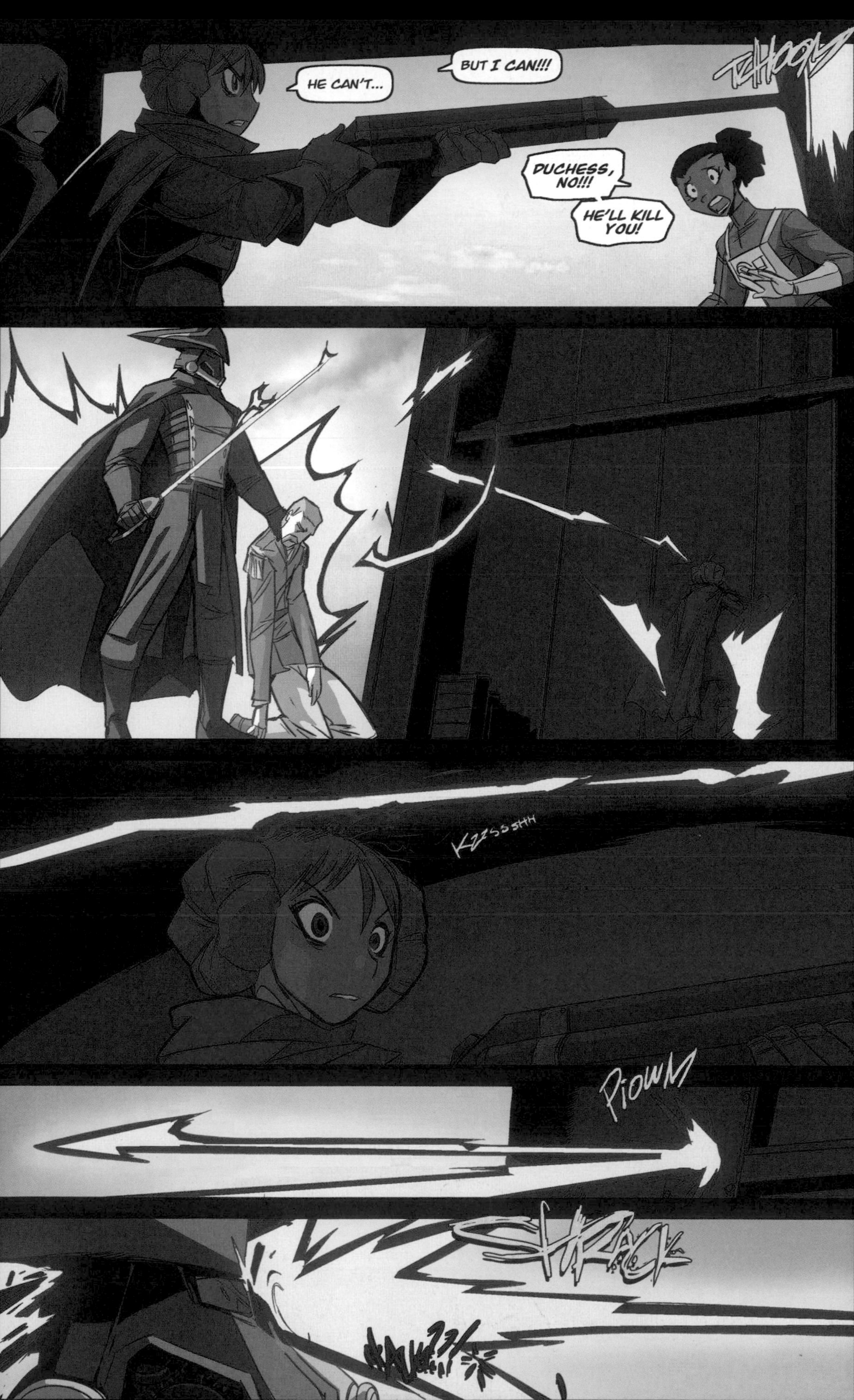
TCHOOOM
HE CAN'T...
BUT I CAN!!!
DUCHESS, NO!!!
HE'LL KILL YOU!
KZZSSSHH
PIOWM
SHRACK

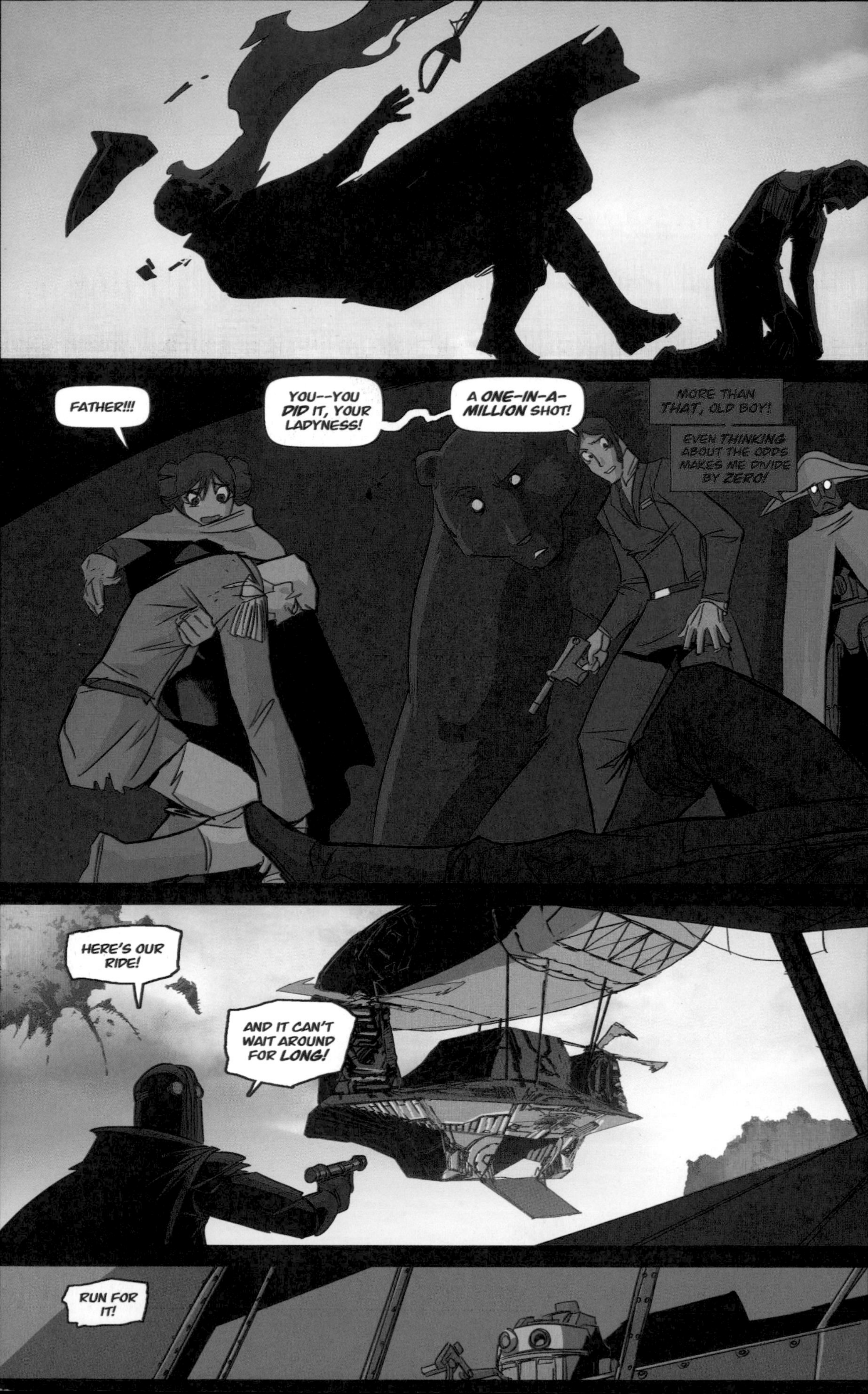
FATHER!!!
YOU--YOU DID IT, YOUR LADYNESS!
A ONE-IN-A-MILLION SHOT!
MORE THAN THAT, OLD BOY!
EVEN THINKING ABOUT THE ODDS MAKES ME DIVIDE BY ZERO!
HERE'S OUR RIDE!
AND IT CAN'T WAIT AROUND FOR LONG!
RUN FOR IT!

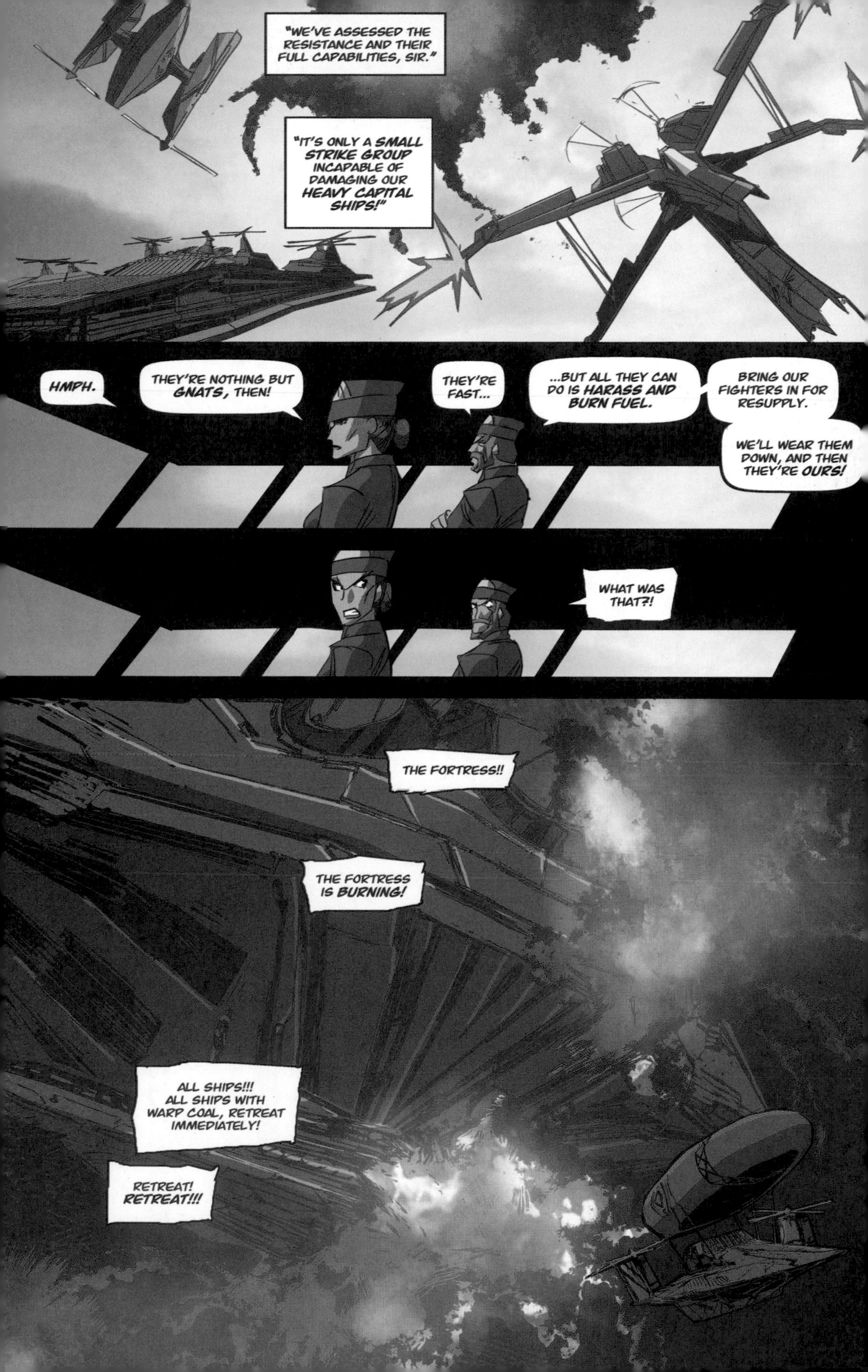
"WE'VE ASSESSED THE RESISTANCE AND THEIR FULL CAPABILITIES, SIR."
"IT'S ONLY A SMALL STRIKE GROUP INCAPABLE OF DAMAGING OUR HEAVY CAPITAL SHIPS!"
HMPH.
THEY'RE NOTHING BUT GNATS, THEN!
THEY'RE FAST...
...BUT ALL THEY CAN DO IS HARASS AND BURN FUEL.
BRING OUR FIGHTERS IN FOR RESUPPLY.
WE'LL WEAR THEM DOWN, AND THEN THEY'RE OURS!
WHAT WAS THAT?!
THE FORTRESS!!
THE FORTRESS IS BURNING!
ALL SHIPS!!! ALL SHIPS WITH WARP COAL, RETREAT IMMEDIATELY!
RETREAT! RETREAT!!!

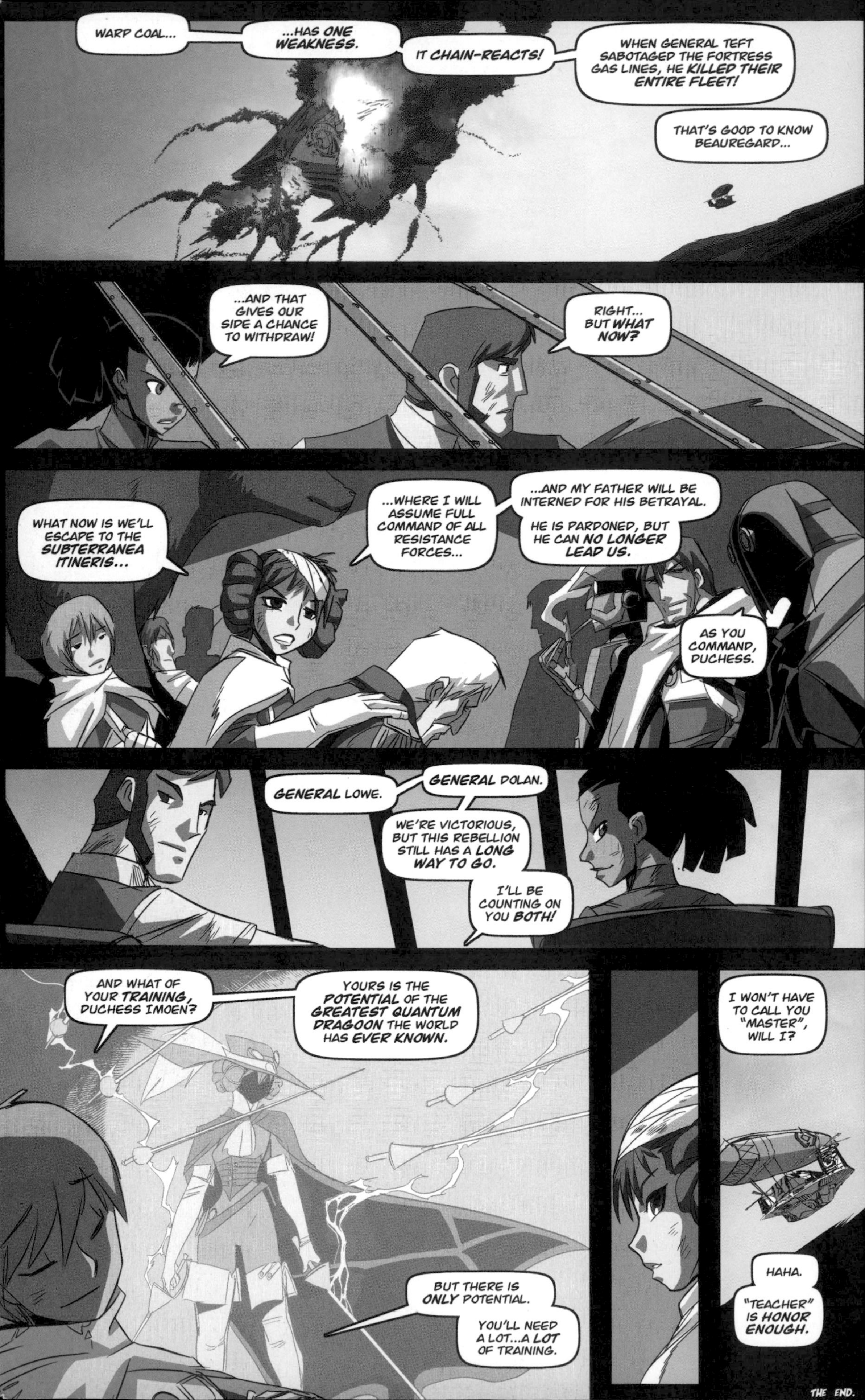
WARP COAL...
...HAS ONE WEAKNESS.
IT CHAIN-REACTS!
WHEN GENERAL TEFT SABOTAGED THE FORTRESS GAS LINES, HE KILLED THEIR ENTIRE FLEET!
THAT'S GOOD TO KNOW BEAUREGARD...
...AND THAT GIVES OUR SIDE A CHANCE TO WITHDRAW!
RIGHT... BUT WHAT NOW?
WHAT NOW IS WE'LL ESCAPE TO THE SUBTERRANEA ITINERIS...
...WHERE I WILL ASSUME FULL COMMAND OF ALL RESISTANCE FORCES...
...AND MY FATHER WILL BE INTERNED FOR HIS BETRAYAL.
HE IS PARDONED, BUT HE CAN NO LONGER LEAD US.
AS YOU COMMAND, DUCHESS.
GENERAL LOWE.
GENERAL DOLAN.
WE'RE VICTORIOUS, BUT THIS REBELLION STILL HAS A LONG WAY TO GO.
I'LL BE COUNTING ON YOU BOTH!
AND WHAT OF YOUR TRAINING, DUCHESS IMOEN?
YOURS IS THE POTENTIAL OF THE GREATEST QUANTUM DRAGOON THE WORLD HAS EVER KNOWN.
BUT THERE IS ONLY POTENTIAL.
YOU'LL NEED A LOT...A LOT OF TRAINING.
I WON'T HAVE TO CALL YOU "MASTER", WILL I?
HAHA.
"TEACHER" IS HONOR ENOUGH.
THE END.

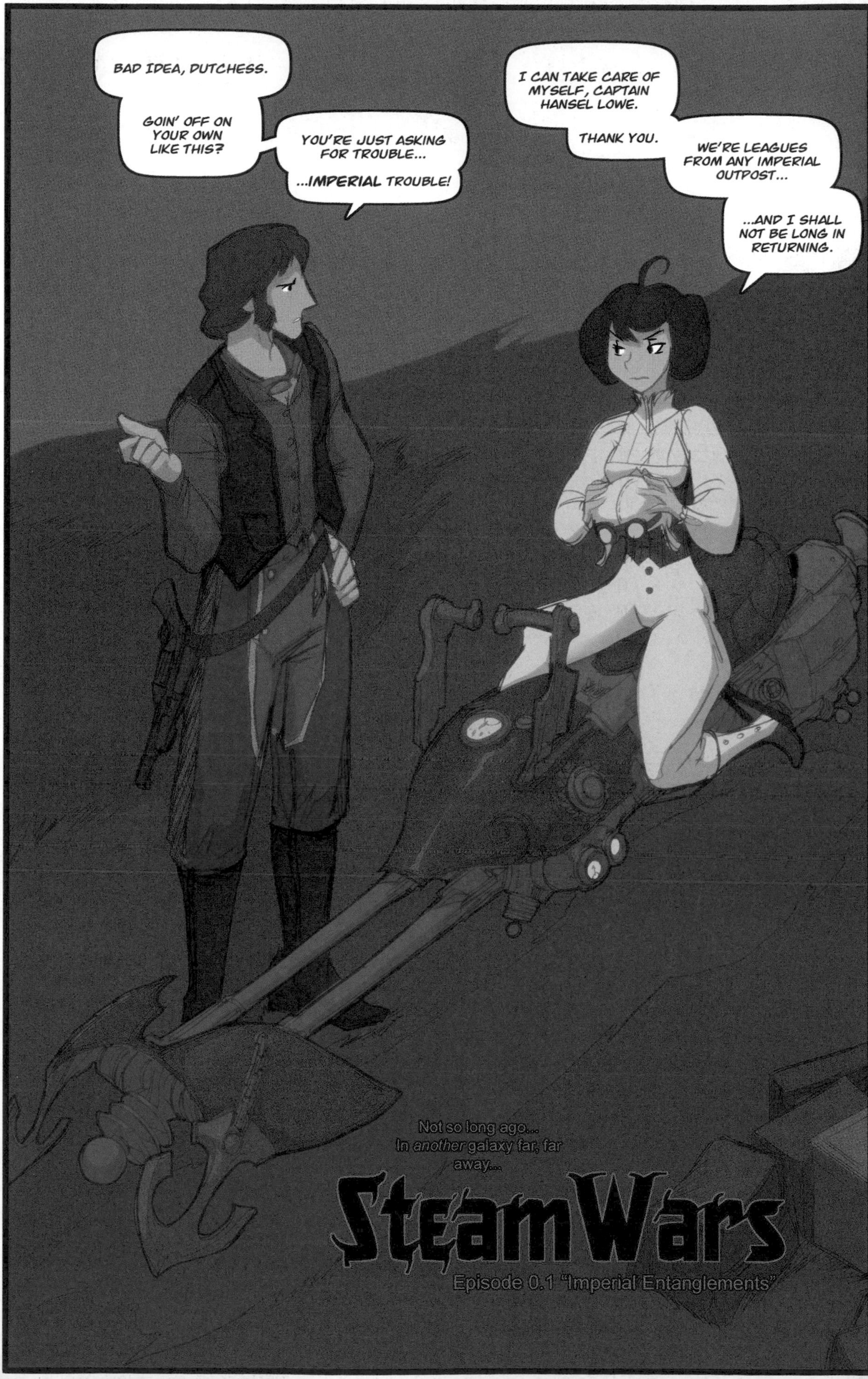
BAD IDEA, DUTCHESS.
GOIN' OFF ON YOUR OWN LIKE THIS?
YOU'RE JUST ASKING FOR TROUBLE...
...IMPERIAL TROUBLE!
I CAN TAKE CARE OF MYSELF, CAPTAIN HANSEL LOWE.
THANK YOU.
WE'RE LEAGUES FROM ANY IMPERIAL OUTPOST...
...AND I SHALL NOT BE LONG IN RETURNING.
Not so long ago... In another galaxy far, far away...
SteamWars
Episode 0.1 "Imperial Entanglements"

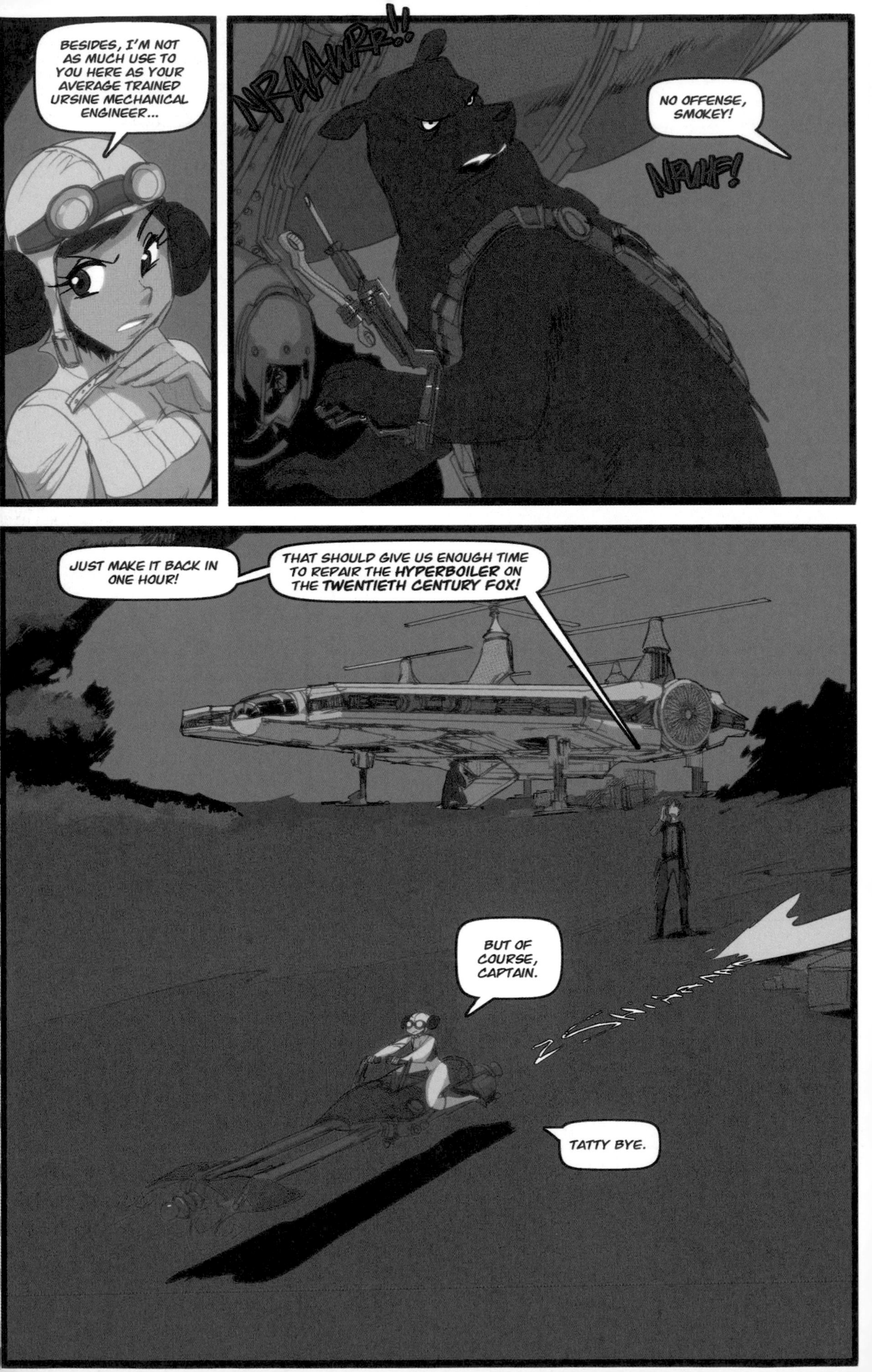
BESIDES, I'M NOT AS MUCH USE TO YOU HERE AS YOUR AVERAGE TRAINED URSINE MECHANICAL ENGINEER...
NRAAWRR!!
NO OFFENSE, SMOKEY!
NRUHF!
JUST MAKE IT BACK IN ONE HOUR!
THAT SHOULD GIVE US ENOUGH TIME TO REPAIR THE HYPERBOILER ON THE TWENTIETH CENTURY FOX!
BUT OF COURSE, CAPTAIN.
TATTY BYE.

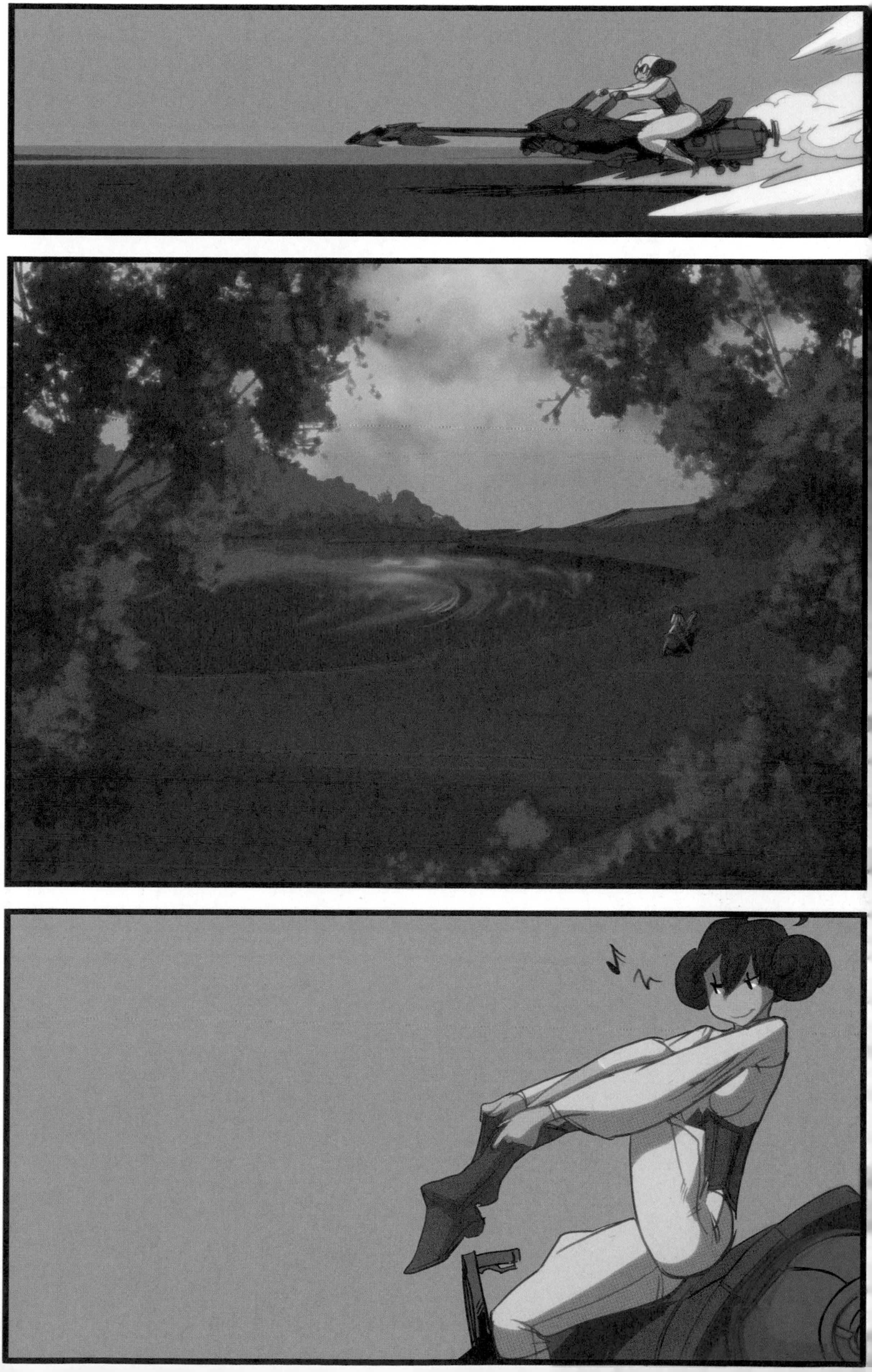

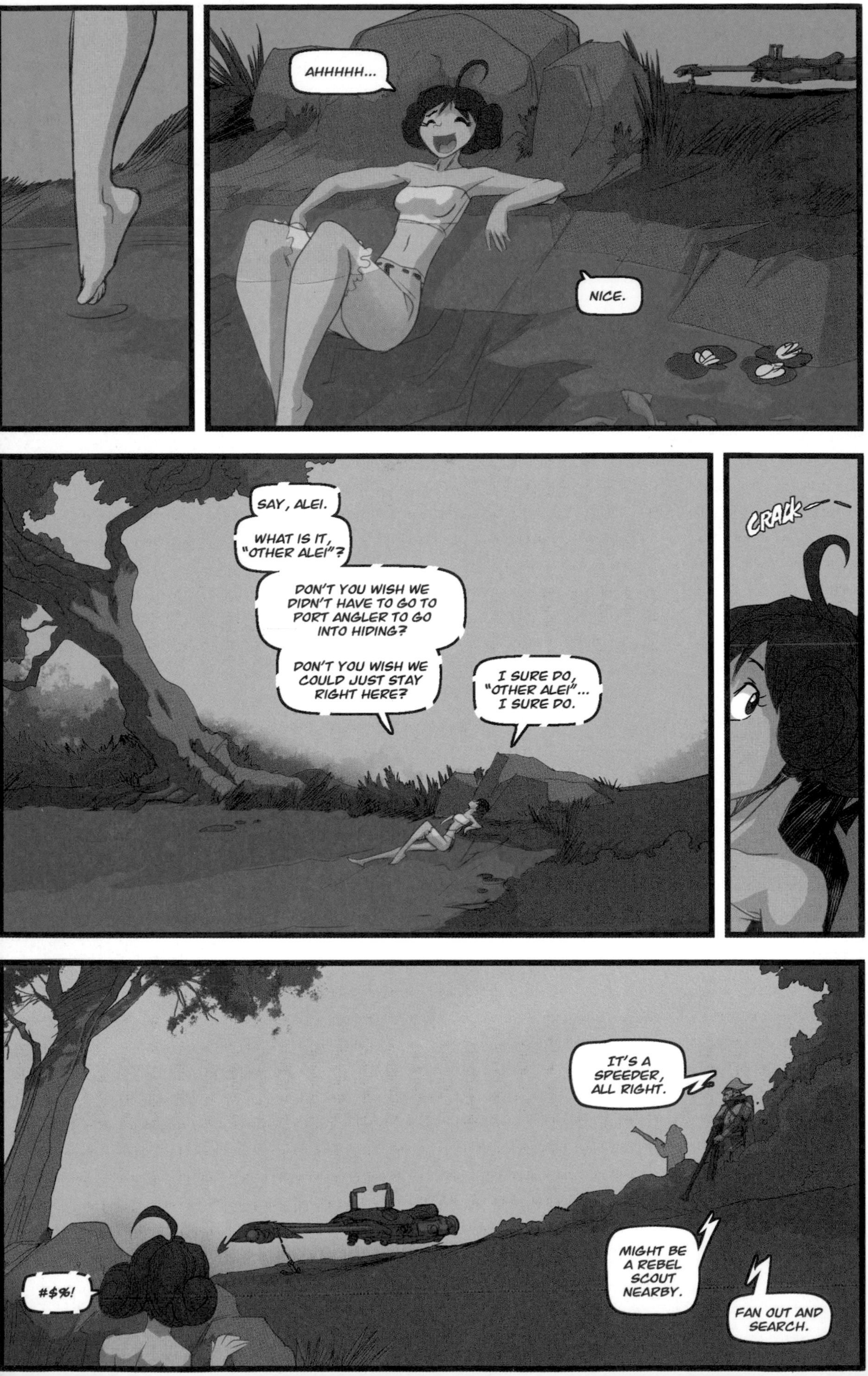
AHHHHH...
NICE.
SAY, ALEI.
WHAT IS IT, "OTHER ALEI"?
DON'T YOU WISH WE DIDN'T HAVE TO GO TO PORT ANGLER TO GO INTO HIDING?
DON'T YOU WISH WE COULD JUST STAY RIGHT HERE?
I SURE DO, "OTHER ALEI"... I SURE DO.
CRACK
IT'S A SPEEDER, ALL RIGHT.
MIGHT BE A REBEL SCOUT NEARBY.
FAN OUT AND SEARCH.
#$%!

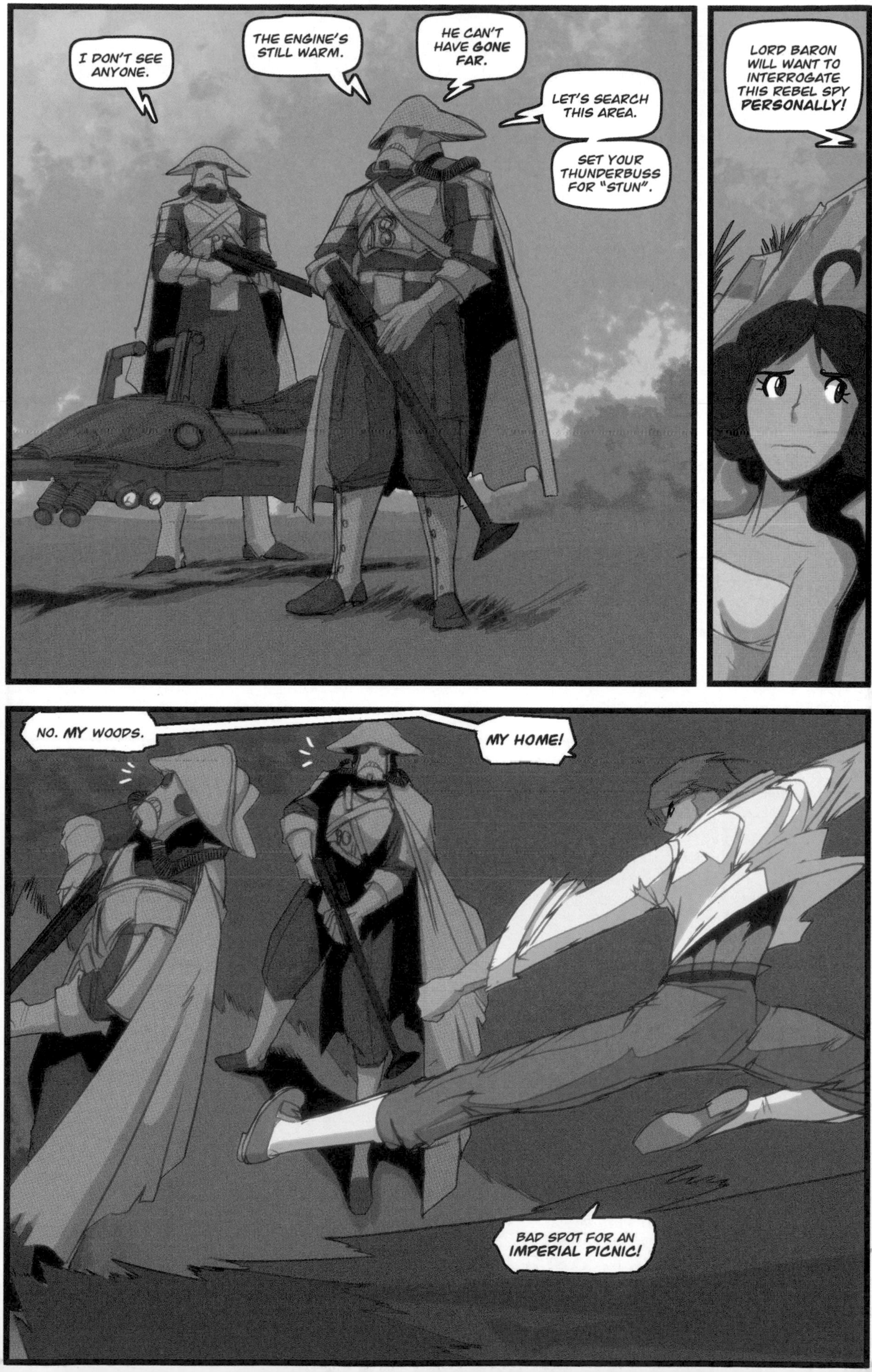

I DON'T SEE ANYONE.
THE ENGINE'S STILL WARM.
HE CAN'T HAVE GONE FAR.
LET'S SEARCH THIS AREA.
SET YOUR THUNDERBUSS FOR "STUN".
LORD BARON WILL WANT TO INTERROGATE THIS REBEL SPY PERSONALLY!
NO. MY WOODS.
MY HOME!
BAD SPOT FOR AN IMPERIAL PICNIC!

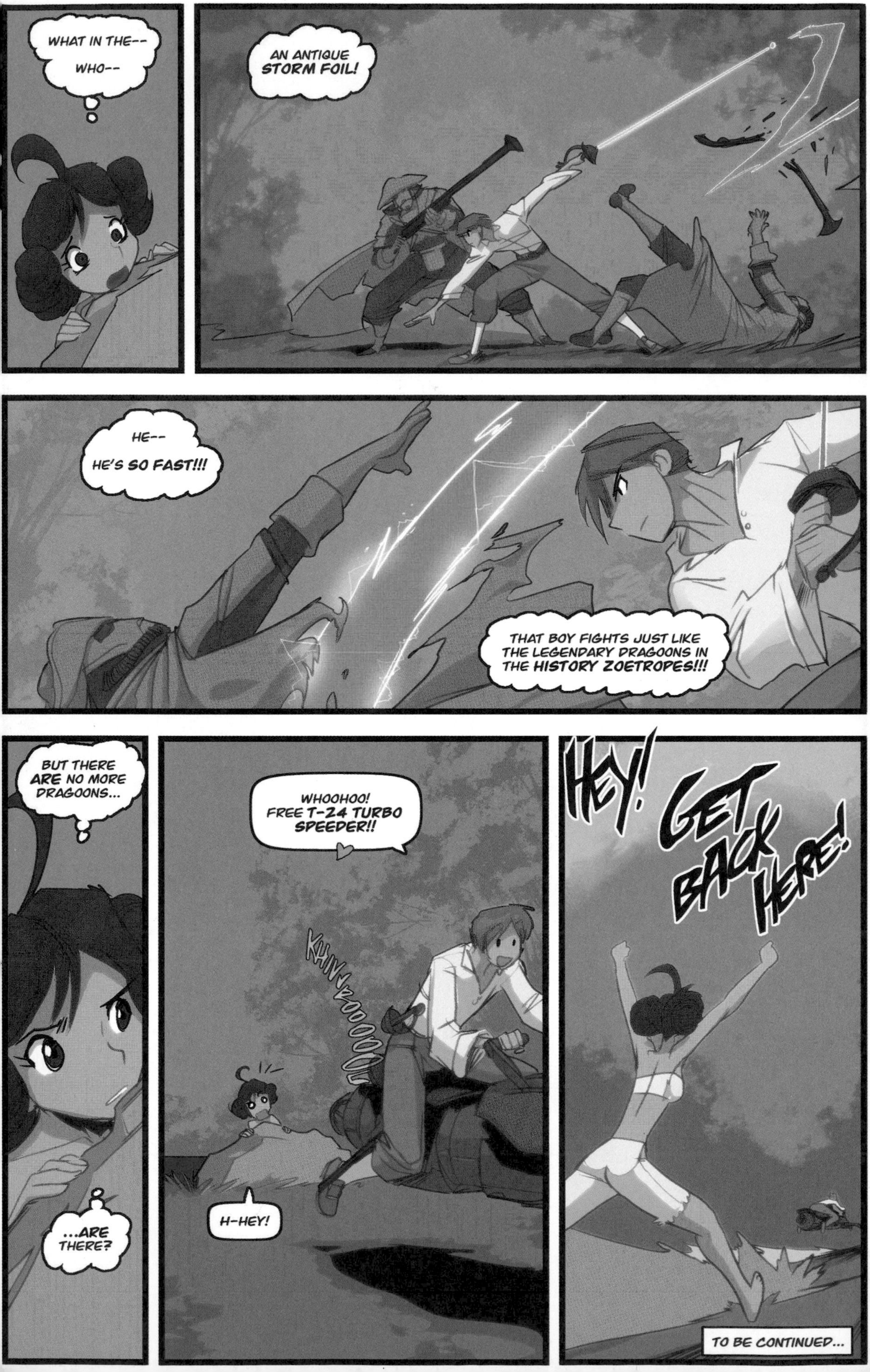
WHAT IN THE--
WHO--
AN ANTIQUE STORM FOIL!
HE--
HE'S SO FAST!!!
THAT BOY FIGHTS JUST LIKE THE LEGENDARY DRAGOONS IN THE HISTORY ZOETROPES!!!
BUT THERE ARE NO MORE DRAGOONS...
...ARE THERE?
WHOOHOO! FREE T-24 TURBO SPEEDER!!
KHIVVROOOOOM
H-HEY!
HEY!
GET BACK HERE!
TO BE CONTINUED...

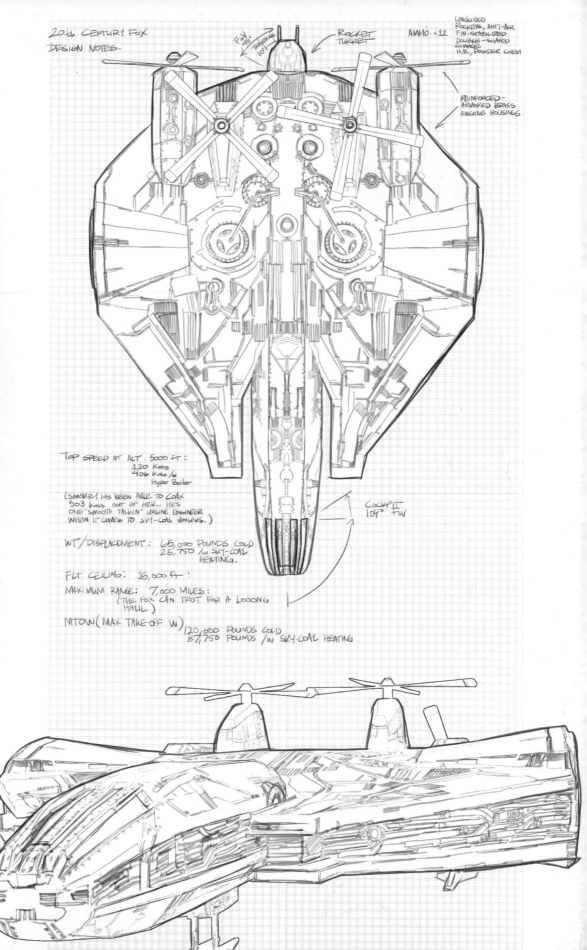

20th CENTURY FOX
DESIGN NOTES.

ROCKET TURRET

AMMO. × 12

UNGUIDED
ROCKETS, ANTI-AIR
FIN-STABILIZED
DOUBLE-SHAPED
CHARGE
H.E., POWDER CHEM

F.O.V.
16°
TRAVERSE 10°

REINFORCED-
ARMORED BRASS
ENGINE HOUSINGS

COCKPIT
109° FOV

TOP SPEED AT ALT. 5000 FT:
120 KNOTS
406 KNOTS /w HYPER BOILER

(SMOKEY HAS BEEN ABLE TO COAX
503 KNOTS OUT OF HER... HE'S
ONE "SMOOTH TALKIN" URSINE ENGINEER
WHEN IT COMES TO SKY-COAL BOILERS.)

WT/DISPLACEMENT: 65,000 POUNDS COLD
25,750 /w SKY-COAL
HEATING.

FLT CEILING: 16,000 FT:

MAXIMUM RANGE: 7,000 MILES:
(THE FOX CAN TROT FOR A LOOONG
HAUL)

MTOW (MAX TAKE-OFF W) 120,650 POUNDS COLD
87,750 POUNDS /w SKY-COAL HEATING

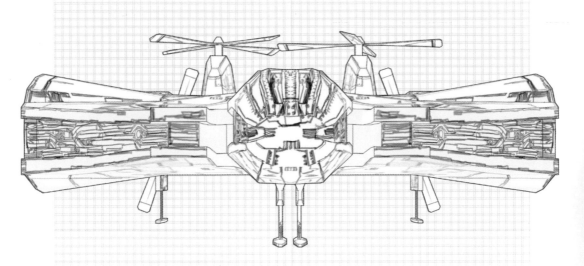

SHIP CLASS: LIGHT FRIGATE/ESCORT, ARMED
MANEUVER RATING: MEDIUM-LIGHT
THRUST RATING: VERY FAST
ARMOR RATING: MEDIUM-LIGHT

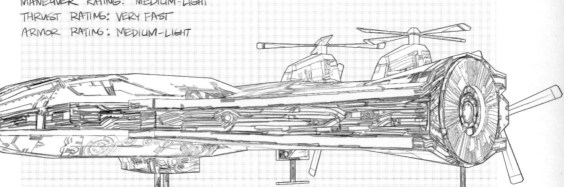

CREW CAP: (MINIMUM 4: 2 PILOT, 1 ENGINEER, 1 GUNNER)
    CLEES, SMOKEY AND I CAN FUNCTION WITH JUST THE THREE OF US
    UNDER IDEAL CONDITIONS... BUT WHEN ARE THINGS IDEAL WITH LEAD FLYING?

MAINTENANCE CONDITION: PERFECT+   (THANKS TO SMOKEY! HE KEEPS THIS BIRD
                                  BETTER THAN ANY HUMAN ENGINEER COULD!)

ENGINE: X2   KASINOV SKY-COAL LIFT TURBINES.
                                CHAMBERS: 30 EACH
                                FIRE BOX: 773
                                SUPERHEAT SURFACE AREA: 870 SQFT
                                AIR TRACTION POWER: 350,000 lbs
                                FACTOR OF ADHESION: 16.07

          X2   MARTININE REVERSED-THRUST STEAM-PROPS
                                CHAMBERS: 42 EACH
                                FIRE BOX: 687
                                  SUPER HEAT SURFACE AREA: 620 SQFT
                                        GEAR-COMPRESSED: 200 SQFT
                                        SHIELDED HYPER-BOILED: 50 SQFT
                                AIR TRACTION POWER: 200,000 lbs — 1.5 million lbs
                                FACTOR OF ADHESION: 12 — 78

These are factory stats / mixed with my own knowledge.
SMOKEY COULD PROBABLY BREAK THESE STATISTICS!

FUEL TYPE: SKY-COAL

            STANDARD FLOAT MOSS PEAT
            WITH 15% VOLATILES MAX.

            SHE CAN FLY WITH 20% — 30% BUT
            THE PERFORMANCE HIT IS HIGH

          ENERGY CONTENT/EXTRACTION
              96,000 Kj/Kg

"HEGEMONY LANDER"
GB-H713 'GOSHAWK'

NOTES BY CAPT. H. LOWE

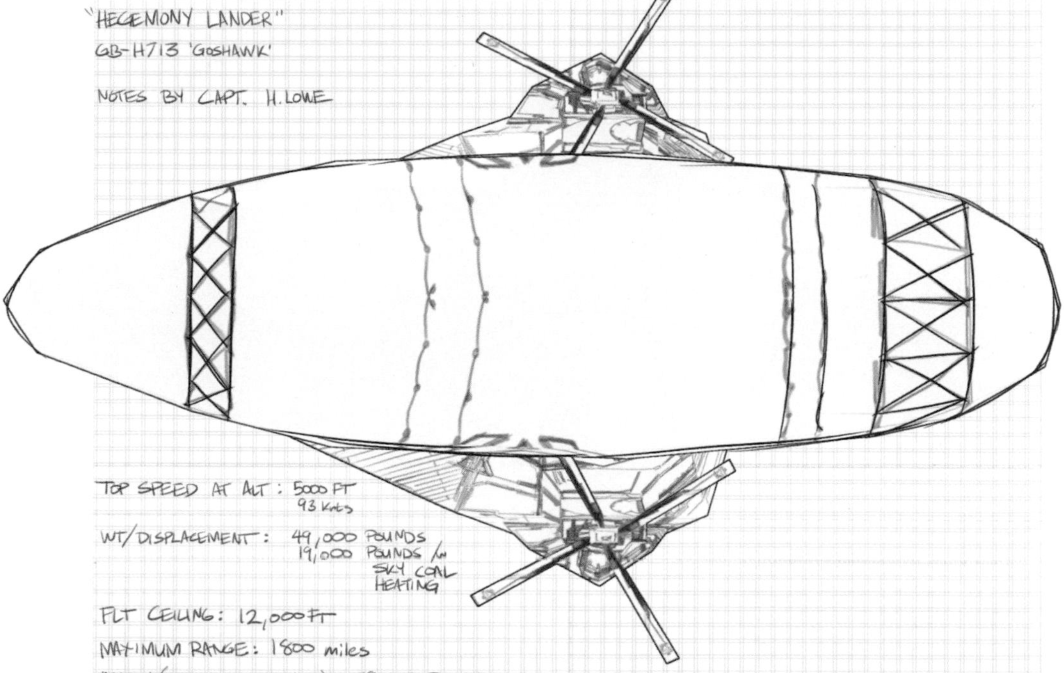

TOP SPEED AT ALT: 5000 FT
93 Knts

WT/DISPLACEMENT: 49,000 POUNDS
19,000 POUNDS /w SKY COAL HEATING

FLT CEILING: 12,000 FT

MAXIMUM RANGE: 1800 miles

MTOW (MAX TAKE-OFF WT): 79,000 POUNDS
39,000 POUNDS /w SKY COAL

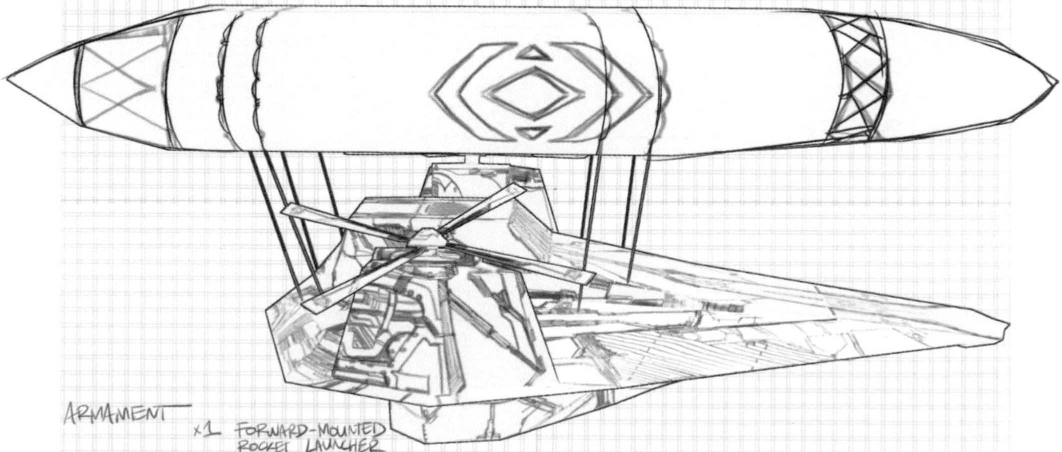

ARMAMENT
x1 FORWARD-MOUNTED ROCKET LAUNCHER (ANTI-AIR)

x6 UNDERCARRIAGE-MOUNTED ANTI-PERS MORTARS

SHIP CLASS: LIGHT FRIGATE/GUN BOAT.

MANEUVER RATING: MEDIUM-HEAVY

THRUST RATING: MEDIUM-SLOW

ARMOR RATING: LIGHT

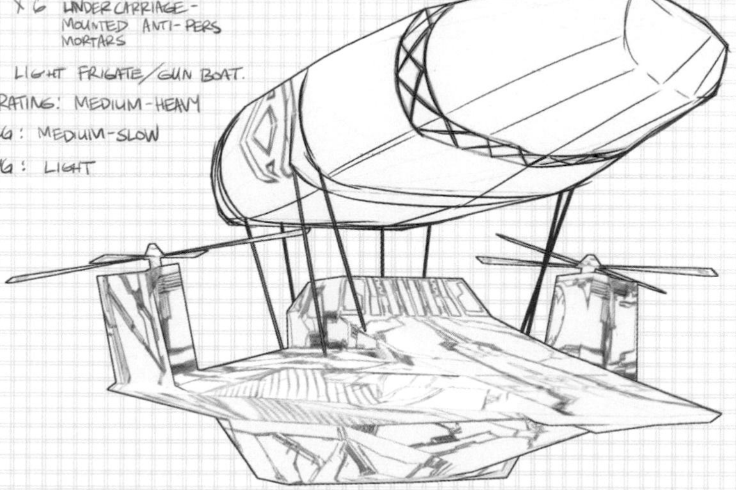

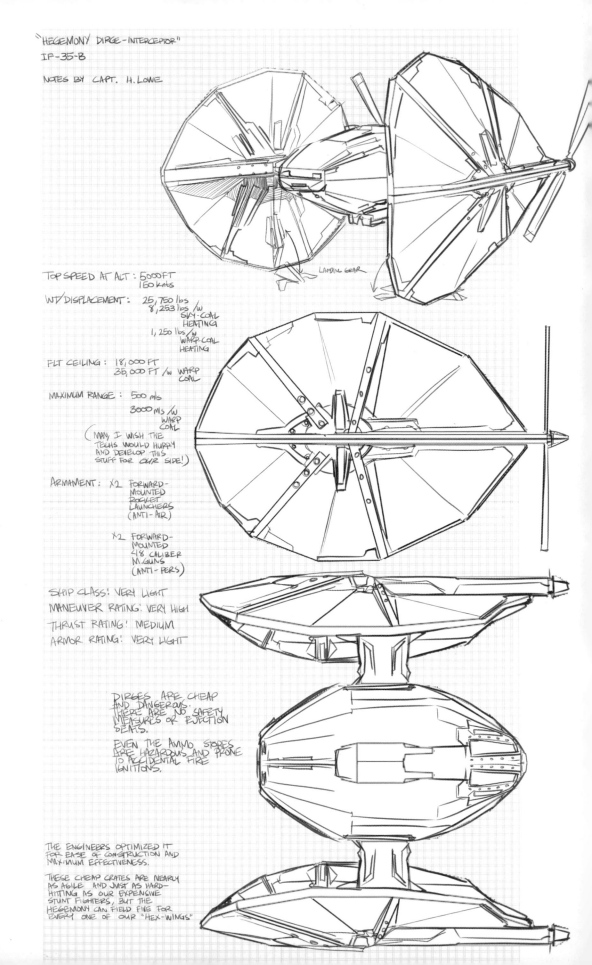

"HEGEMONY DIRGE-INTERCEPTOR"

IF-35-B

NOTES BY CAPT. H. LOWE

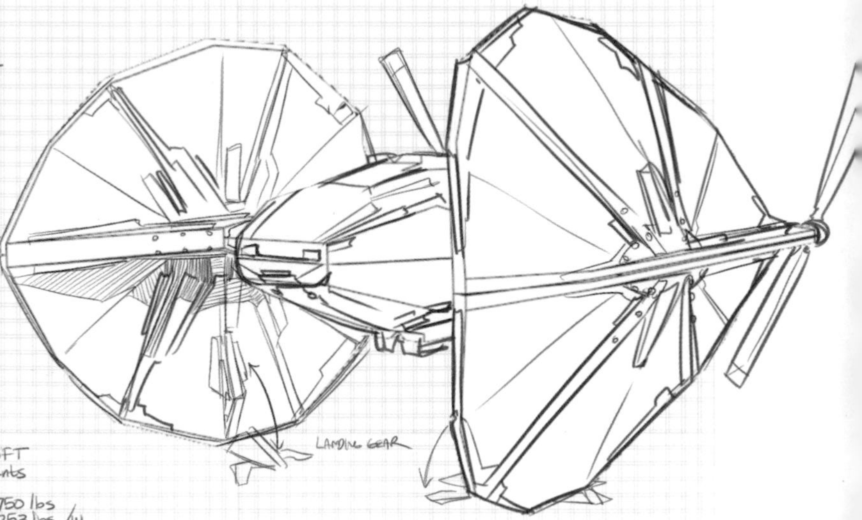
LANDING GEAR

TOP SPEED AT ALT: 5000FT
150 knts

WT/DISPLACEMENT: 25,750 lbs
8,253 lbs /w SKY-COAL HEATING
1,250 lbs /w WARP-COAL HEATING

FLT CEILING: 18,000 FT
35,000 FT /w WARP COAL

MAXIMUM RANGE: 500 mls
3000 mls /w WARP COAL

(MAN, I WISH THE TECHS WOULD HURRY AND DEVELOP THIS STUFF FOR OUR SIDE!)

ARMAMENT: X2 FORWARD-MOUNTED ROCKET LAUNCHERS (ANTI-AIR)

X2 FORWARD-MOUNTED .48 CALIBER M.GUNS (ANTI-PERS)

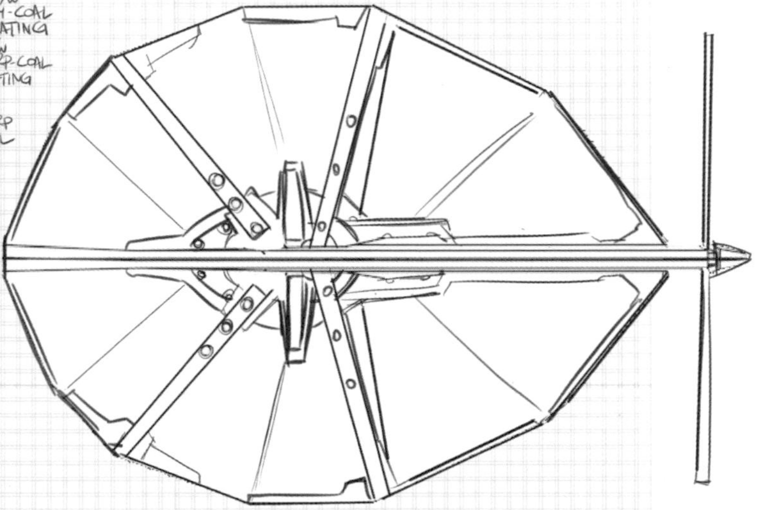

SHIP CLASS: VERY LIGHT

MANEUVER RATING: VERY HIGH

THRUST RATING: MEDIUM

ARMOR RATING: VERY LIGHT

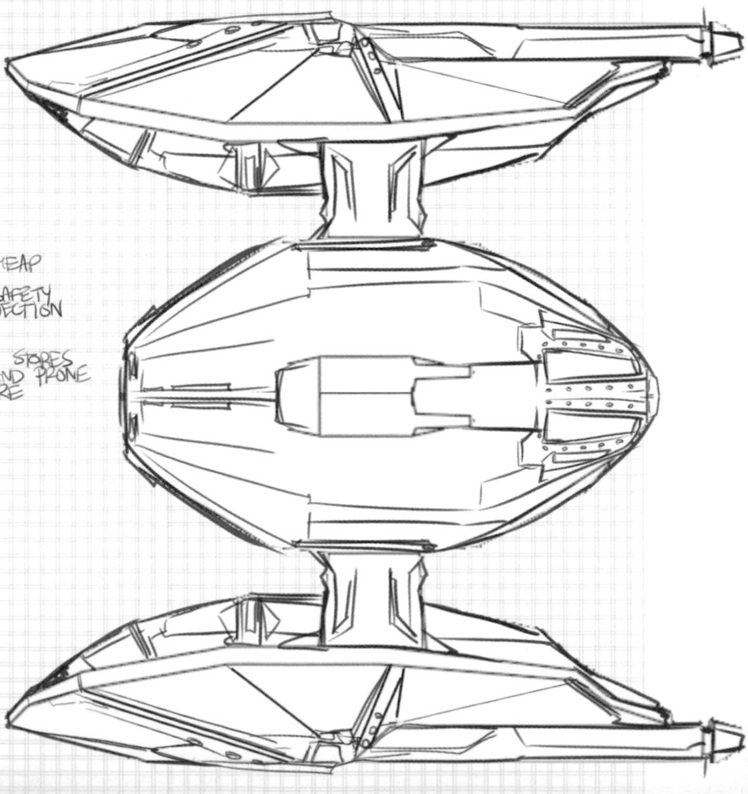

DIRGES ARE CHEAP AND DANGEROUS. THERE ARE NO SAFETY MEASURES OR EJECTION SEATS.

EVEN THE AMMO STORES ARE HAZARDOUS AND PRONE TO ACCIDENTAL FIRE IGNITIONS.

THE ENGINEERS OPTIMIZED IT FOR EASE OF CONSTRUCTION AND MAXIMUM EFFECTIVENESS.

THESE CHEAP CRATES ARE NEARLY AS AGILE AND JUST AS HARD-HITTING AS OUR EXPENSIVE STUNT FIGHTERS, BUT THE HEGEMONY CAN FIELD FIVE FOR EVERY ONE OF OUR "HEX-WINGS"

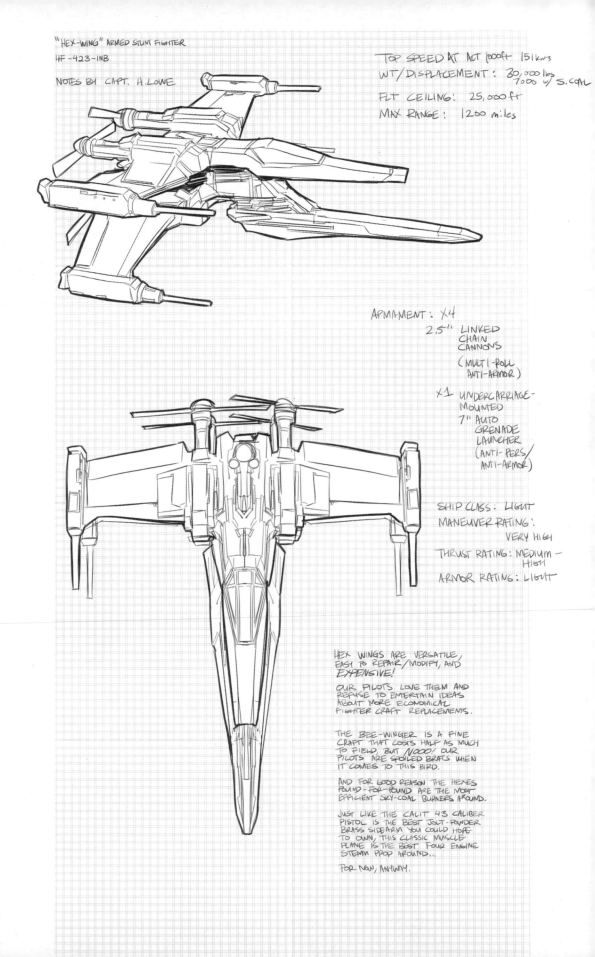

"HEX-WING" ARMED STUNT FIGHTER

HF-423-1NB

NOTES BY CAPT. H. LOWE

TOP SPEED AT ALT 1000ft 151 knts

WT/DISPLACEMENT: 30,000 lbs
7000 w/ S. COAL

FLT CEILING: 25,000 ft

MAX RANGE: 1200 miles

ARMAMENT: X4
2.5" LINKED
CHAIN
CANNONS

(MULTI-ROLL
ANTI-ARMOR)

X1 UNDERCARRIAGE-
MOUNTED
7" AUTO
GRENADE
LAUNCHER
(ANTI-PERS/
ANTI-ARMOR)

SHIP CLASS: LIGHT
MANEUVER RATING:
VERY HIGH
THRUST RATING: MEDIUM —
HIGH
ARMOR RATING: LIGHT

HEX WINGS ARE VERSATILE,
EASY TO REPAIR/MODIFY, AND
EXPENSIVE!

OUR PILOTS LOVE THEM AND
REFUSE TO ENTERTAIN IDEAS
ABOUT MORE ECONOMICAL
FIGHTER CRAFT REPLACEMENTS.

THE BEE-WINGER IS A FINE
CRAFT THAT COSTS HALF AS MUCH
TO FIELD, BUT NOOO! OUR
PILOTS ARE SPOILED BRATS WHEN
IT COMES TO THIS BIRD.

AND FOR GOOD REASON THE HEXES
POUND-FOR-POUND ARE THE MOST
EFFICIENT SKY-COAL BURNERS AROUND.

JUST LIKE THE CALIT 43 CALIBER
PISTOL IS THE BEST JOLT-POWDER
BRASS SIDEARM YOU COULD HOPE
TO OWN, THIS CLASSIC MUSCLE
PLANE IS THE BEST FOUR ENGINE
STEAM PROP AROUND...

FOR NOW, ANYWAY.

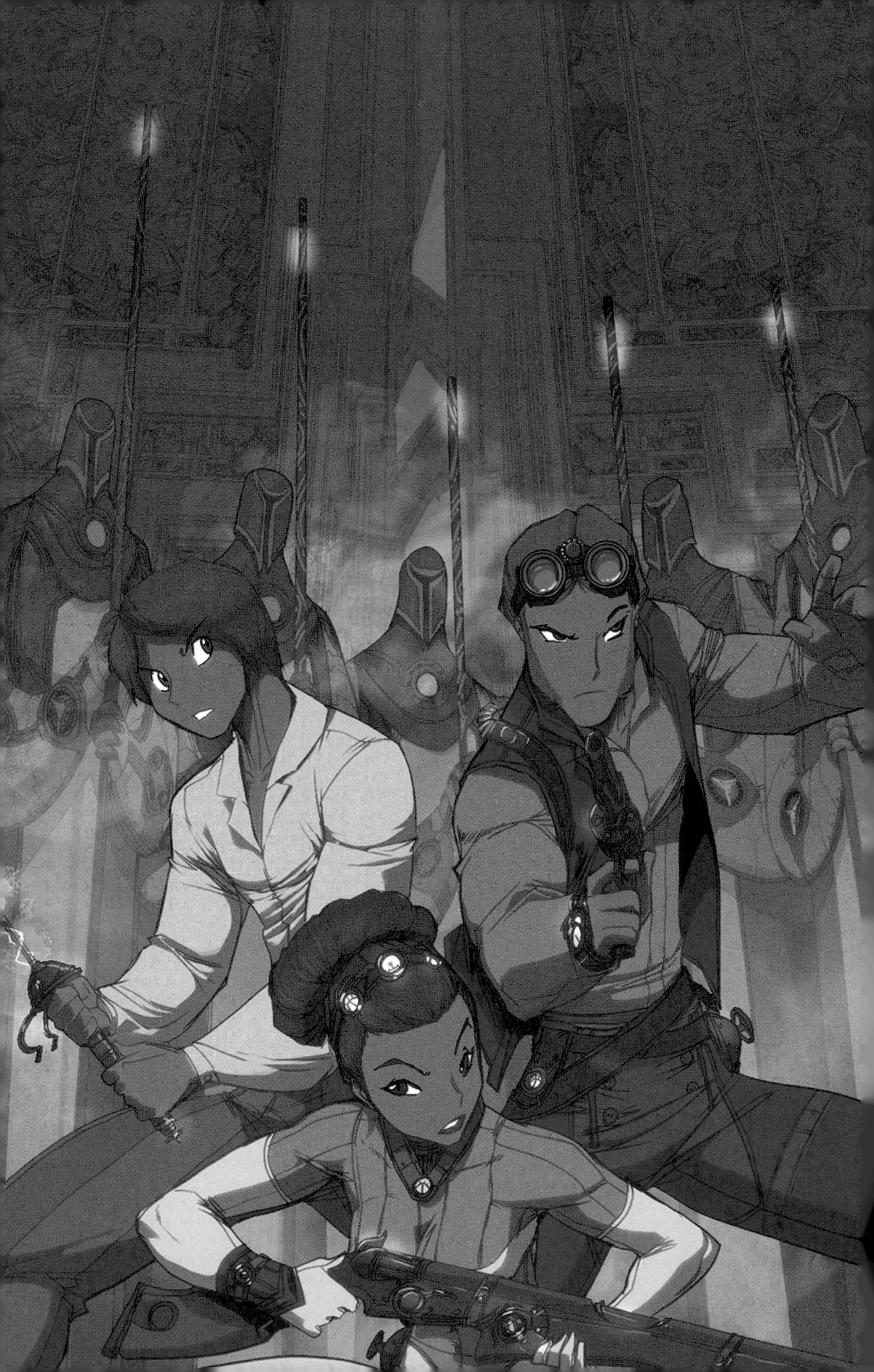

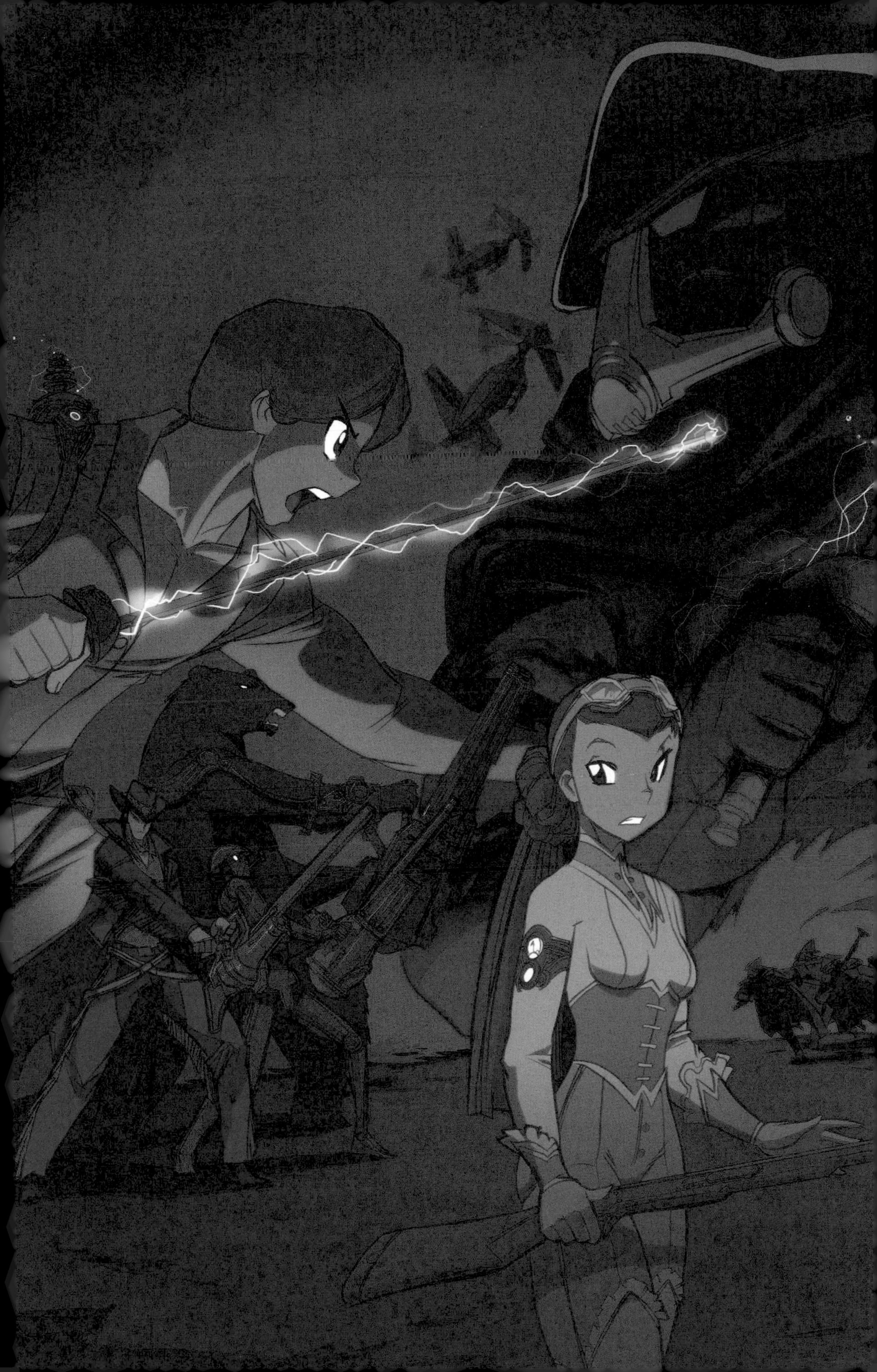

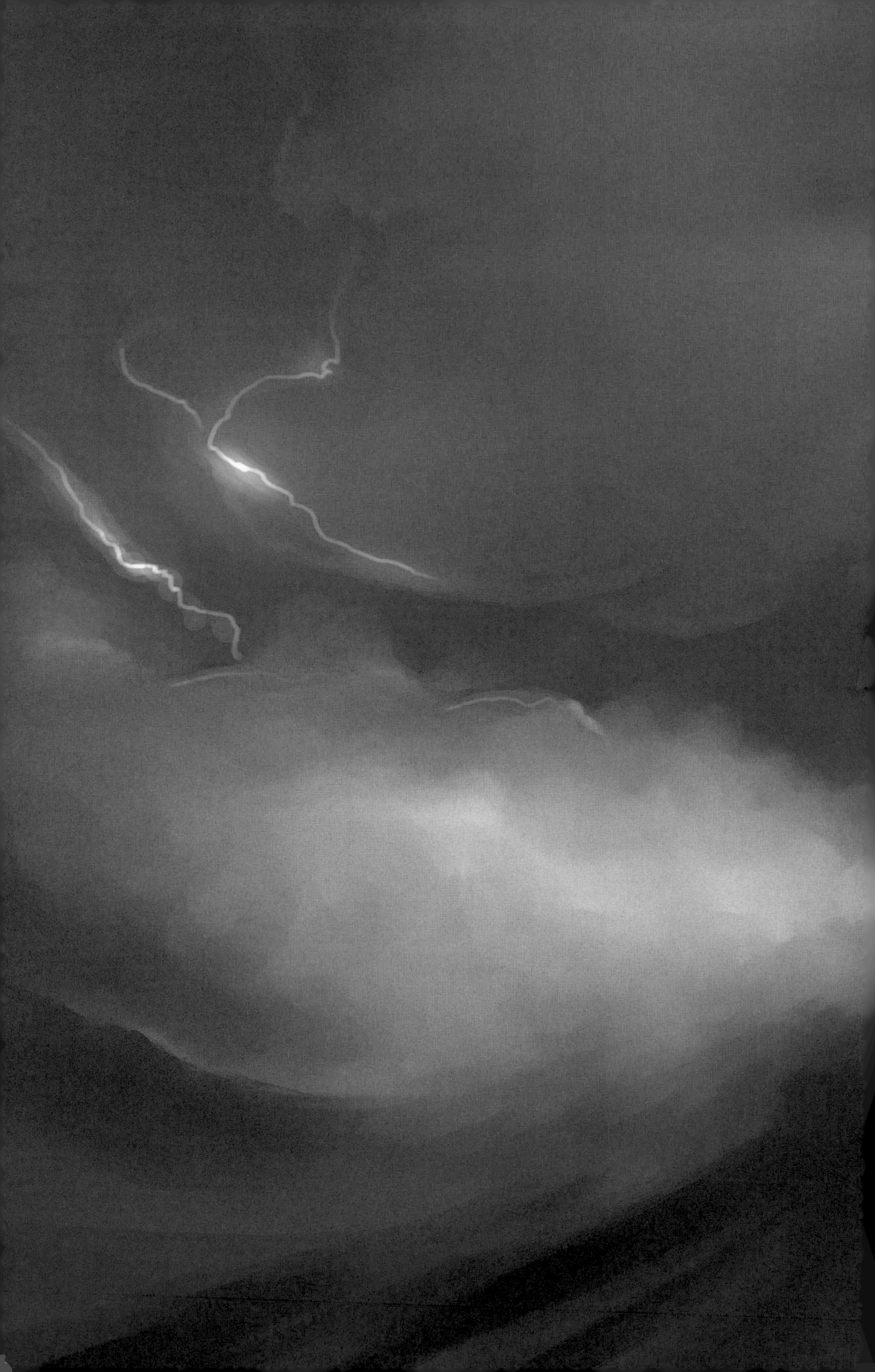

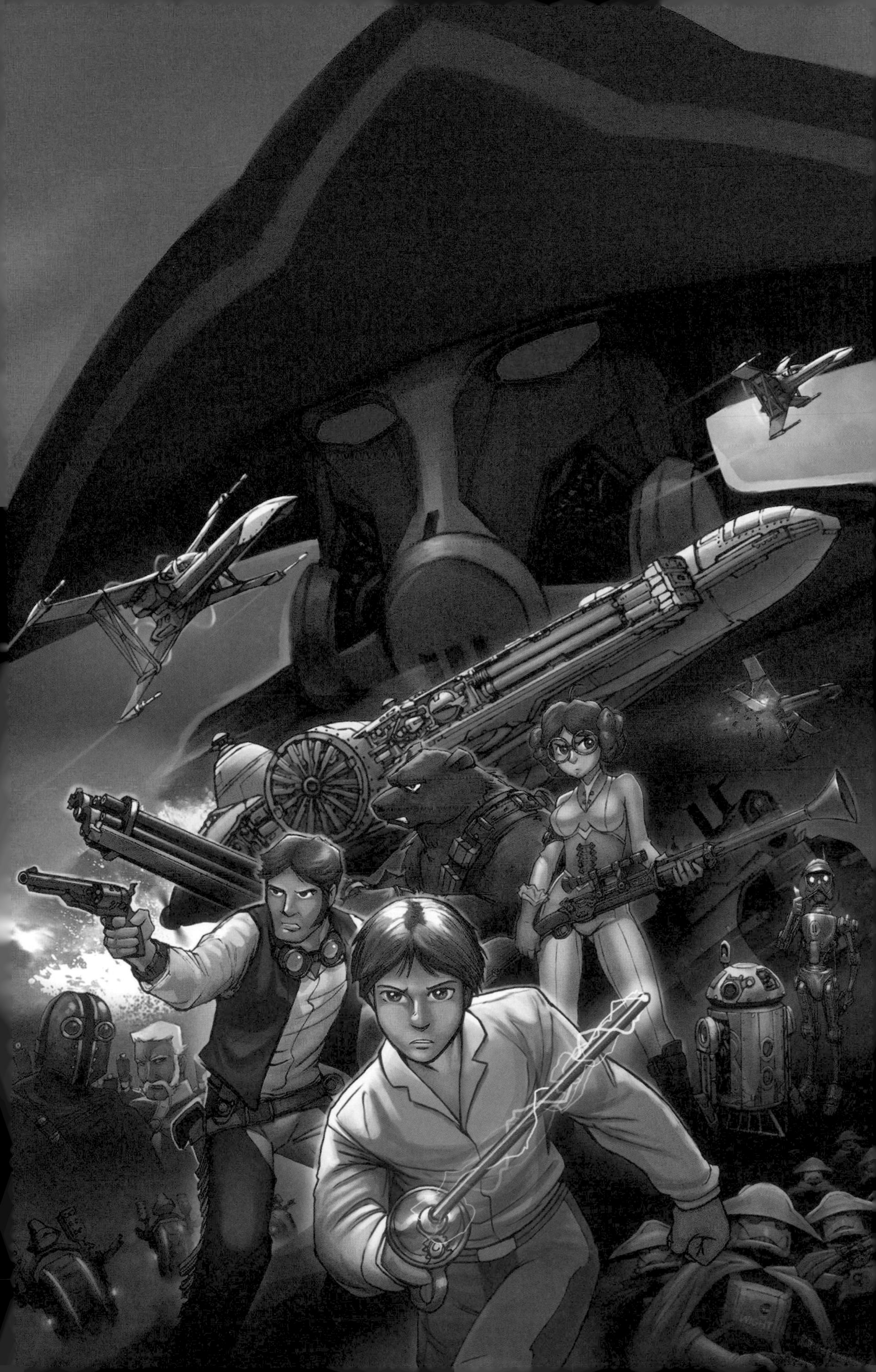

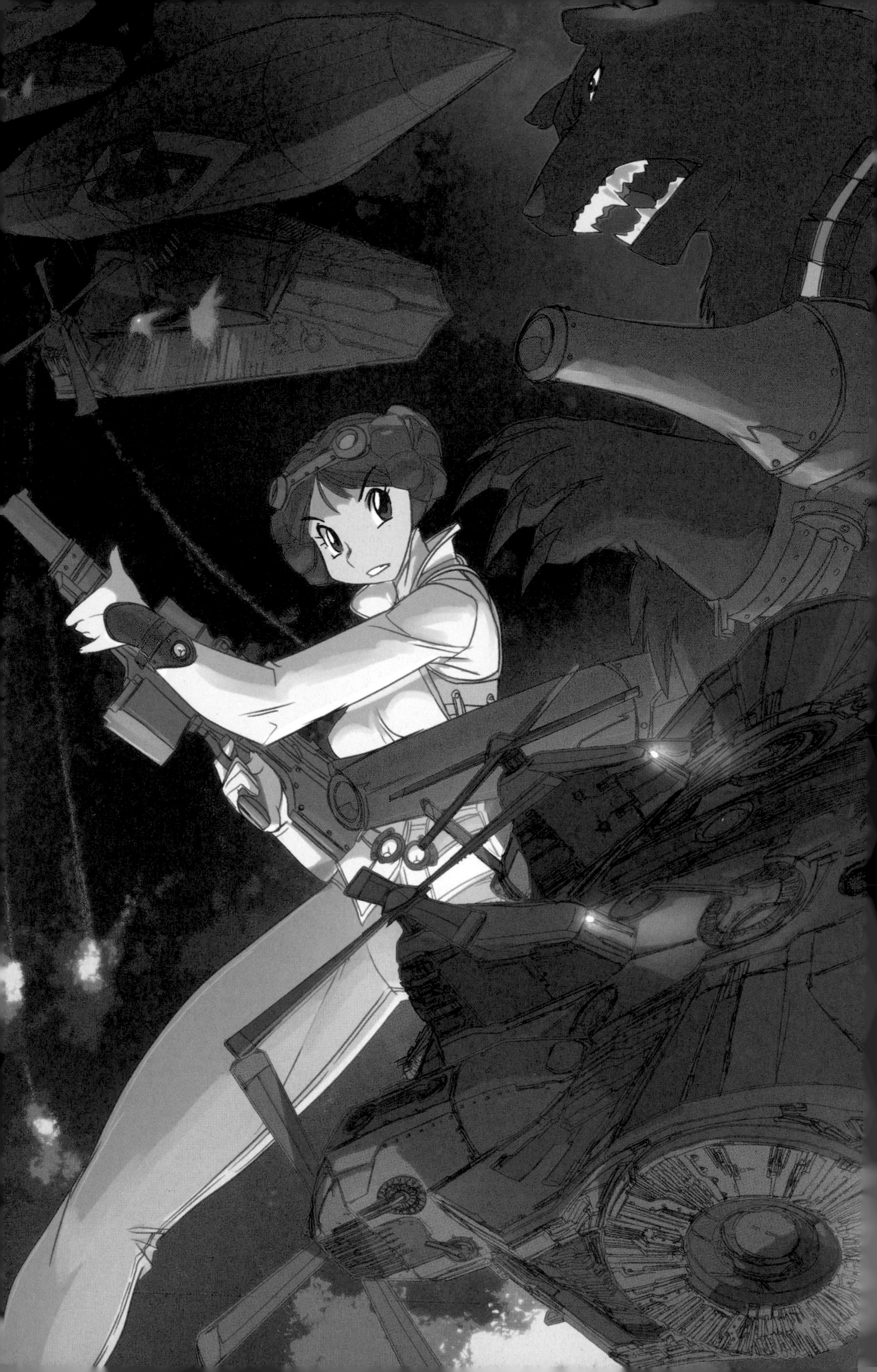

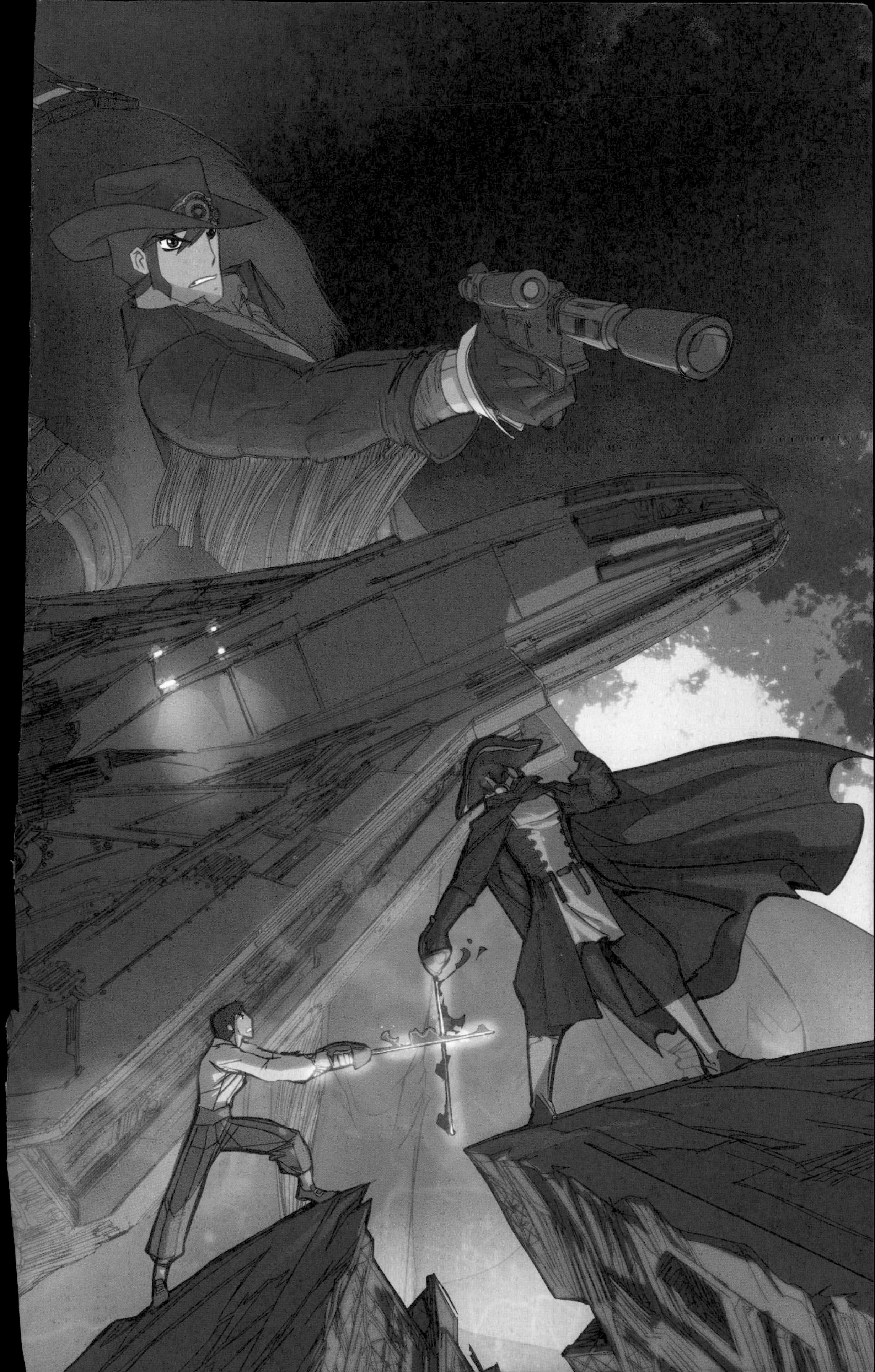

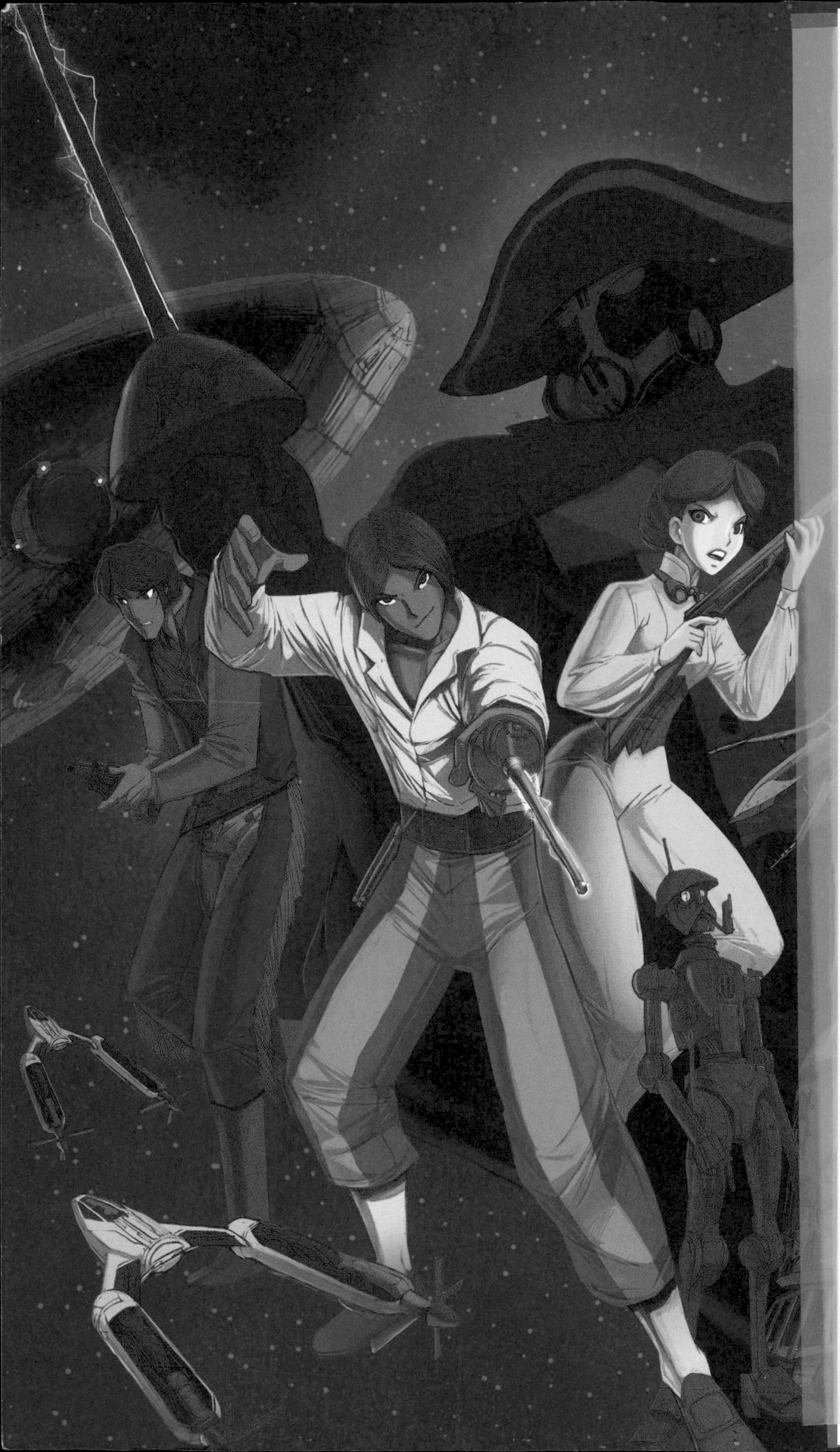